I0885780

GraphersRock.

RASTERIZE

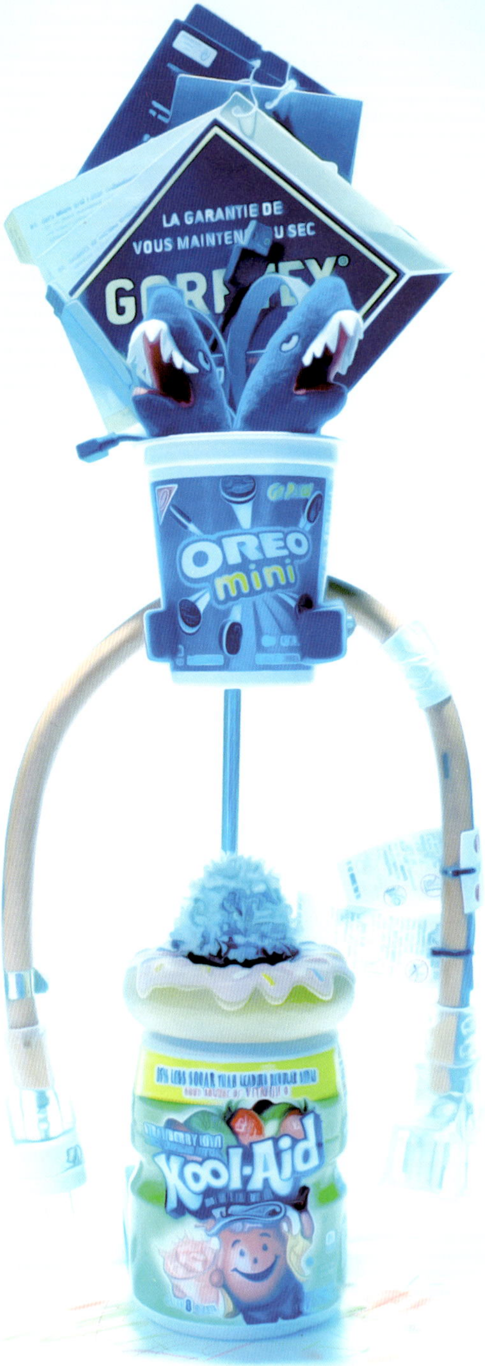
LA GARANTIE DE
OREO
mini
Kool-Aid

はじめに

GraphersRockは巧みで、危険だ。多様なクライアントと共謀しながら、
その世界に彼らと僕らを巻き込む。身近なところで言うならば、
Maltine Recordsにおけるアートワークもその1つだろう。

その世界とは何か?
テクノカルチャー/サイバーパンク/オカルト/インターネット/ストリート/80年代/90年代
といった象徴的な言葉をタグのように並べることは
その世界への入口としては有用に機能するだろうが本質を表すには何かが足りない。

そう。汚れないインクがデスクトップのレイヤー上にまき散らされ、
ネットワークから無意識の予兆が膨張しながらディスプレイに憑依したかと思いきや、
急に0と1の隙間から現れる不穏な静寂さに息をのむ。
そうした言葉に言い表せない行為と感覚がそれらを形作っている。
この本で僕らはその一端を眺めることができるだろう。

そして、この先もGraphersRockから生み出されるイメージたちが
時代の歩調をバグらせながら凡庸でない未来へと投影されていくことを期待している。

tomad (MaltineRecords)

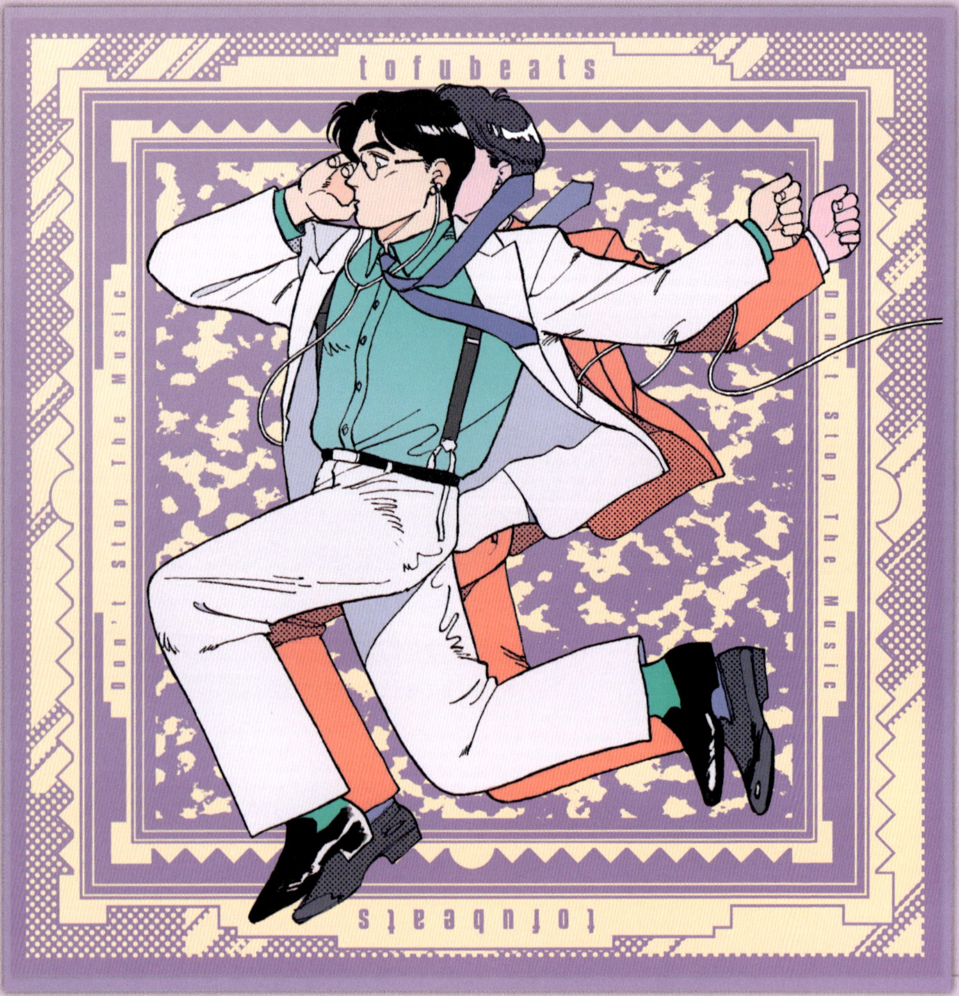

tofubeats / Don't Stop The Music
CDジャケット ｜ ワーナーミュージック・ジャパン / アンボルデ ｜ 2013

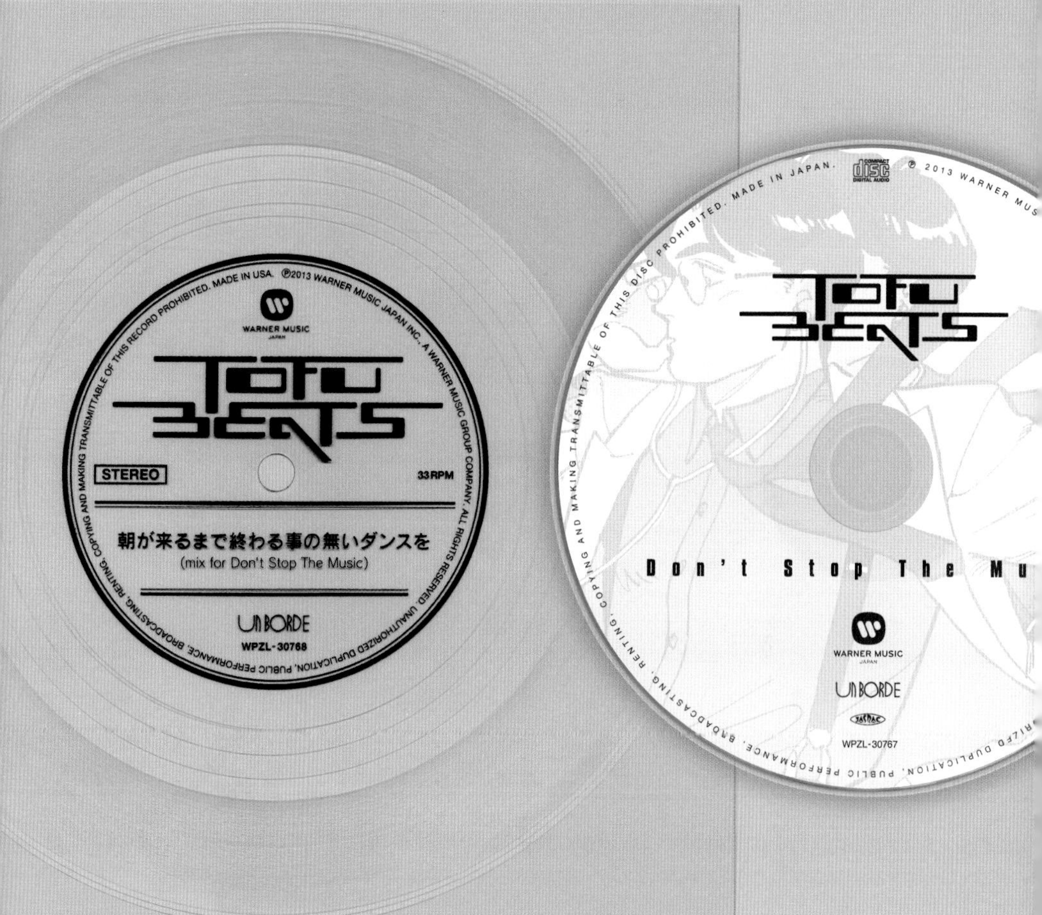
TOFU BEATS
WARNER MUSIC JAPAN
STEREO
33RPM
朝が来るまで終わる事の無いダンスを
(mix for Don't Stop The Music)
UNBORDE
WPZL-30768
COPYING AND MAKING TRANSMITTABLE OF THIS RECORD PROHIBITED. MADE IN USA. ℗2013 WARNER MUSIC JAPAN INC., A WARNER MUSIC GROUP COMPANY. ALL RIGHTS RESERVED. UNAUTHORIZED DUPLICATION, PUBLIC PERFORMANCE, BROADCASTING, RENTING,
TOFU BEATS
Don't Stop The Mu
WARNER MUSIC JAPAN
UNBORDE
WPZL-30767
COPYING AND MAKING TRANSMITTABLE OF THIS DISC PROHIBITED. MADE IN JAPAN.
℗ 2013 WARNER MUS
RIZED DUPLICATION, PUBLIC PERFORMANCE, BROADCASTING, RENTING,

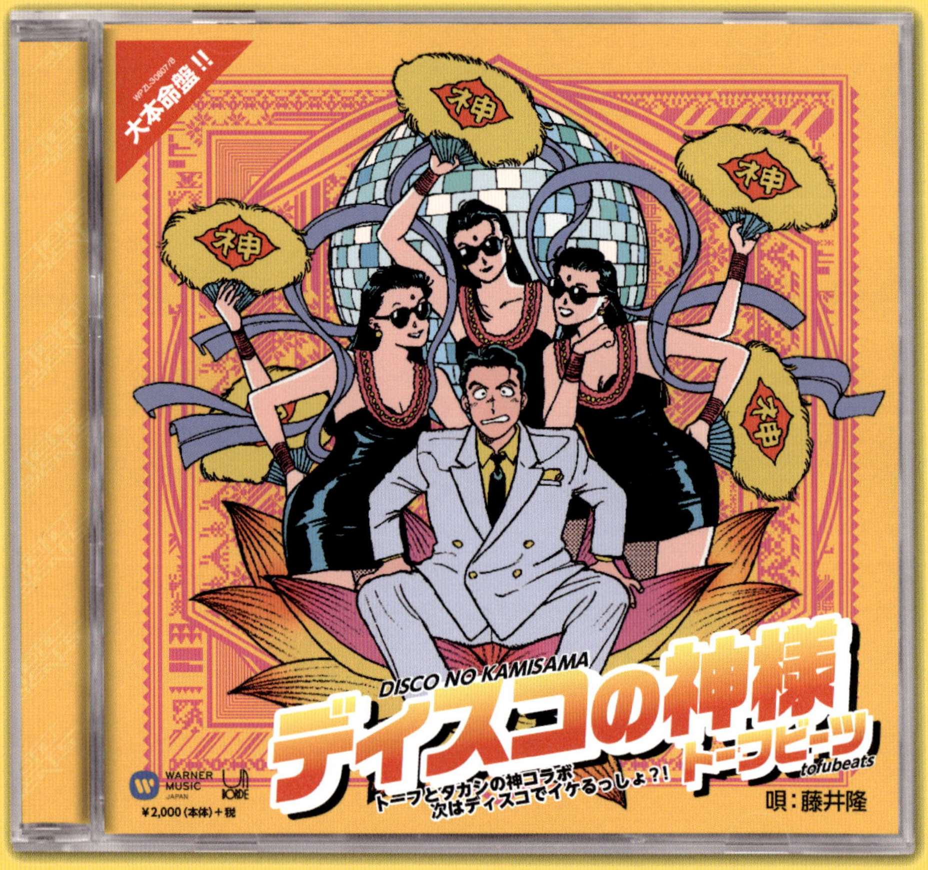

tofubeats / ディスコの神様
CDジャケット | ワーナーミュージック・ジャパン / アンボルデ | 2014

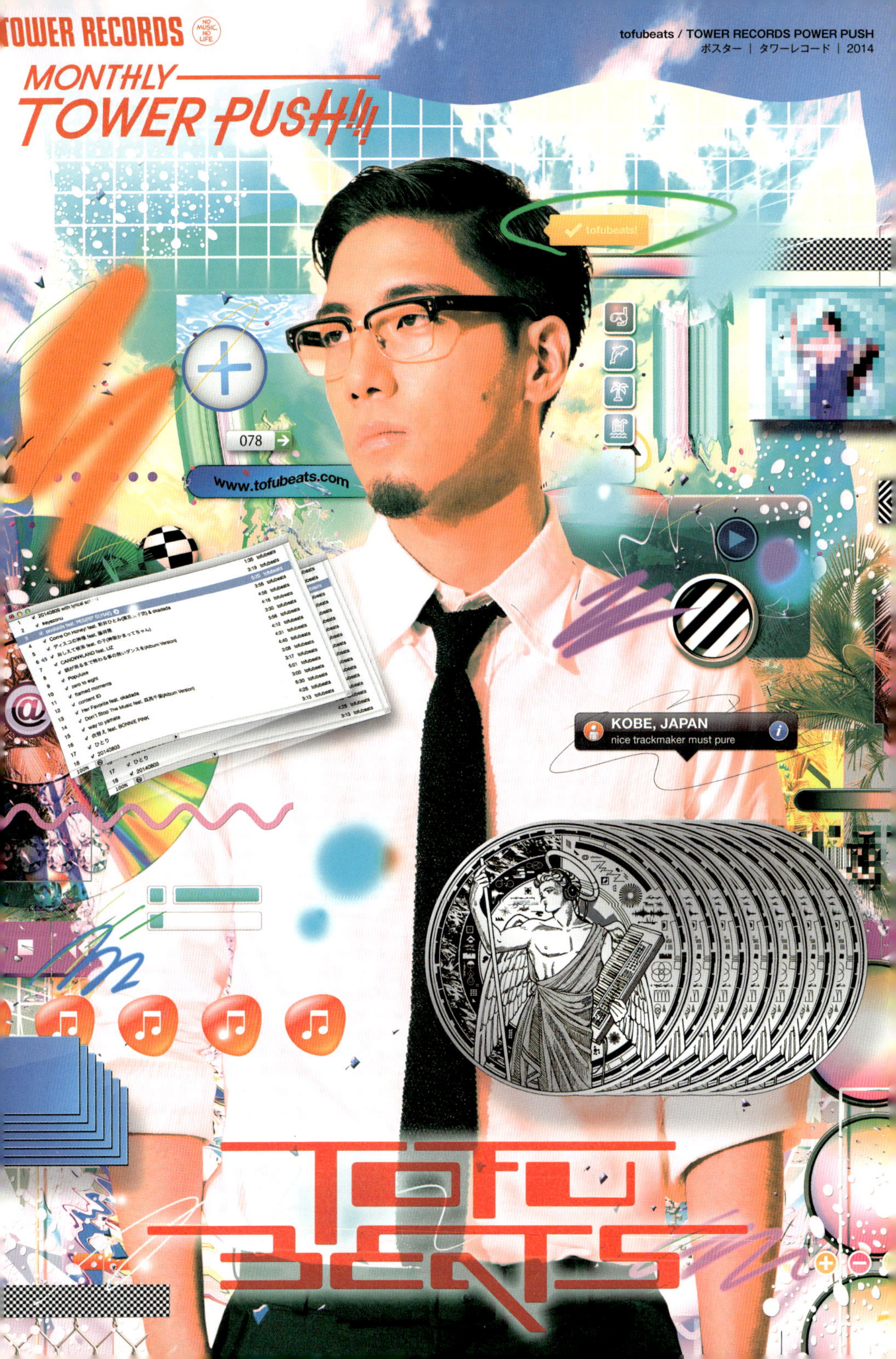

tofubeats / TOWER RECORDS POWER PUSH
ポスター ｜ タワーレコード ｜ 2014

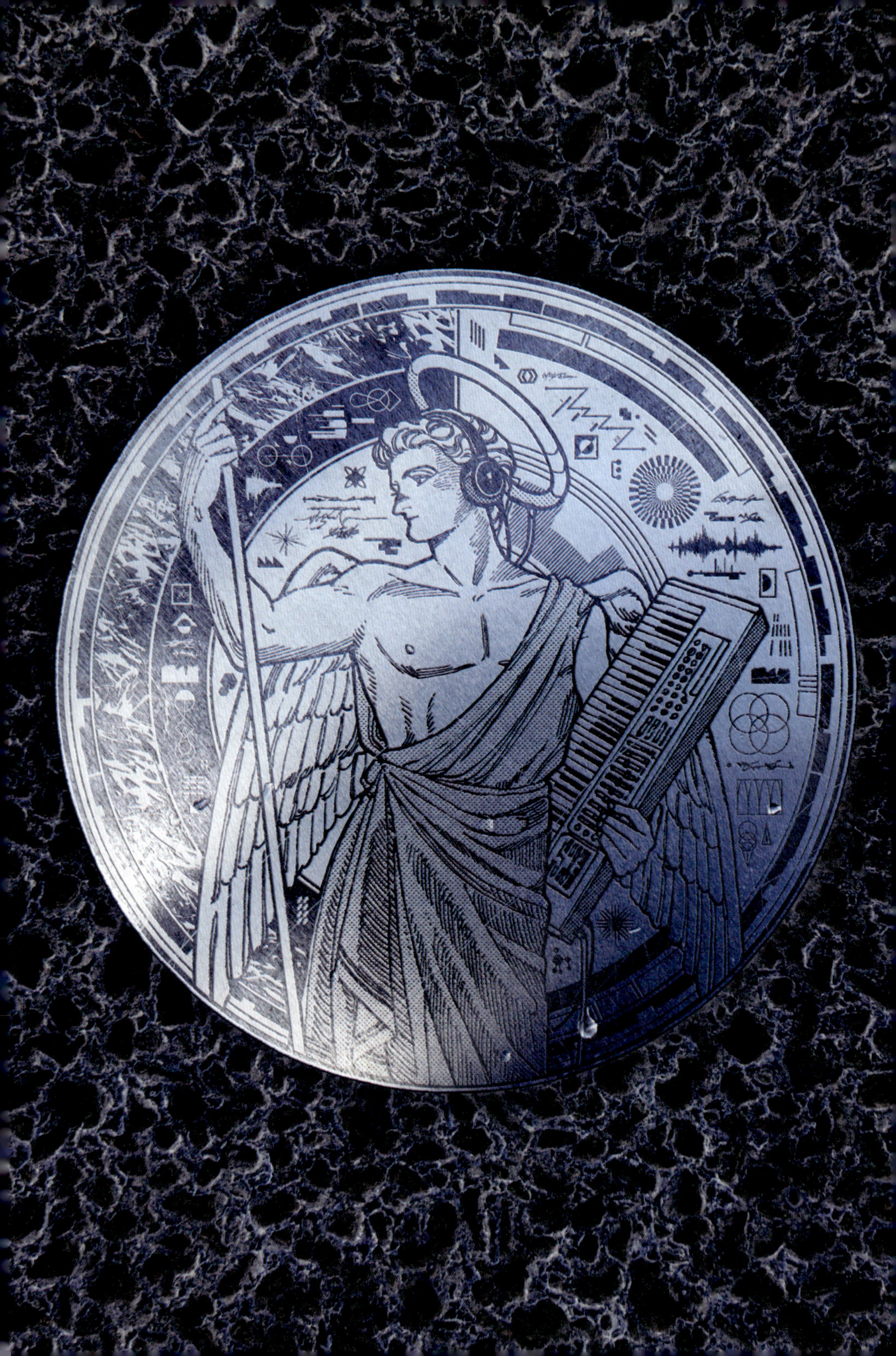

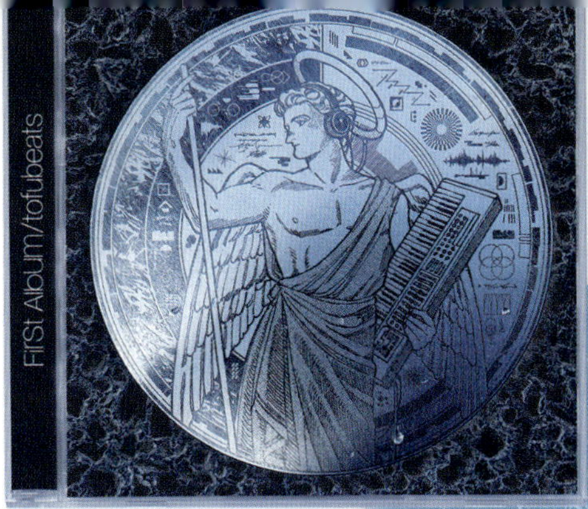

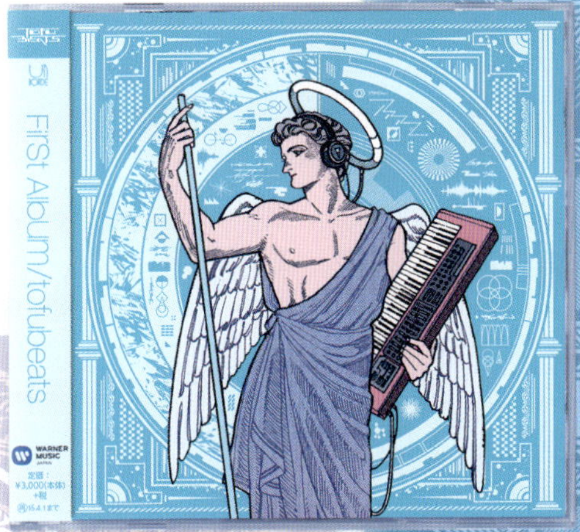

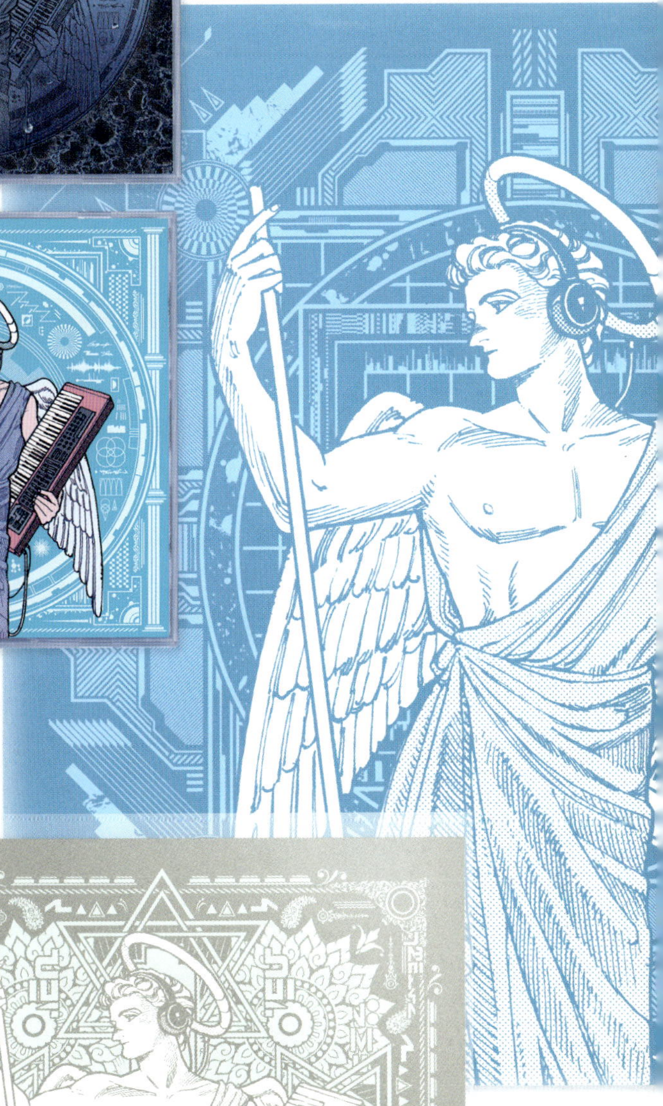

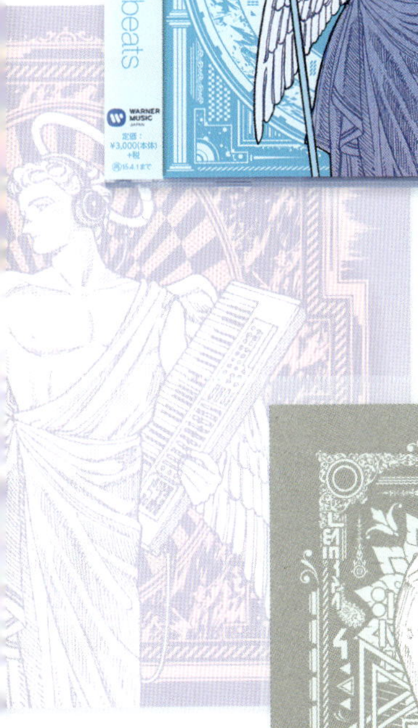

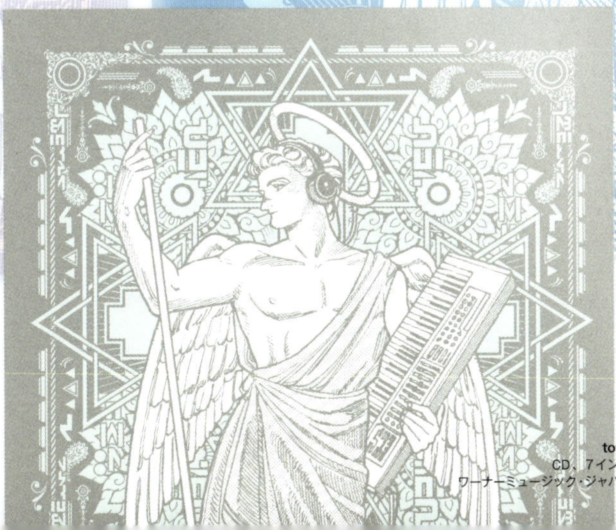

tofubeats / First Album
CD、7インチ、12インチジャケット
ワーナーミュージック・ジャパン / アンボルデ ｜ 2014

POS

tofubeats

baby - I woke up and it's not even early in the AM
Ah feel like I wasted my time
Not everything goes well in life
But looking back gets you nowhere

DISC 1 / CD Audio

DANCE&DANCE / intro

POSITIVE feat. Dream Ami

T.D.M. feat. okadada

Too Many Girls feat. KREVA

STAKEHOLDER

Throw your laptop on the fire feat. 小室哲哉

I know you / skit

Without U feat. Skylar Spence

すてきなメゾン feat. 玉城ティナ

くりかえしのMUSIC feat. 岸田繁(くるり)

閑話休題 / skit

別の人間 feat. 中納良恵(EGO-WRAPPIN')

baby - I woke up and it's not even early in the AM
Ah feel like I wasted my time
Not everything goes well in life
But looking back gets you nowhere

Even when you are feeling down
Be positive and
everything's going to be all right
It's okay to think like that isn't it?

Hey cheer up
World is going to be a better place
Will you dance with me today?
I want to expect good things to happen in the future
Go hang out a little
Just because two of us are laughing together
It's going to be okay tonight
Let's dancinthruthenight

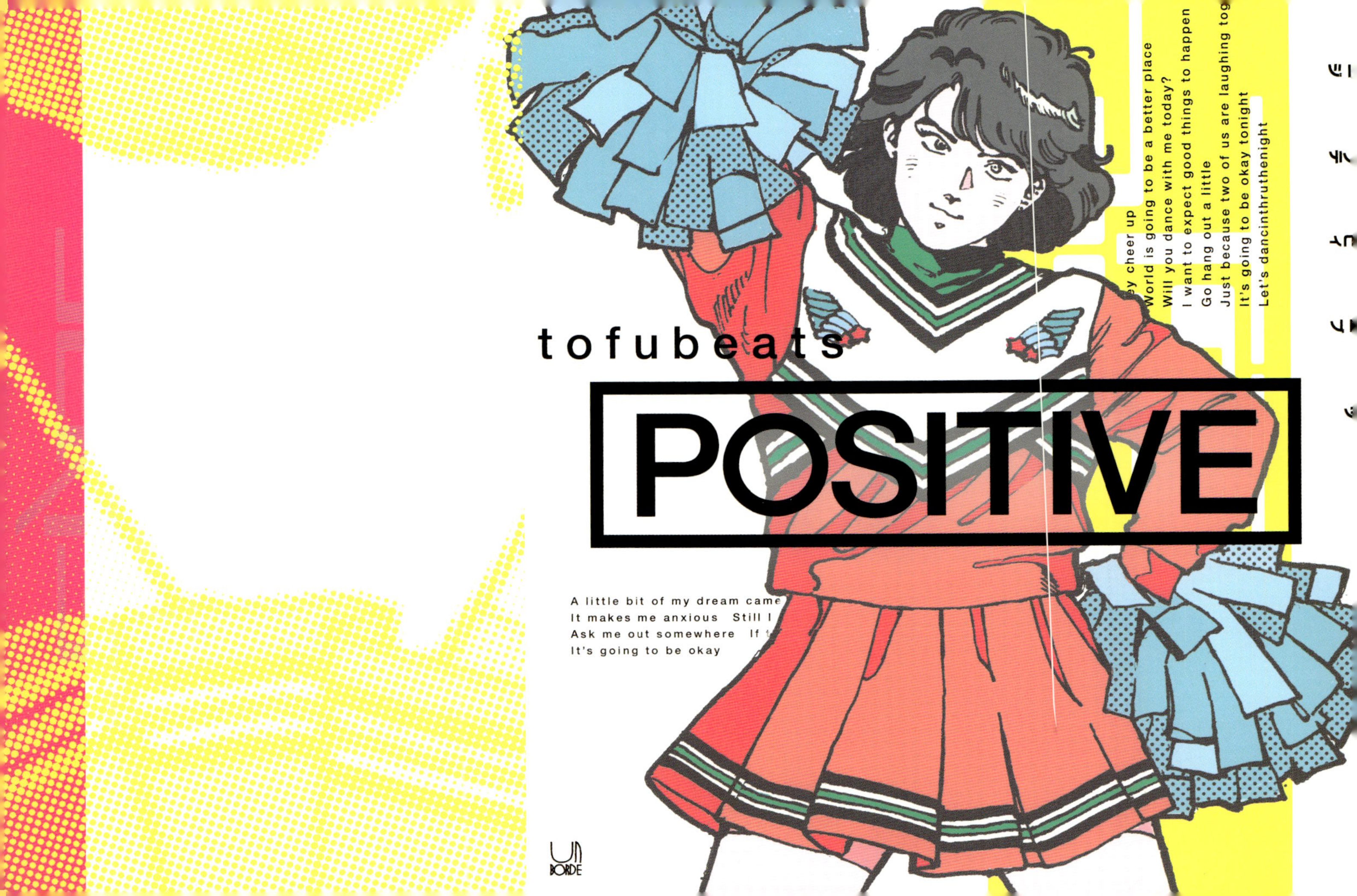
tofubeats
POSITIVE
A little bit of my dream came
It makes me anxious Still I
Ask me out somewhere If
It's going to be okay
ey cheer up
World is going to be a better place
Will you dance with me today?
I want to expect good things to happen
Go hang out a little
Just because two of us are laughing tog
It's going to be okay tonight
Let's dancinthruthenight
UN BORDE

tofubeats / POSITIVE
CDジャケット ｜ ワーナーミュージック・ジャパン / アンボルデ ｜ 2015

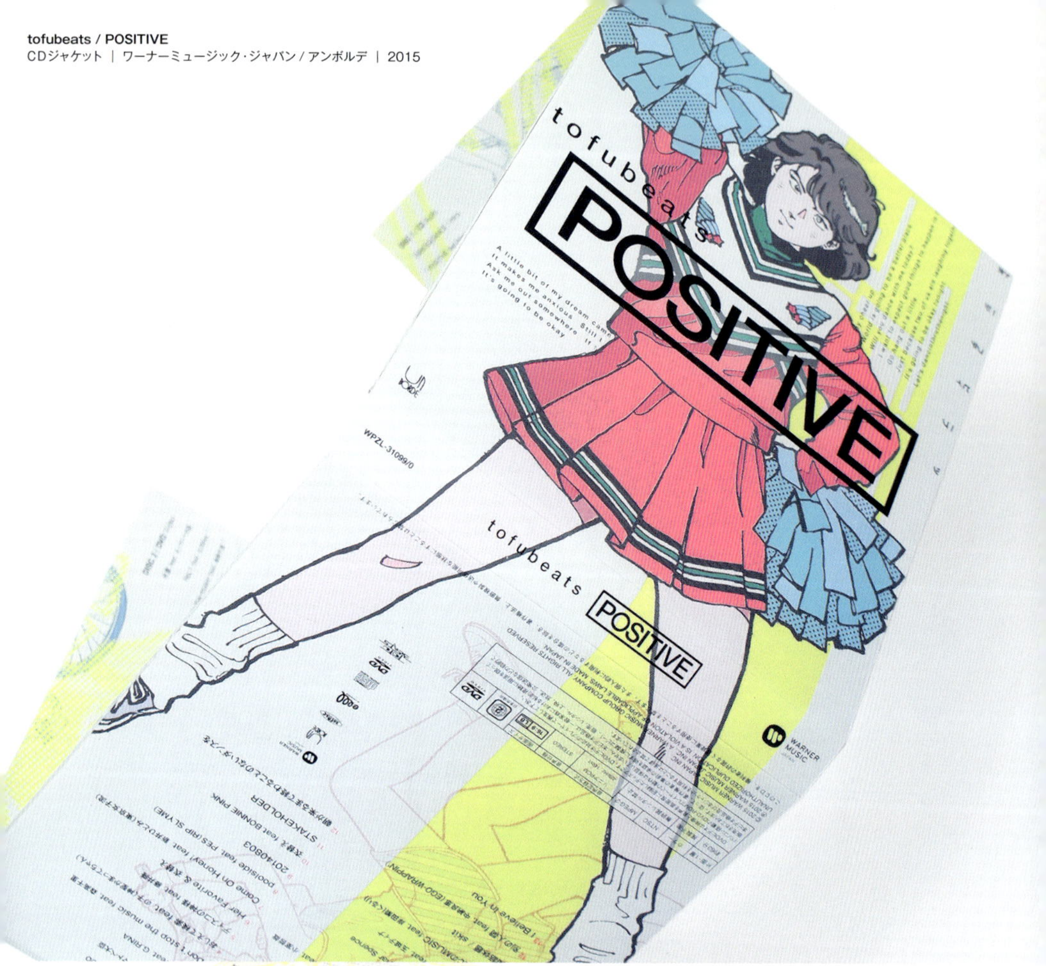

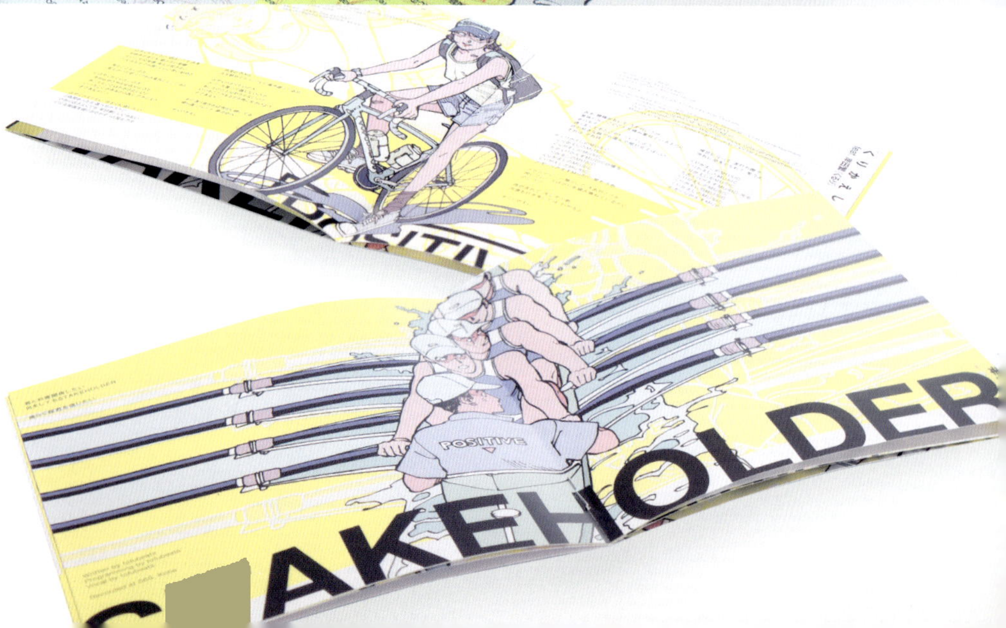

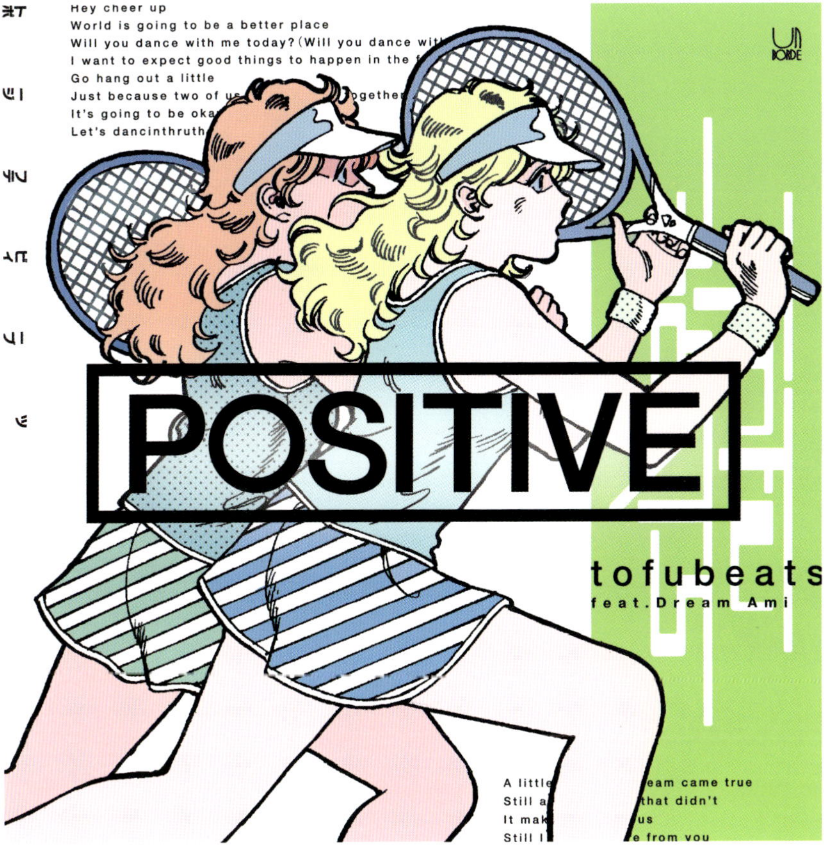

tofubeats / POSITIVE feat. Dream Ami
配信ジャケット ｜ ワーナーミュージック・ジャパン / アンボルデ ｜ 2015

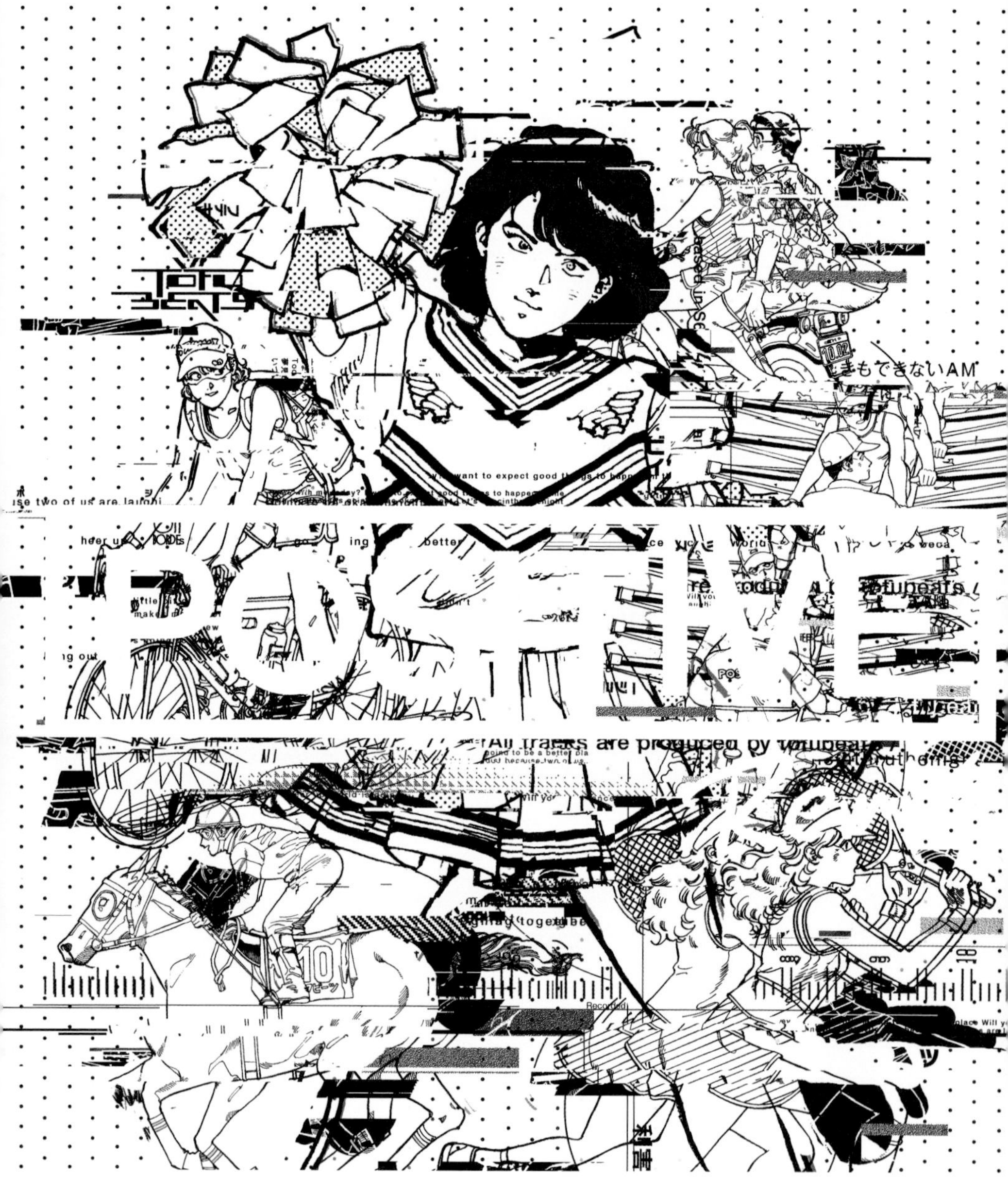
POSITIVE
All tracks are produced by tofubeats
まもできないAM
want to expect good things to happen
se two of us are laughi

tofubeats / **POSITIVE** REMIXES

トーフビーツ
ポジテイブ
リミキシーズ

[1] POSITIVE feat. Dream Ami - **中田ヤスタカ(CAPSULE) REMIX**

[2] T.D.M. feat. okadada - **okadada enxtended mix**

[3] Too Many Girls feat. KREVA - **The Anticipation Illicit Tsuboi REMIX**

[4] STAKEHOLDER - **小室哲哉 REMIX**

[5] Throw your laptop on the fire feat. 小室哲哉 - **PART2STYLE Sound REMIX**

[6] Without U feat. Skylar Spence - **in the blue shirt REMIX**

[7] すてきなメゾン feat. 玉城ティナ - **tofubeats REMIX**

[8] くりかえしのMUSIC feat. 岸田繁(くるり) - **tofubeats REMIX**

[9] 別の人間 feat. 中納良恵(EGO-WRAPPIN') - **PUNCH & MIGHTY REMIX**

[10] I Believe In You - **cherryboy function REMIX**

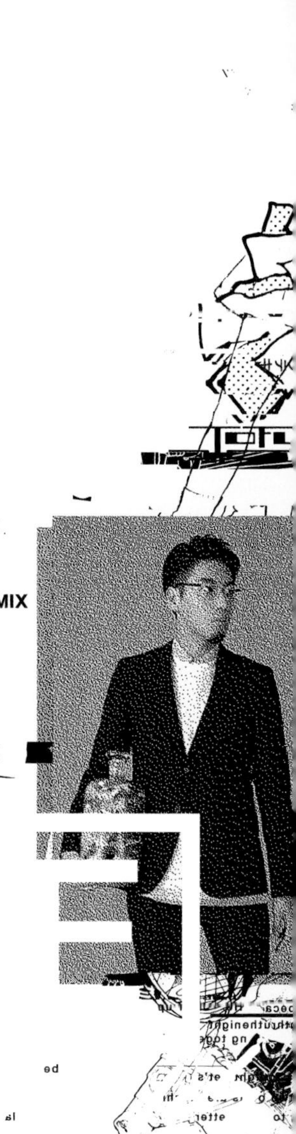

Mastering : Ryuich Tanaka (MIXERS LAB.)

additional musician
M-3 Guitar : Kashif(PPP), Drums : なかじまはじめ
M-9 Mixed by EVISBEATS
M-? window remix : dust.c

Dream Ami by the courtesy of rhythm zone / AVEX MUSIC CREATIVE INC.
KREVA by the courtesy of PONY CANYON INC.
Shigeru Kishida(Quruli) by the courtesy of Speedstar Records / Victor Entertainment
Yoshie Nakano (EGO-WRAPPIN') by the courtesy of NOFRAMES / TOY'S FACTORY / Minor Swing

℗© 2016 WARNER MUSIC JAPAN INC., A WARNER MUSIC GROUP COMPANY.
ALL RIGHTS RESERVED.UNAUTHORIZED DUPLICATION IS A VIOLATION OF APPLICABLE LAWS. MADE IN JAPAN.

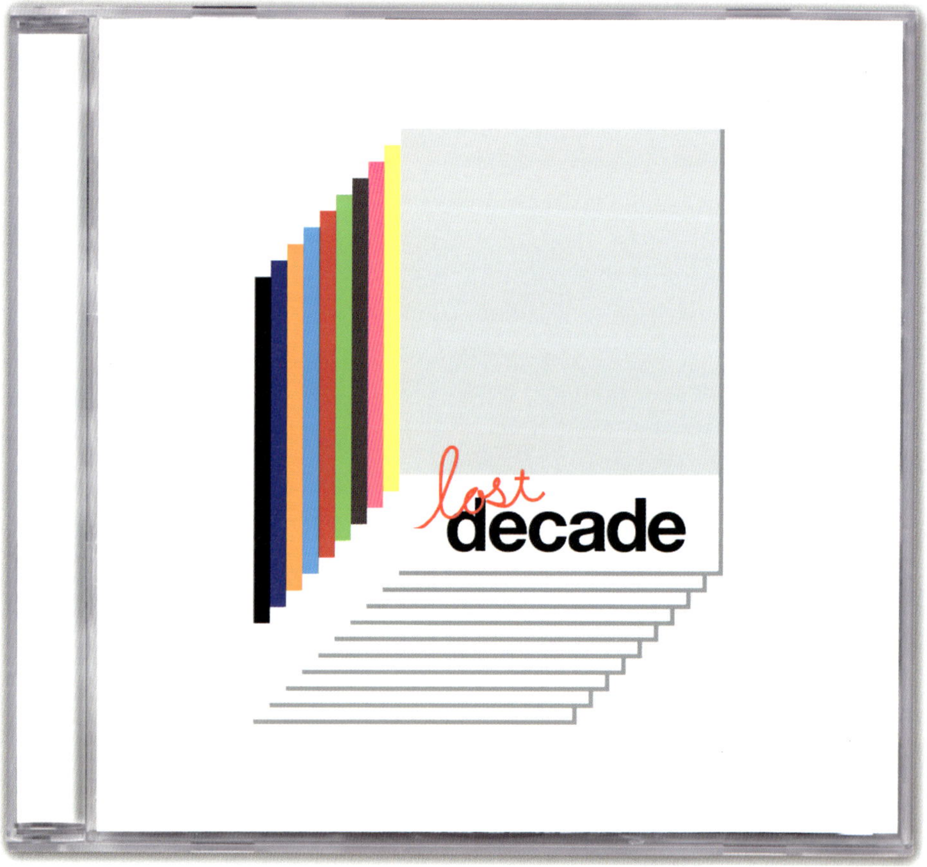

tofubeats / lost decade
CDジャケット | 2013

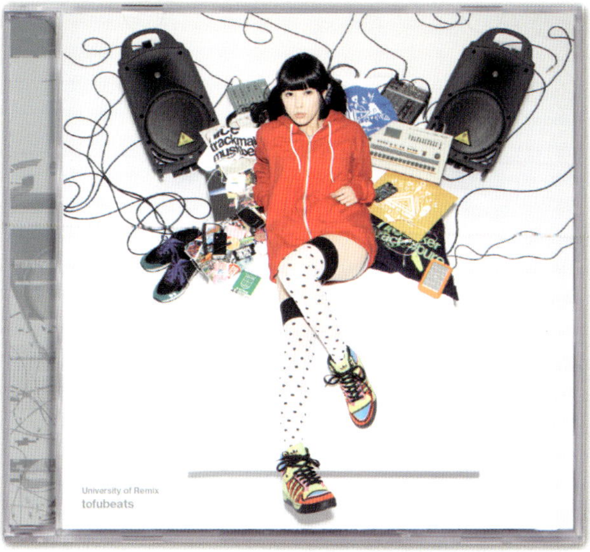

tofubeats / University of Remix
CDジャケット ｜ SME Records Inc. ｜ 2013
©2013 SME Records Inc.

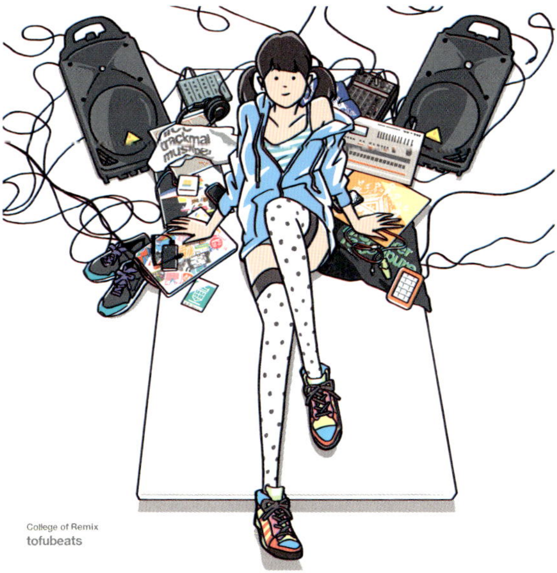

tofubeats / College of Remix
配信ジャケット ｜ ONEPEACE.INC ｜ 2013

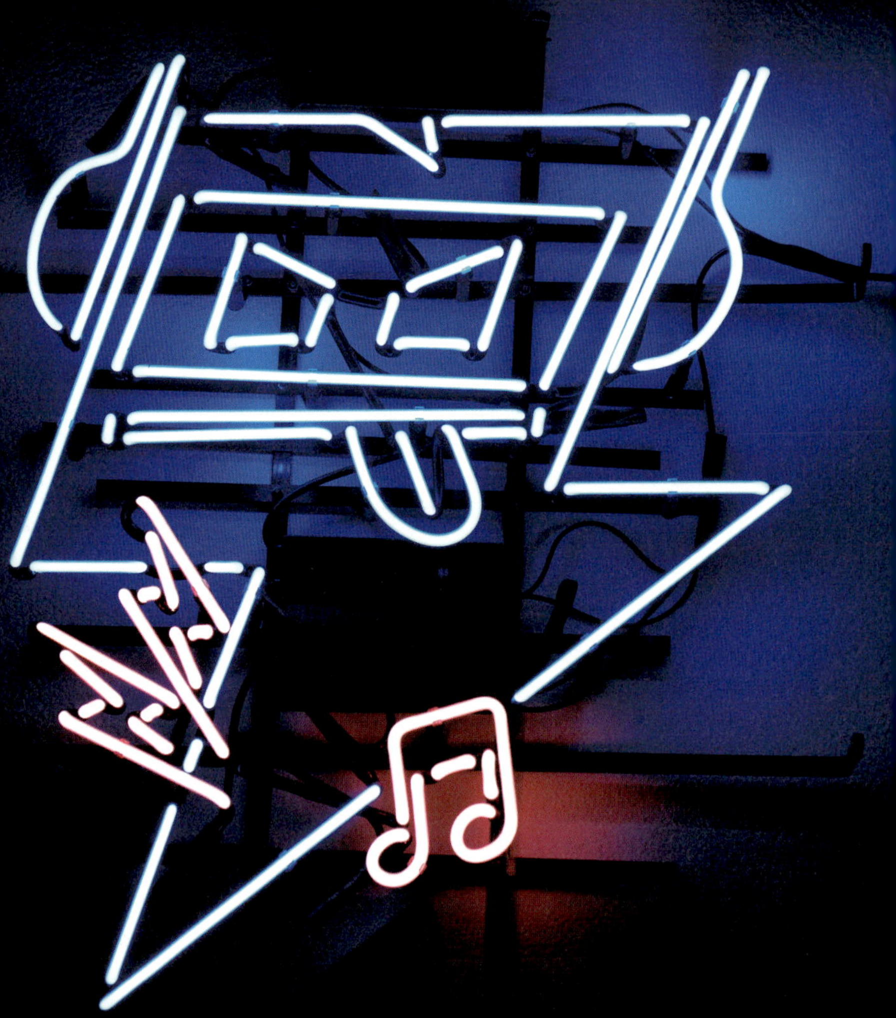

Maltine Records Neon sign
Maltine Records | 2015

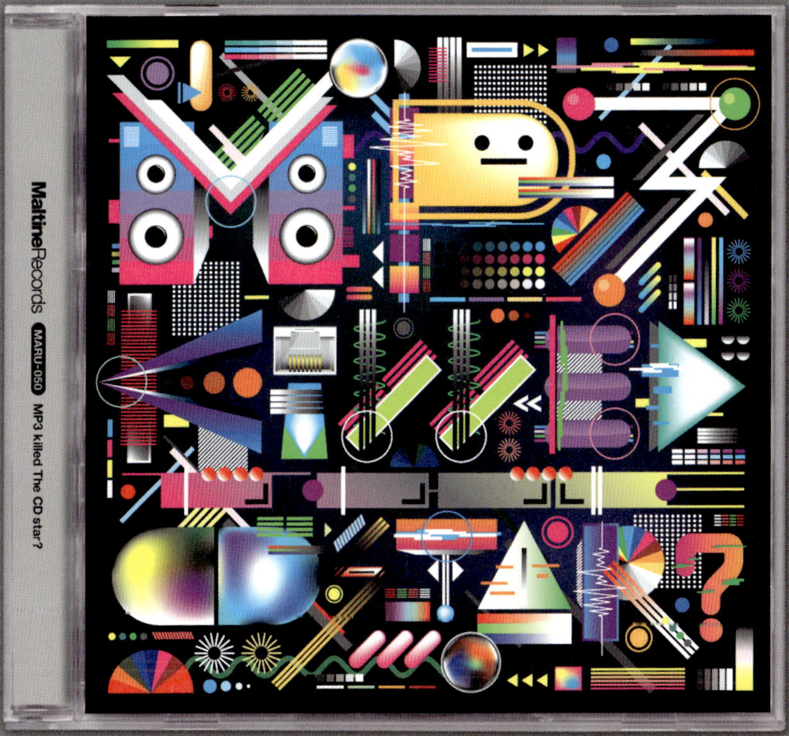

MP3 killed The CD star?
CDジャケット ｜ Maltine Records ｜ 2010

Maltine Records Sticker

ステッカー | Maltine Records | 2008

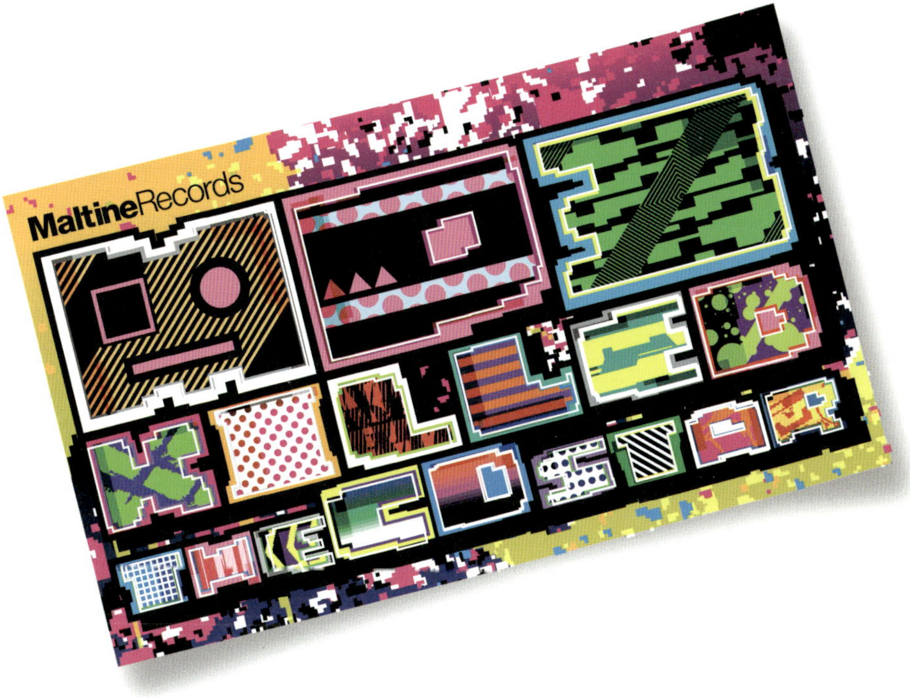

Maltine Records Sticker
ステッカー | Maltine Records | 2009

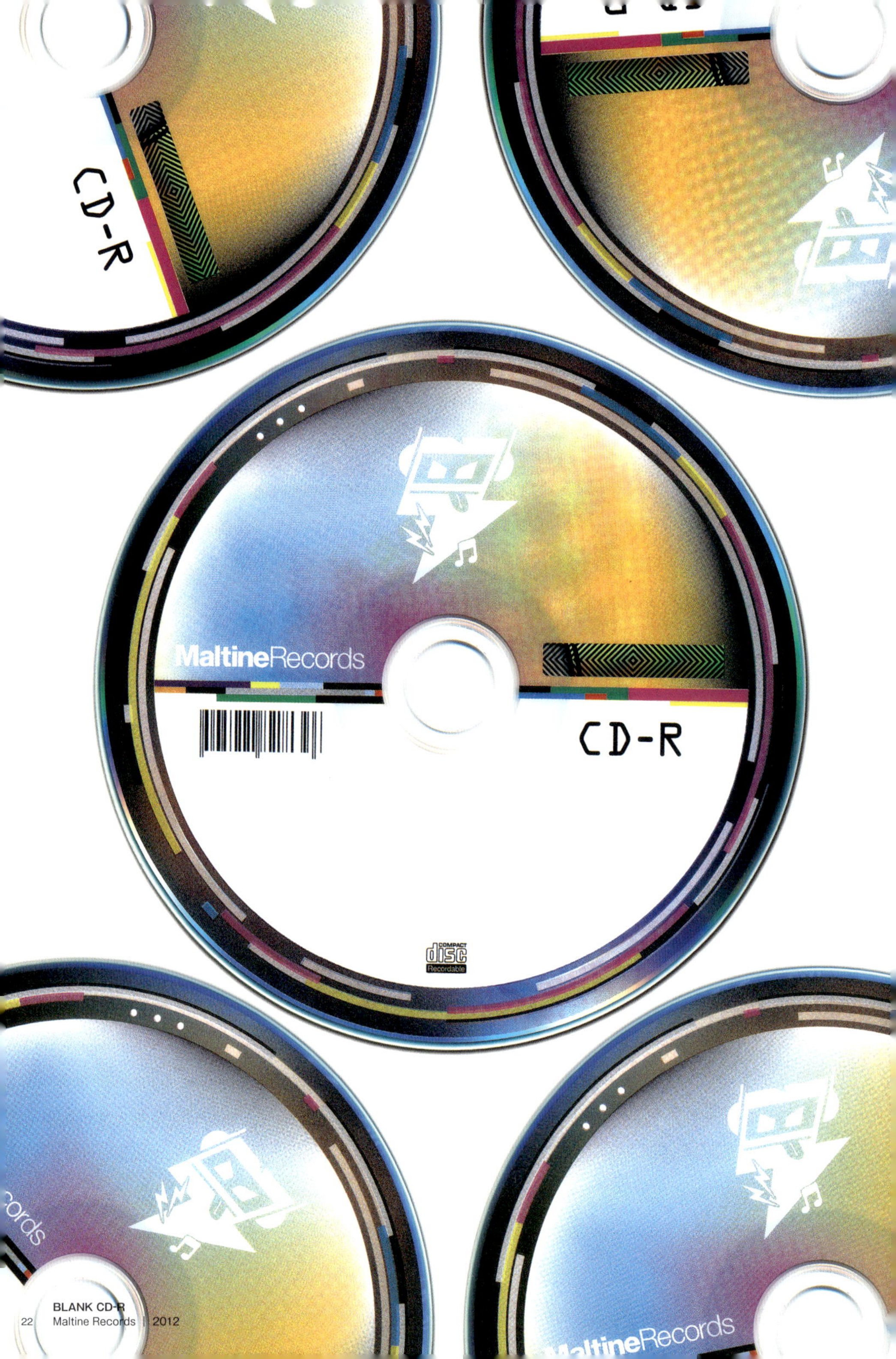

BLANK CD-R
Maltine Records | 2012

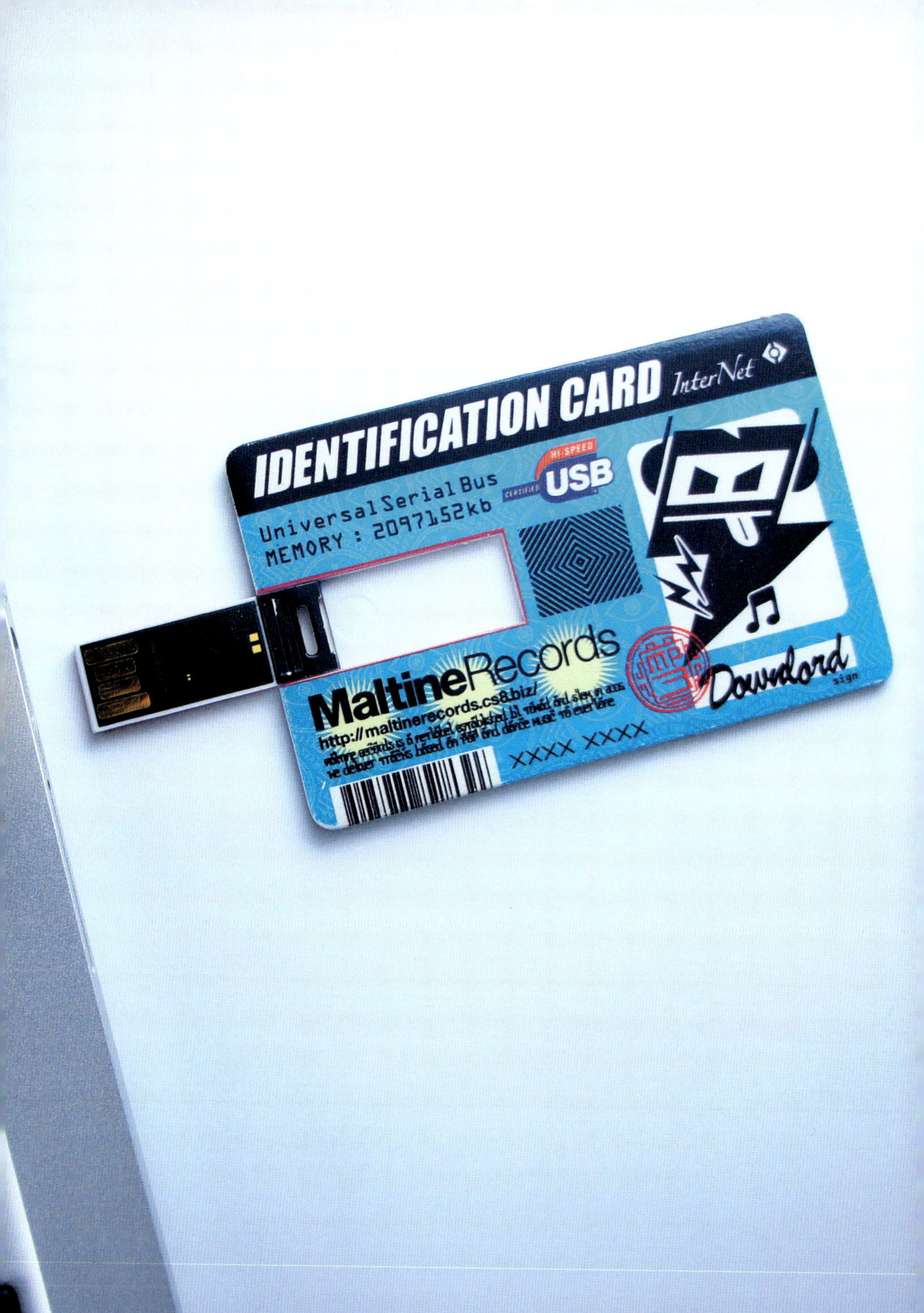
IDENTIFICATION CARD
InterNet
HI-SPEED
CERTIFIED USB
Universal Serial Bus
MEMORY : 2097152kb
MaltineRecords
http://maltinerecords.cs8.biz/
XXXX XXXX
Downlord
sign

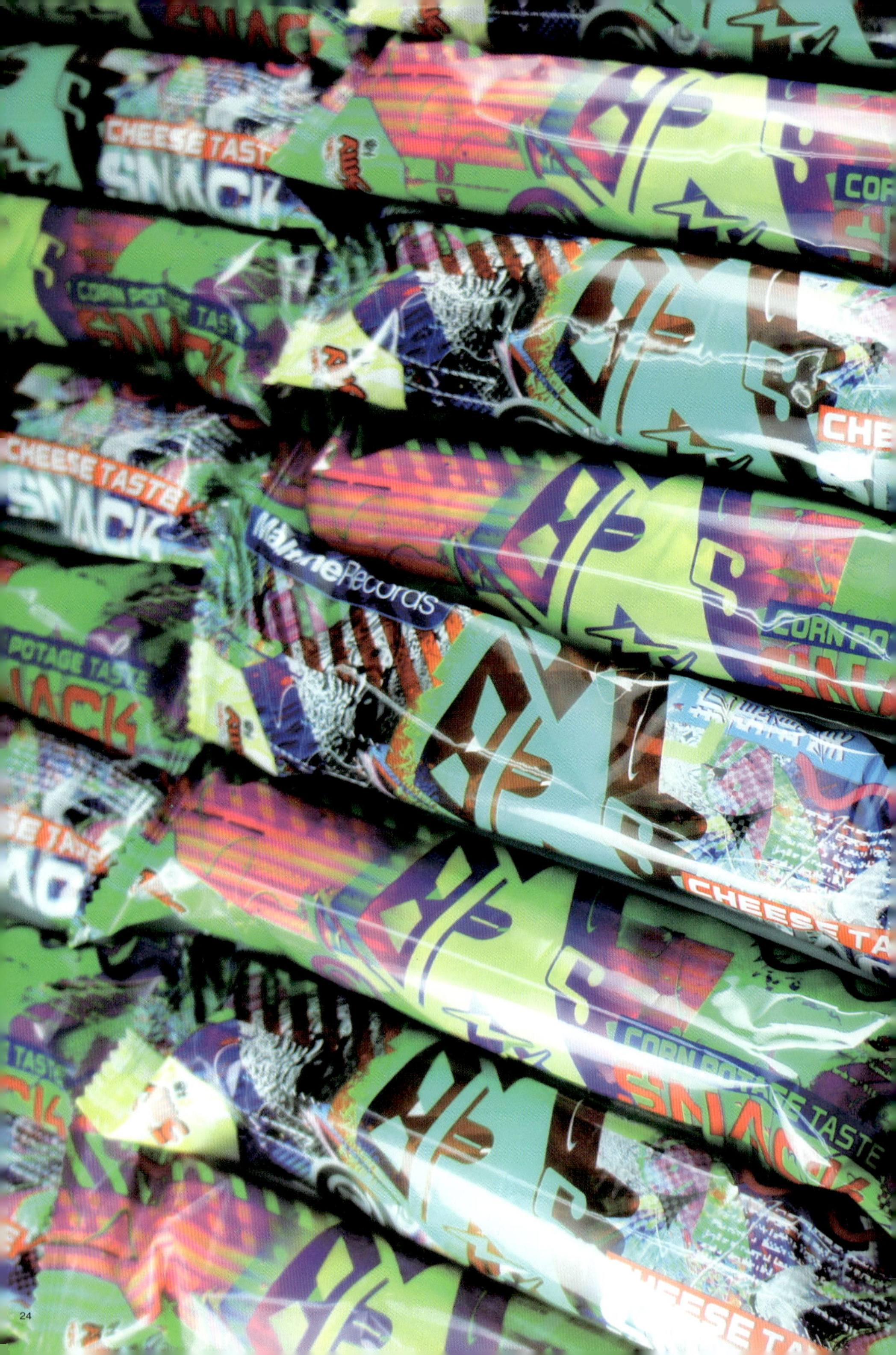
CHEESE TASTE
SNACK
Maltine Records
CORN POTAGE TASTE
SNACK

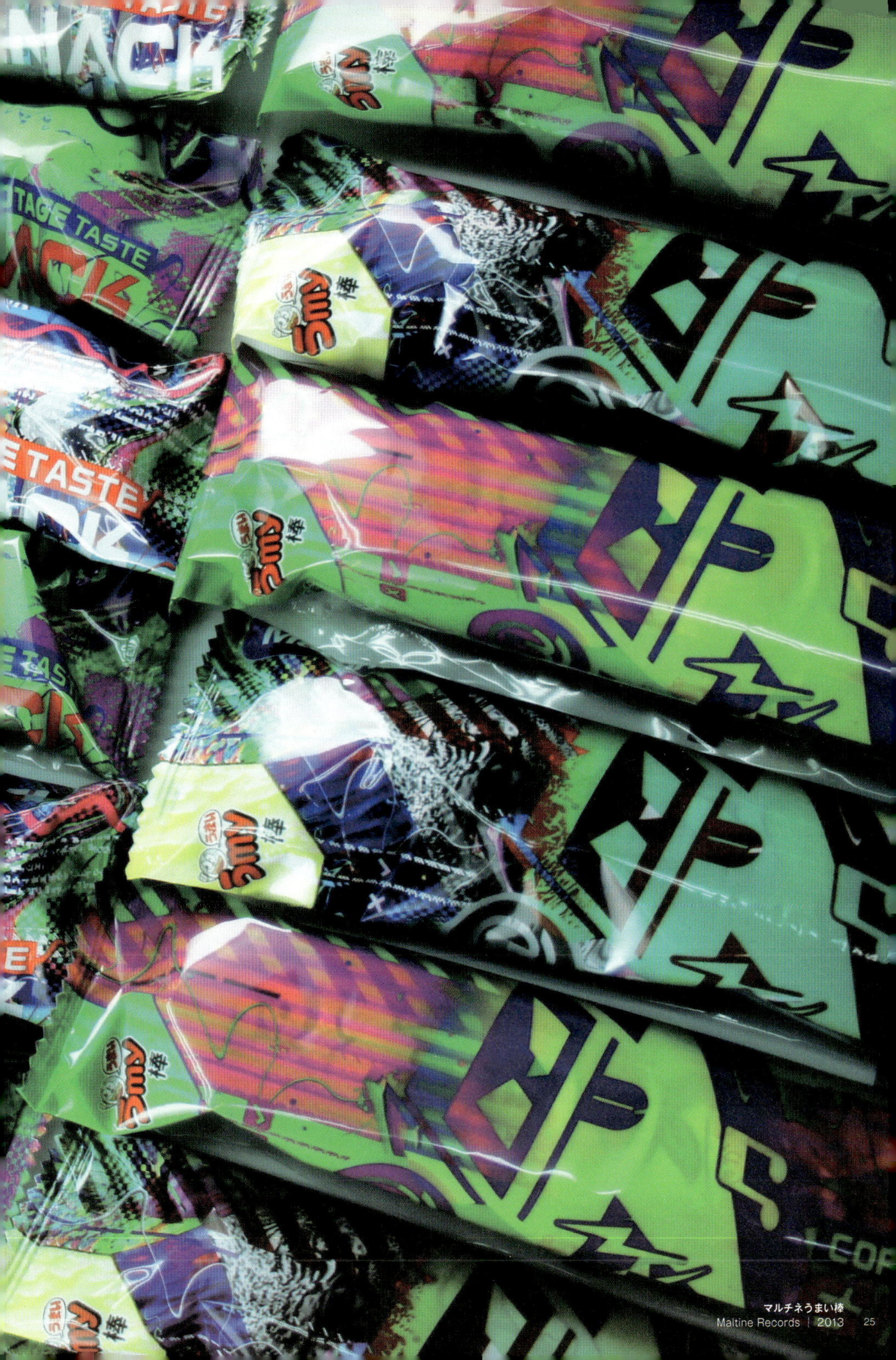

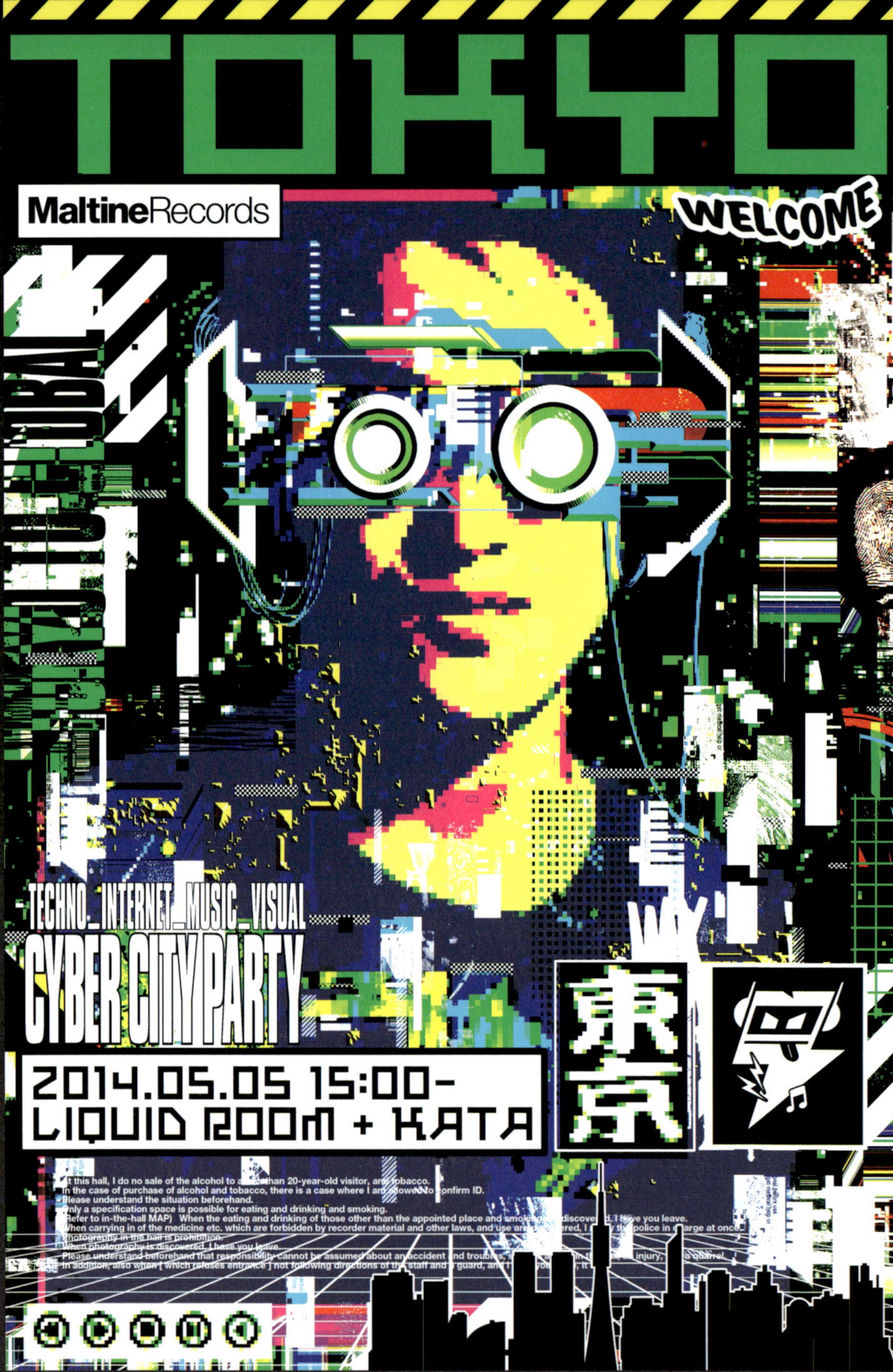
TOKYO
MaltineRecords
WELCOME
TECHNO_INTERNET_MUSIC_VISUAL
CYBER CITY PARTY
2014.05.05 15:00-
LIQUID ROOM + KATA
東京
Please understand the situation beforehand.
Only a specification space is possible for eating and drinking and smoking.
Photography in the hall is prohibition.
When photography is discovered, I have you leave.

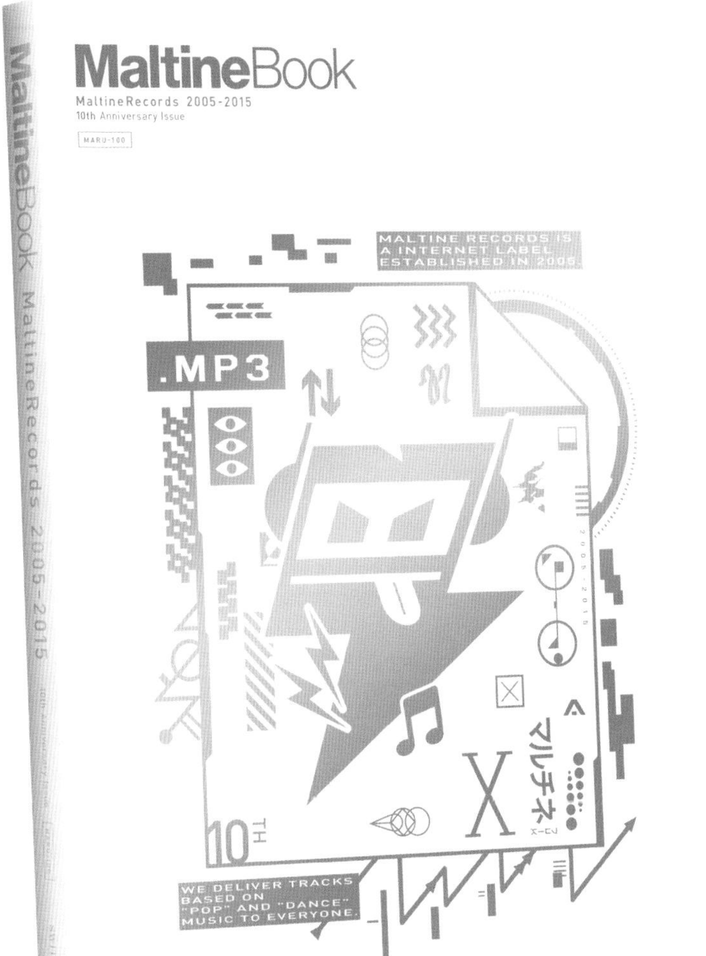
MaltineBook
MaltineRecords 2005-2015
10th Anniversary Issue
MARU-100
MALTINE RECORDS IS
A INTERNET LABEL
ESTABLISHED IN 2005.
.MP3
マルチネ
10TH
WE DELIVER TRACKS
BASED ON
"POP" AND "DANCE"
MUSIC TO EVERYONE.
MaltineBook MaltineRecords 2005-2015

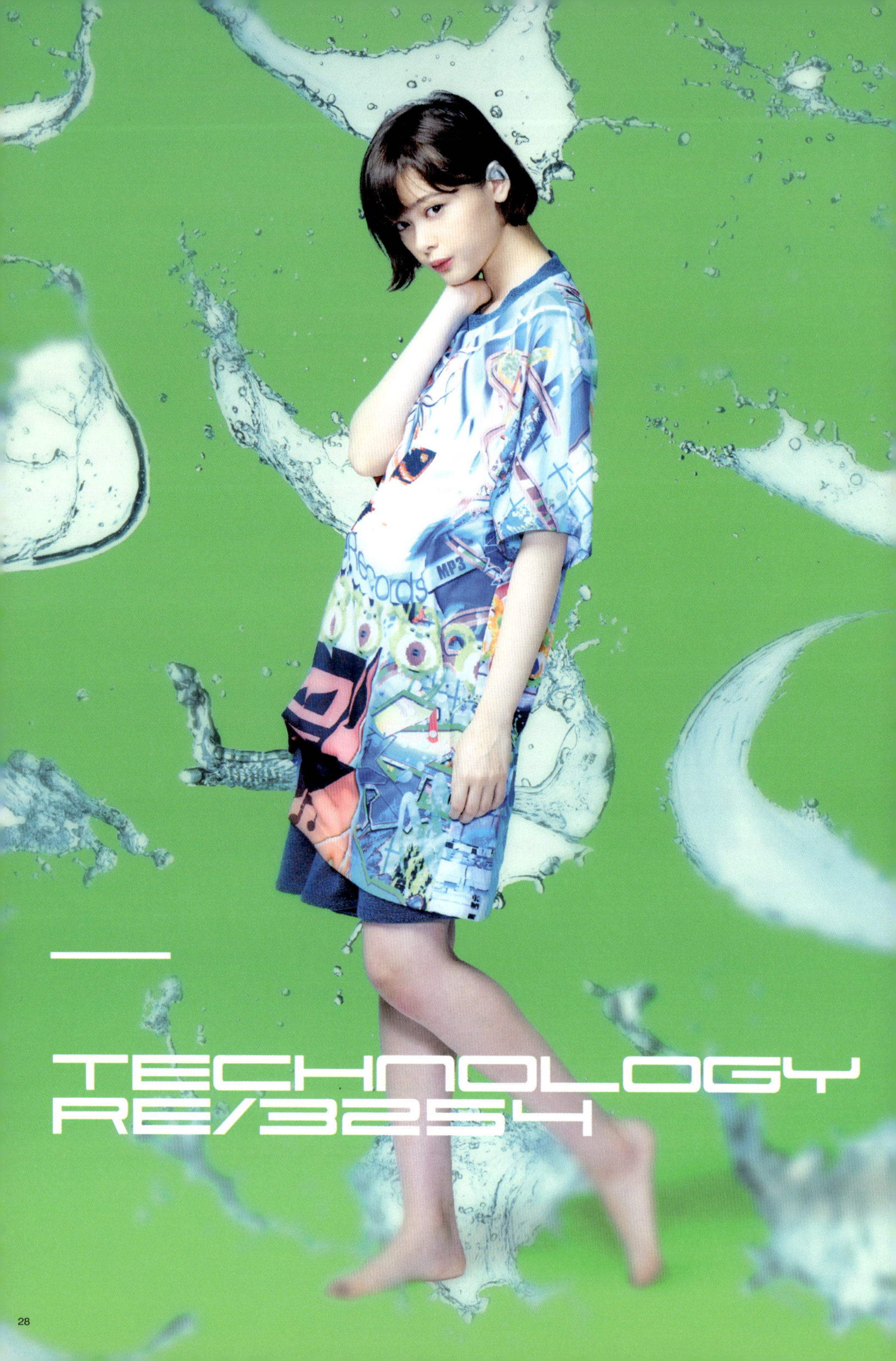

TECHNOLOGY RE/32254

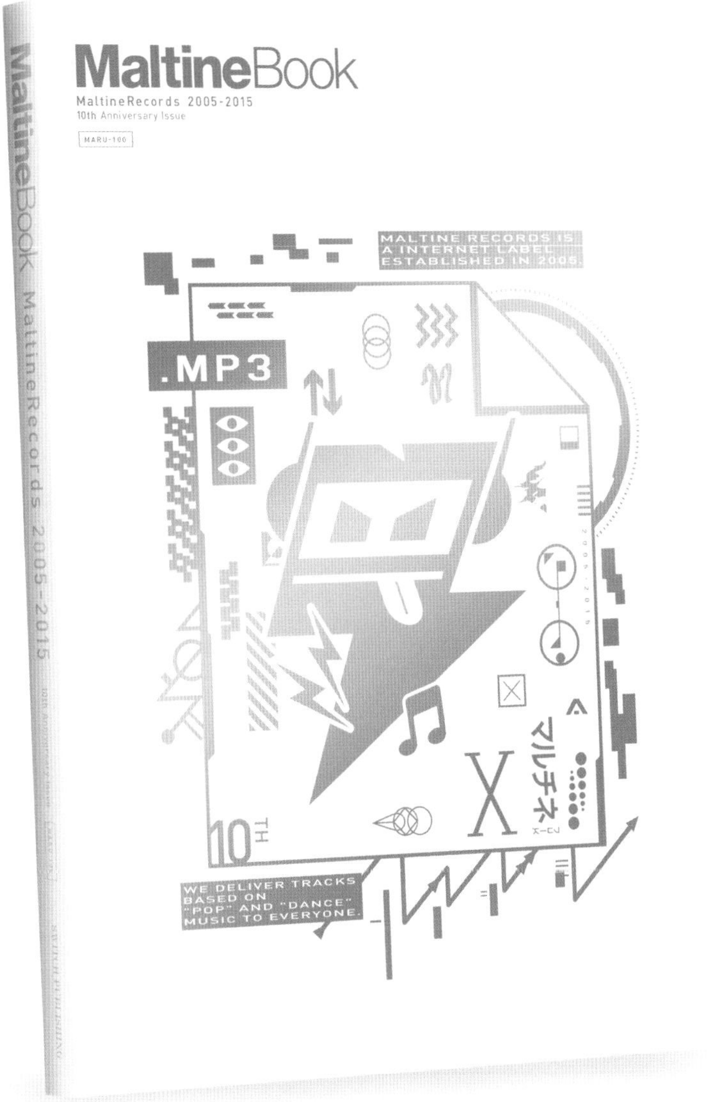

Maltine Book
ムック本装」 | スイッチ・パブリッシング | 2015

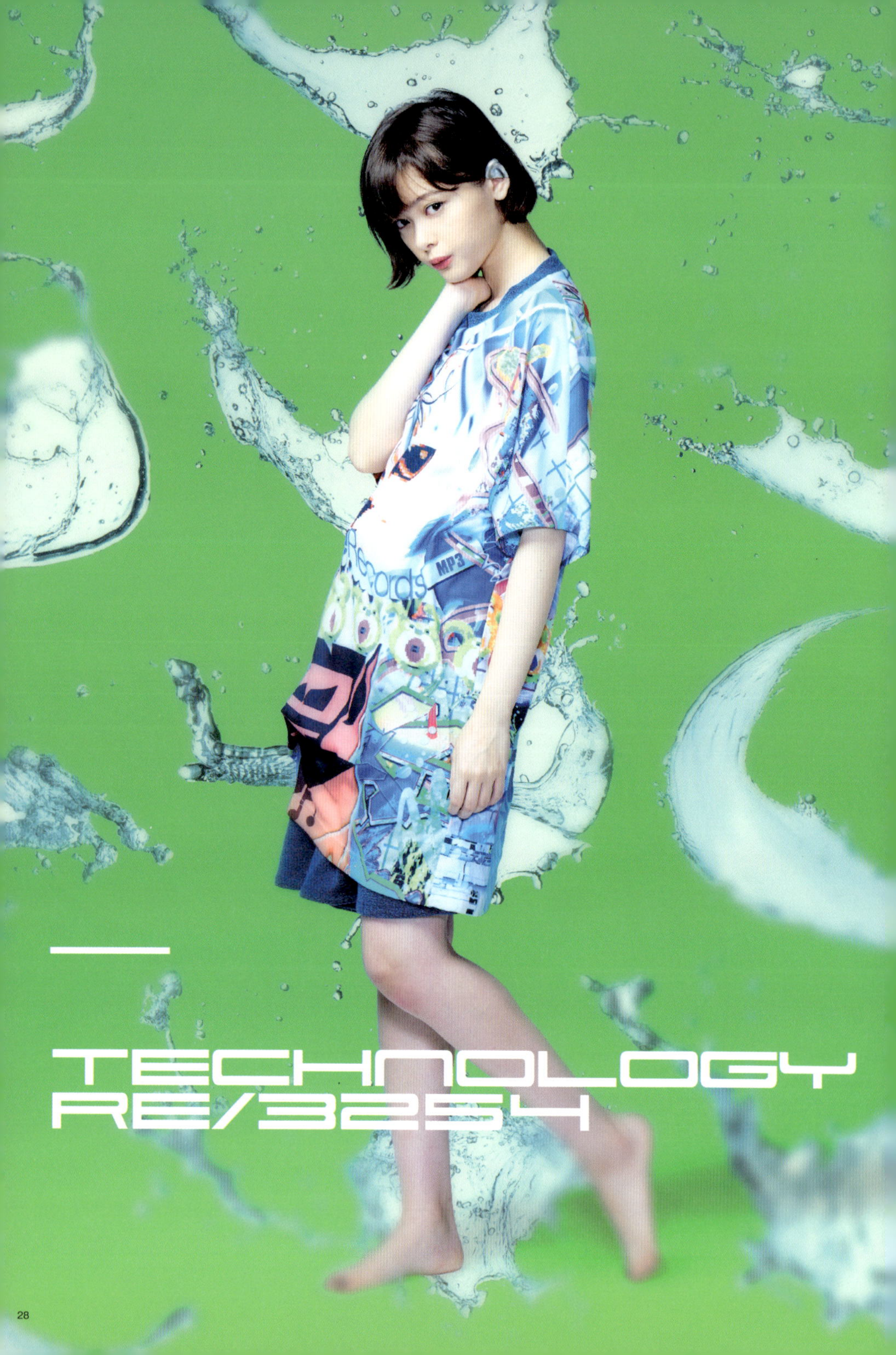

TECHNOLOGY RE/32254

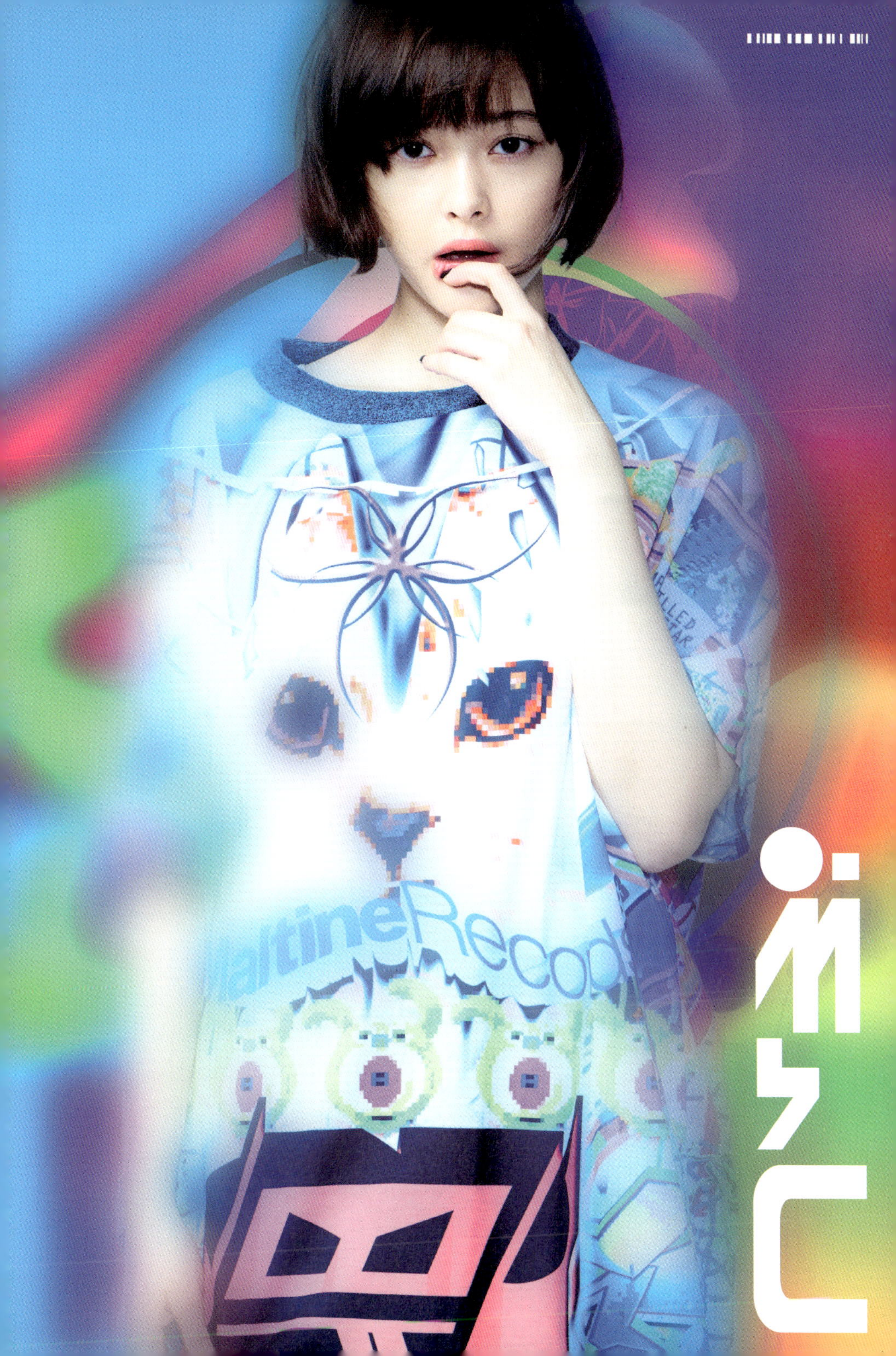

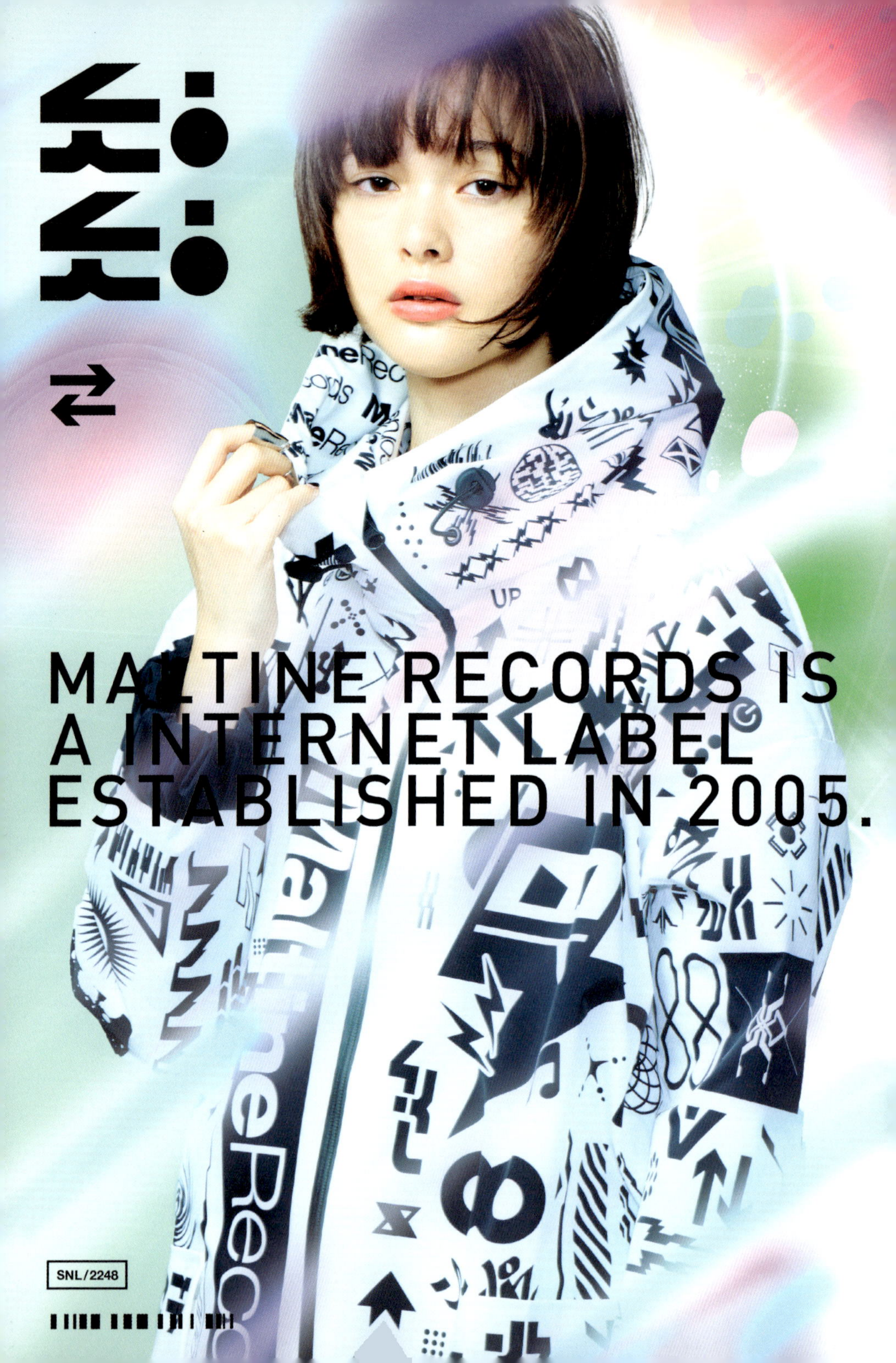
MALTINE RECORDS IS
A INTERNET LABEL
ESTABLISHED IN 2005.
SNL/2248

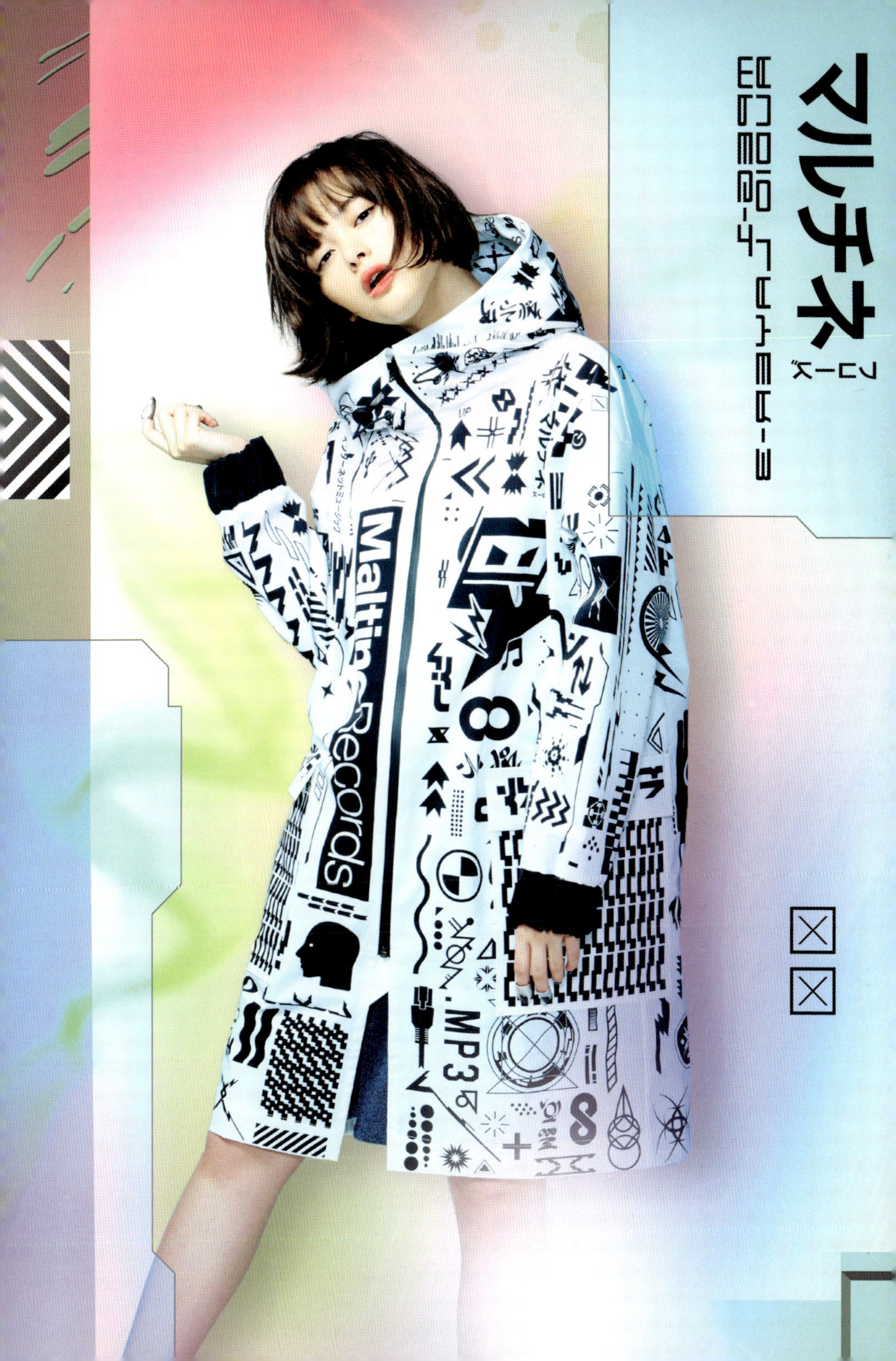
マルチネ
フード
Maltine Records
MP3

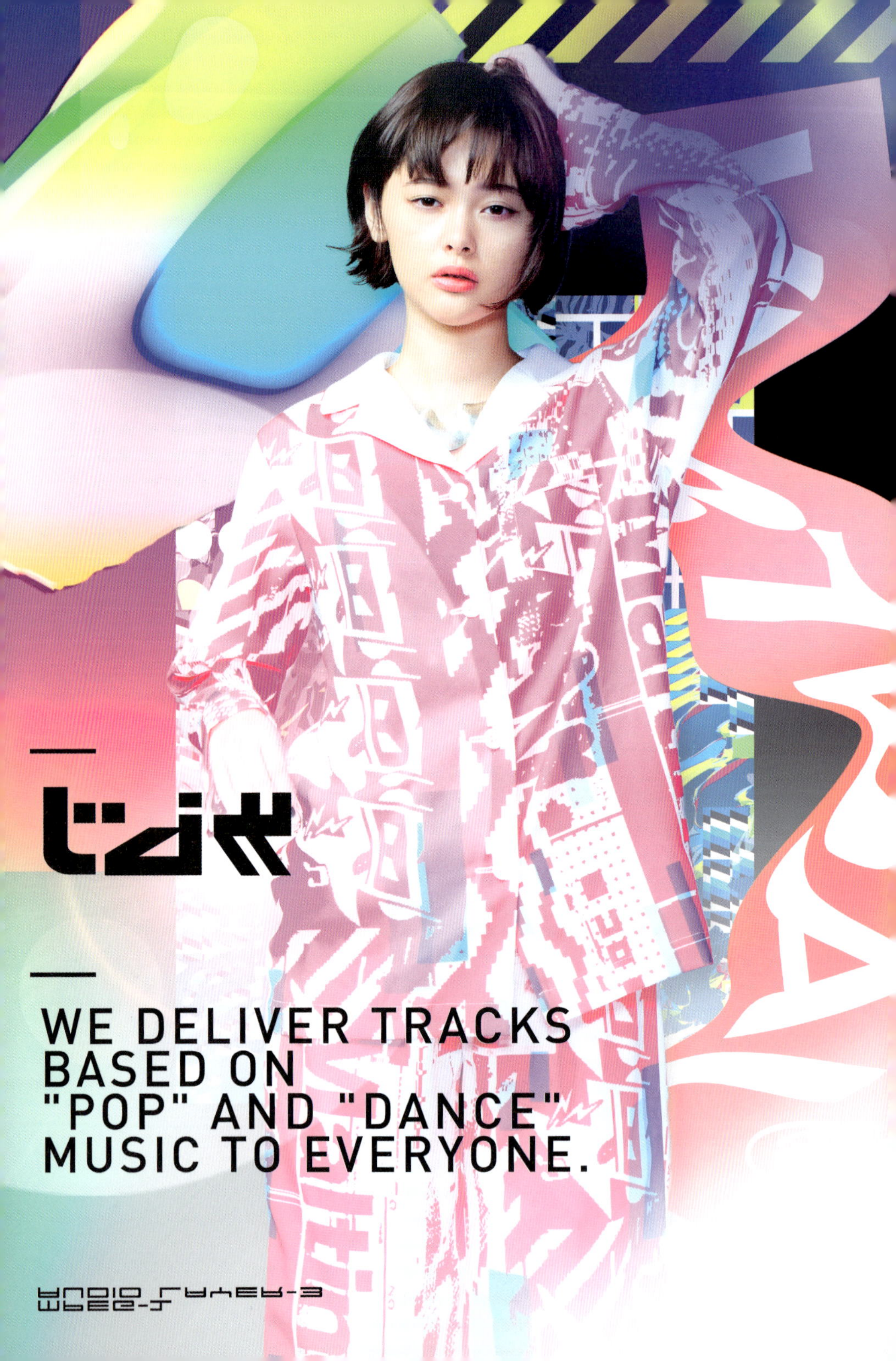
WE DELIVER TRACKS
BASED ON
"POP" AND "DANCE"
MUSIC TO EVERYONE.

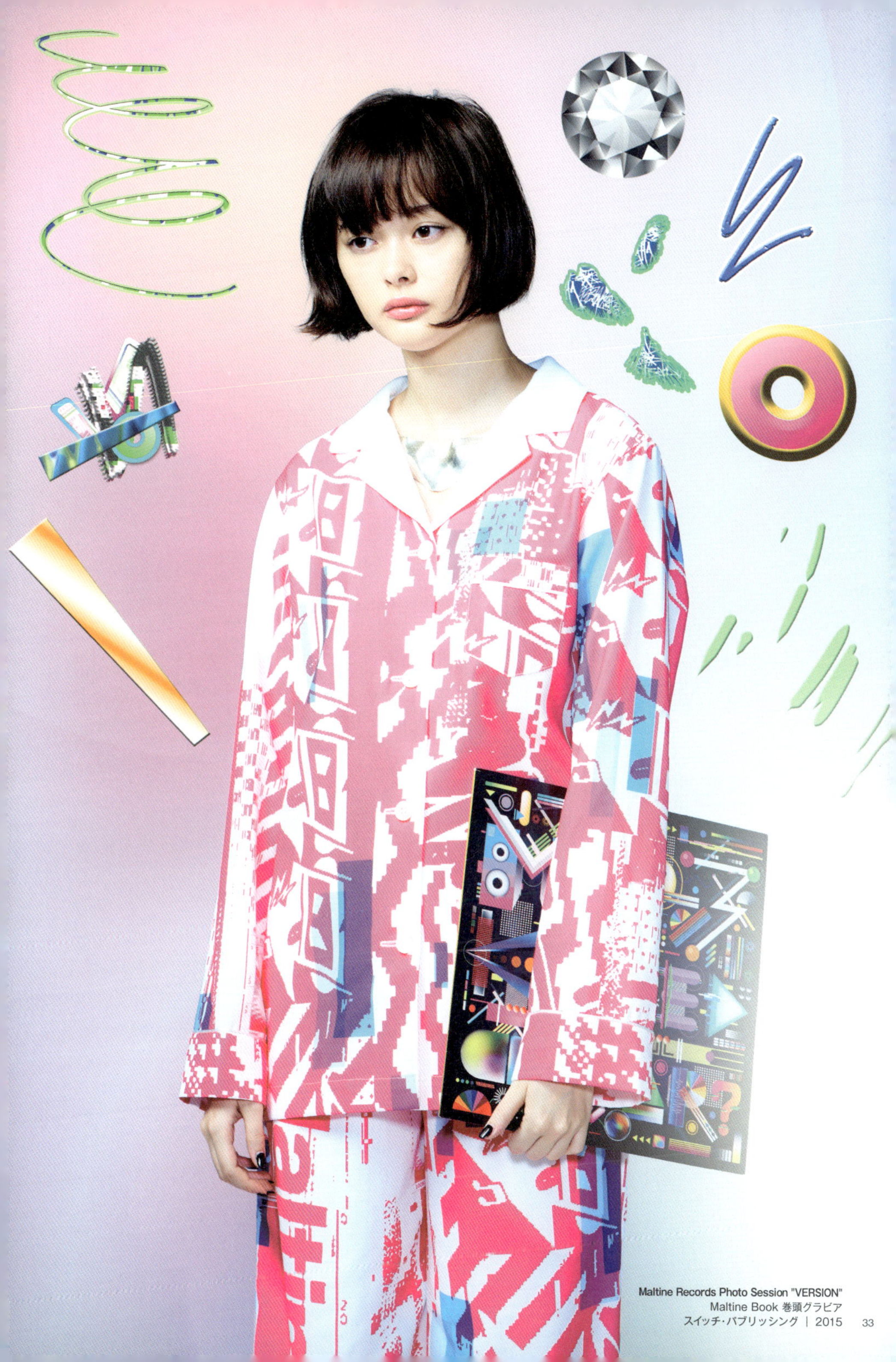

Maltine Records Photo Session "VERSION"
Maltine Book 巻頭グラビア
スイッチ・パブリッシング | 2015

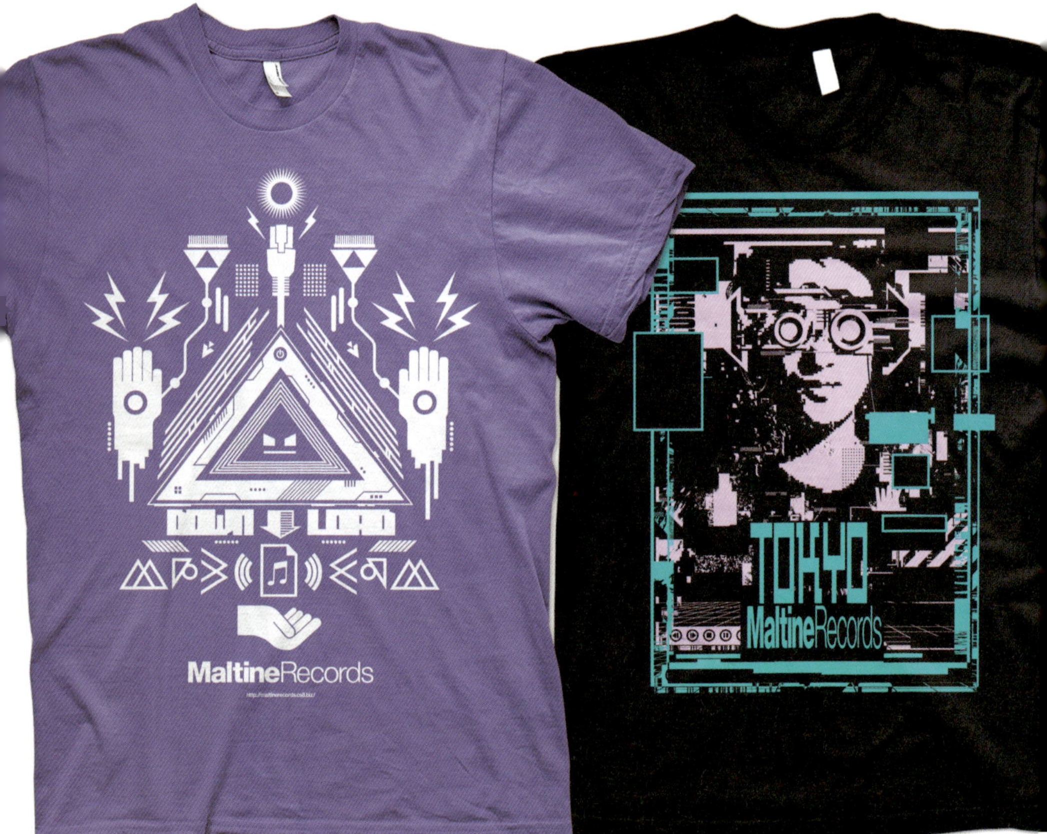
MaltineRecords
TOKYO
MaltineRecords

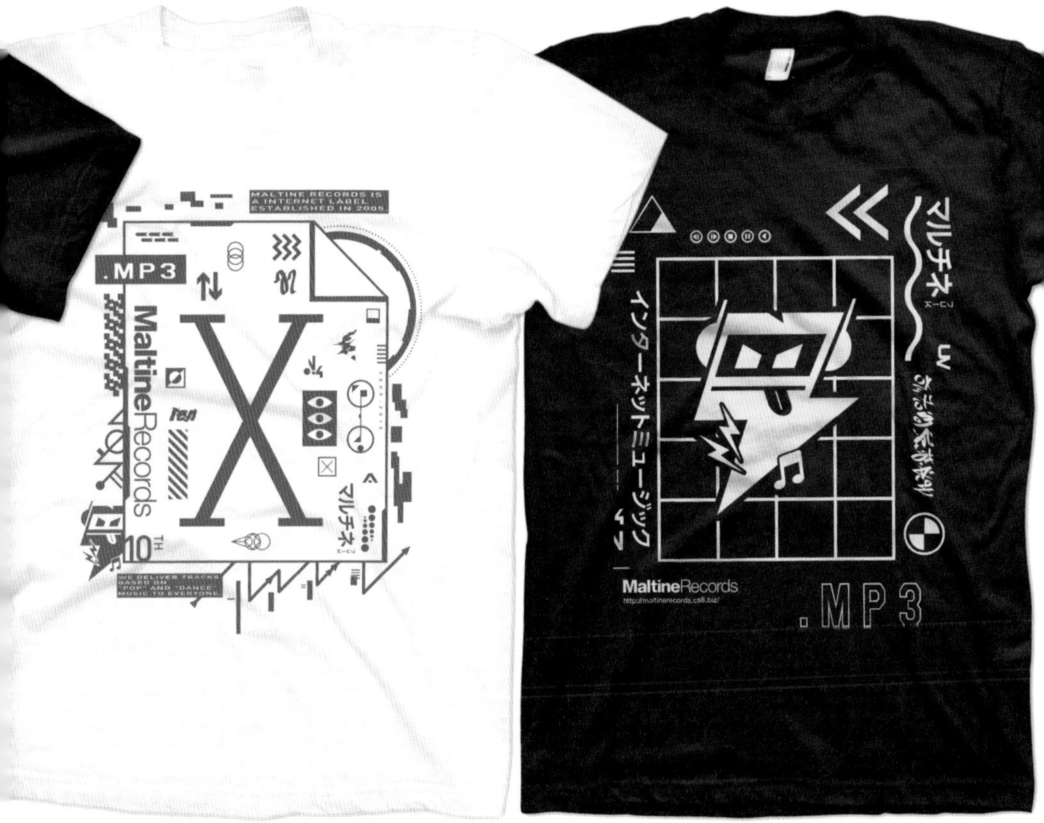

Maltine Records T-shirt
Tシャツ | Maltine Records | 2010–2015

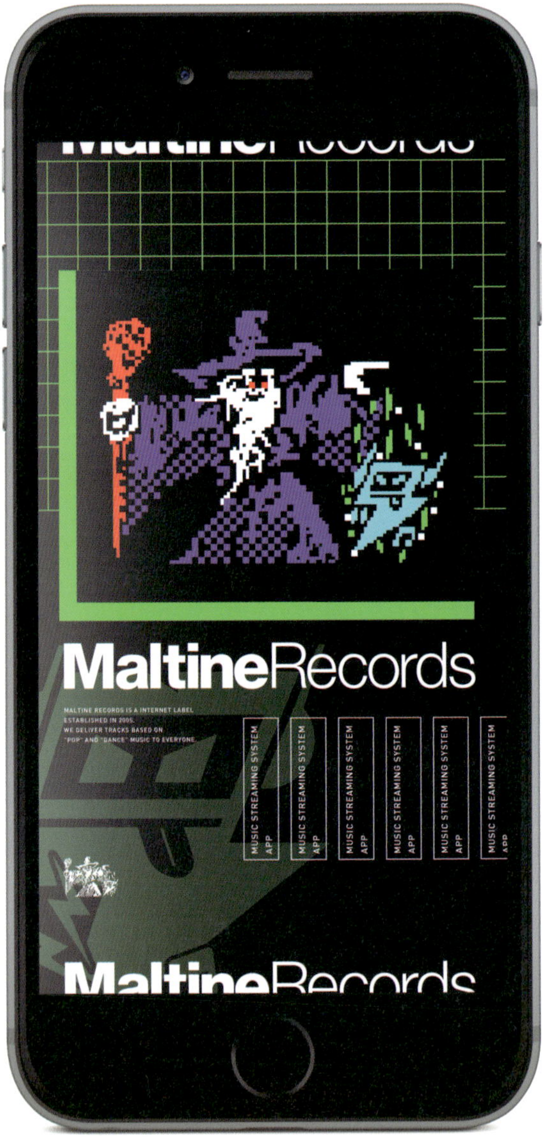

Maltine App
ストリーミングアプリ起動画面 | Maltine Records | 2016

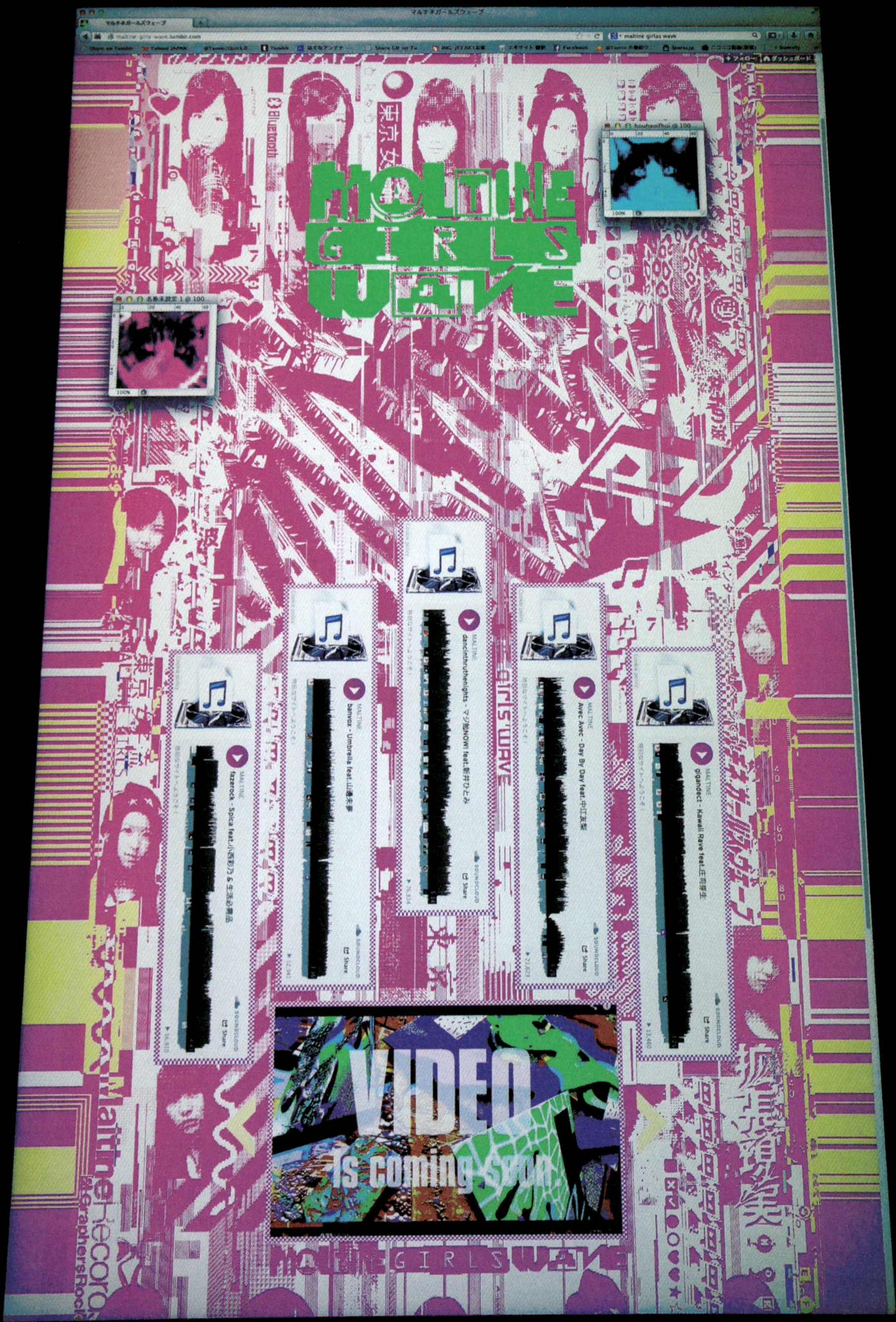
MALTINE GIRLS WAVE
VIDEO
is coming soon

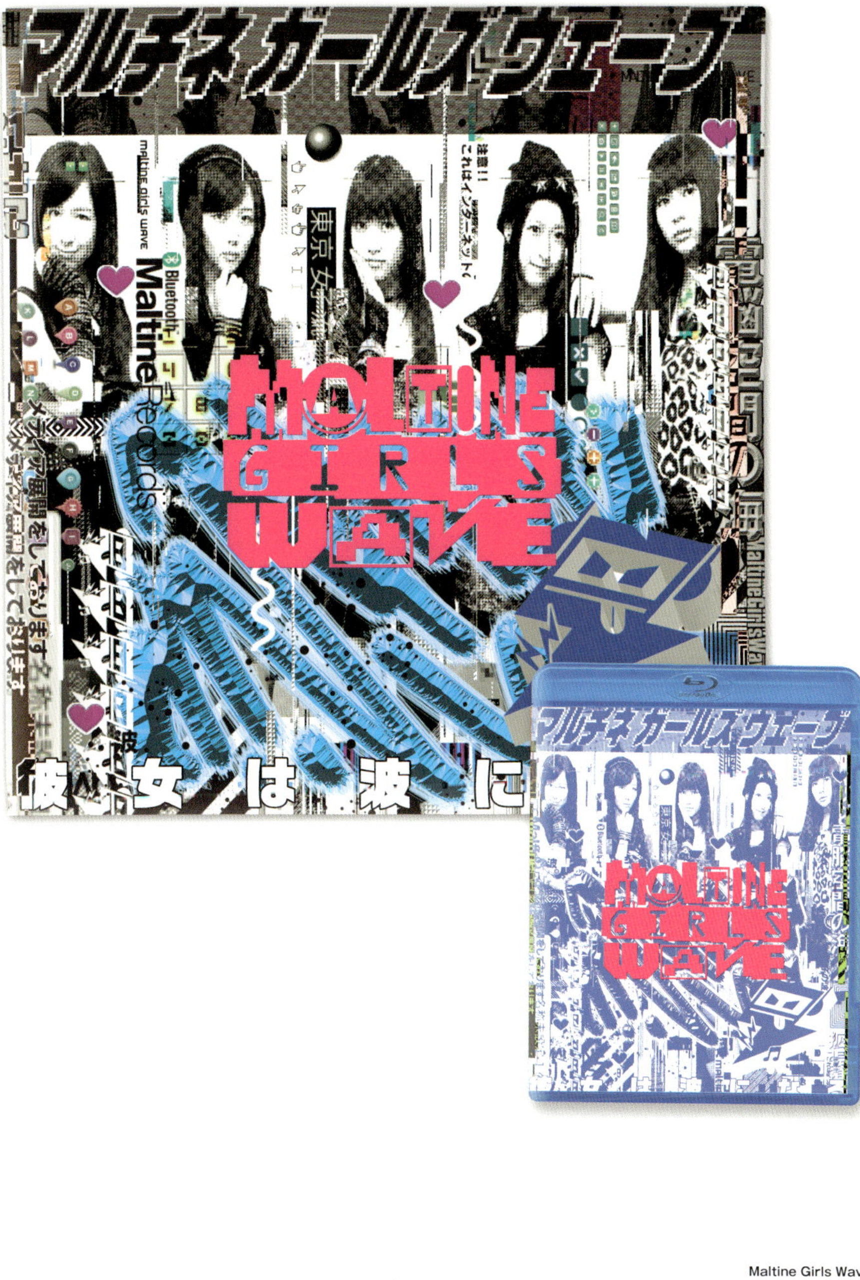

Maltine Girls Wave
キャンペーンサイト、12インチアナログ、ブルーレイジャケット｜avex trax｜2013

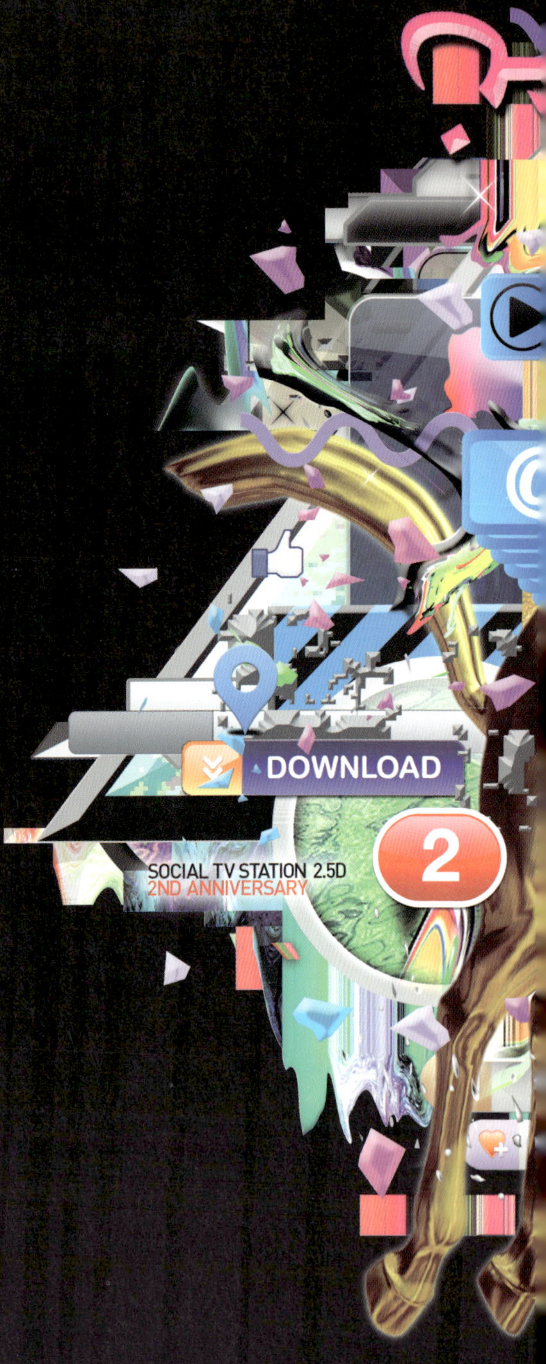
DOWNLOAD
2
SOCIAL TV STATION 2.5D
2ND ANNIVERSARY

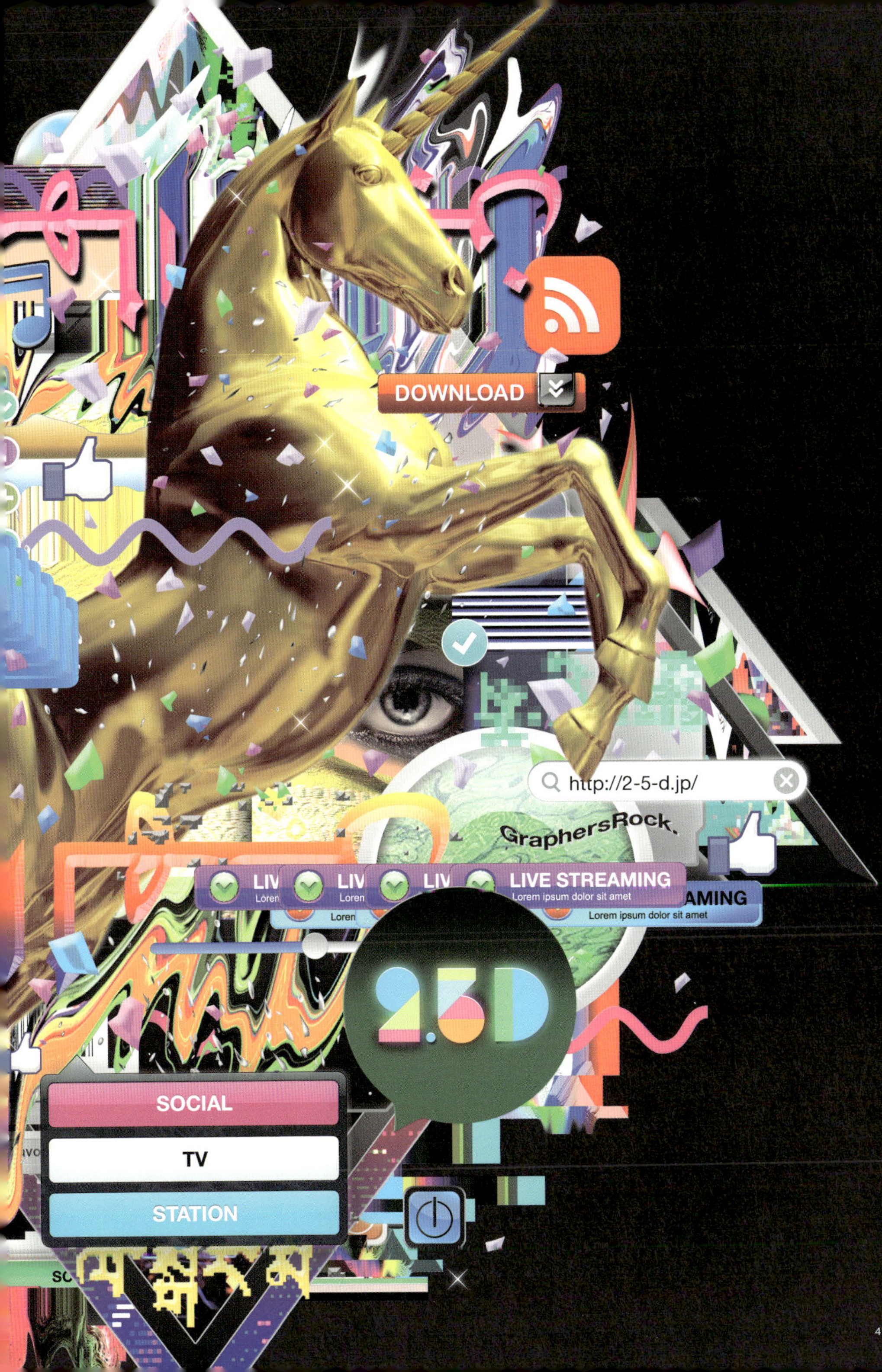
DOWNLOAD
http://2-5-d.jp/
GraphersRock.
LIVE STREAMING
Lorem ipsum dolor sit amet
AMING
Lorem ipsum dolor sit amet
2.5D
SOCIAL
TV
STATION

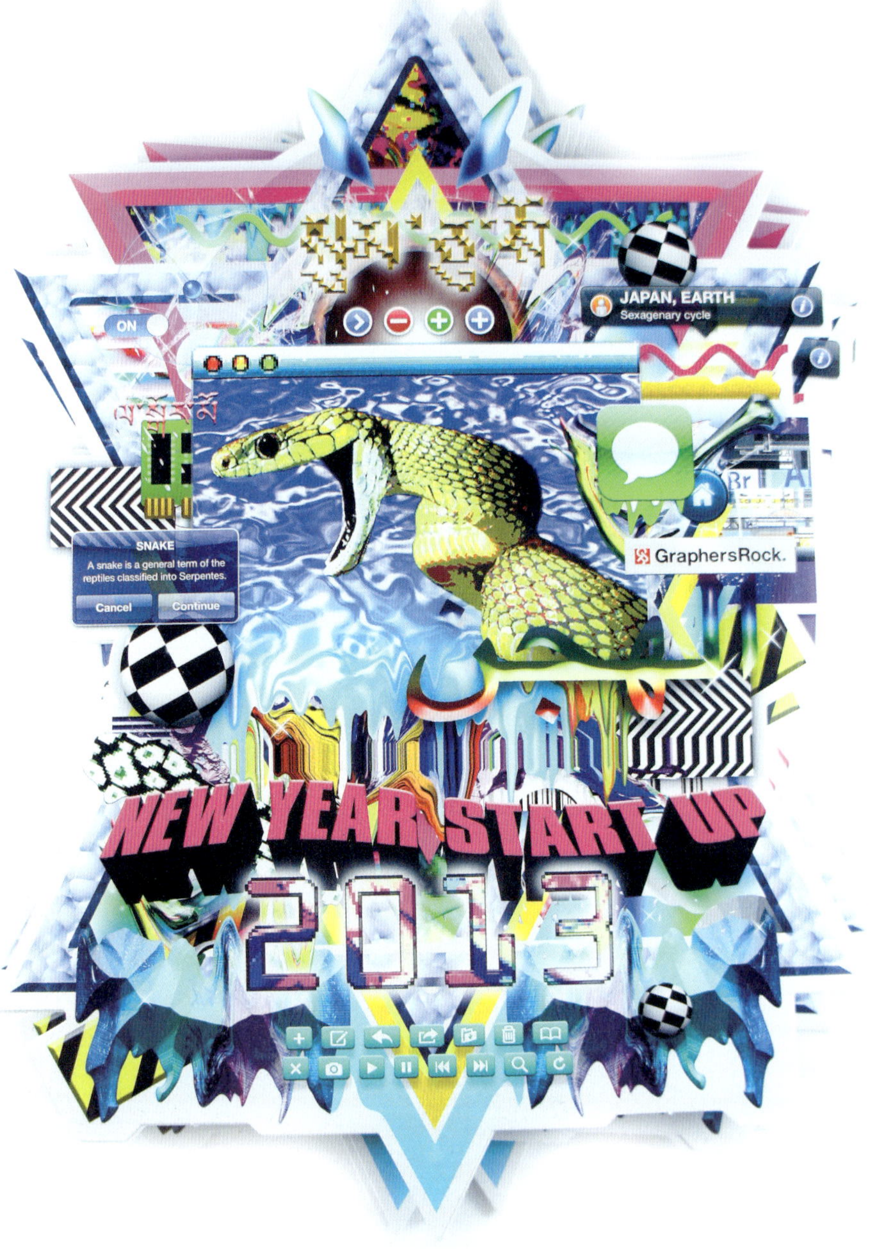
JAPAN, EARTH
Sexagenary cycle
ON
SNAKE
A snake is a general term of the reptiles classified into Serpentes.
Cancel
Continue
GraphersRock.
NEW YEAR START UP
2013

年賀状 2013

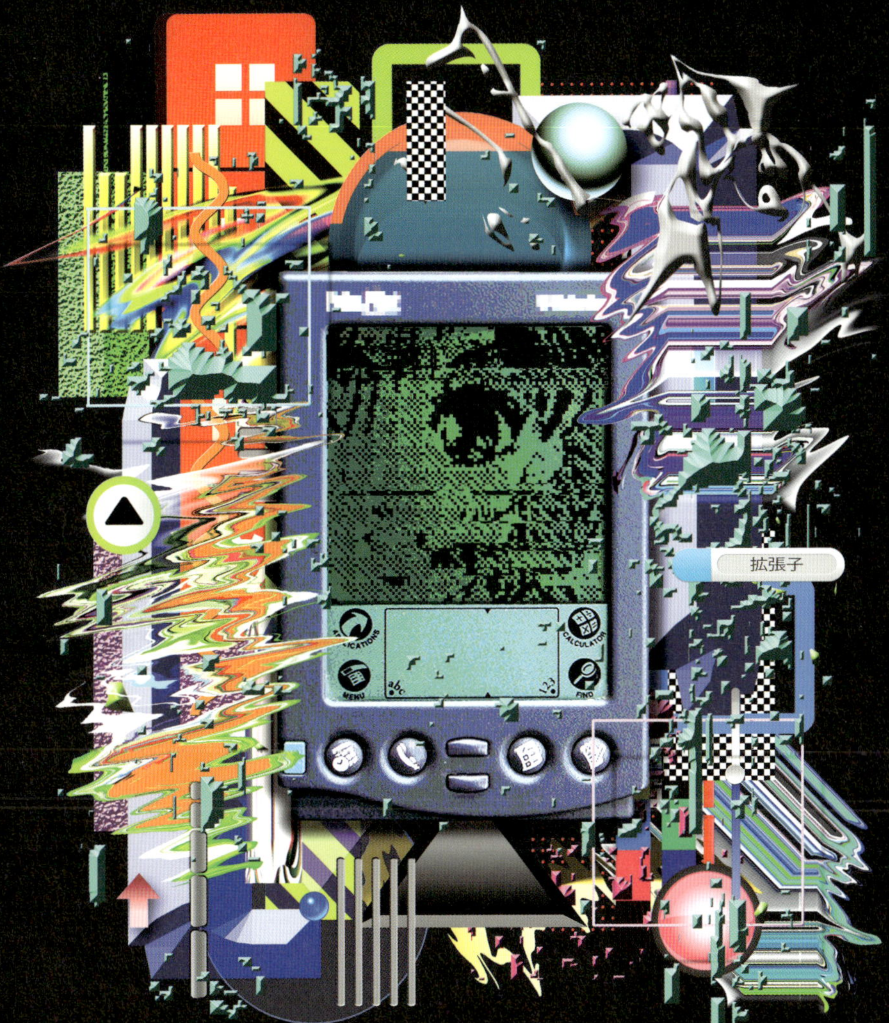

PALM PILOT
GraphersRock | 2014

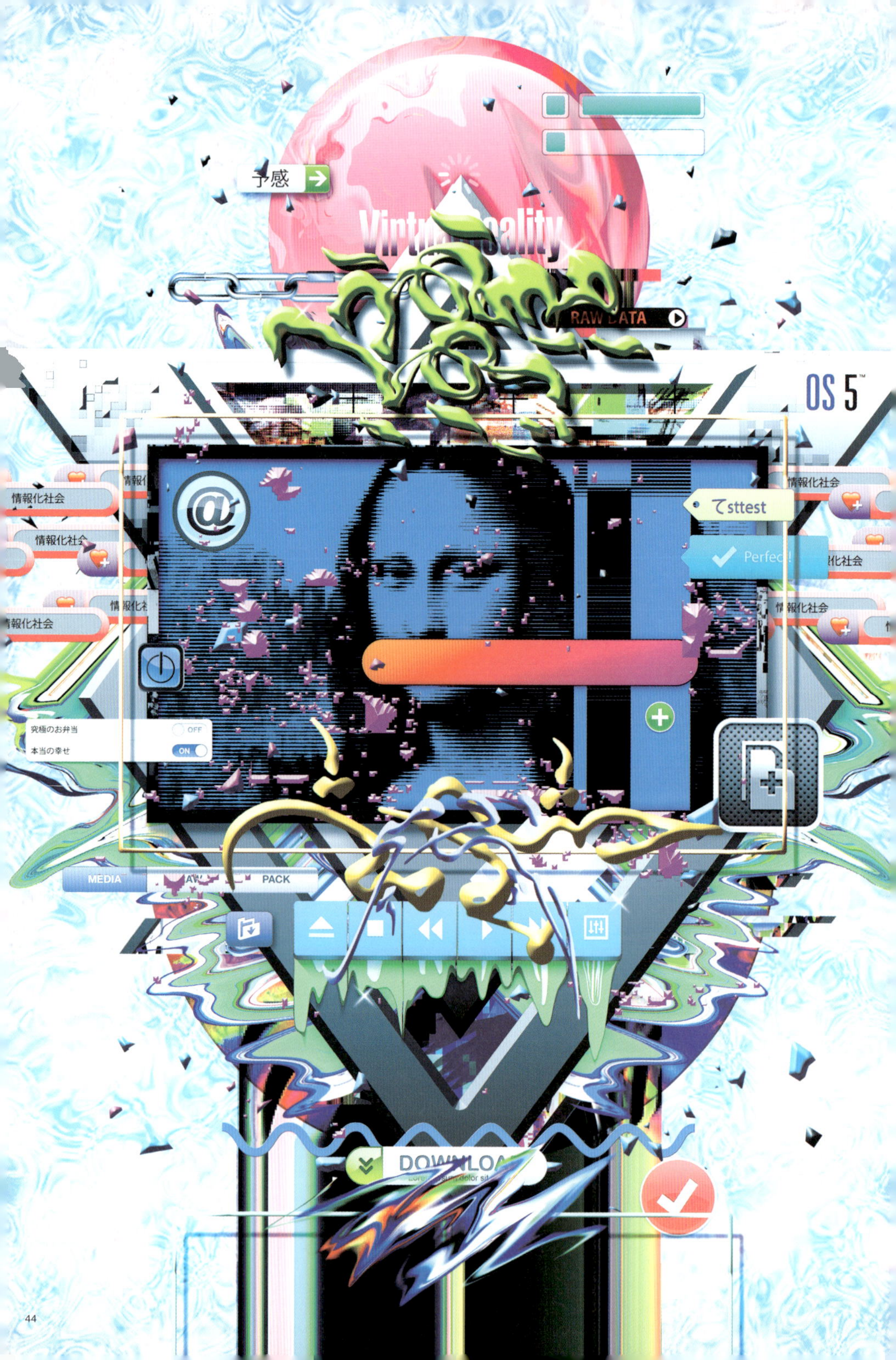
予感
RAW DATA
OS 5™
情報化社会
情報化社会
情報化社会
てsttest
究極のお弁当
OFF
本当の幸せ
ON
MEDIA
PACK

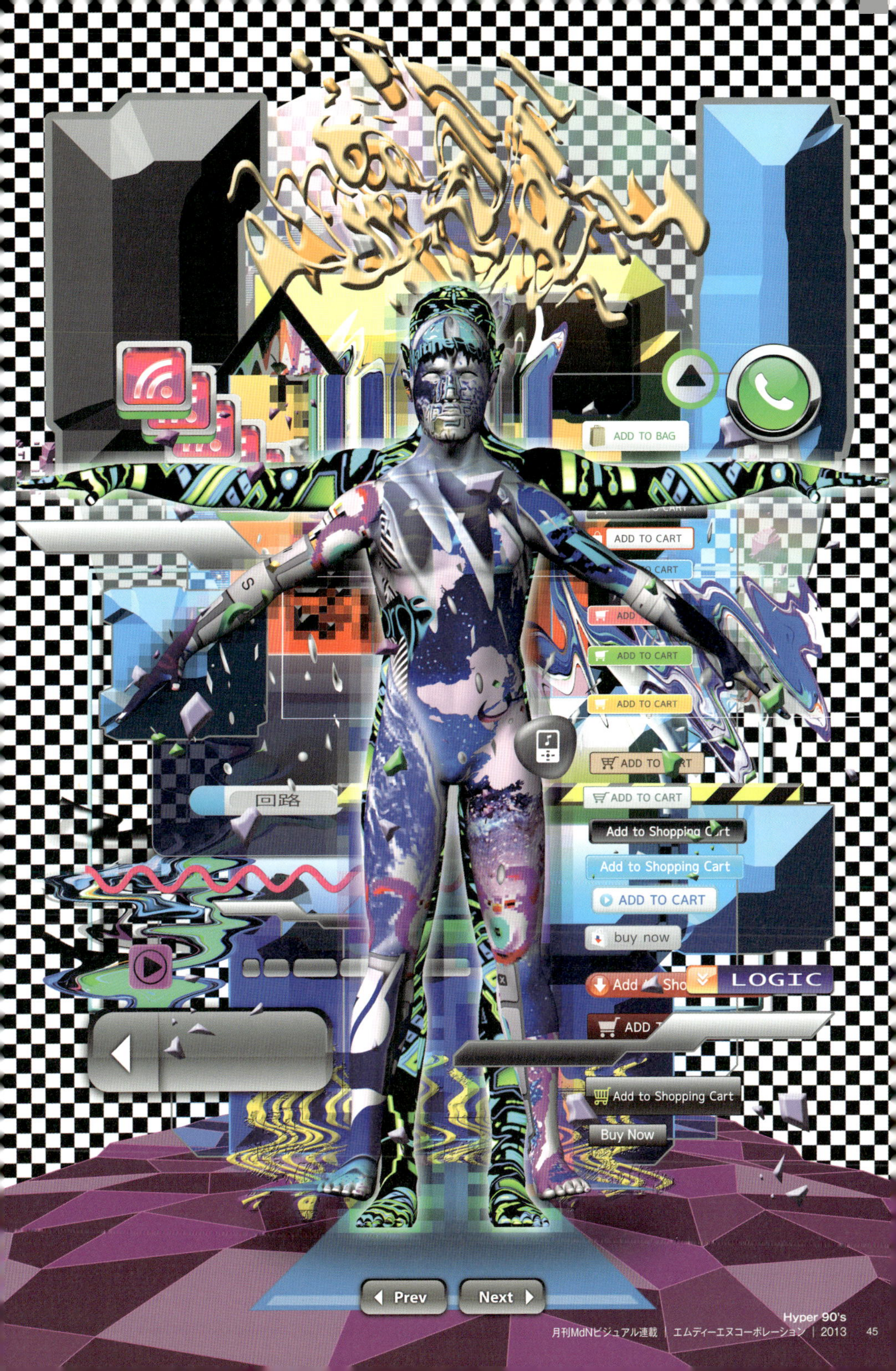
ADD TO BAG
ADD TO CART
ADD TO CART
ADD TO CART
ADD TO CART
ADD TO CART
Add to Shopping Cart
Add to Shopping Cart
ADD TO CART
buy now
LOGIC
Add to Shopping Cart
Buy Now
回路
Prev
Next

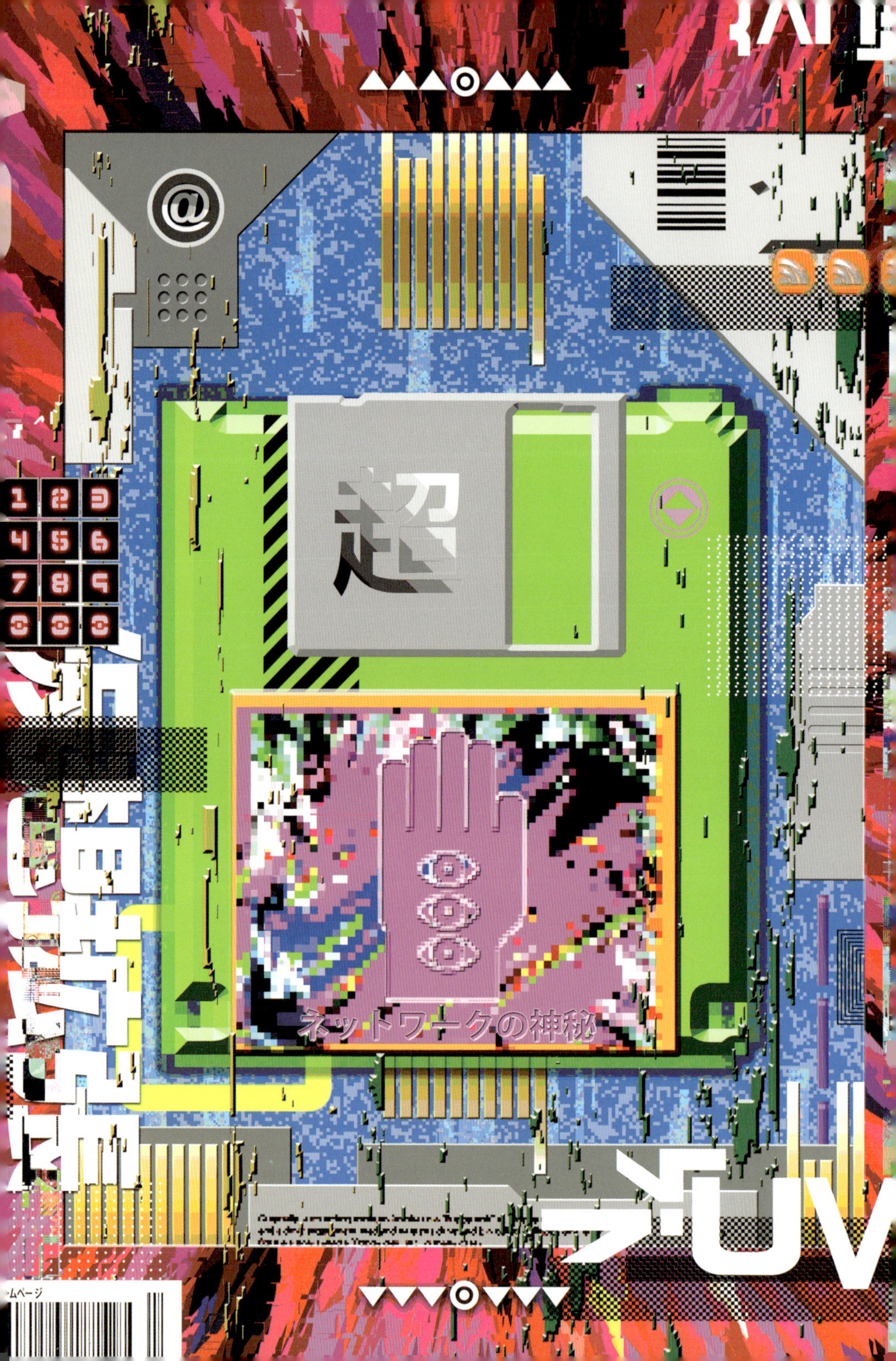
超
ネットワークの神秘

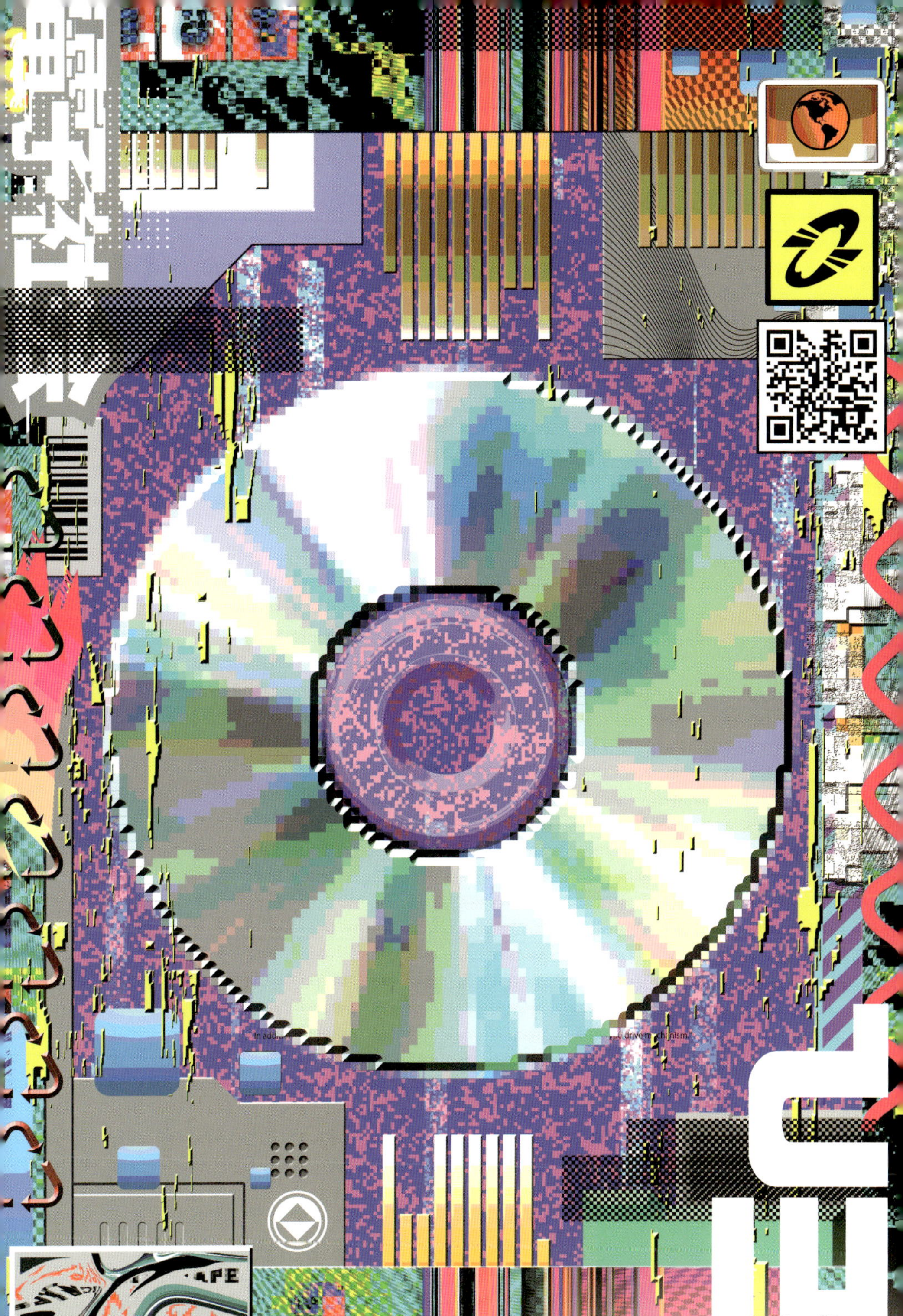

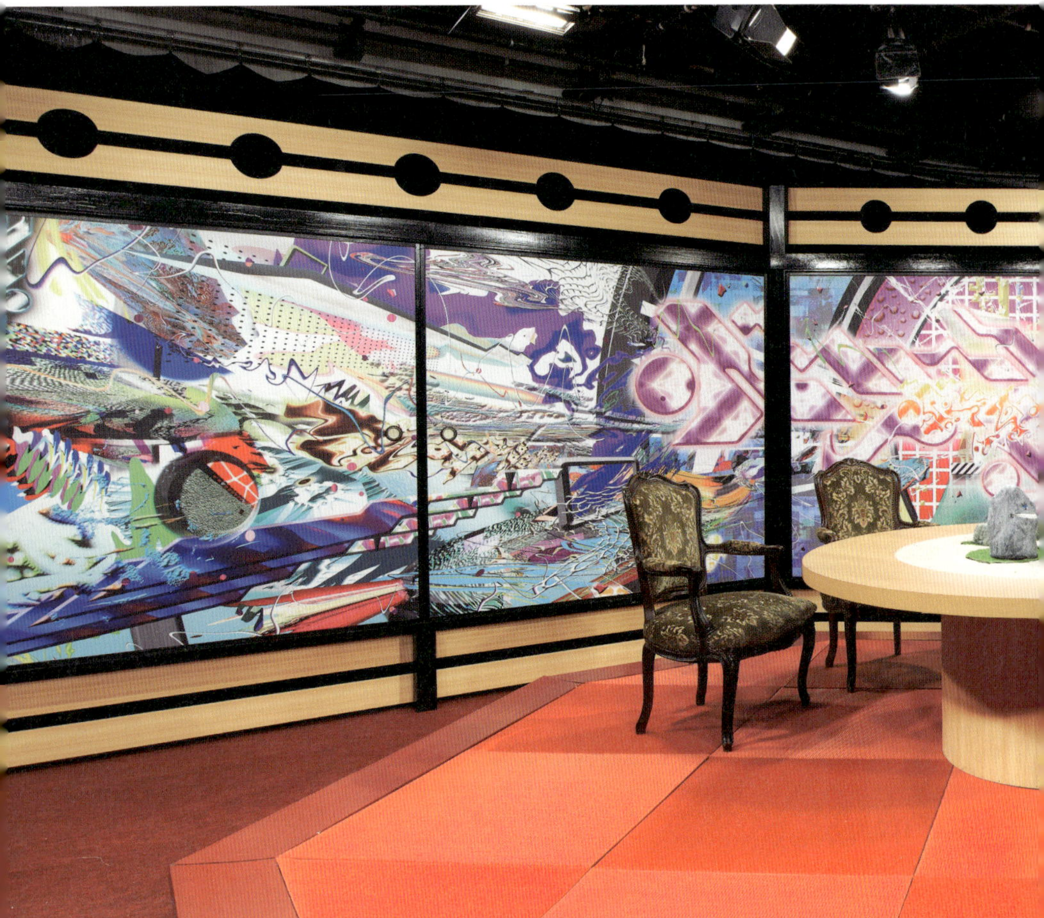

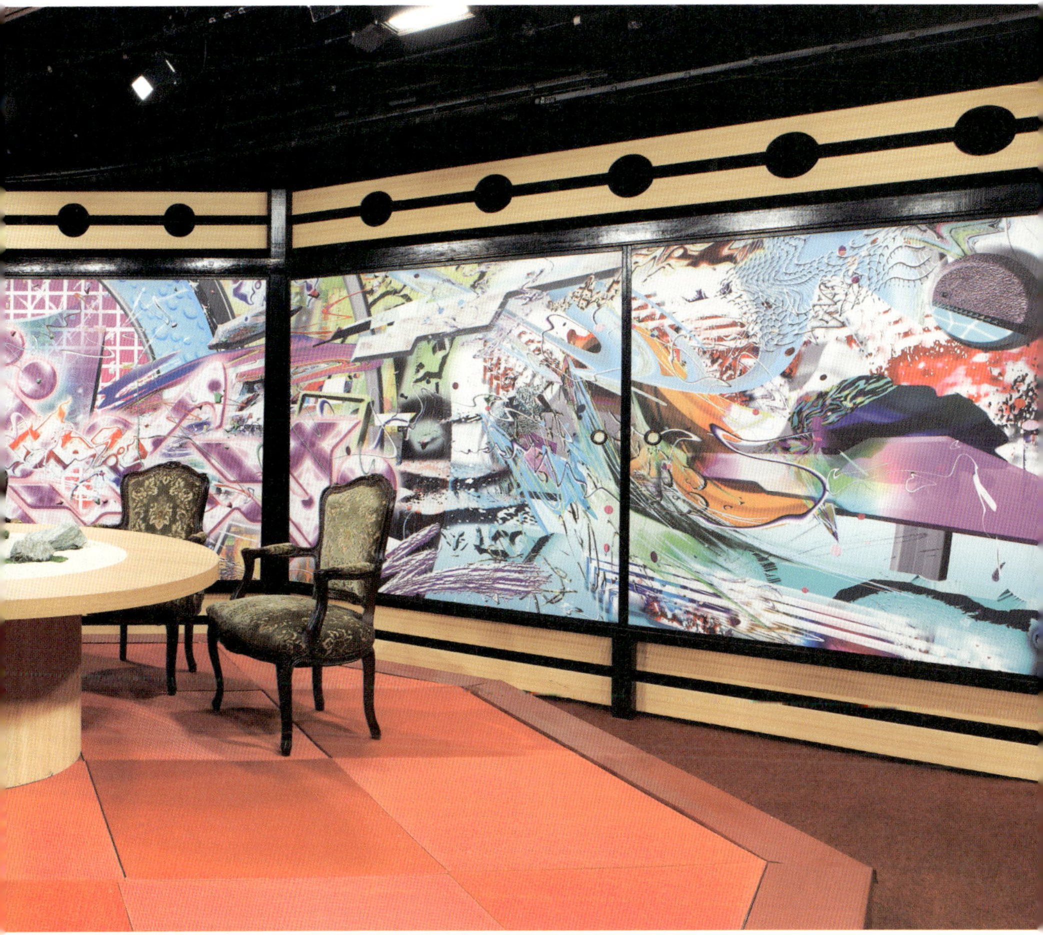

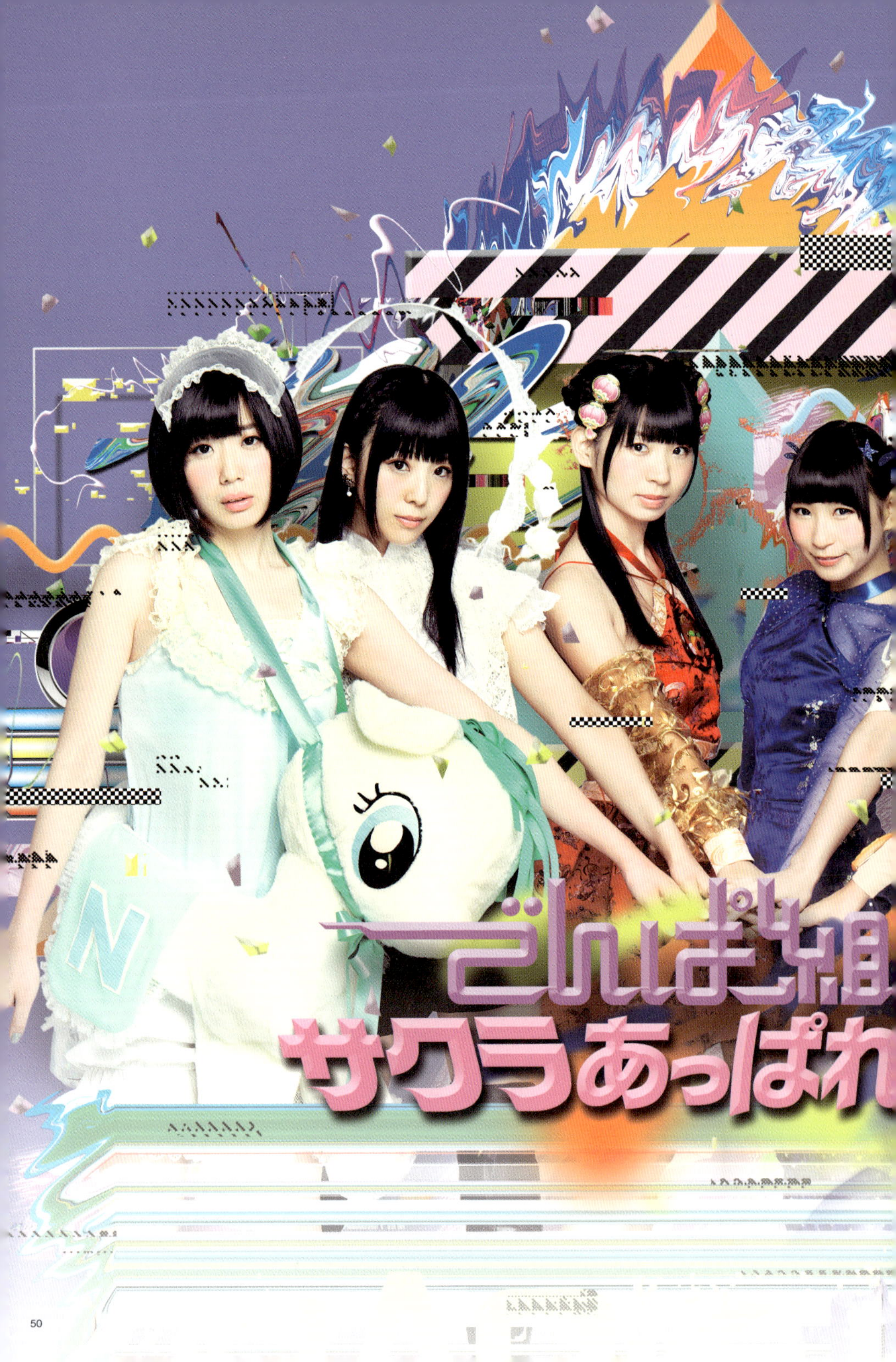
でんぱ組
サクラあっぱれ

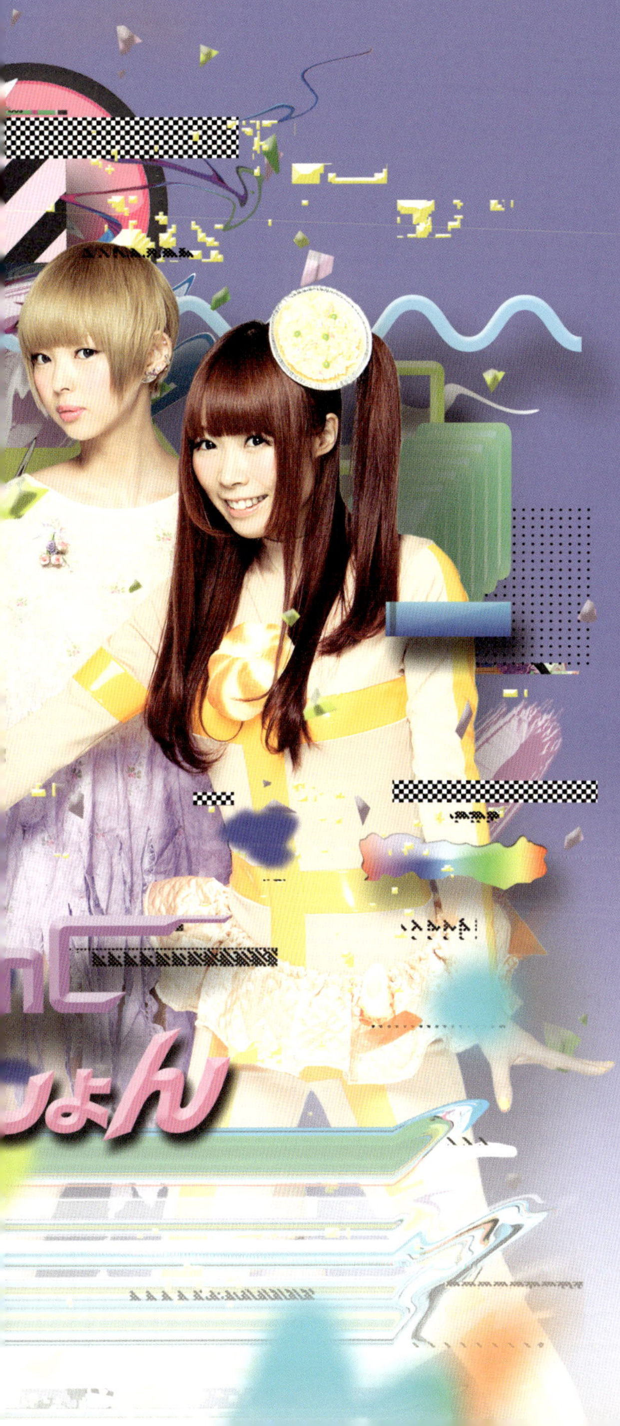

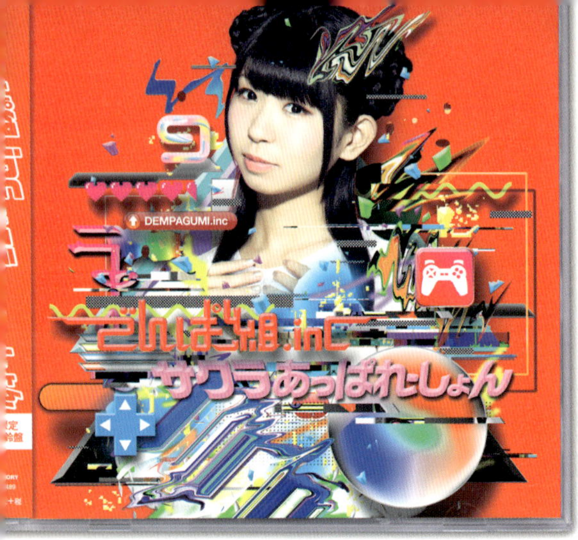
DEMPAGUMI.inc
でんぱ組.inc
サクラあっぱれーしょん

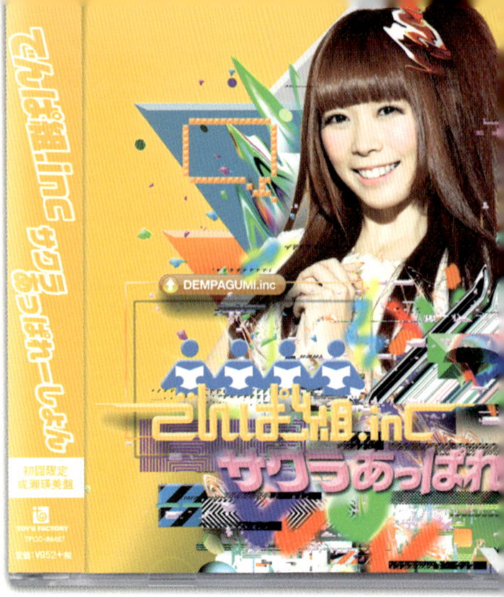
でんぱ組.inc サクラあっぱれーしょん
初回限定
成瀬瑛美盤
TOY'S FACTORY
定価：¥952＋税
DEMPAGUMI.inc
でんぱ組.inc
サクラあっぱれ

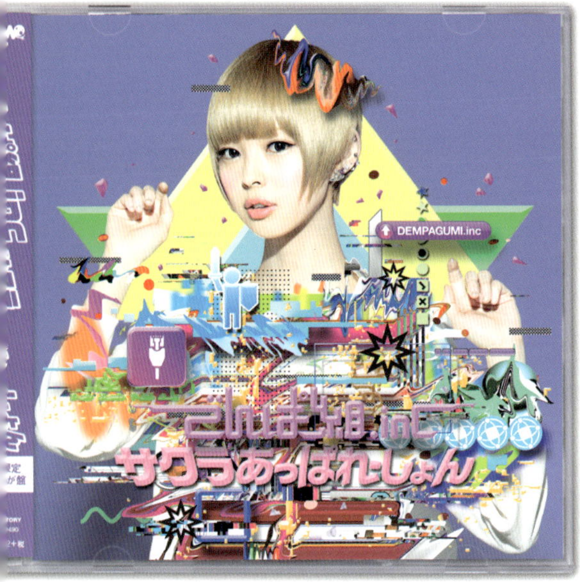
DEMPAGUMI.inc
でんぱ組.inc
サクラあっぱれーしょん

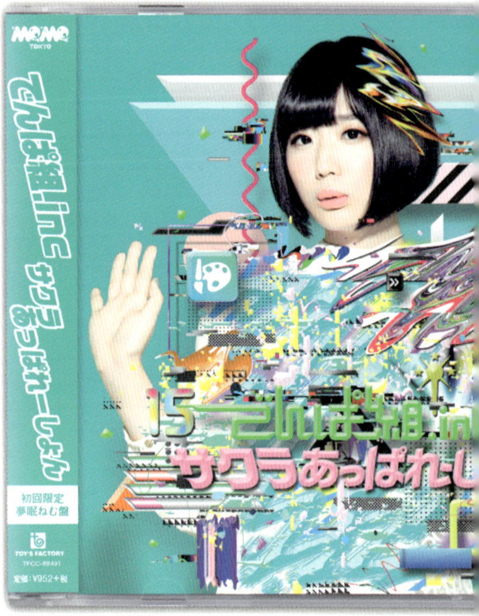
でんぱ組.inc サクラあっぱれーしょん
初回限定
夢眠ねむ盤
TOY'S FACTORY
TFCC-89491
定価：¥952＋税
でんぱ組.inc
サクラあっぱれーし

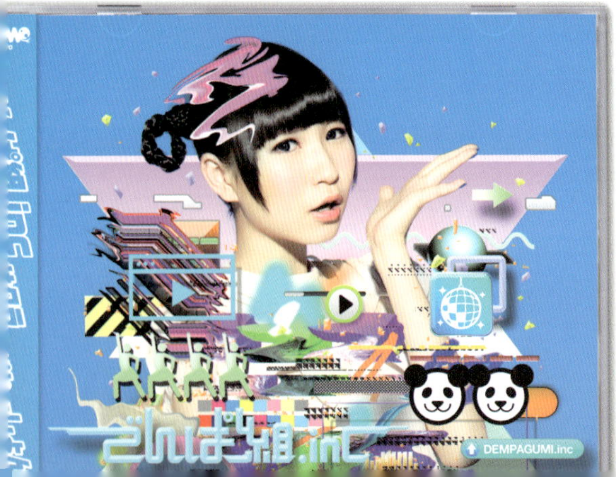
でんぱ組.inc
DEMPAGUMI.inc

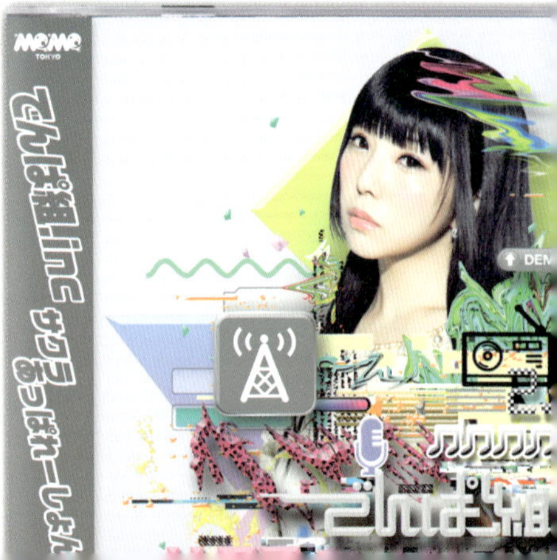
でんぱ組.inc サクラあっぱれーしょん
でんぱ組

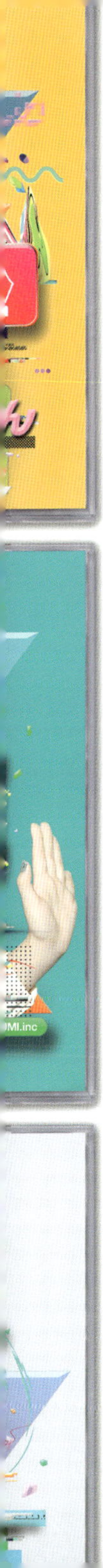

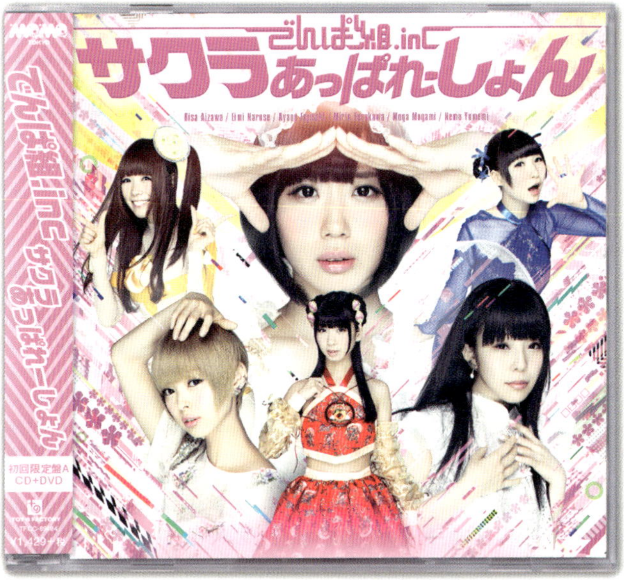

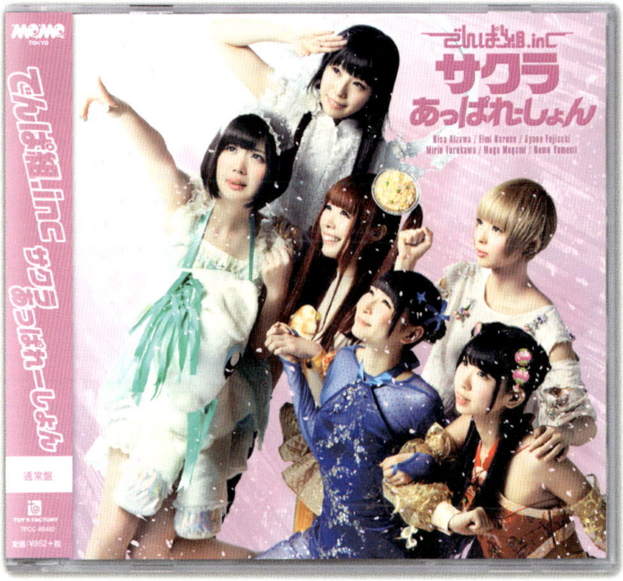

でんぱ組.inc / サクラあっぱれーしょん
CDジャケット ｜ トイズファクトリー ｜ 2014

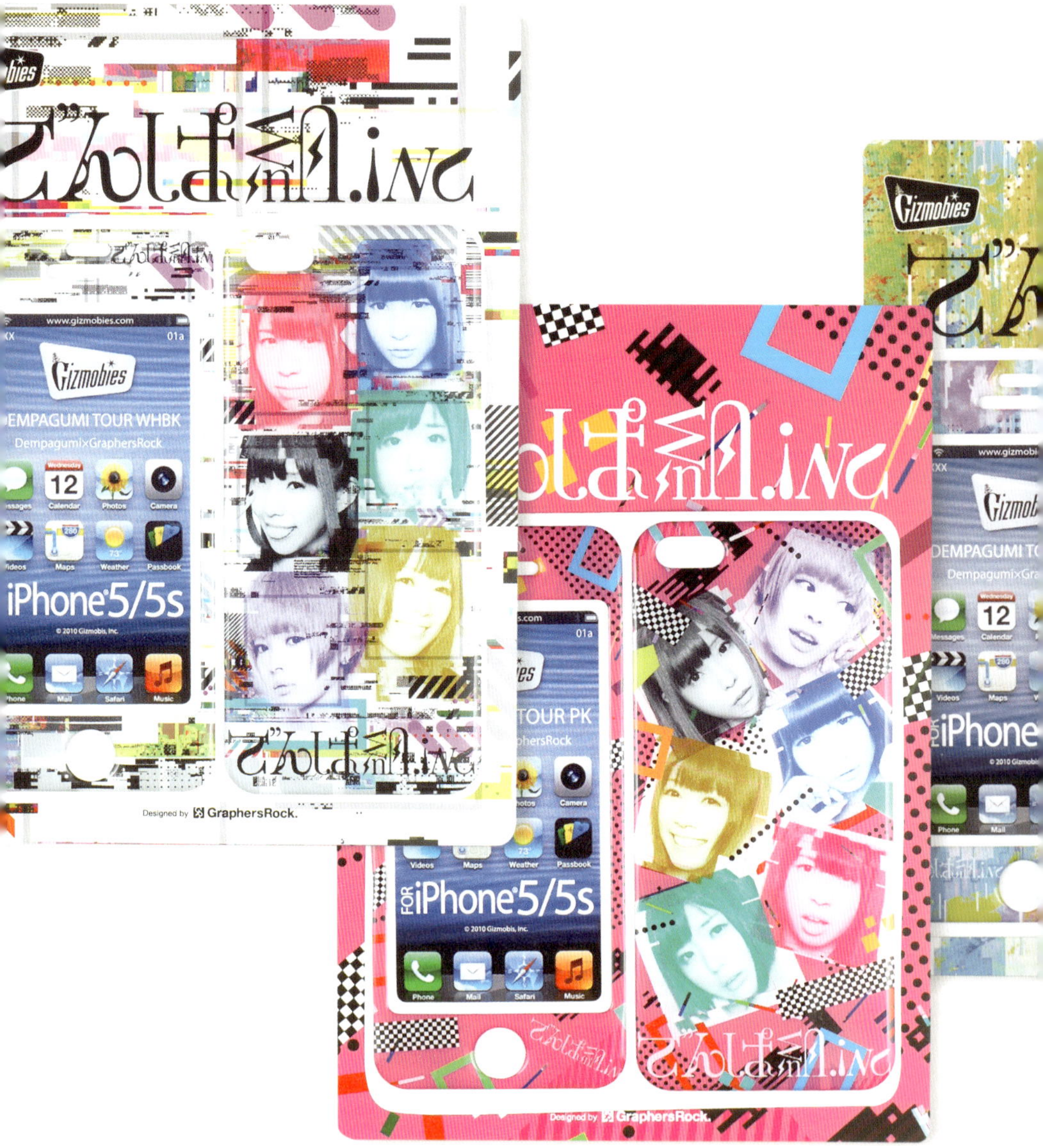
でんぱ組.inc
www.gizmobies.com
Gizmobies
DEMPAGUMI TOUR WHBK
Dempagumi×GraphersRock
iPhone 5/5s
© 2010 Gizmobis, Inc.
Designed by GraphersRock.
TOUR PK
FOR iPhone 5/5s
Designed by GraphersRock.

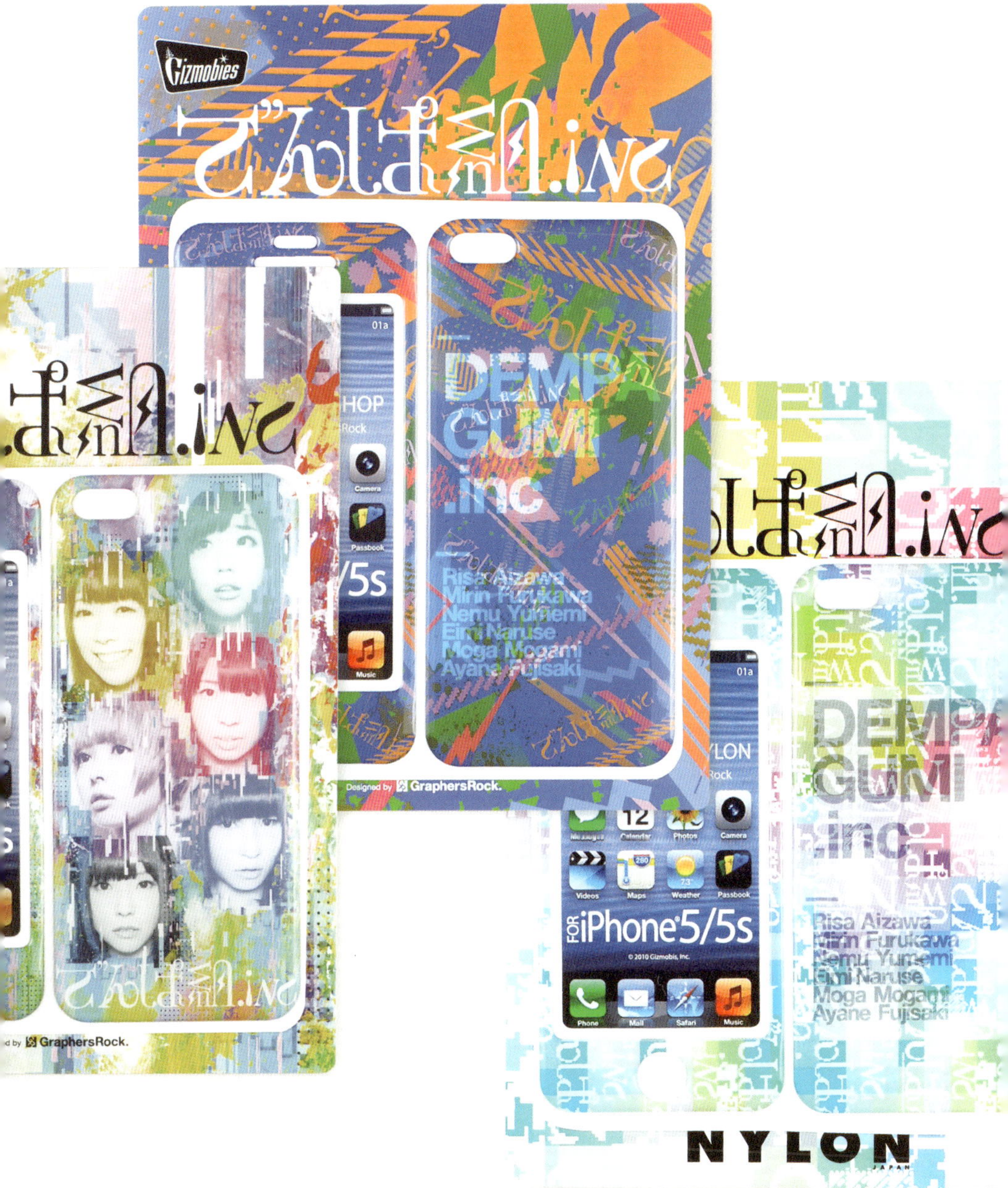

でんぱ組 .inc Gizmobies
iPhone プロテクター ｜ DEARSTAGE ｜ 2013
©DEARSTAGE

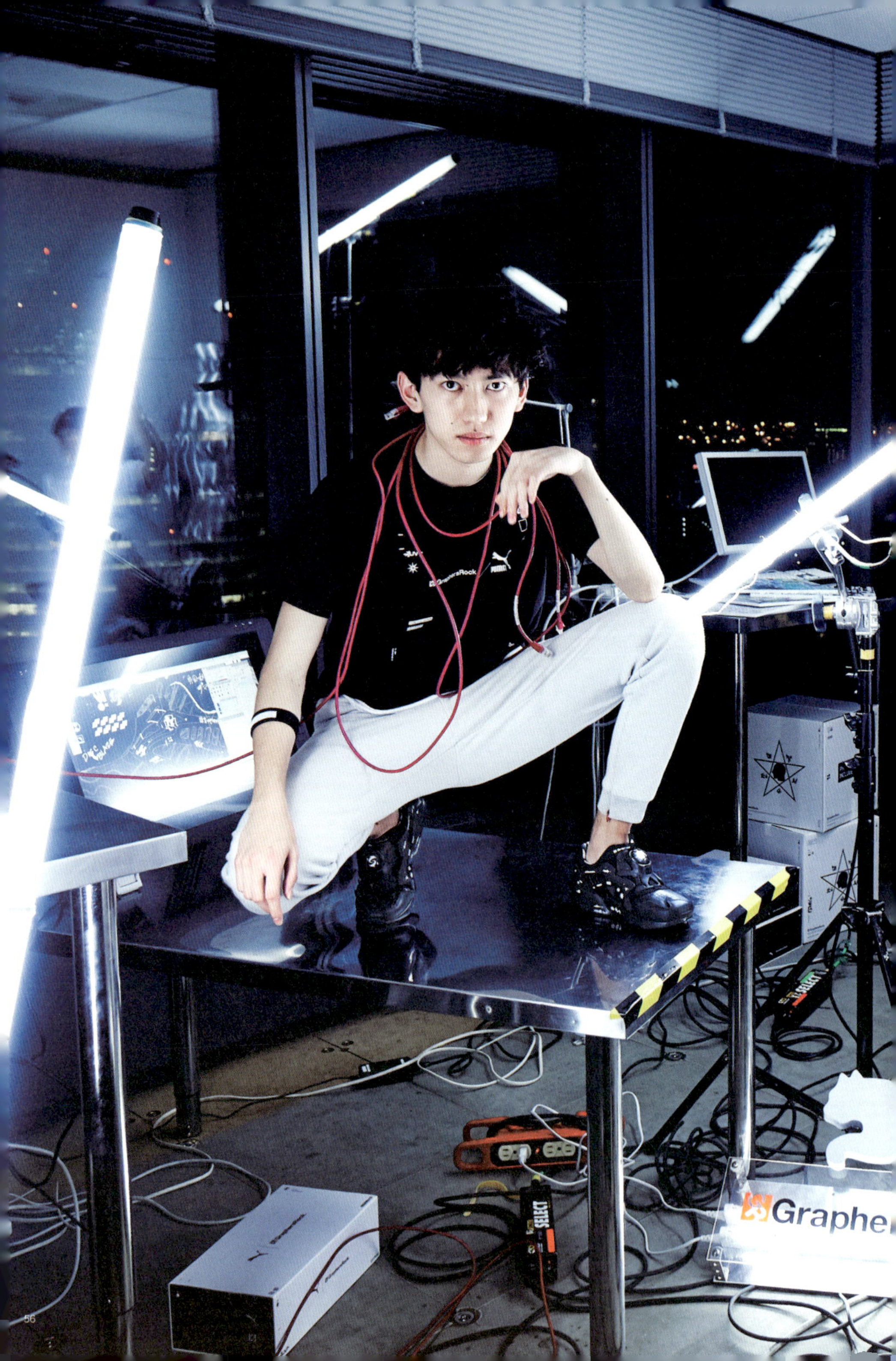
Graphe
SELECT

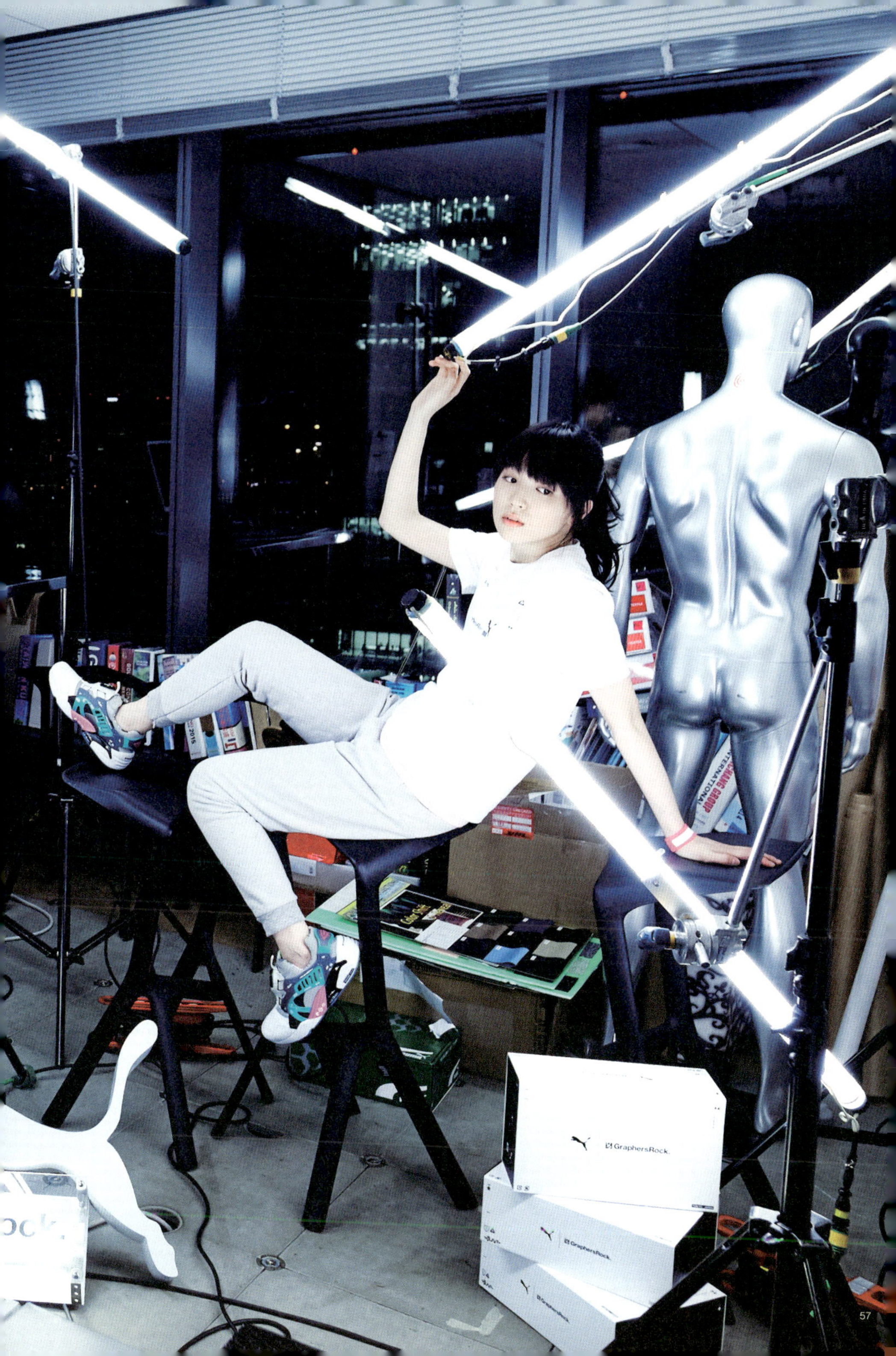
GraphersRock.

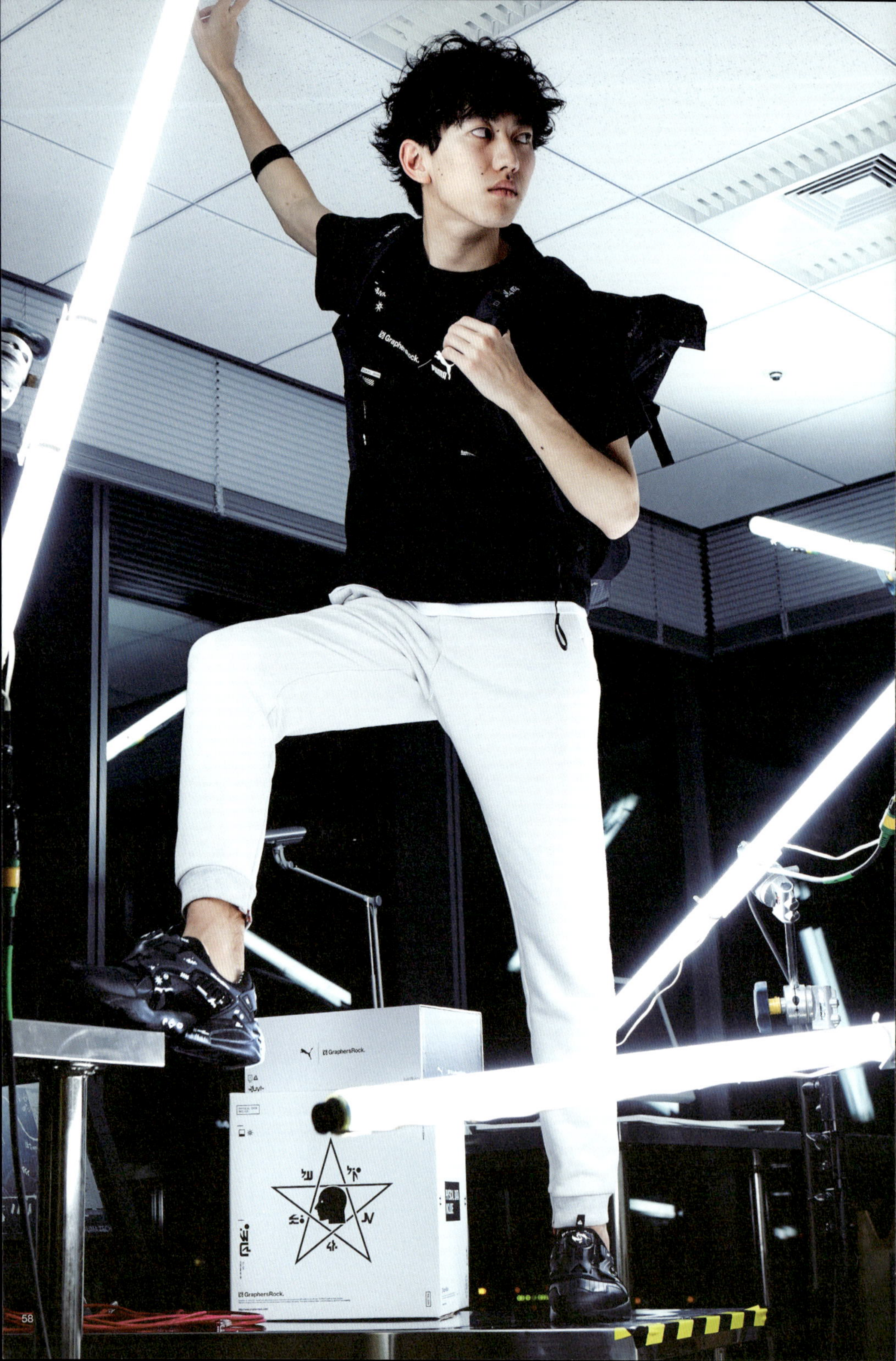
GraphersRock.
GraphersRock.
GraphersRock.

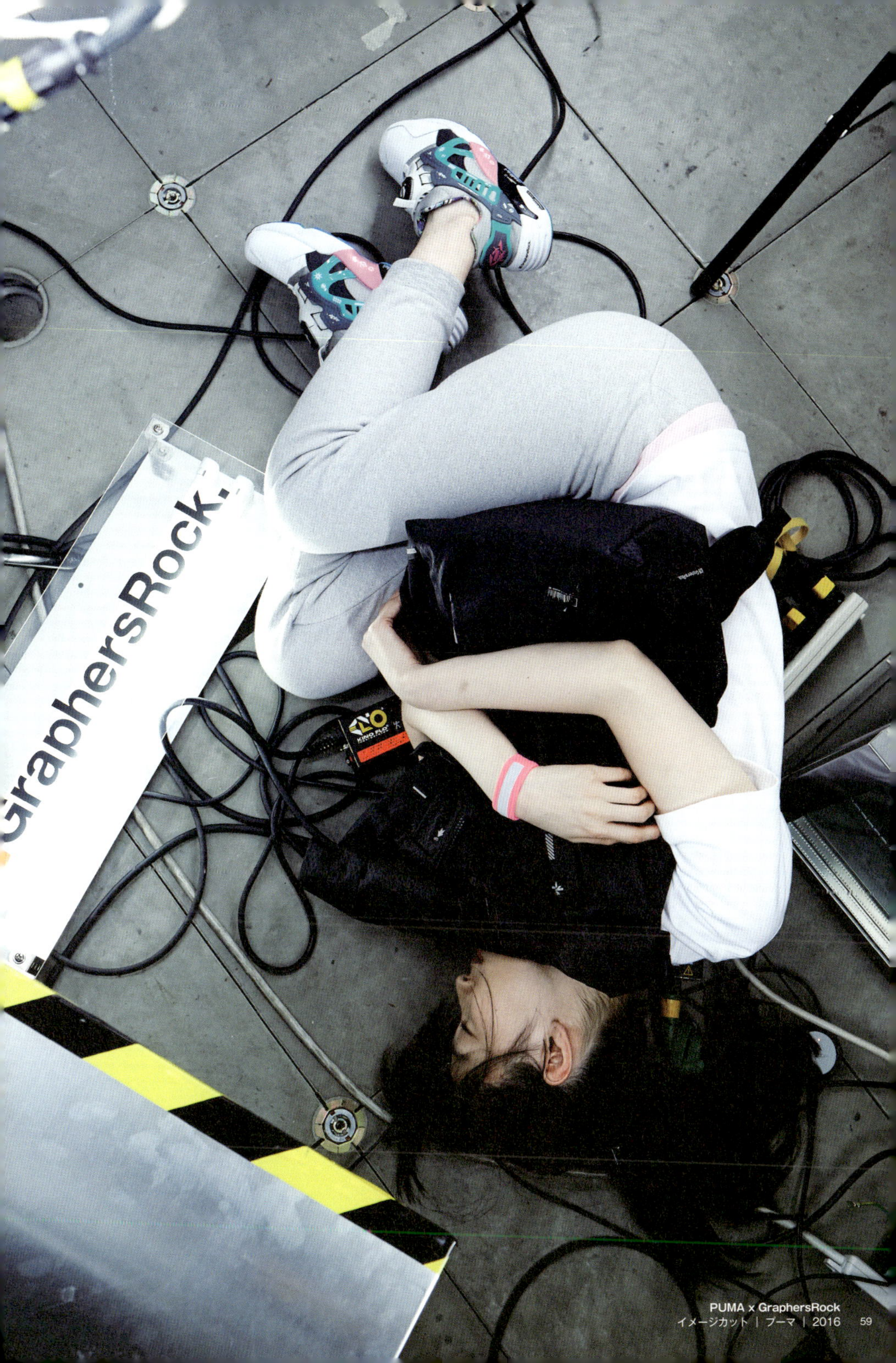
GraphersRock.

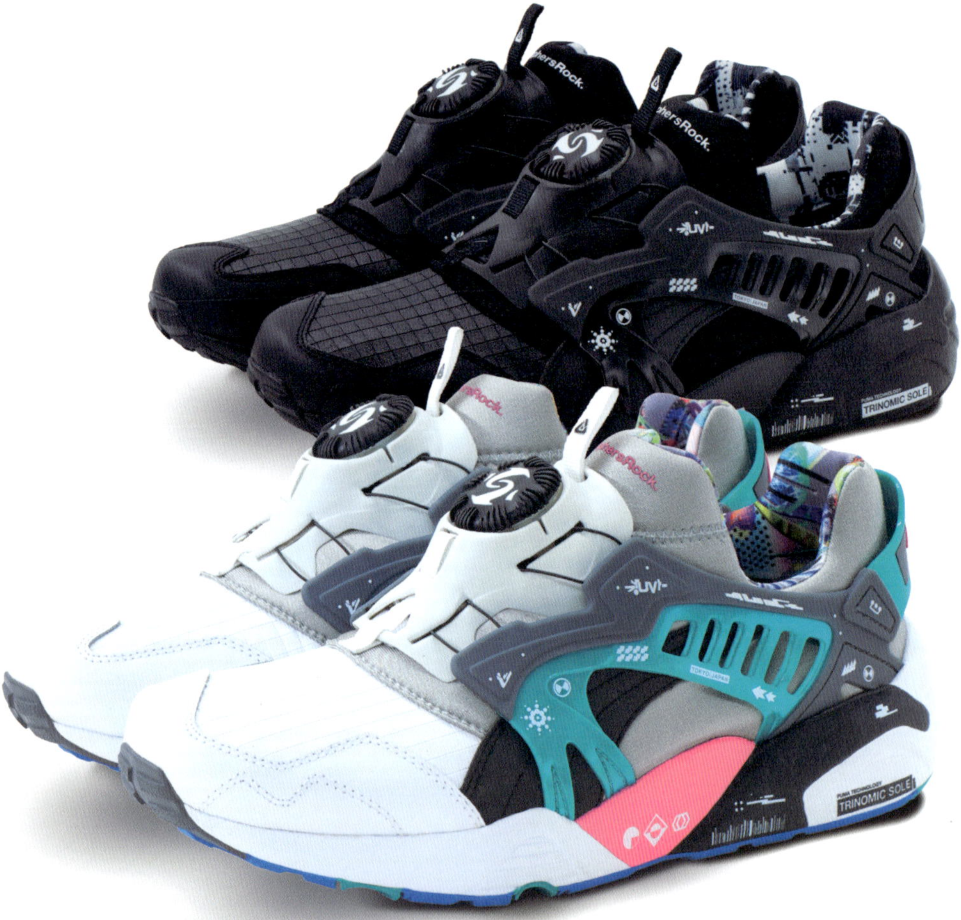

Disc by GraphersRock
 シューズ | プーマ | 2016

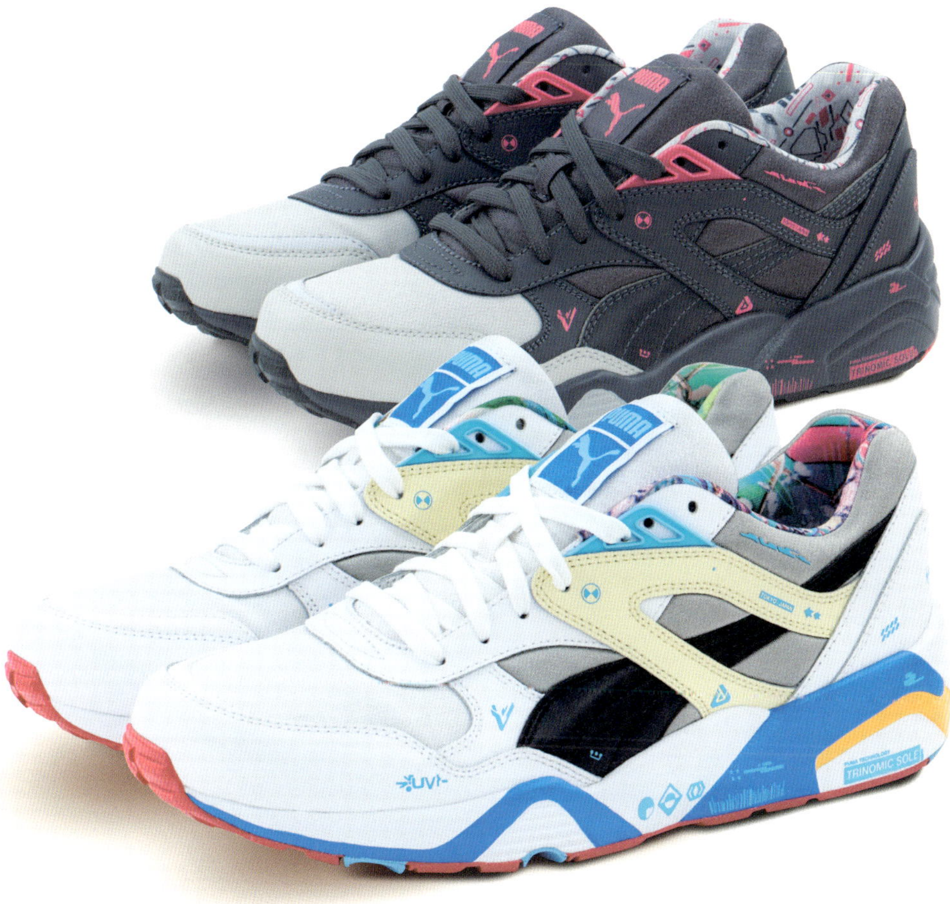

R698 by GraphersRock
シューズ | プーマ | 2016

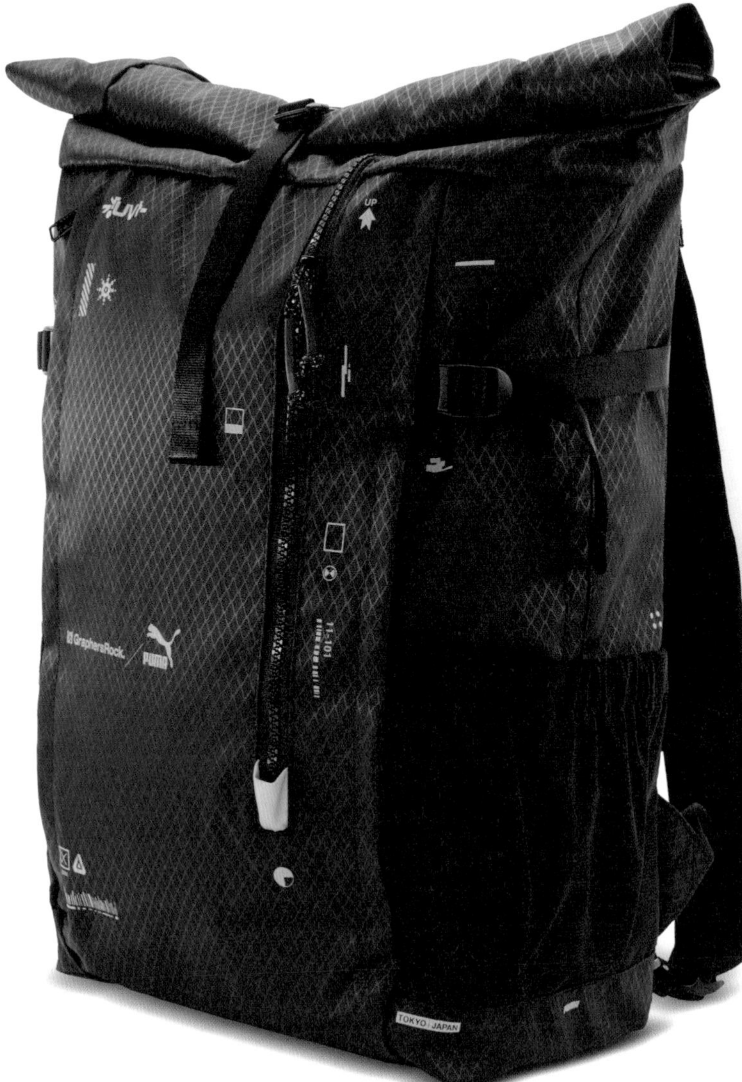

PUMA x GraphersRock Backpack
バックパック ｜ プーマ ｜ 2016

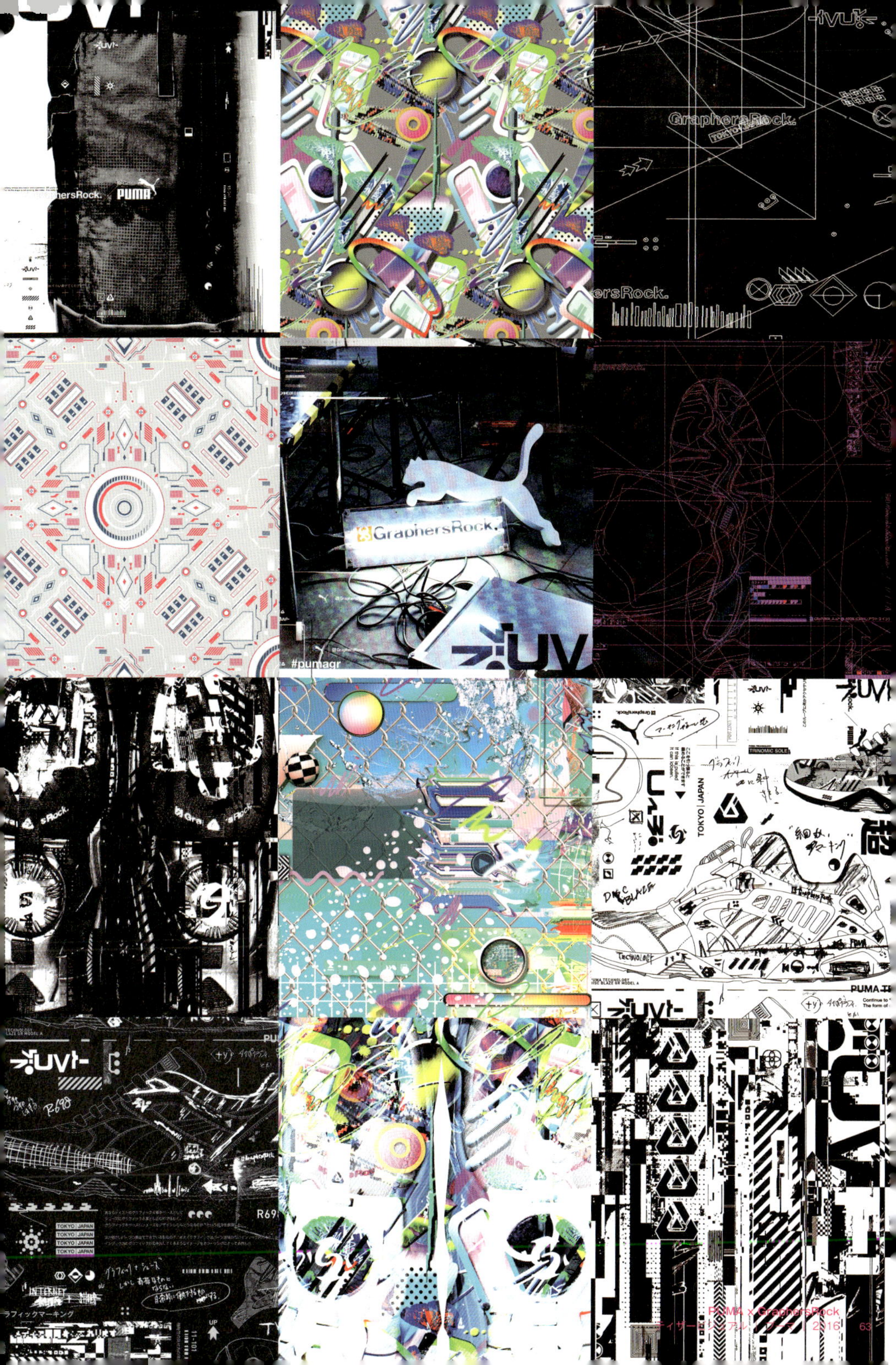

PUMA x GraphersRock
ティザービジュアル | プーマ | 2016

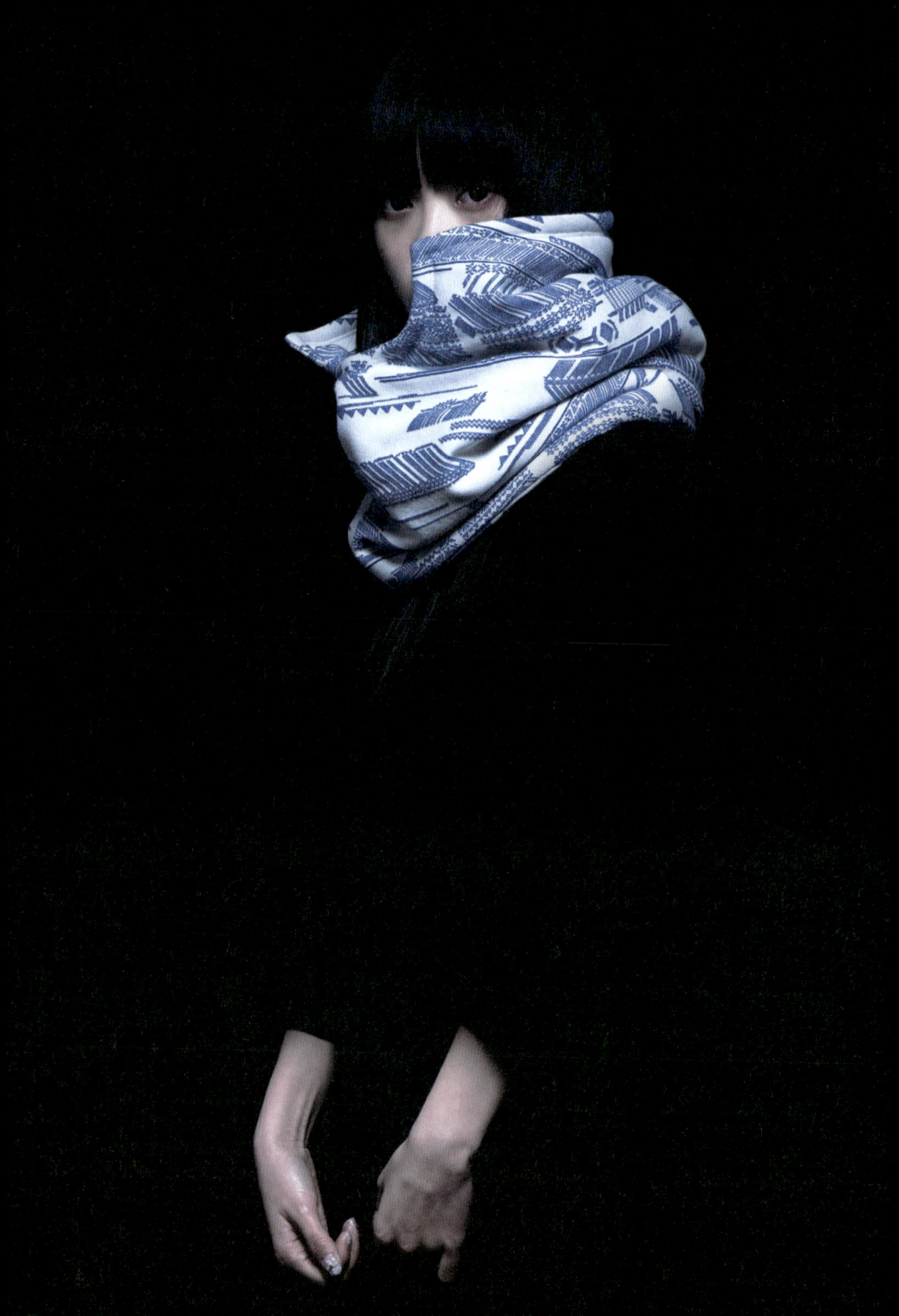

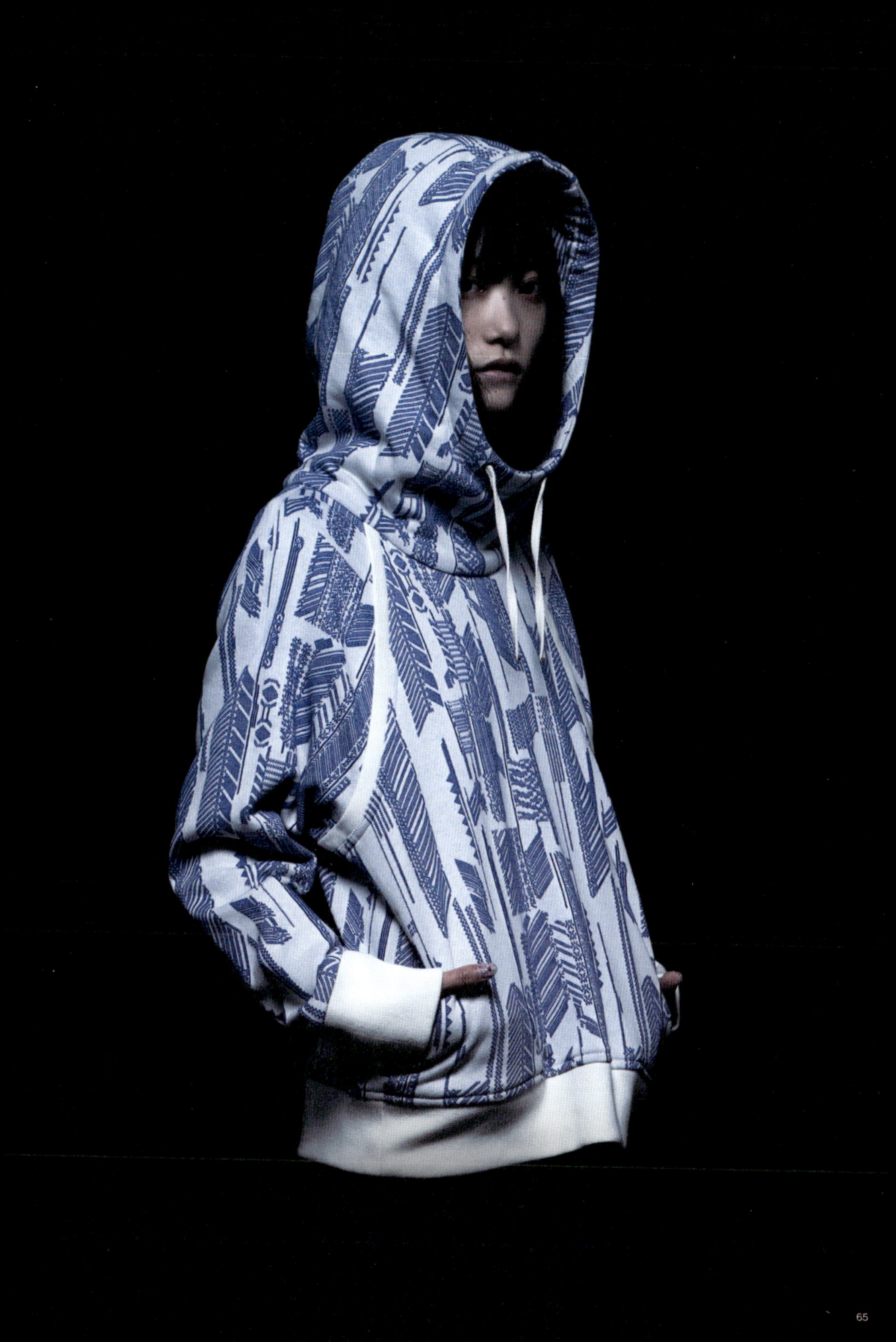

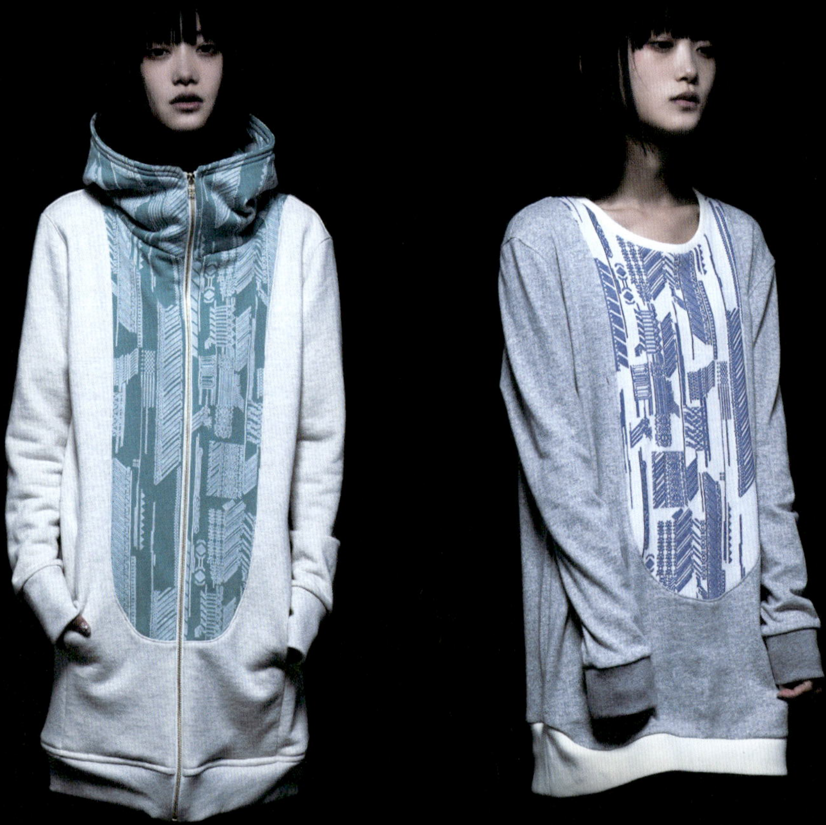

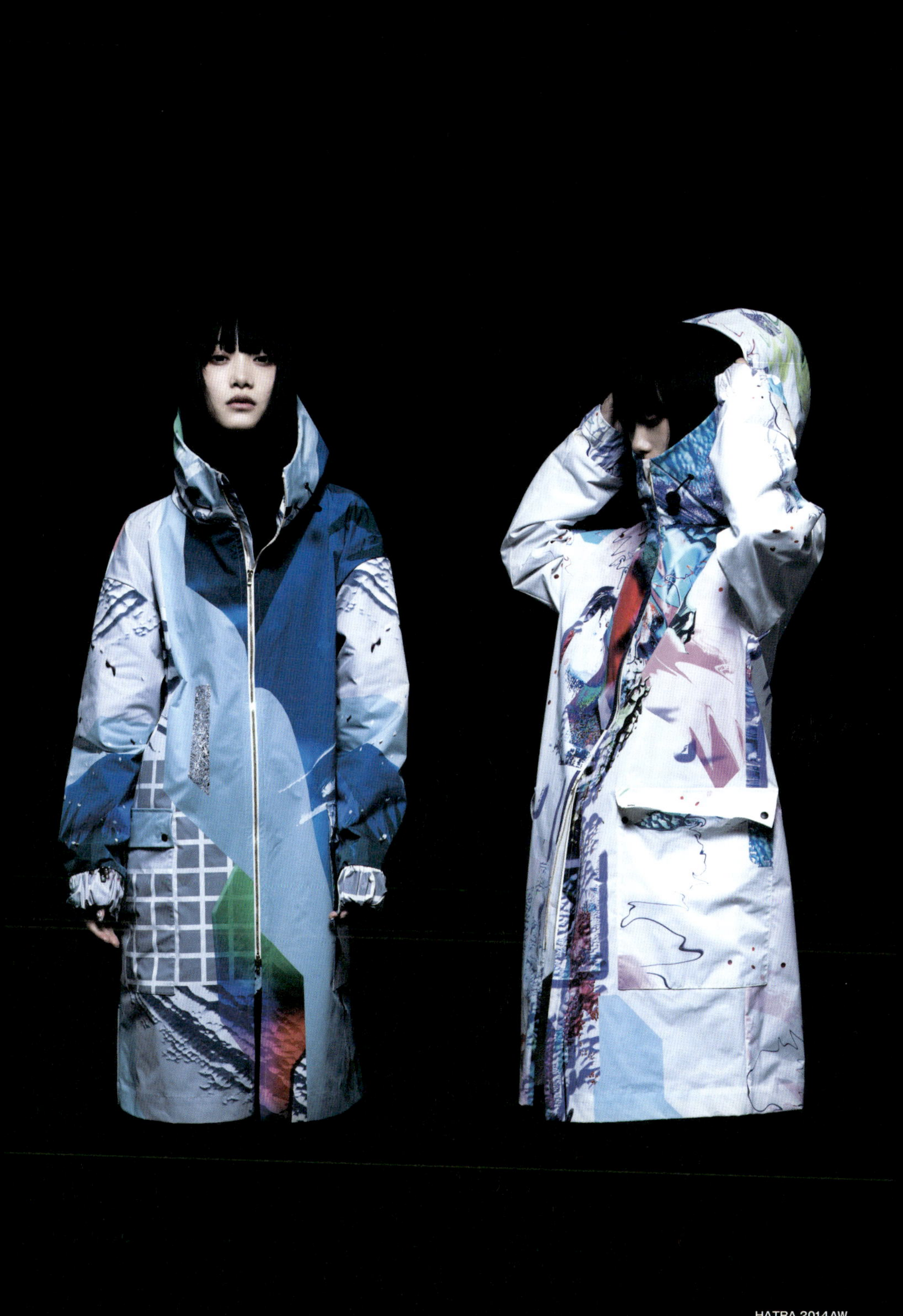

HATRA 2014AW

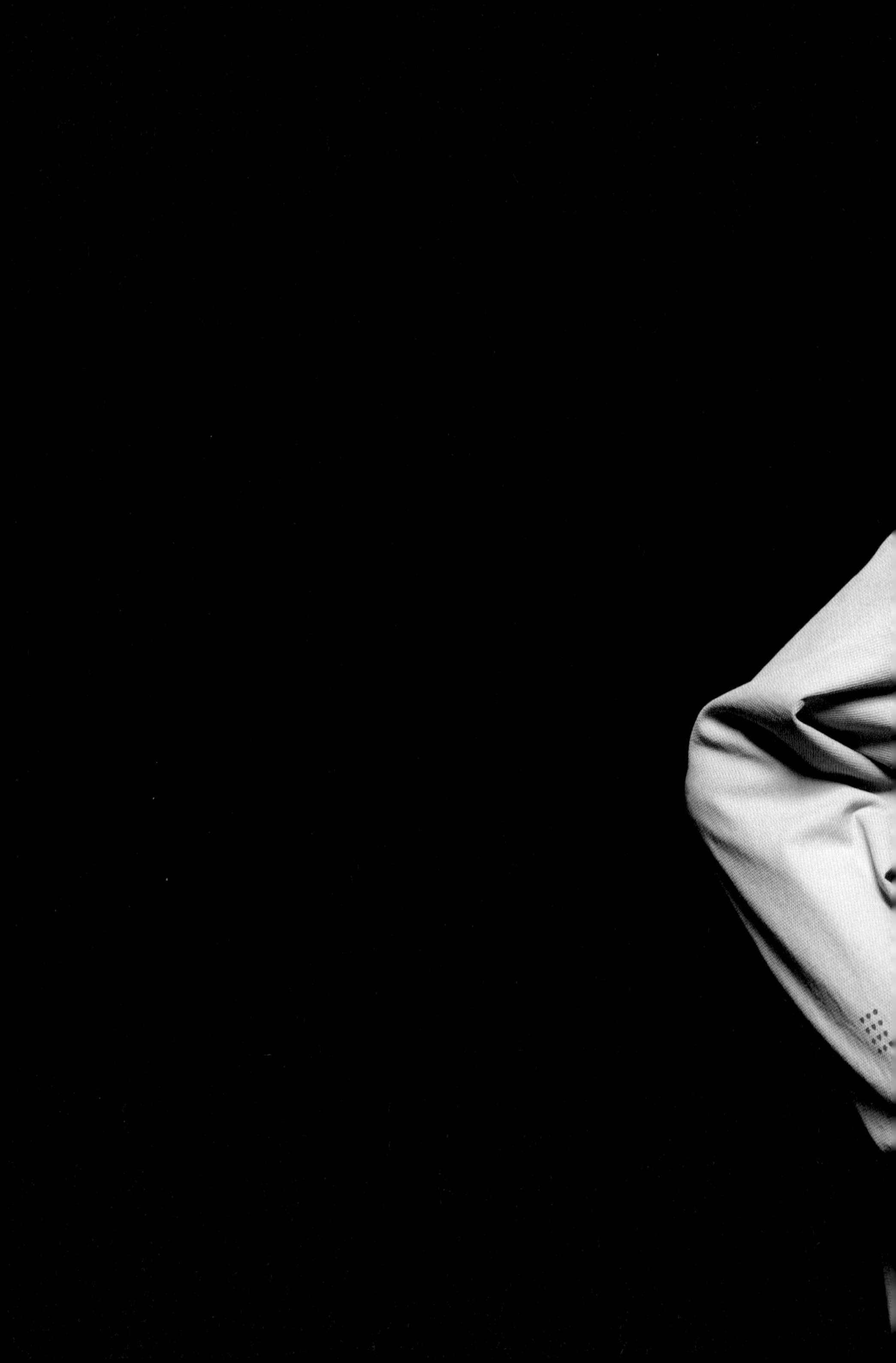

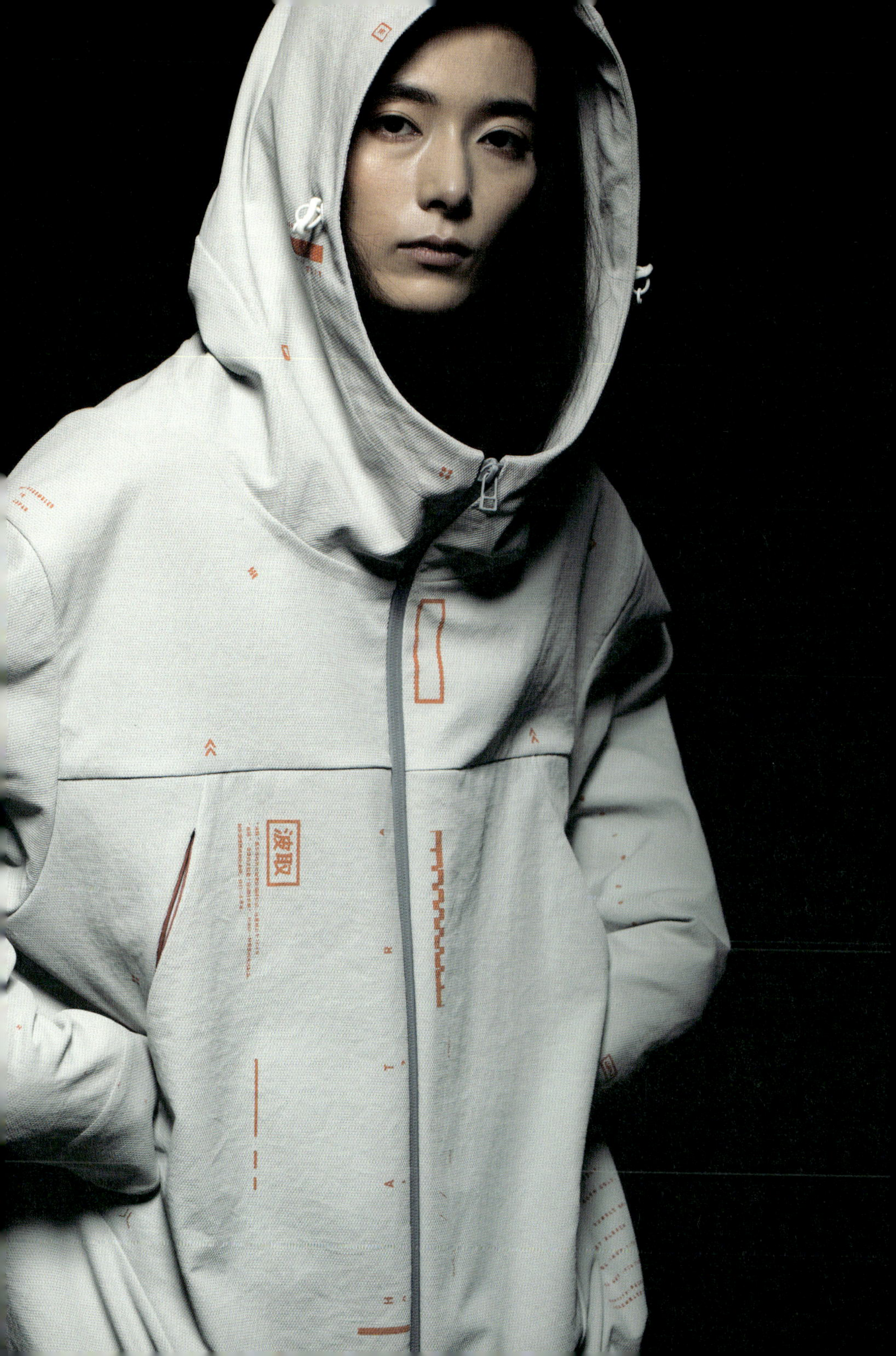
波取

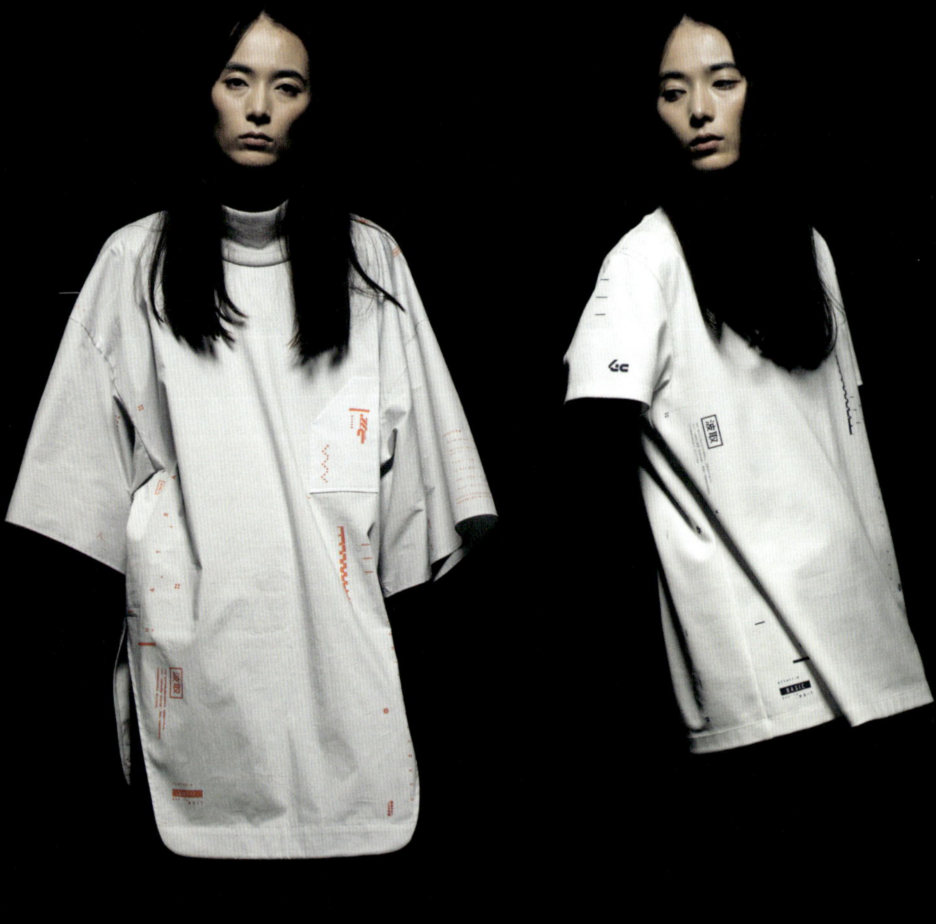

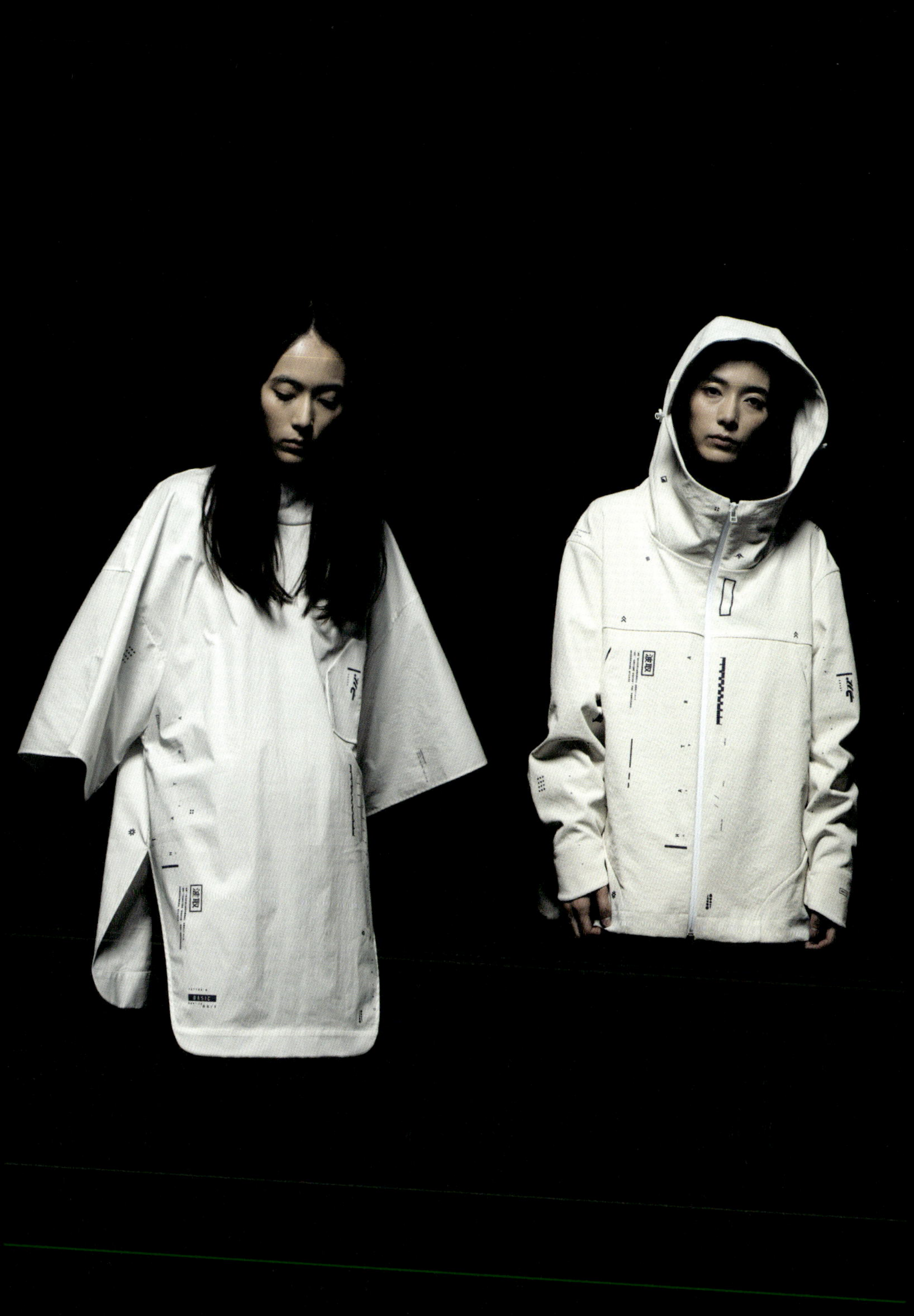

HATRA 2016SS

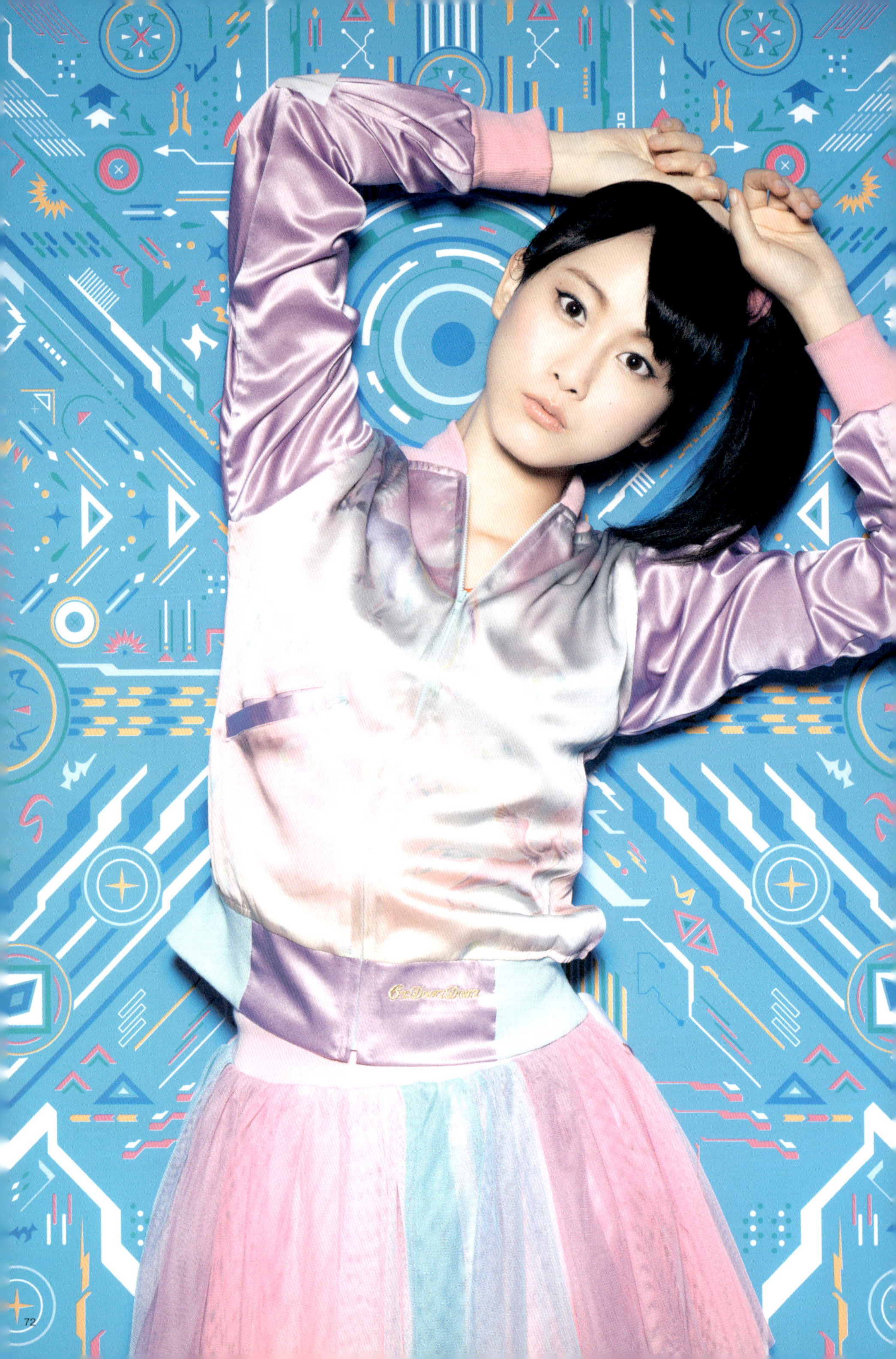

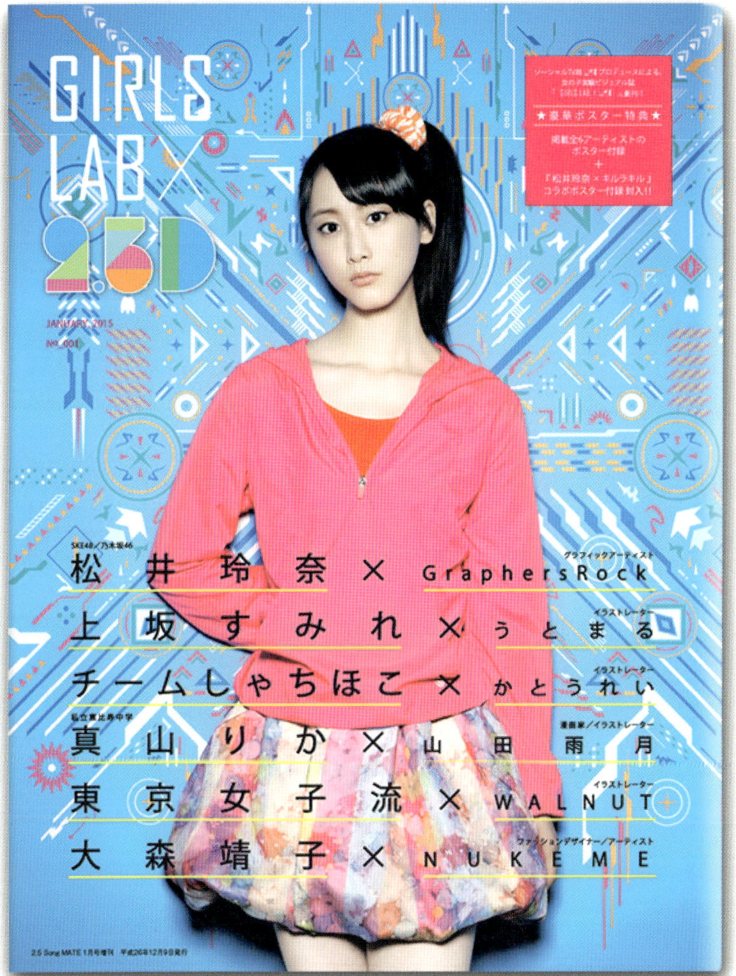
GIRLS LAB × 2.5D
JANUARY. 2015
№. 001
★豪華ポスター特典★
掲載全6アーティストの
ポスター付録
+
『松井玲奈×キルラキル』
コラボポスター付録封入!!
SKE48／乃木坂46
松井玲奈×GraphersRock
グラフィックアーティスト
上坂すみれ×うとまる
イラストレーター
チームしゃちほこ×かとうれい
イラストレーター
私立恵比寿中学
真山りか×山田雨月
漫画家／イラストレーター
東京女子流×WALNUT
イラストレーター
大森靖子×NUKEME
ファッションデザイナー／アーティスト
2.5 Song MATE 1月号増刊 平成26年12月9日発行

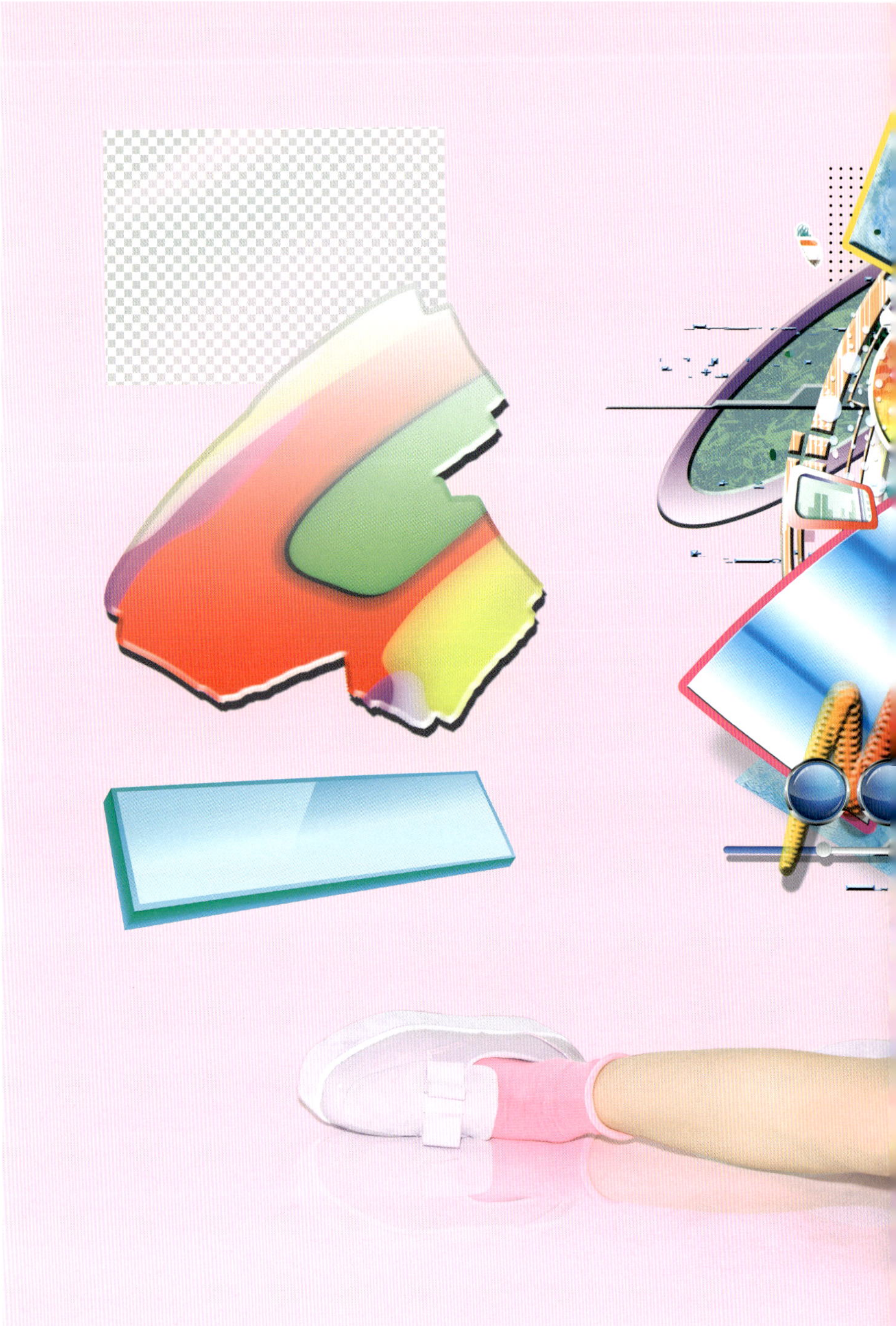

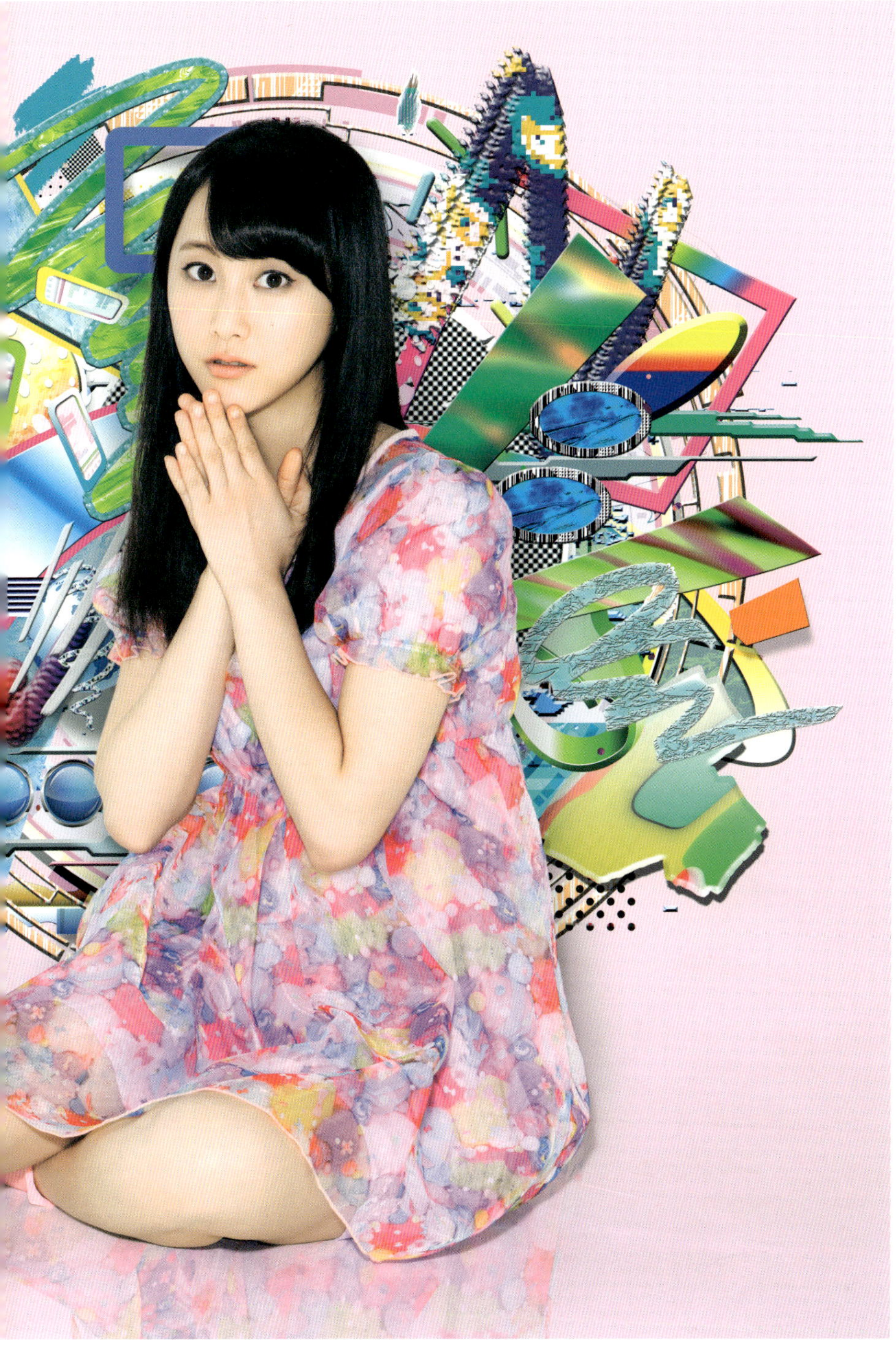

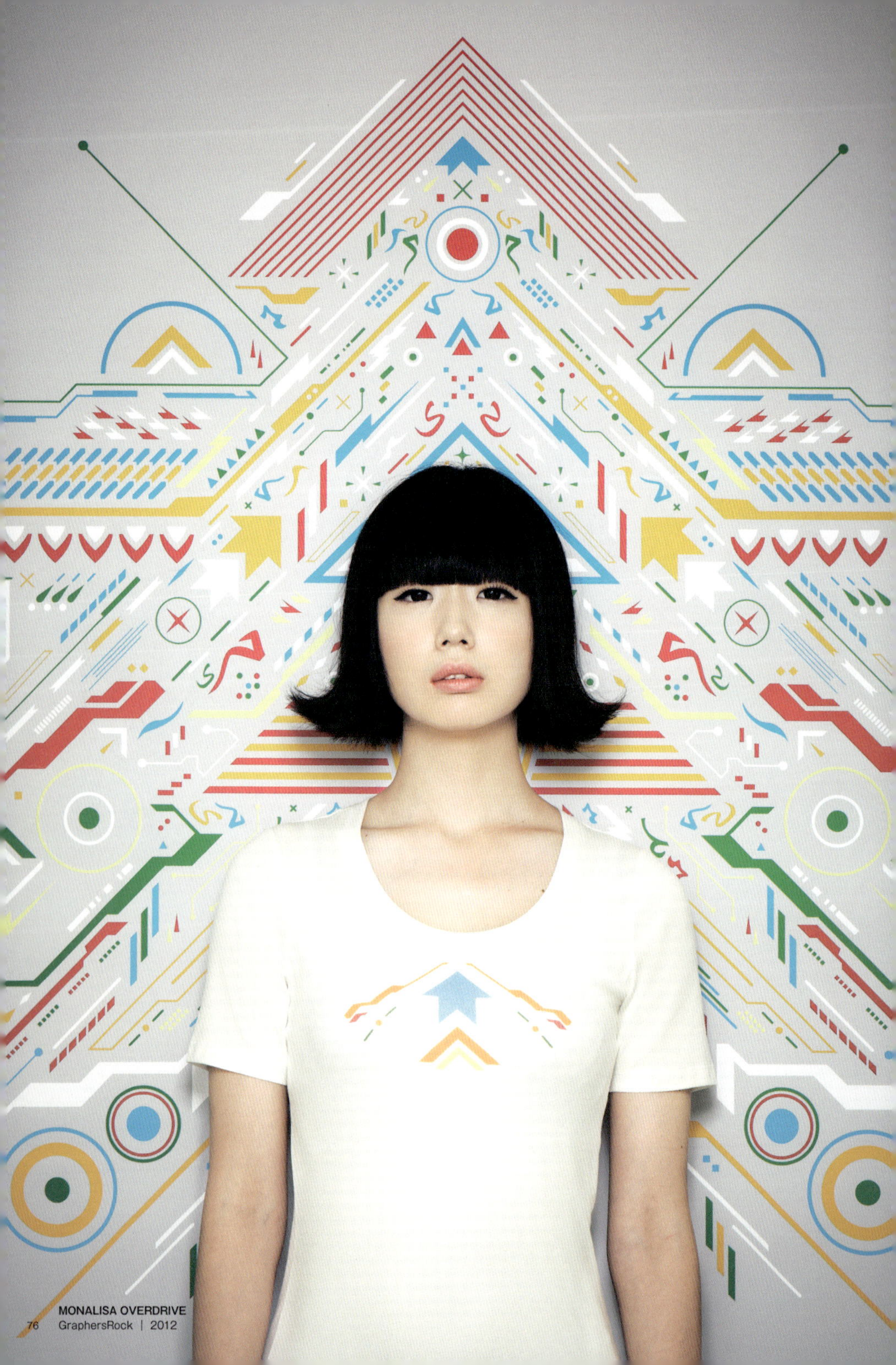

MONALISA OVERDRIVE
GraphersRock | 2012

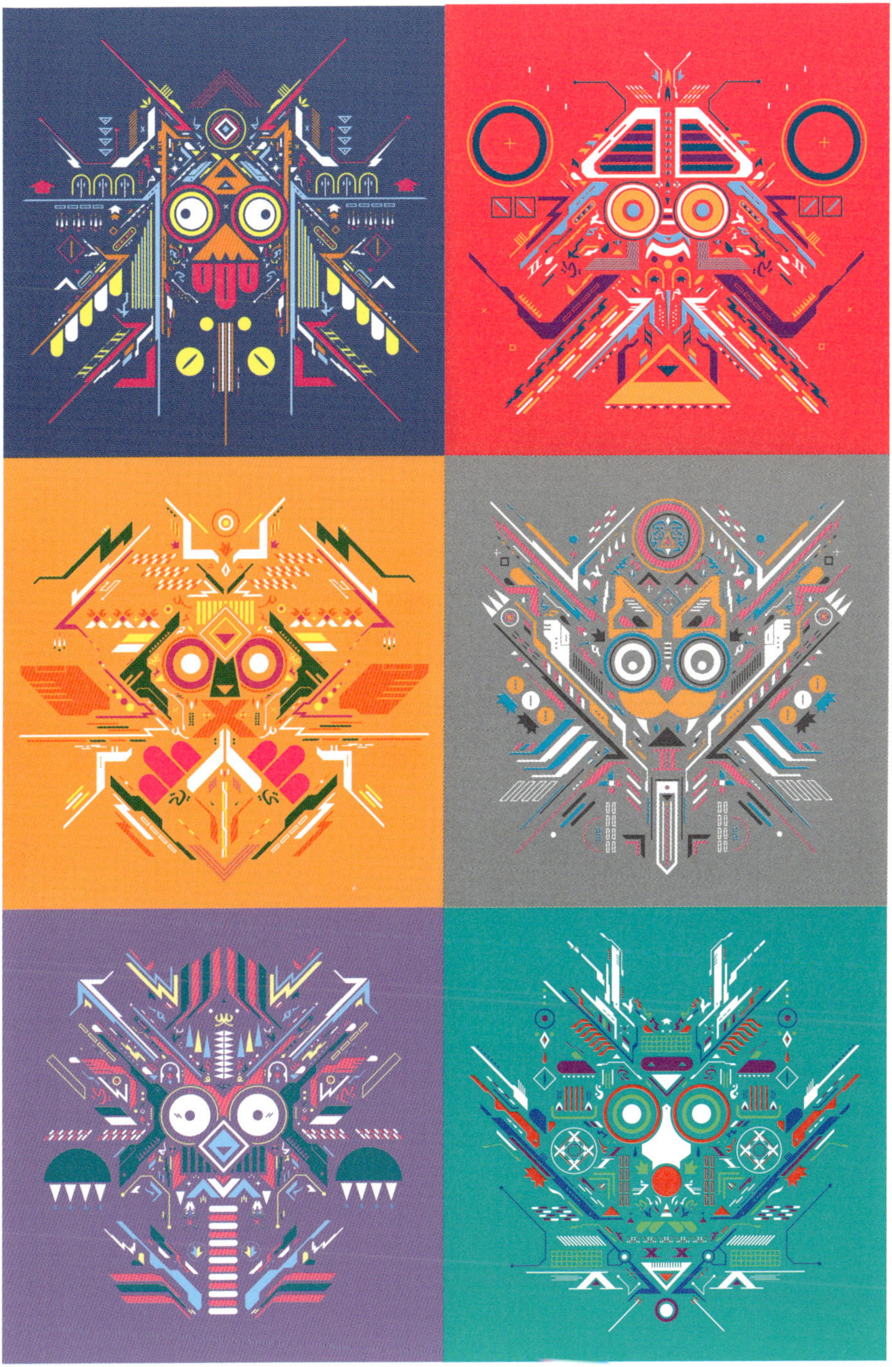

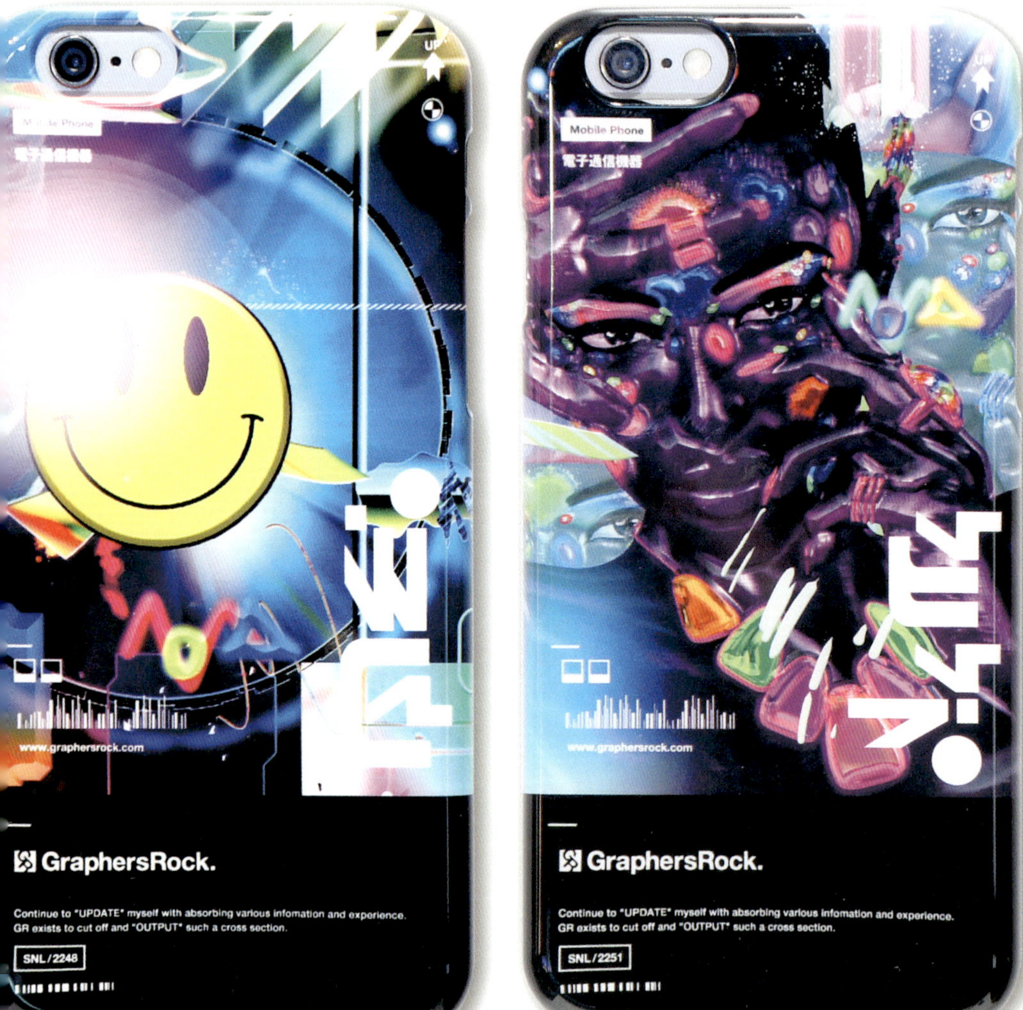
Mobile Phone
電子通信機器
www.graphersrock.com
GraphersRock.
Continue to "UPDATE" myself with absorbing various infomation and experience.
GR exists to cut off and "OUTPUT" such a cross section.
SNL/2248
Mobile Phone
電子通信機器
www.graphersrock.com
GraphersRock.
Continue to "UPDATE" myself with absorbing various infomation and experience.
GR exists to cut off and "OUTPUT" such a cross section.
SNL/2251

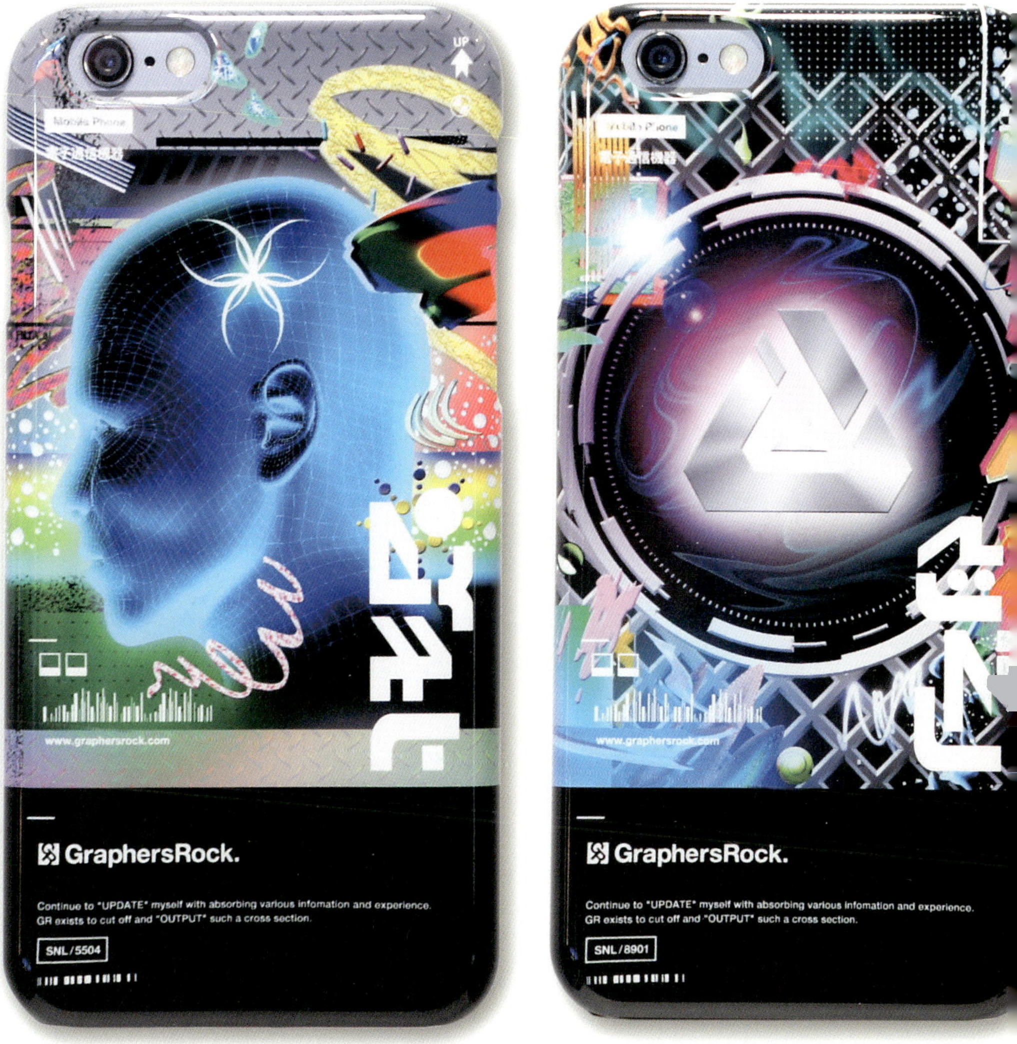

VIDEO CARD PKG 1-4
iPhoneケース | CINRA.STORE | 2015

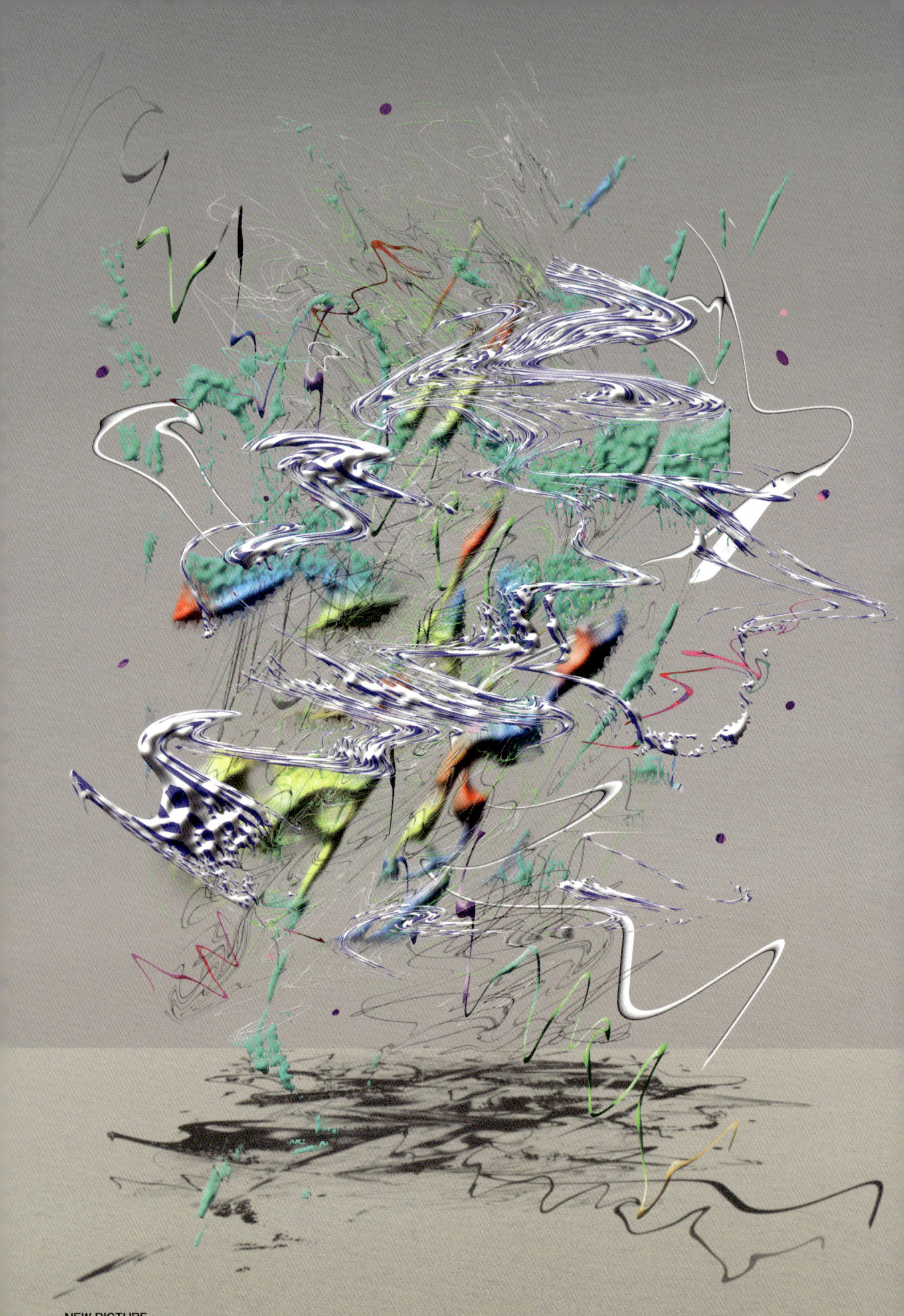

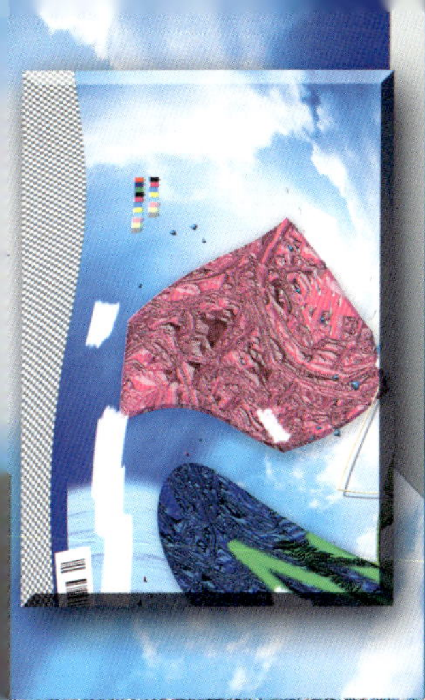
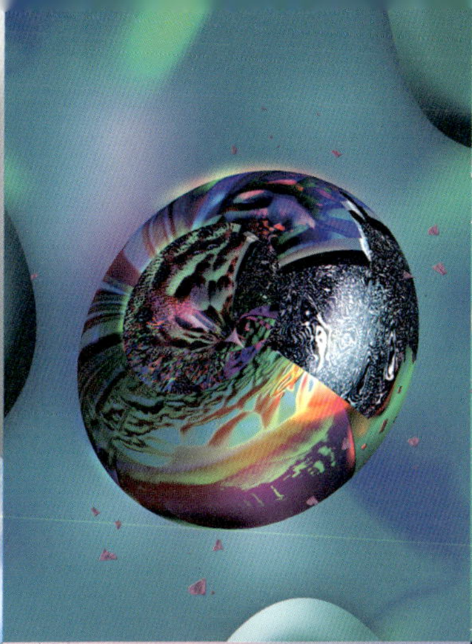
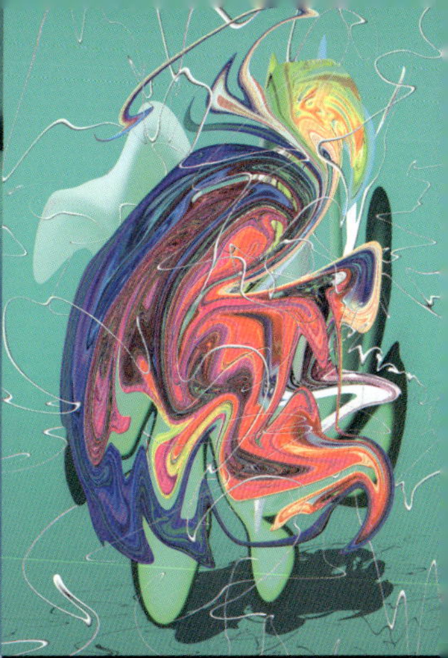
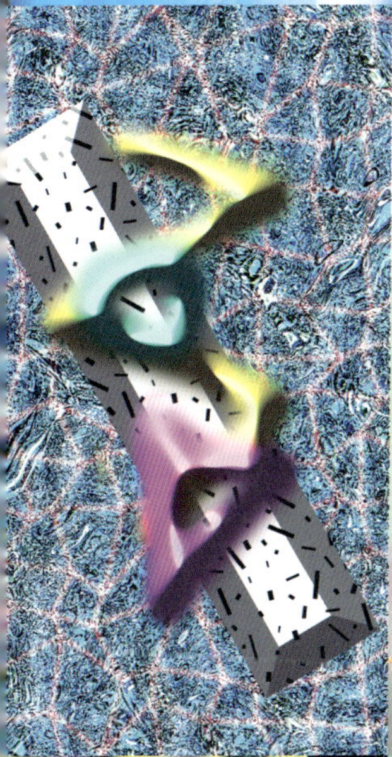
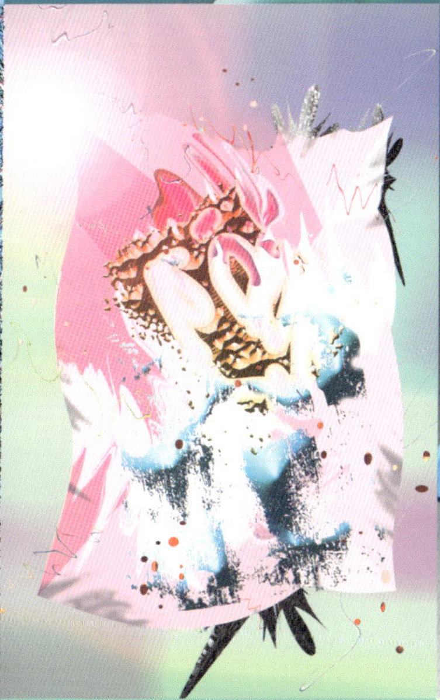
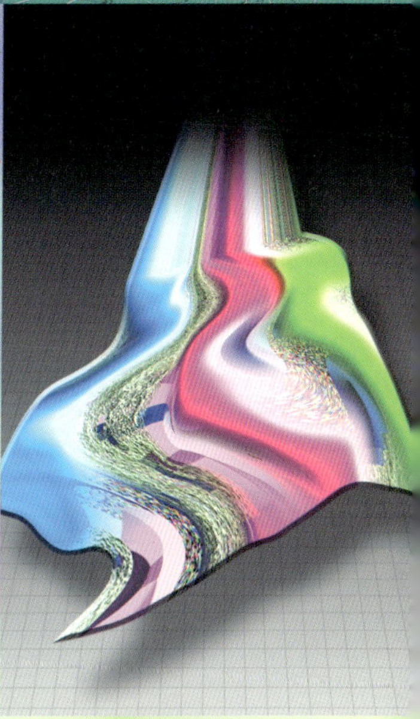
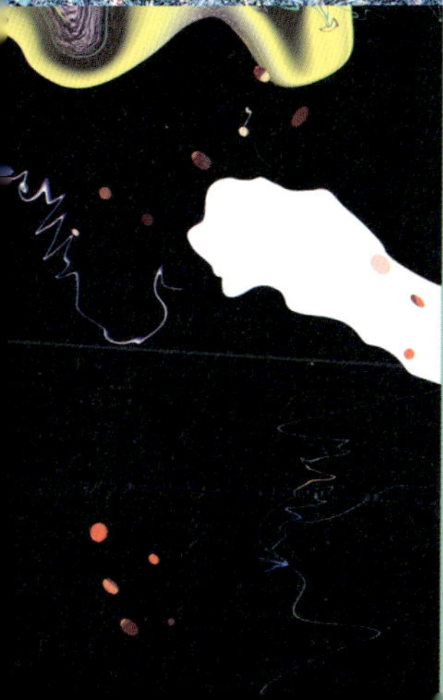

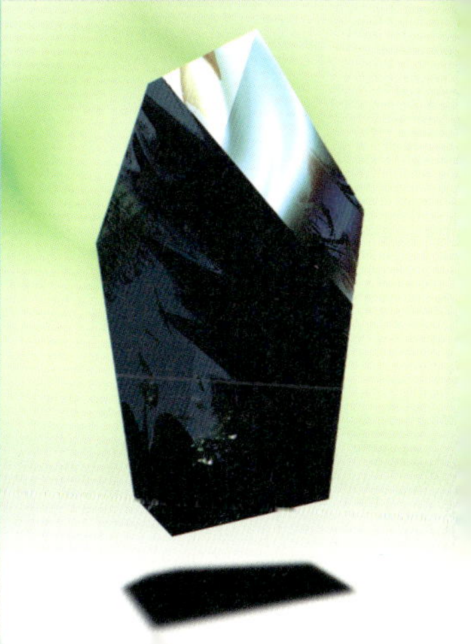

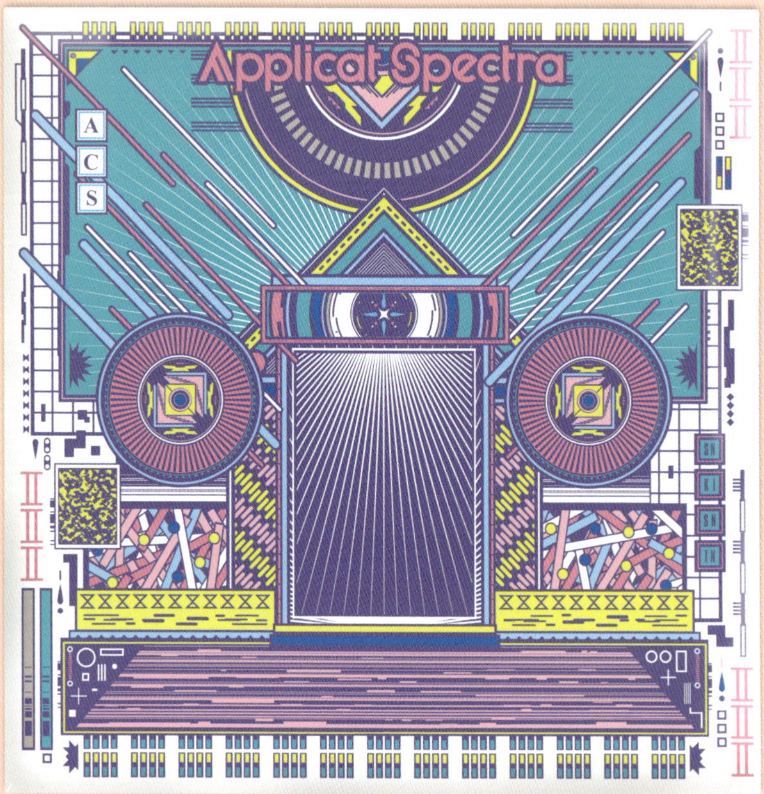

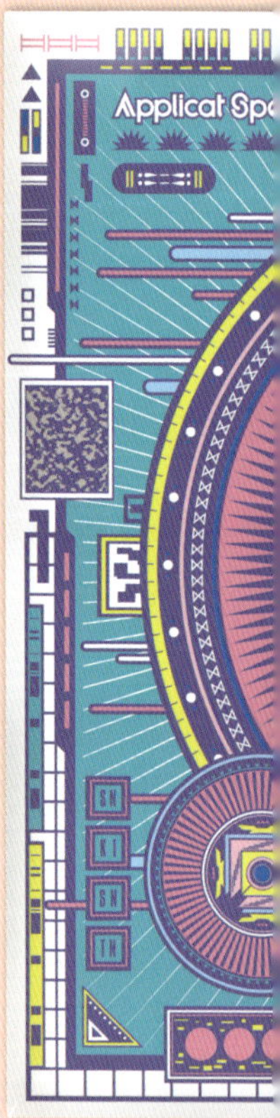

Applicat Spectra / アポステリオep
CDジャケット ｜ 2015

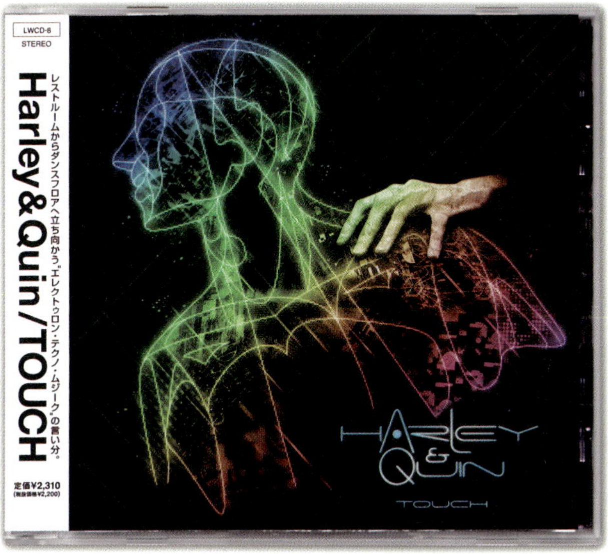

Harley&Quin / TOUCH
CDジャケット ｜ SWC ｜ 2008

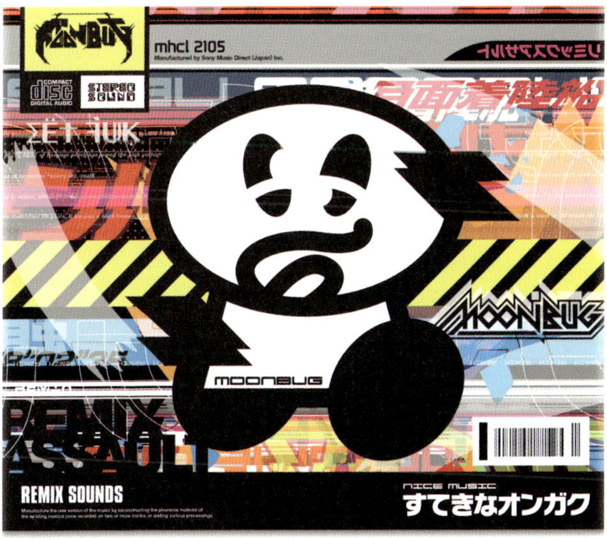

MOONBUG / REMIX ASSAULT
CDジャケット ｜ ソニー・ミュージックダイレクト ｜ 2013
©Sony Music Direct (Japan) Inc.

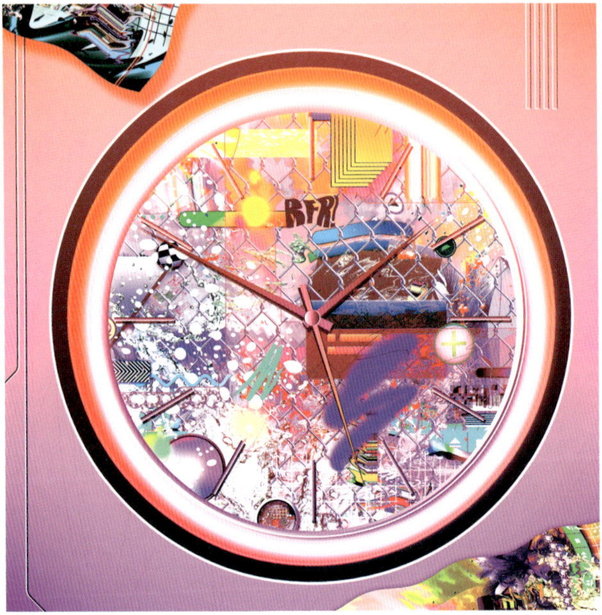

RunFoxRun! / Crayola Sunrise
配信ジャケット ｜ Maltine Records ｜ 2014

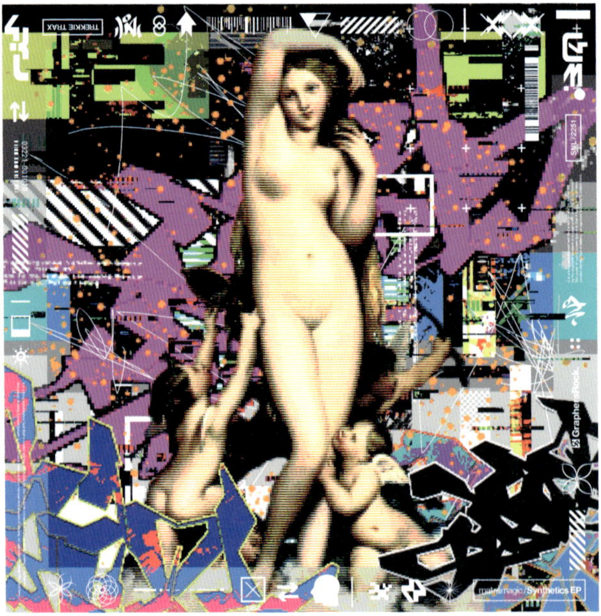

Matra magic / Synthetics EP
配信ジャケット ｜ TREKKIE TRAX ｜ 2015

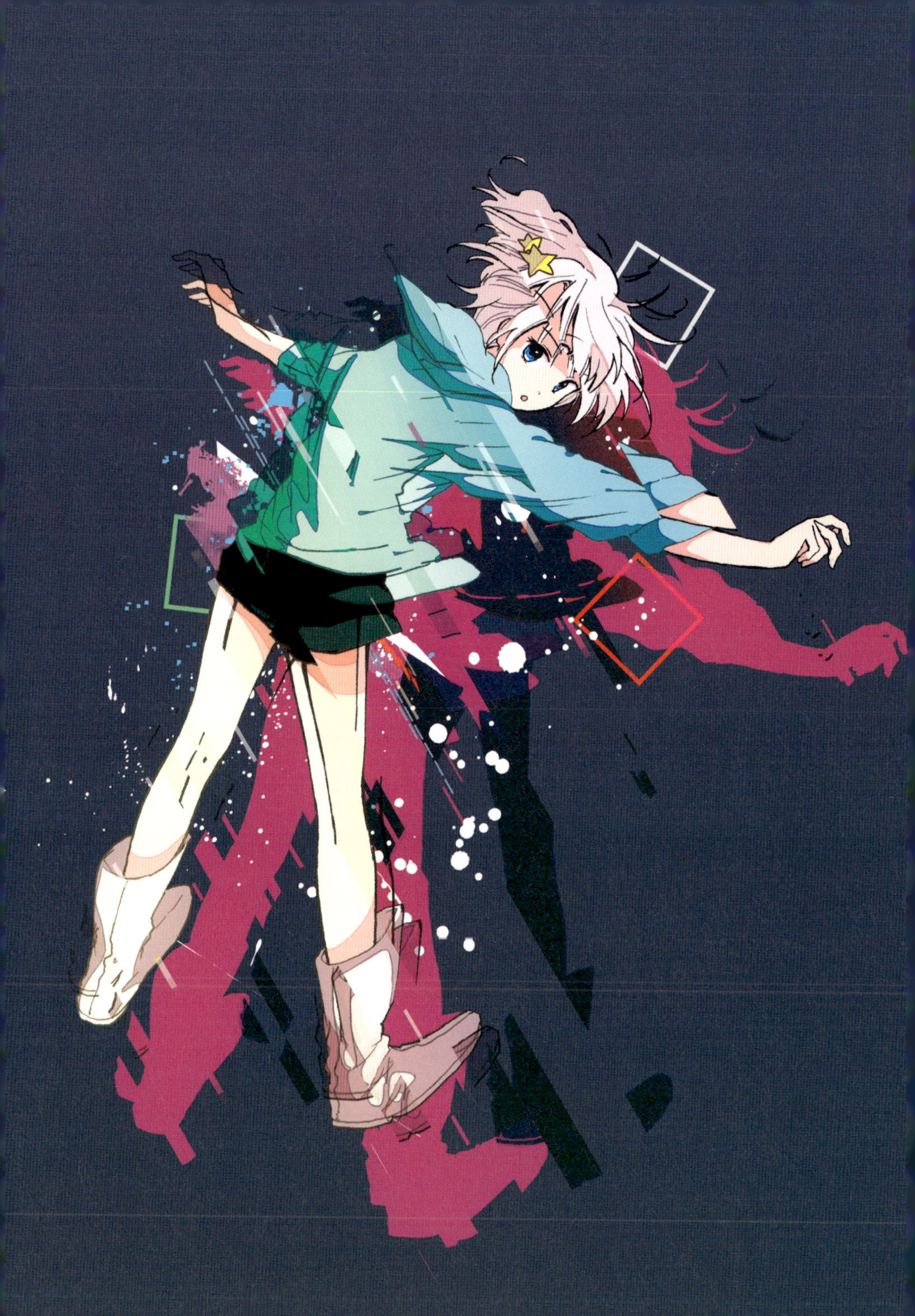

Aquastella / Magical Flight
CDジャケット ｜ 2012

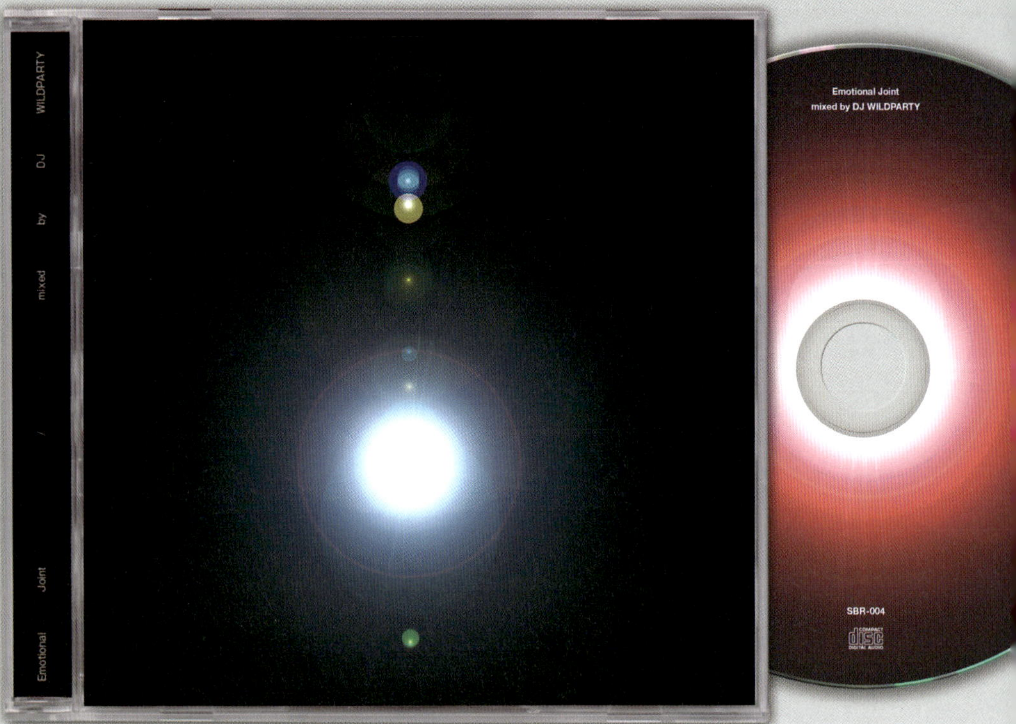

DJ WILDPARTY / EMOTIONAL JOINT

CDジャケット ｜ 2013

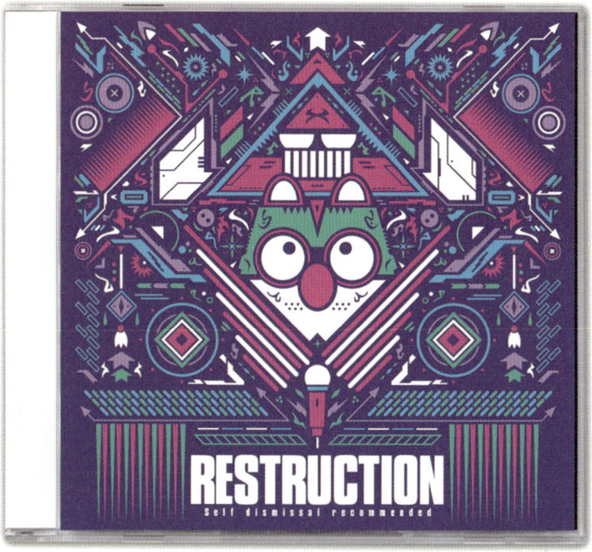

DOTAMA x USK / リストラクション
CDジャケット ｜ 術ノ穴｜ 2012

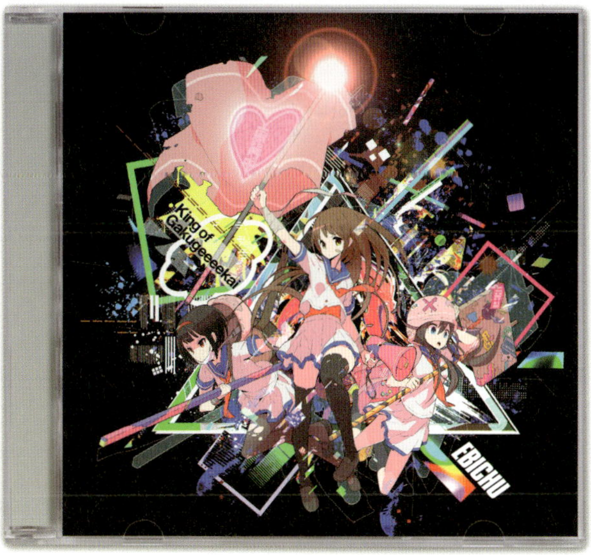

私立恵比寿中学 / Go!Go!Here We Go! ロック・リー / 大人はわかってくれない
CDジャケット ｜ DefSTAR Records ｜ 2012

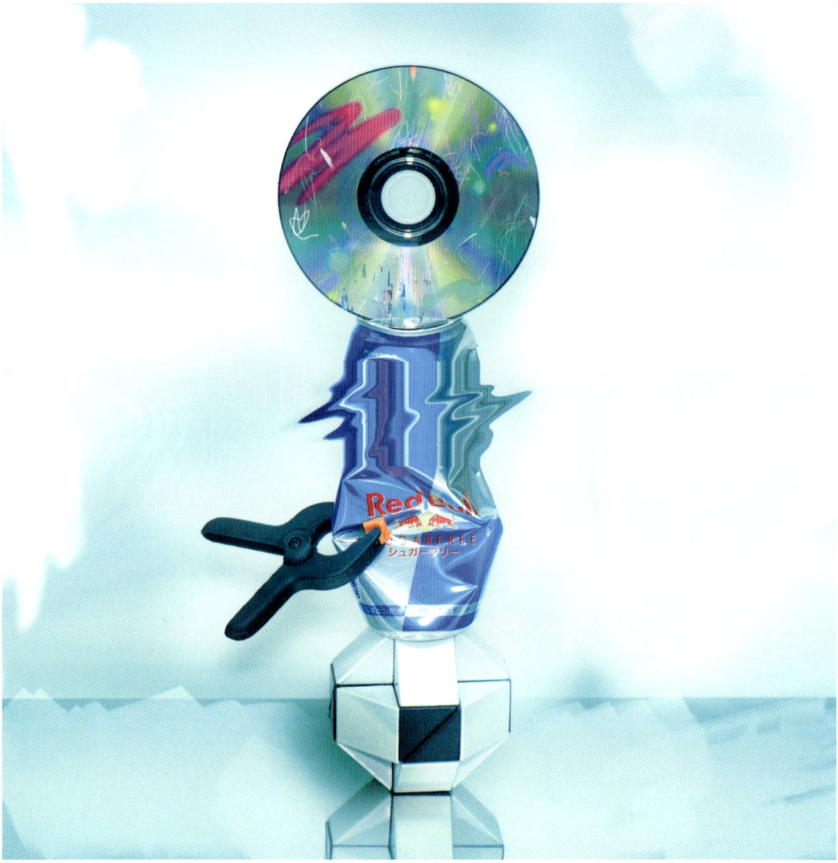

mirrorball inferno / CLASSICS
配信ジャケット | 2014

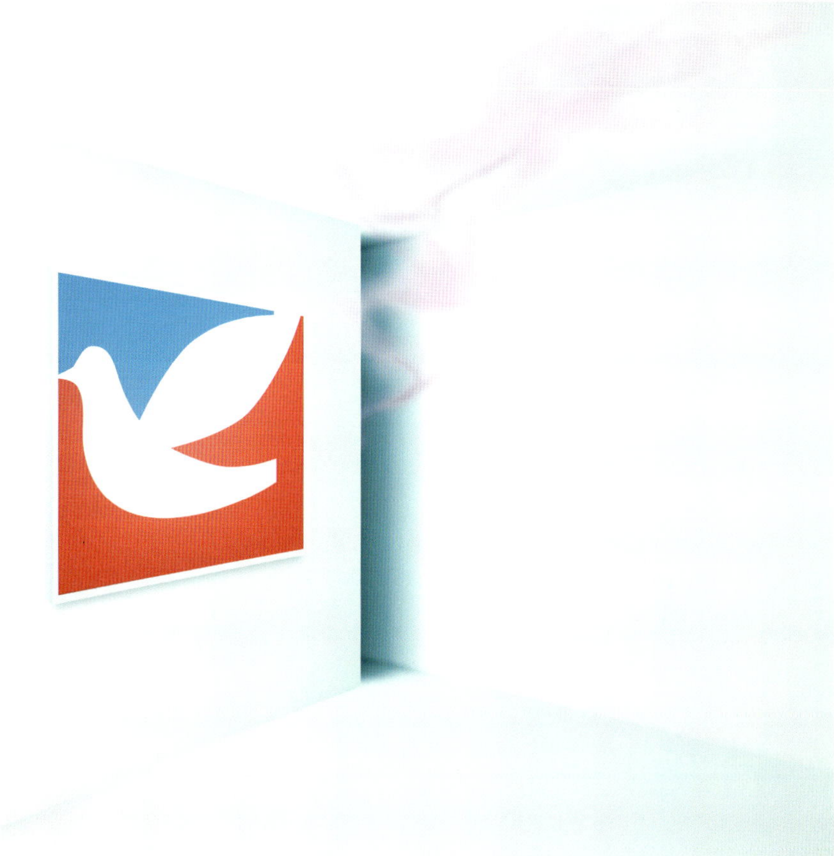

mirrorball inferno / SUPER SALEOUT
配信ジャケット ｜ Maltine Records ｜ 2010

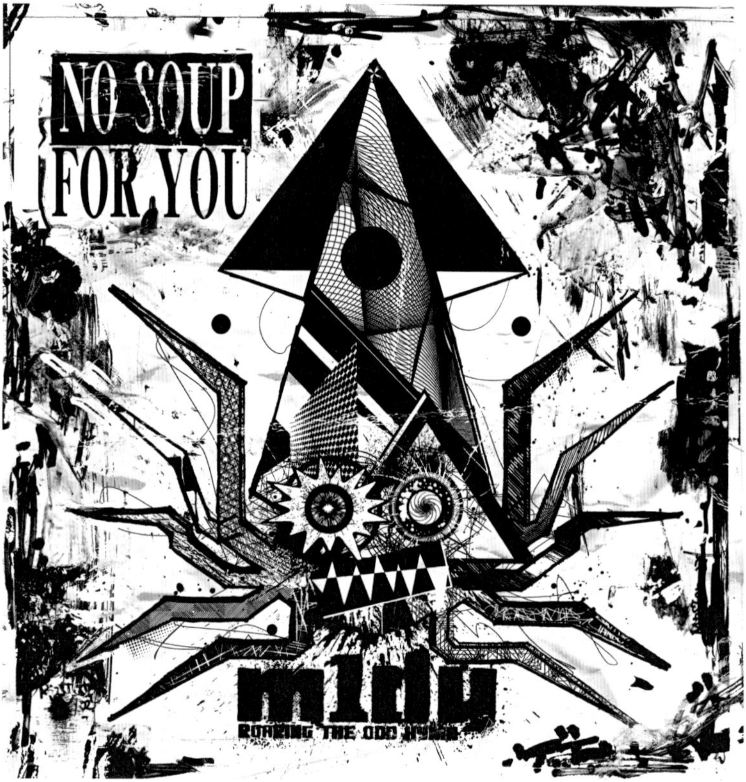

m1dy / NO SOUP FOR YOU
CDジャケット | MADDEST CHICKNDOM | 2008

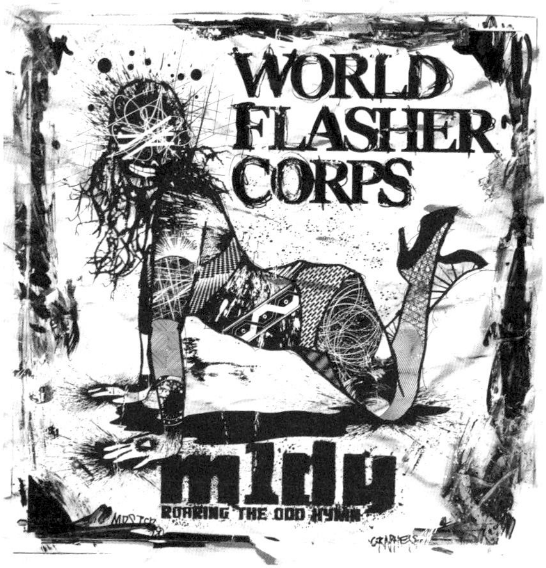

m1dy / WORLD FLASHER CORPS
CDジャケット | MADDEST CHICKNDOM | 2008

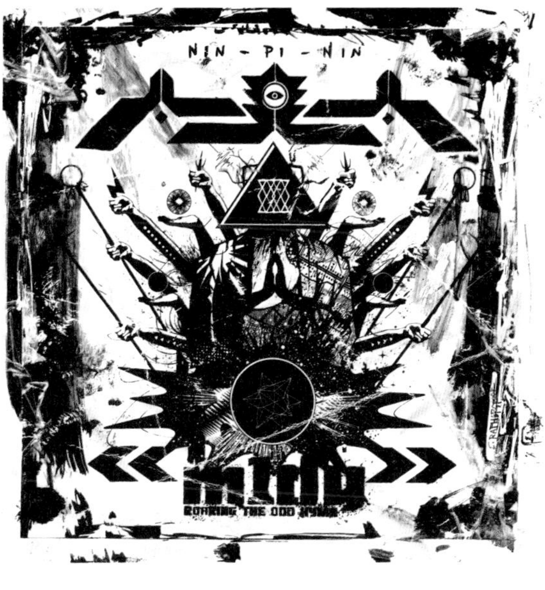

m1dy / 人非人
CDジャケット | MADDEST CHICKNDOM | 2009

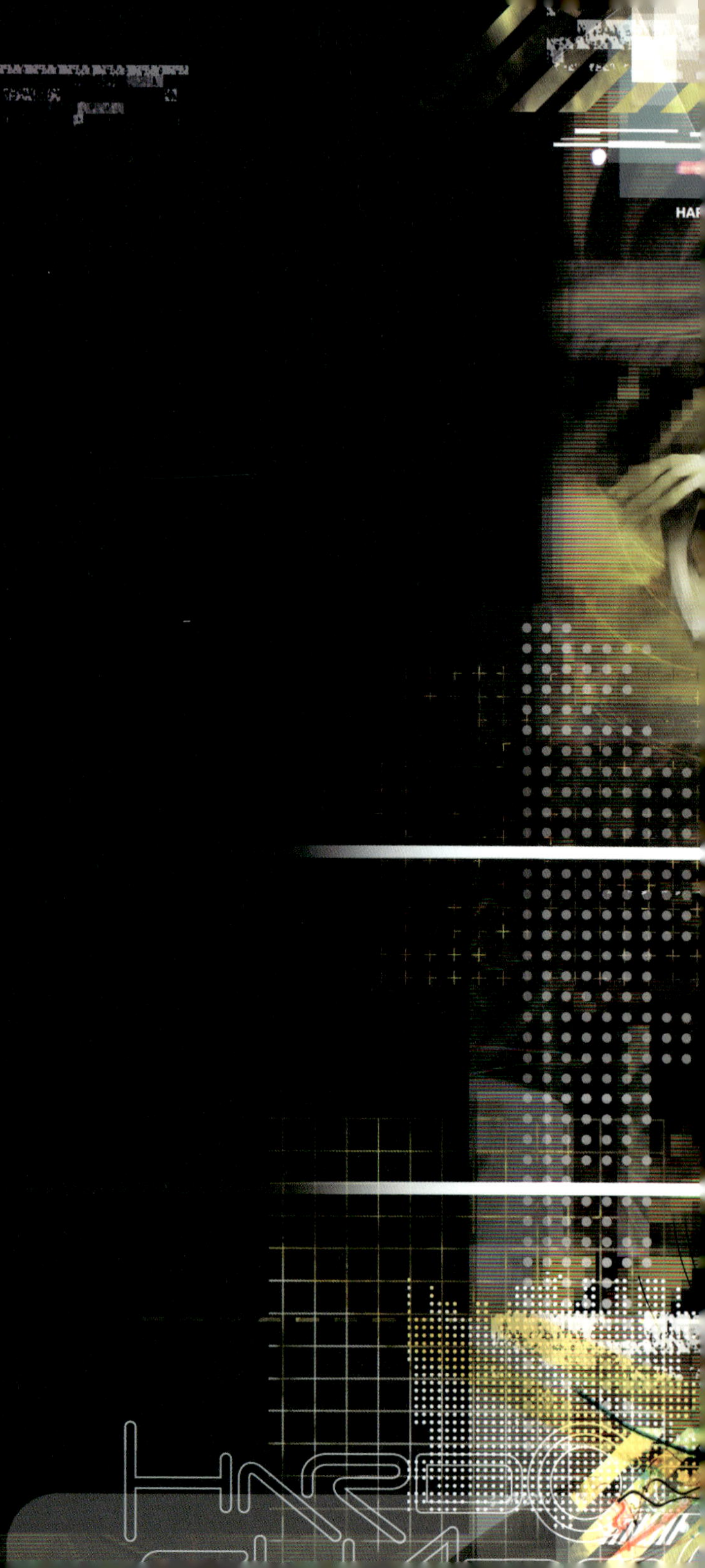

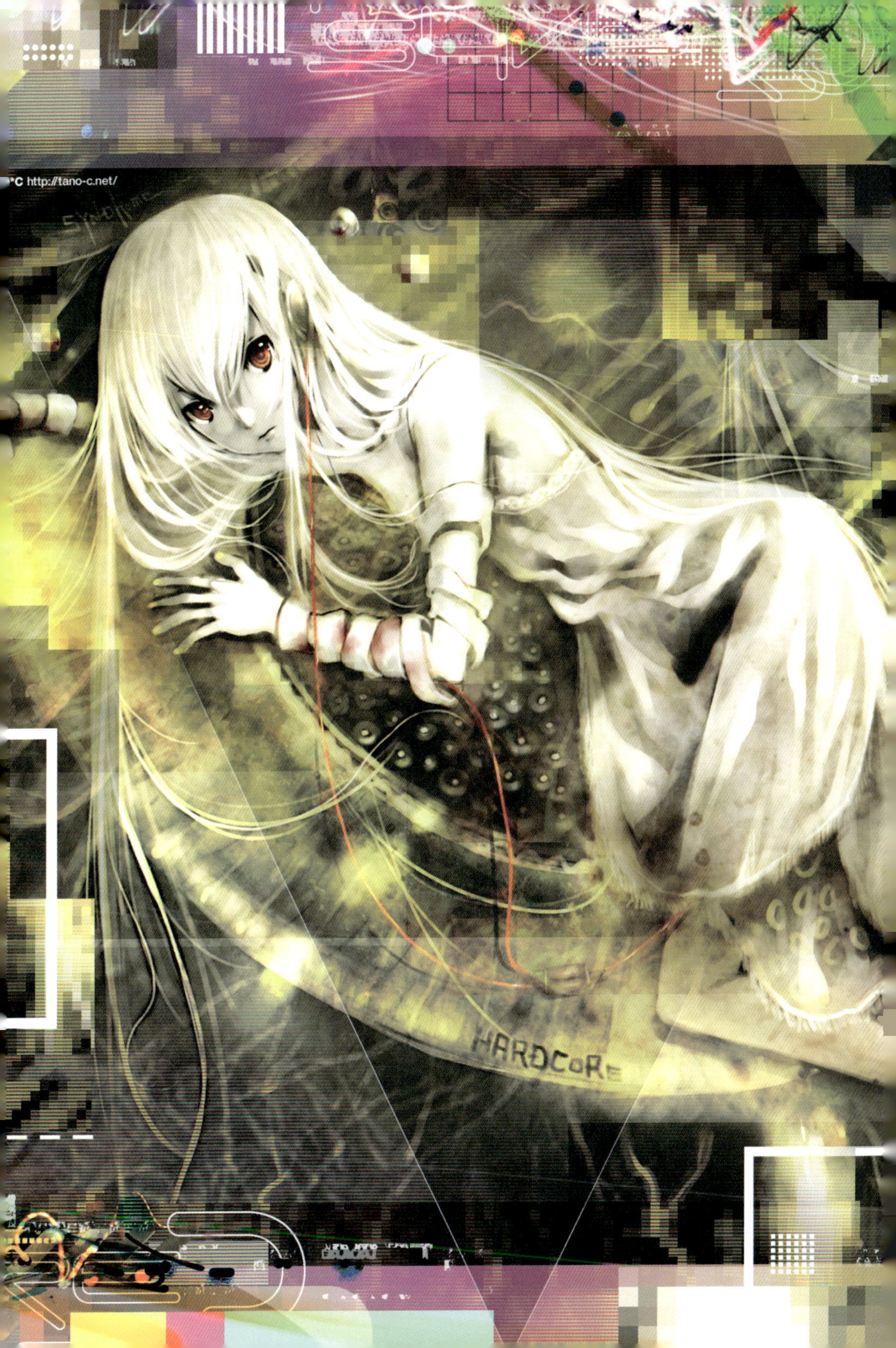
*C http://tano-c.net/
HARDCoRE

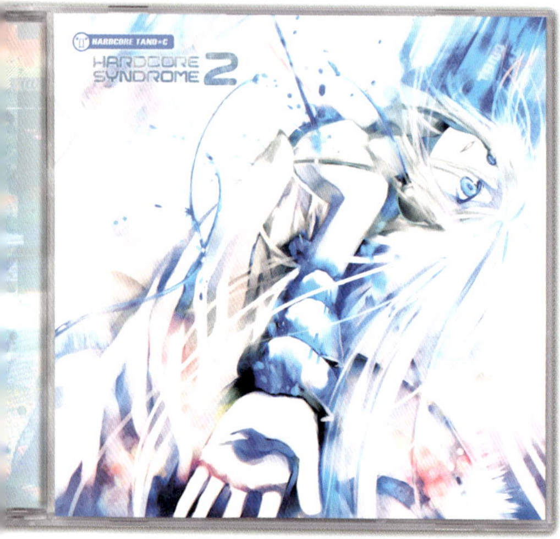
HARDCORE TANO*C
HARDCORE SYNDROME 2

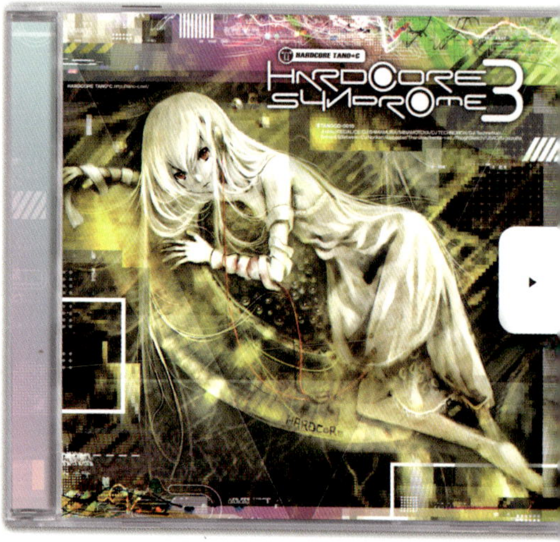
HARDCORE TANO*C
HARDCORE SYNDROME 3

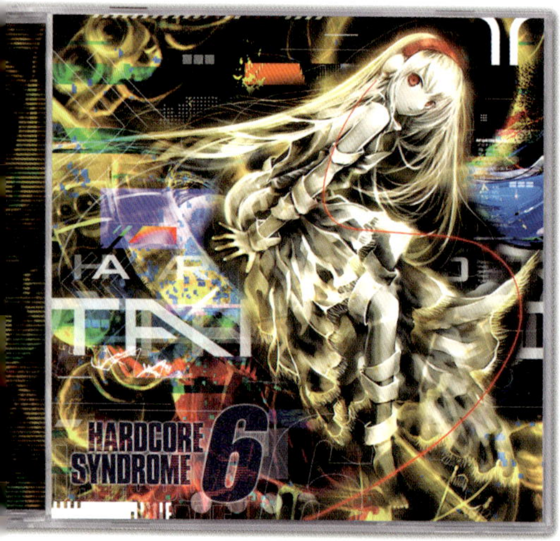
HARDCORE SYNDROME 6

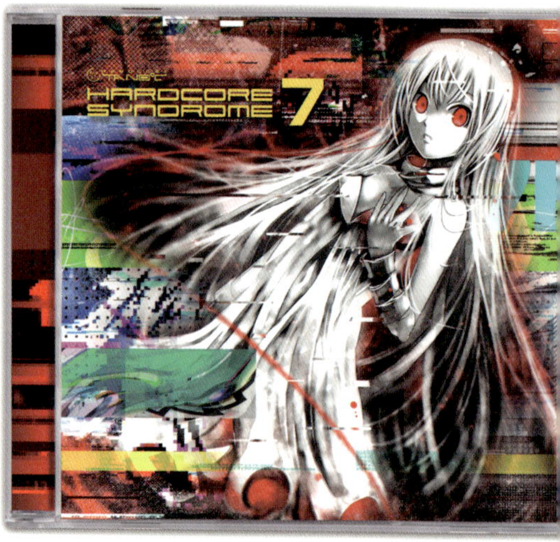
HARDCORE SYNDROME 7

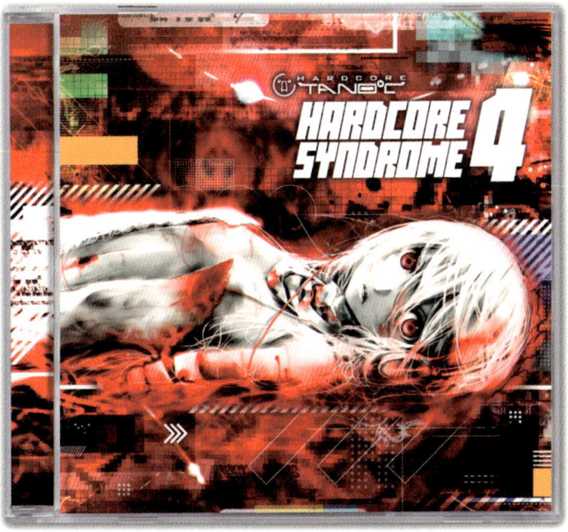

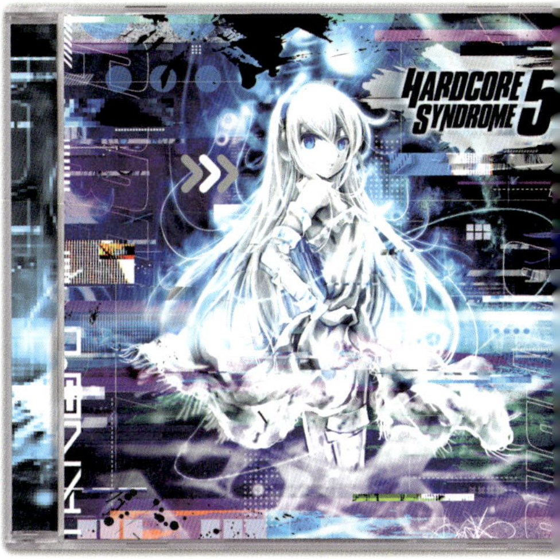

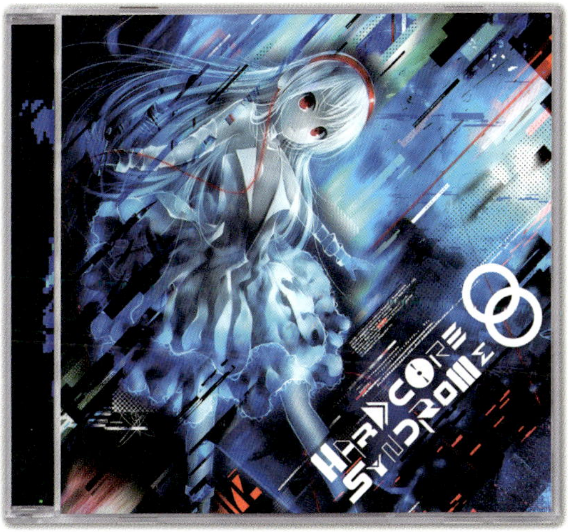

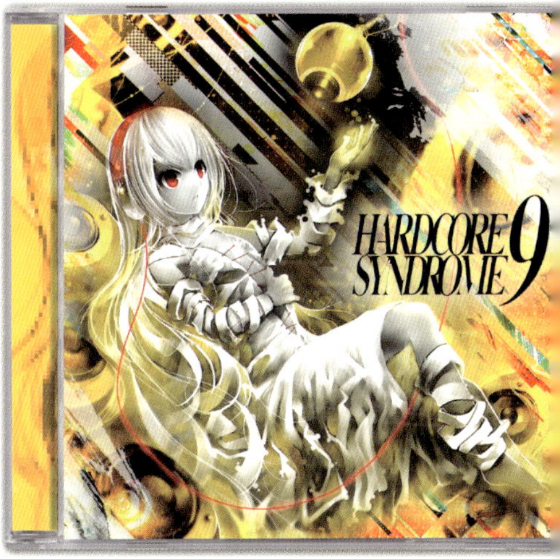

HARDCORE SYNDROME シリーズ
CDジャケット ｜ HARDCORE TANO*C（ハードコアタノシー）｜ 2008 - 2015

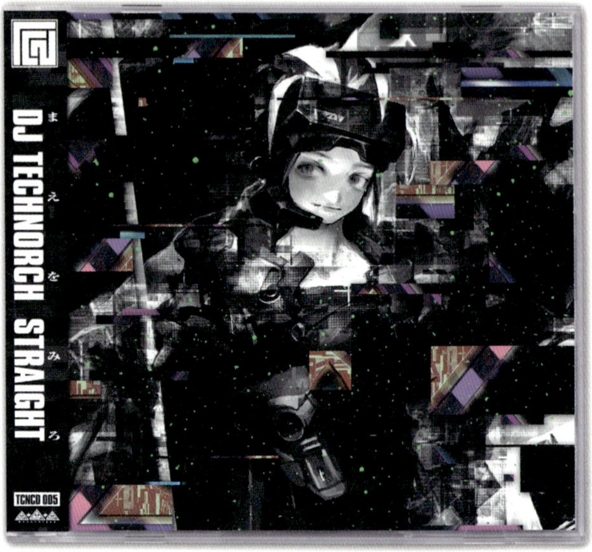

DJ TECHNORCH / STRAIGHT
CDジャケット ｜ 999 Recordings ｜ 2010

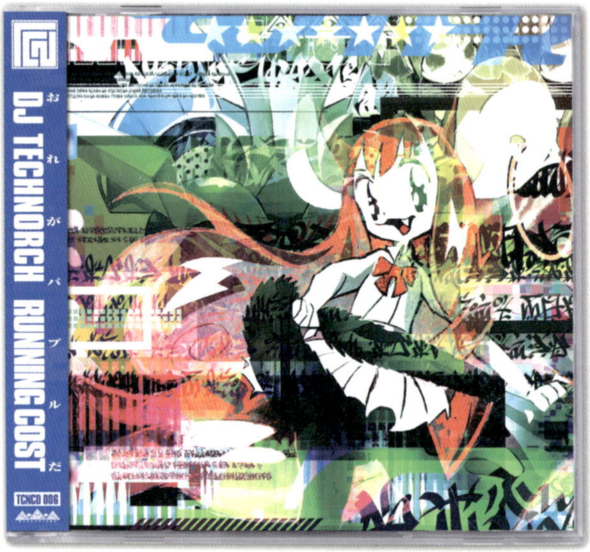

DJ TECHNORCH / RUNNING COST
CDジャケット ｜ 999 Recordings ｜ 2010

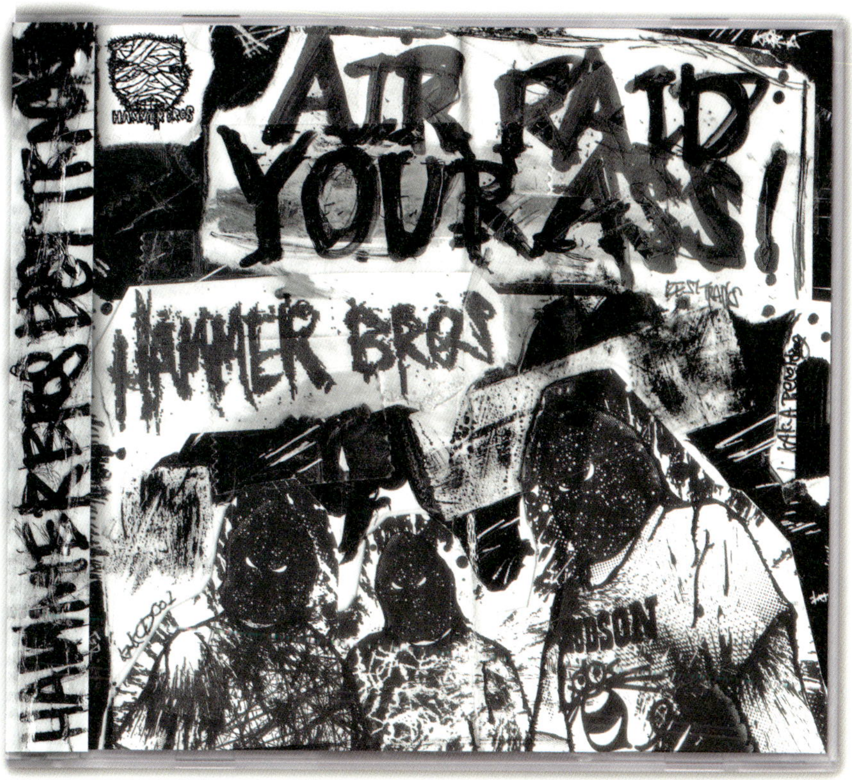

HAMMER BROS / AIR RAID YOUR ASS!
CDジャケット | DefSTAR Records | 2006

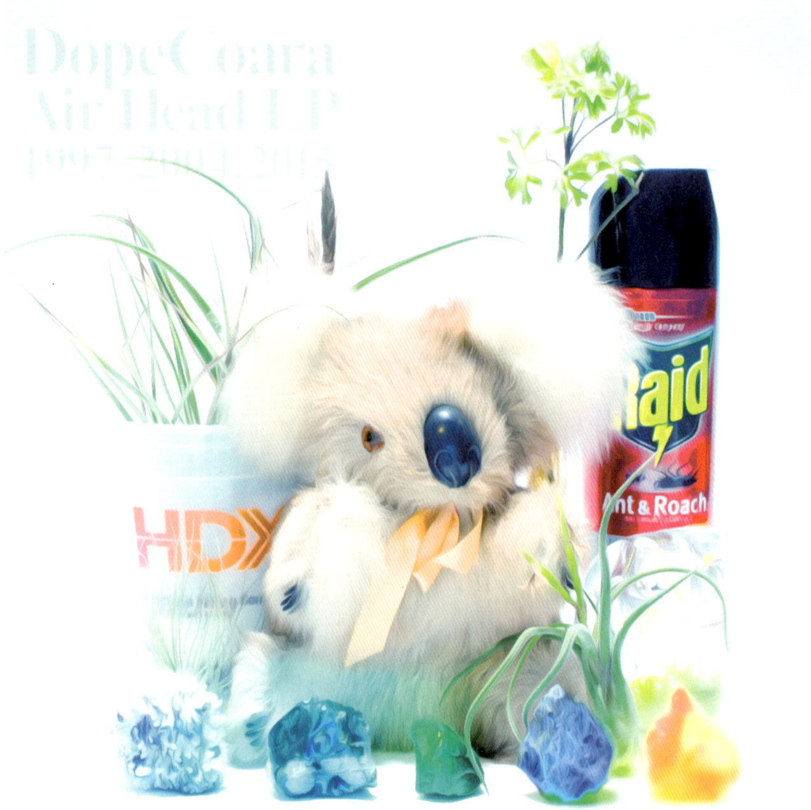

Dope Coara / Air Head LP 1997-2004、2015
配信ジャケット ｜ MURDER CHANNEL ｜ 2015

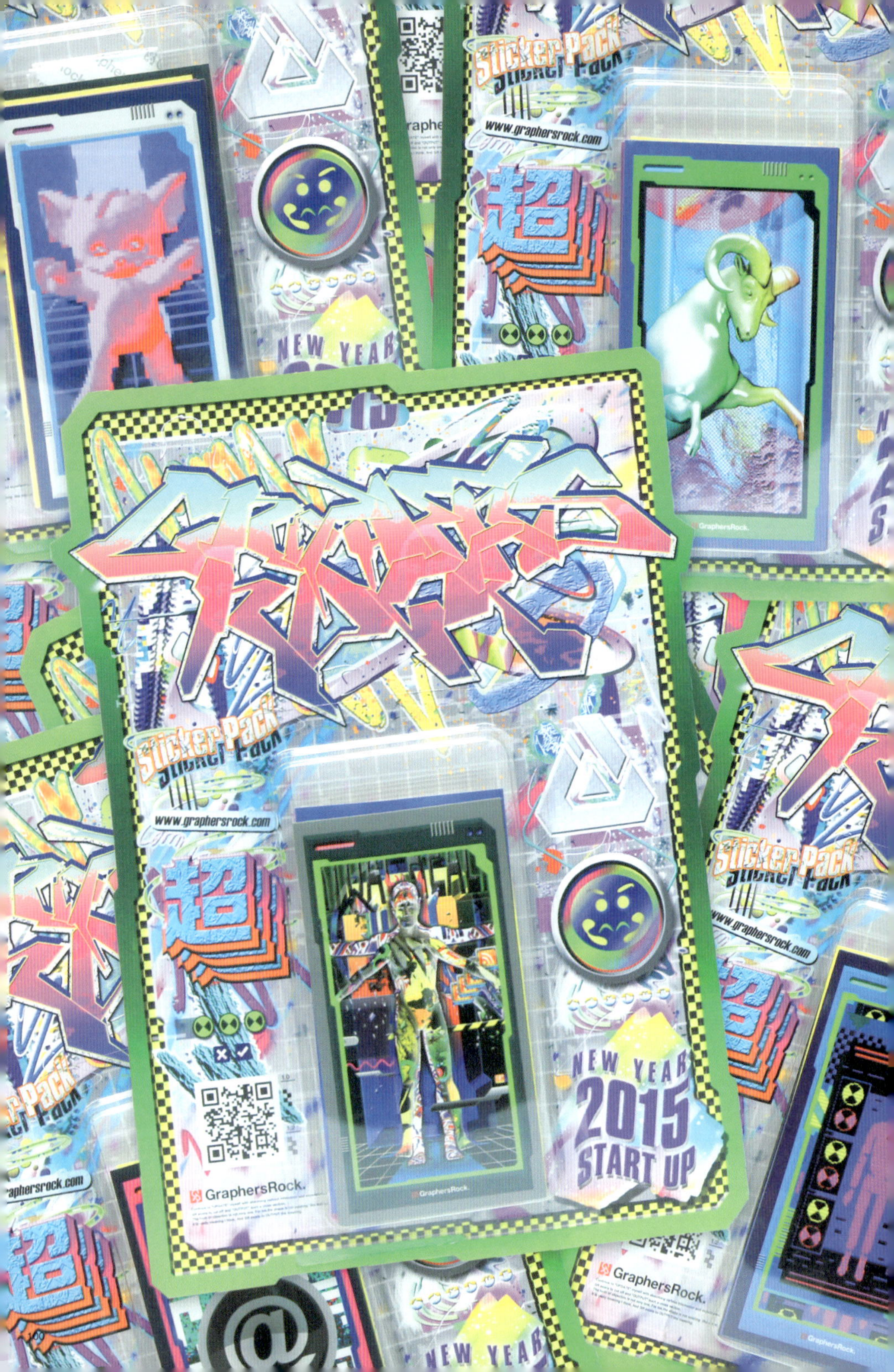
Sticker Pack
www.graphersrock.com
超
NEW YEAR
2015
START UP
GraphersRock.

ステッカーパック年賀状2015
GraphersRock | 2015

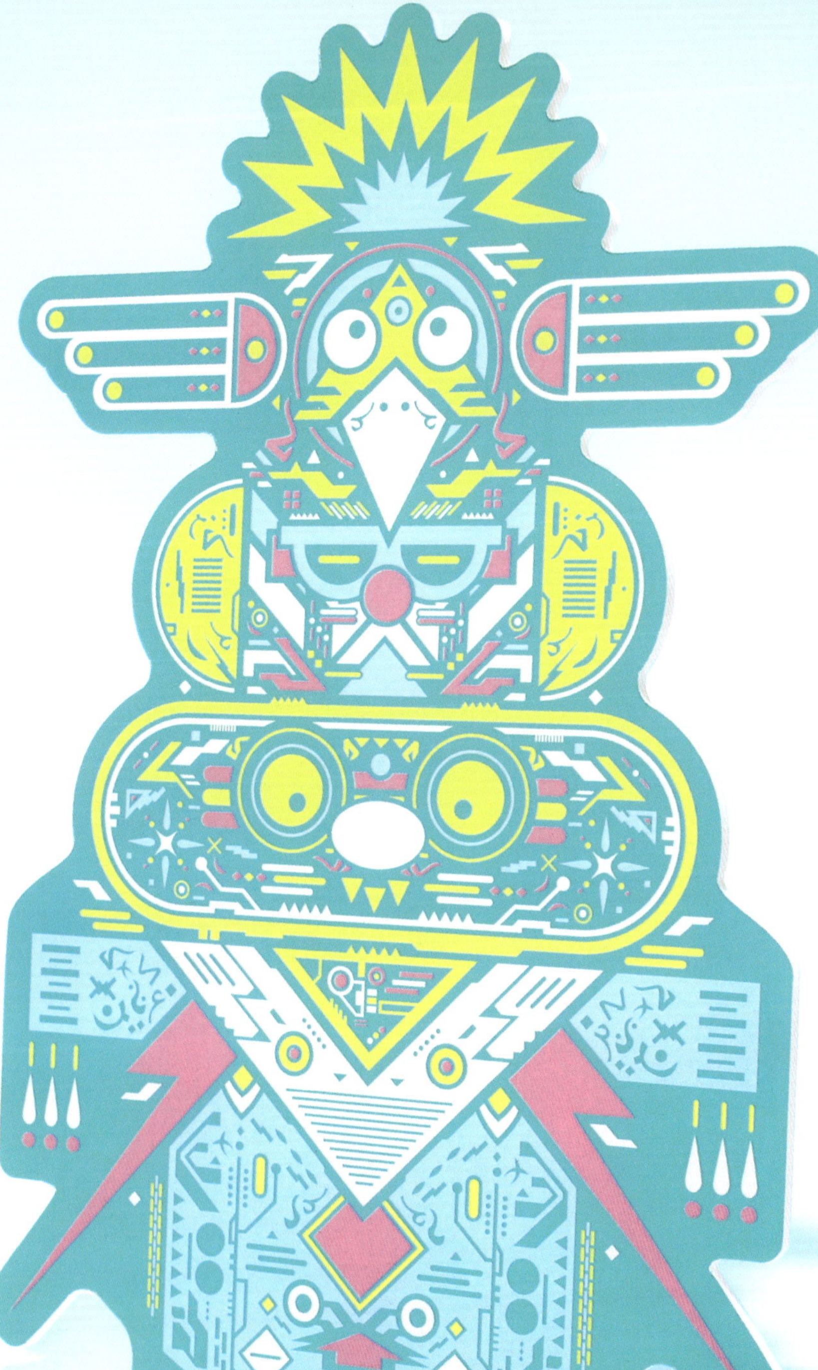

年賀状 2016

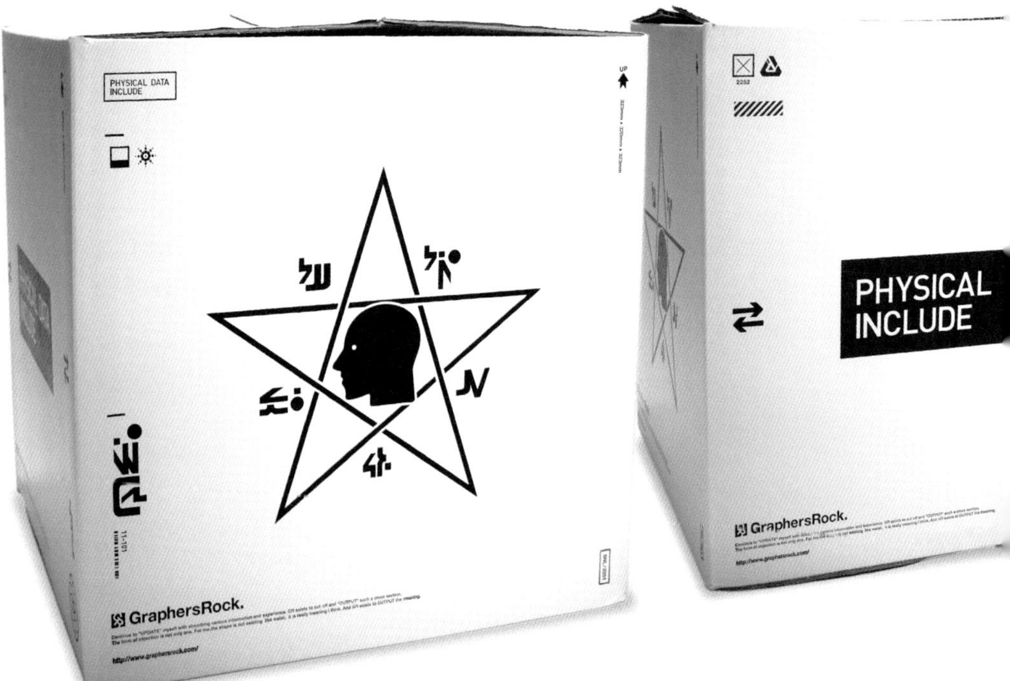

PHYSICAL DATA INCLUDE
LPケースダンボール | GraphersRock | 2015

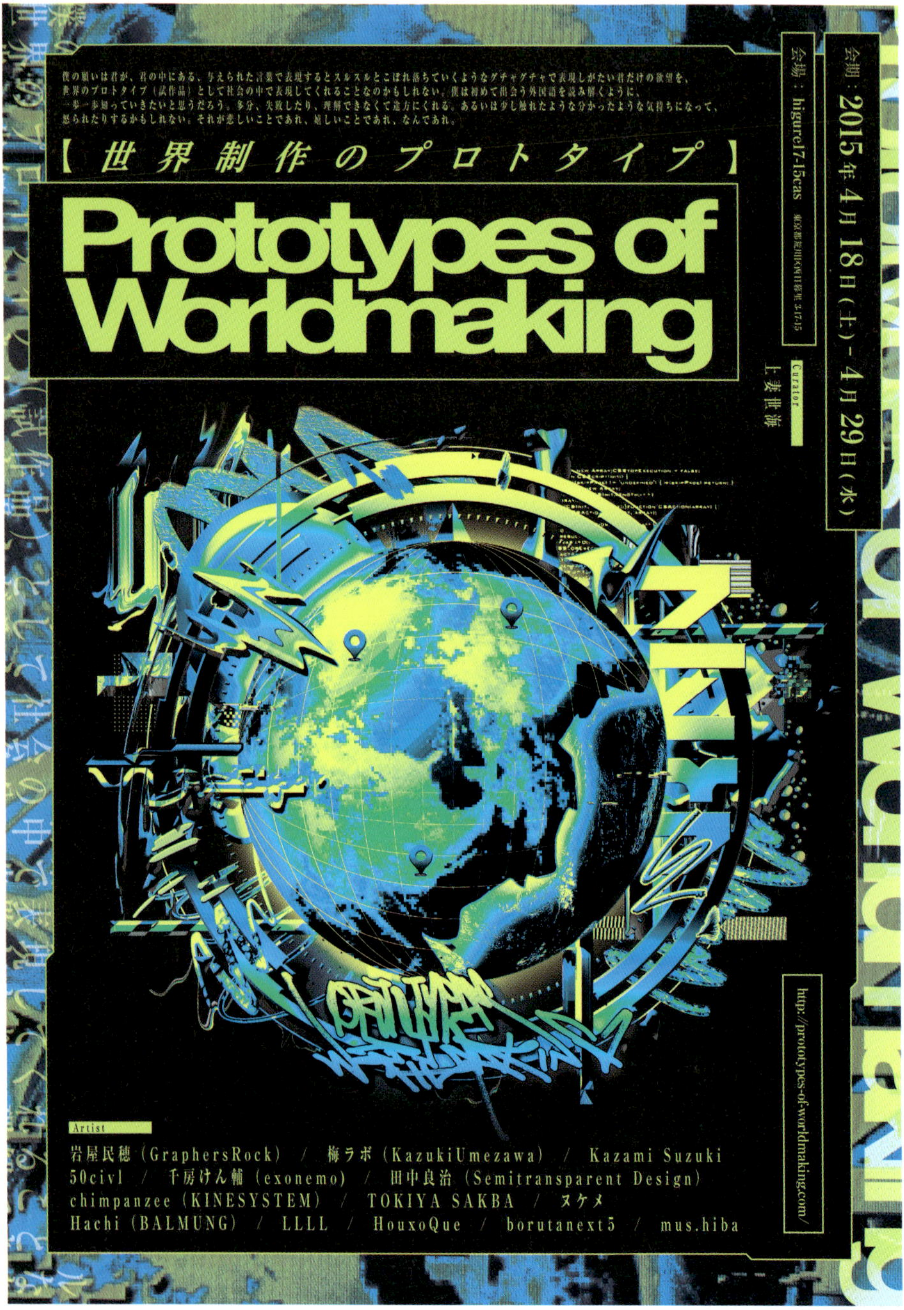

世界制作のプロトタイプ

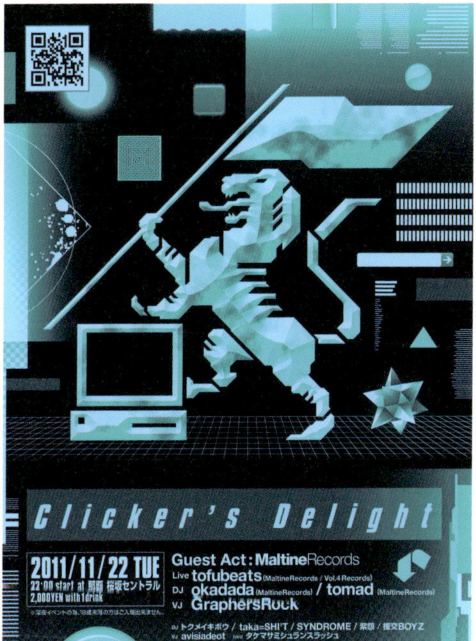

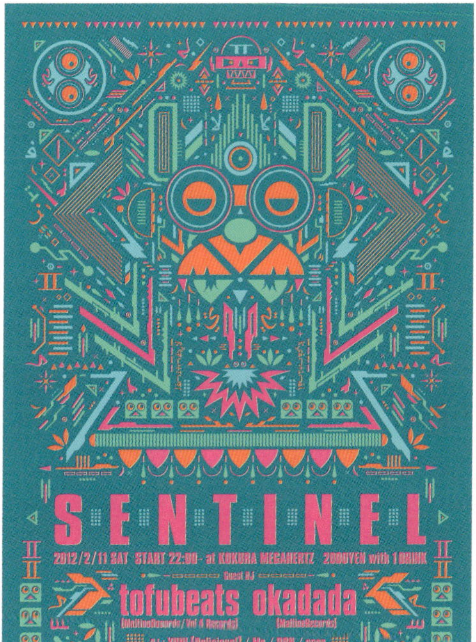

Clicker's Delight
イベントフライヤー ｜ 2011

SENTINEL
イベントフライヤー ｜ 2011

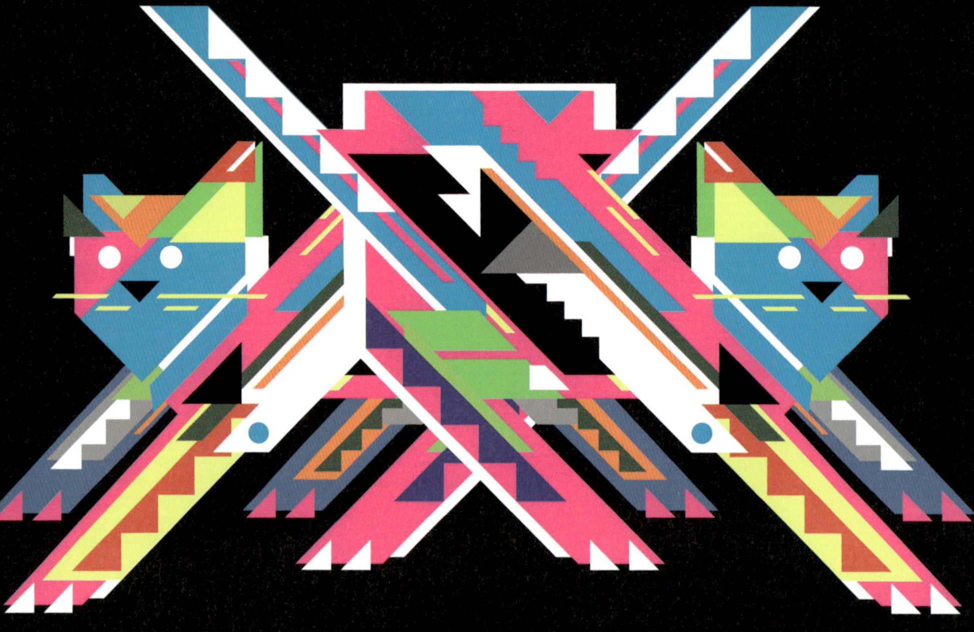

Applicat Spectra Netscape
イベントビジュアル | 2012

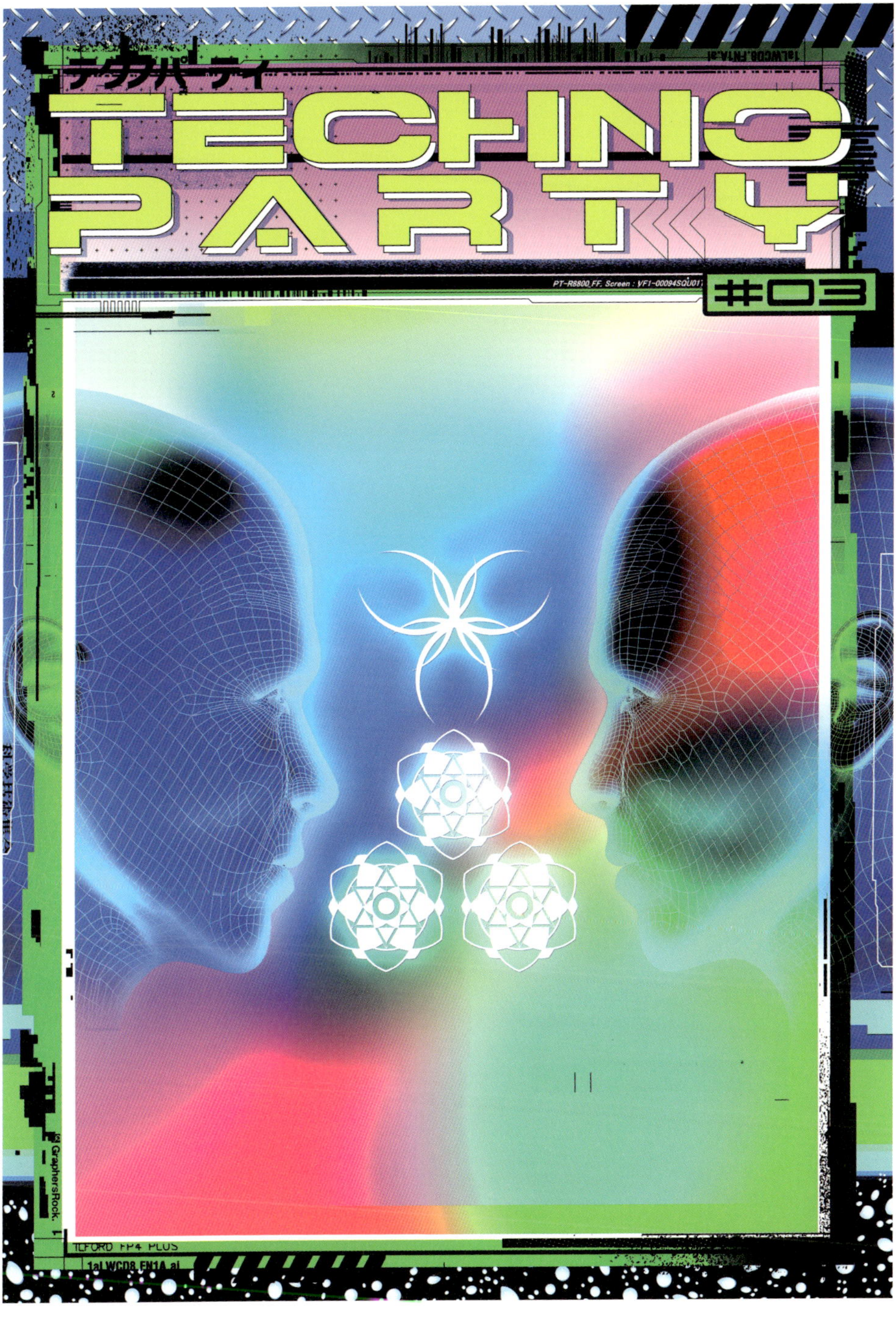
テクノパーティ
TECHNO PARTY
#03
PT-R8800_FF, Screen : VF1-00094SQU01
GraphersRock.
ILFORD FP4 PLUS
1al WCD8 FN1A al

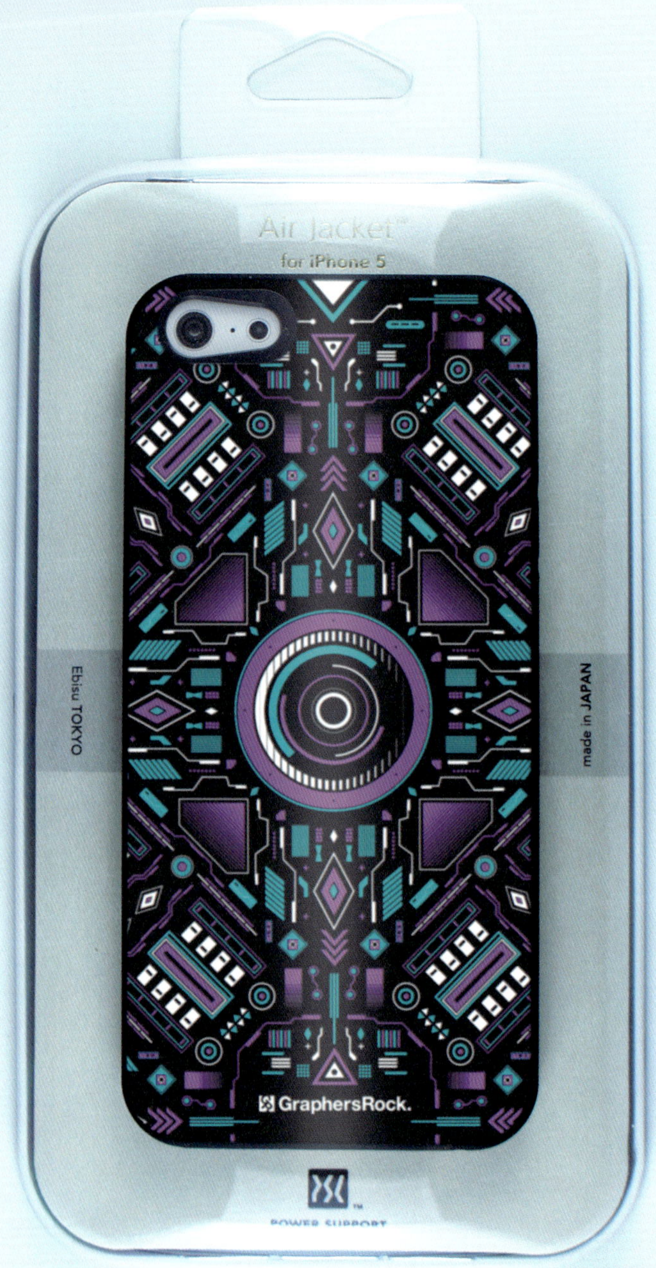

Air Jacket
iPhone ケース ｜ GraphersRock ｜ 2011

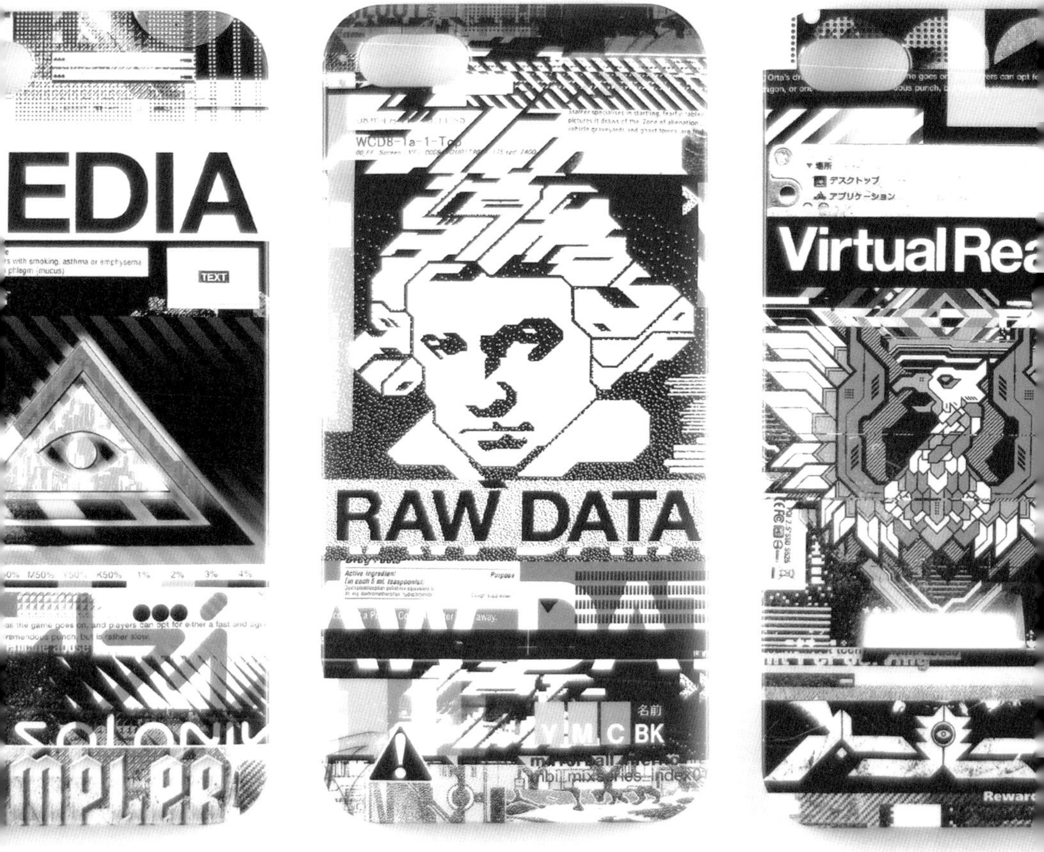

MEDIA , RAW DATA , Virtual Reality
iPhone ケース ｜ CINRA.STORE ｜ 2013

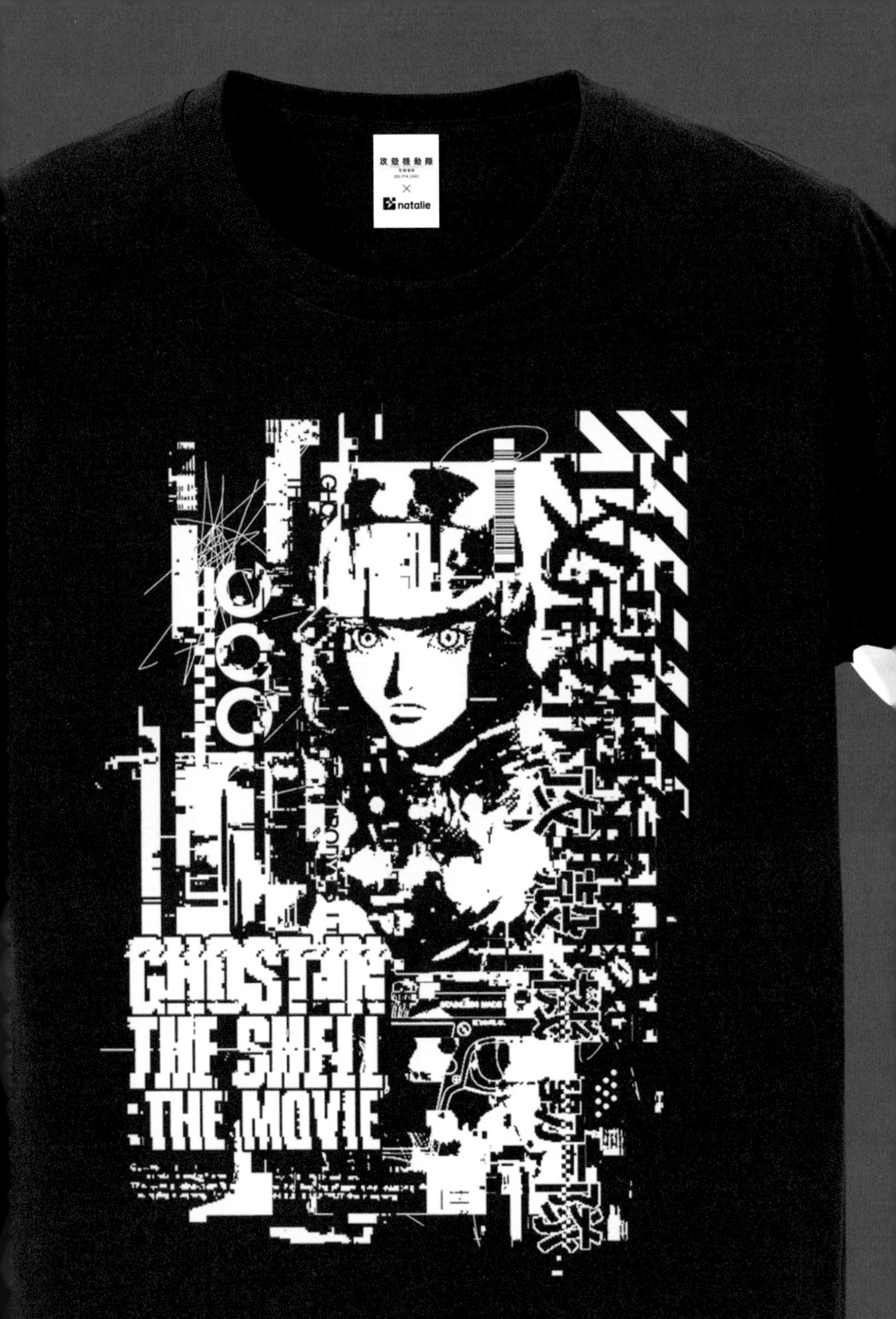
攻殻機動隊
×
natalie
GHOST IN
THE SHELL
THE MOVIE

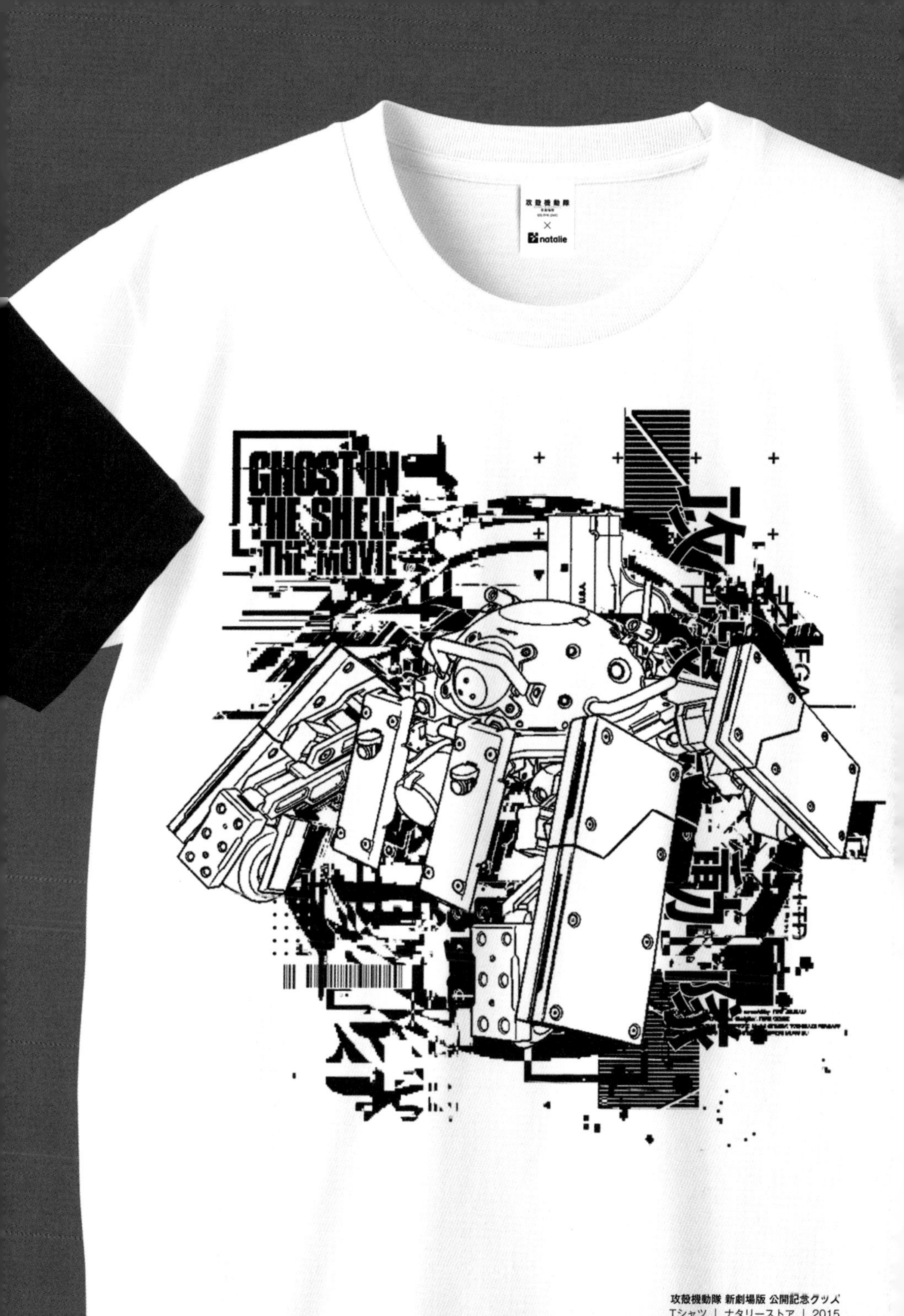

攻殻機動隊 新劇場版 公開記念グッズ
Tシャツ ｜ ナタリーストア ｜ 2015
© 士郎正宗・Production I.G／講談社・「攻殻機動隊 新劇場版」製作委員会

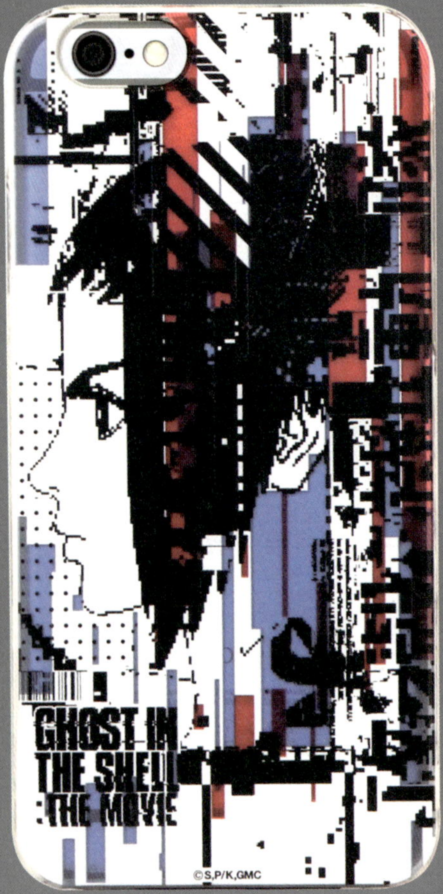

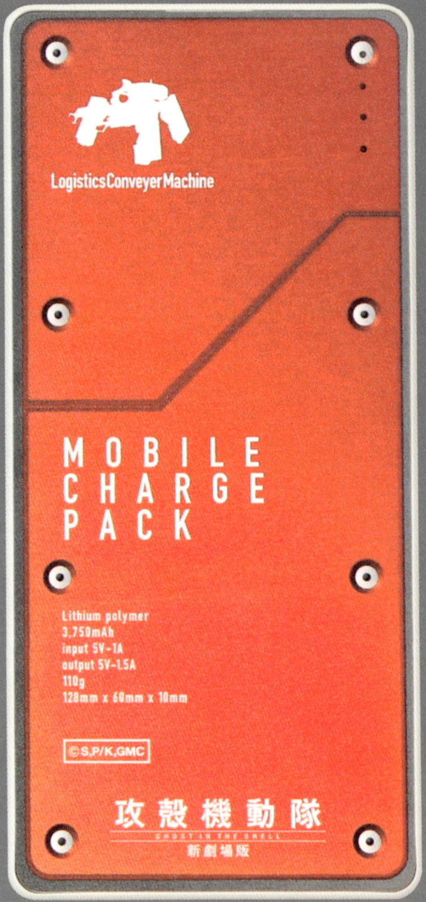

攻殻機動隊 新劇場版 公開記念グッズ
iPhone ケース、モバイルバッテリー ¦ ナタリーストア ¦ 2015
 ©士郎正宗・Production I.G ／講談社・「攻殻機動隊 新劇場版」製作委員会

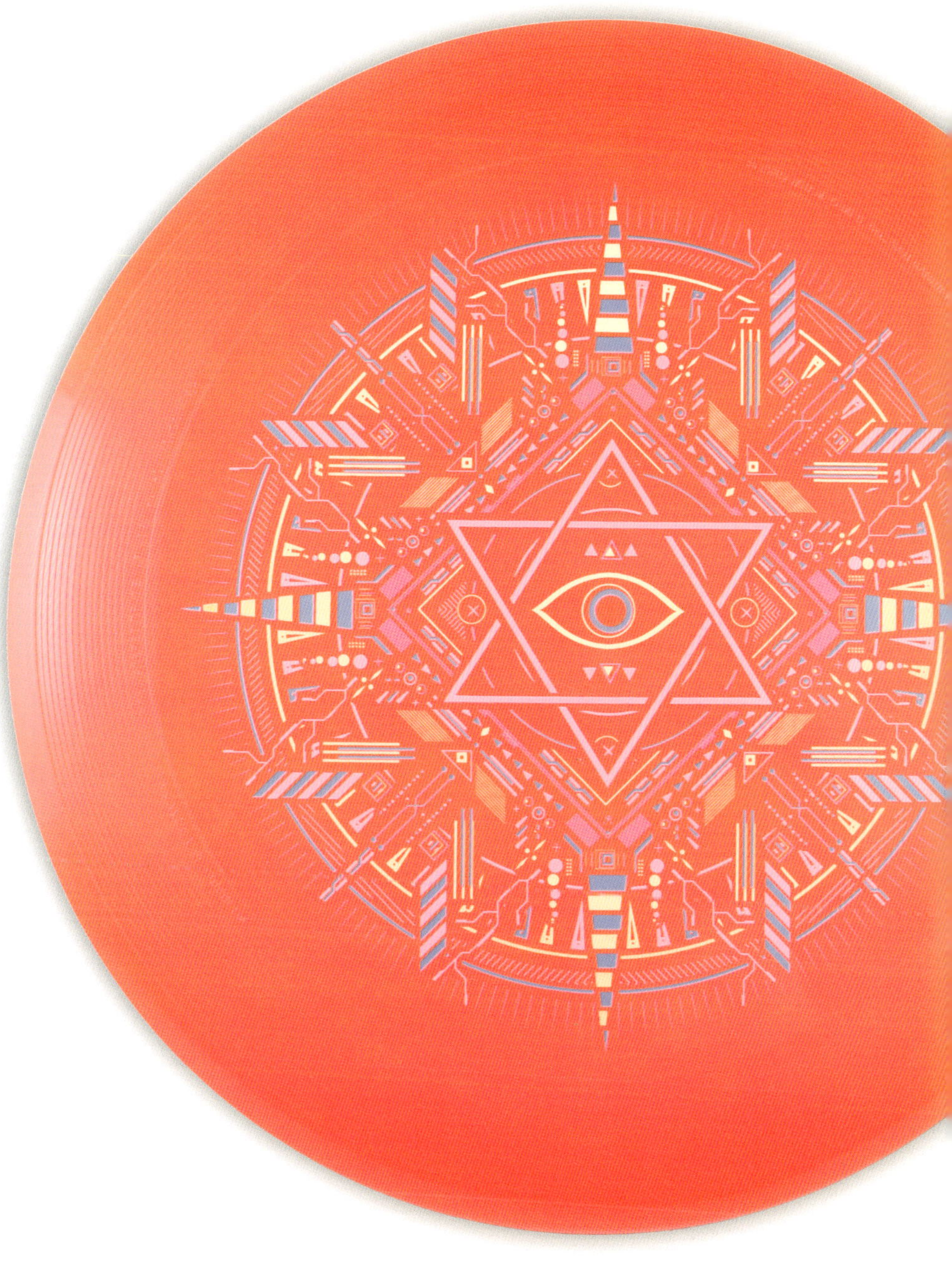

Black Magic

フリスビー ｜ Spin Collectif TOKYO ｜ 2012

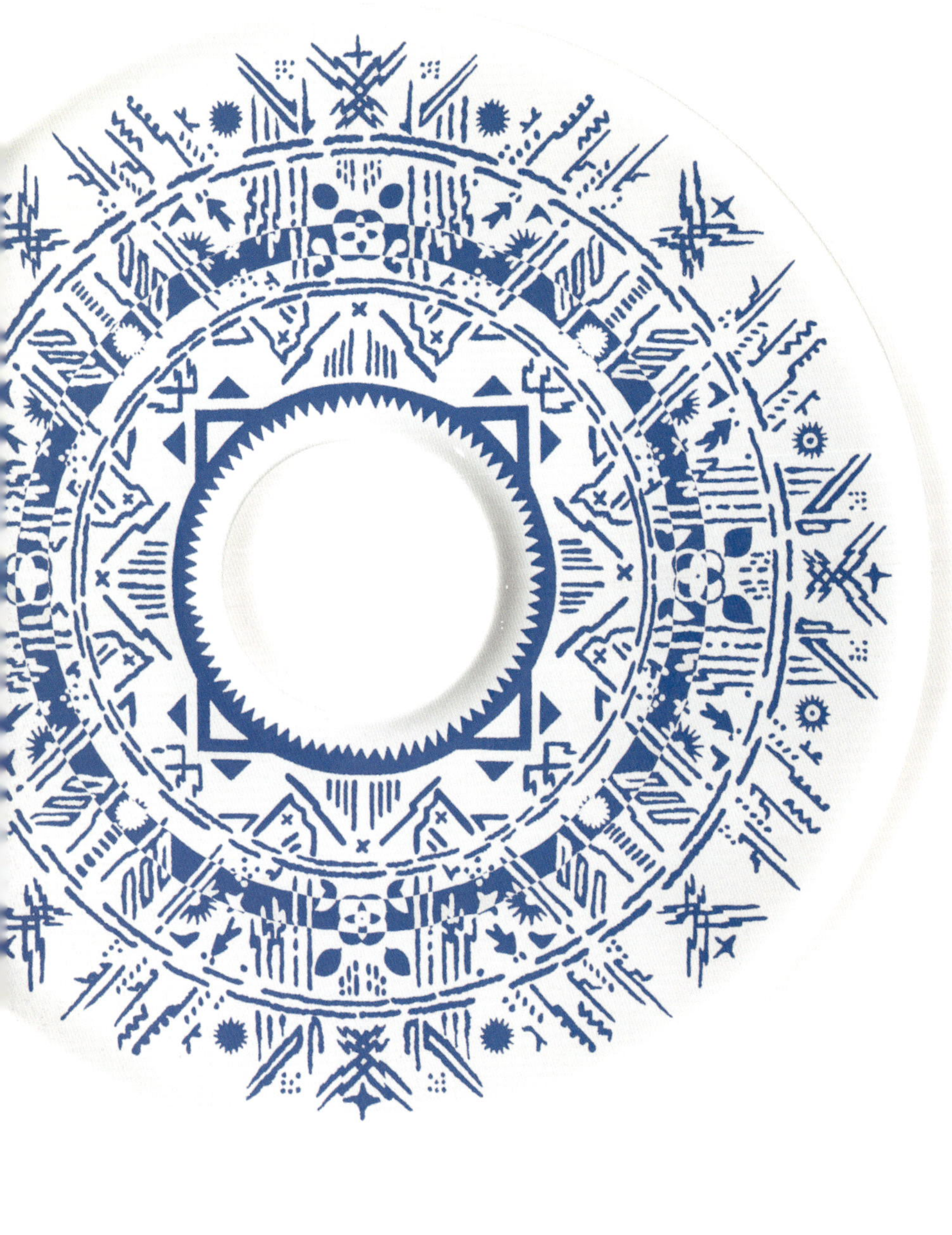

7inch PLATE
陶磁器 | PEOPLEAP Project | 2015

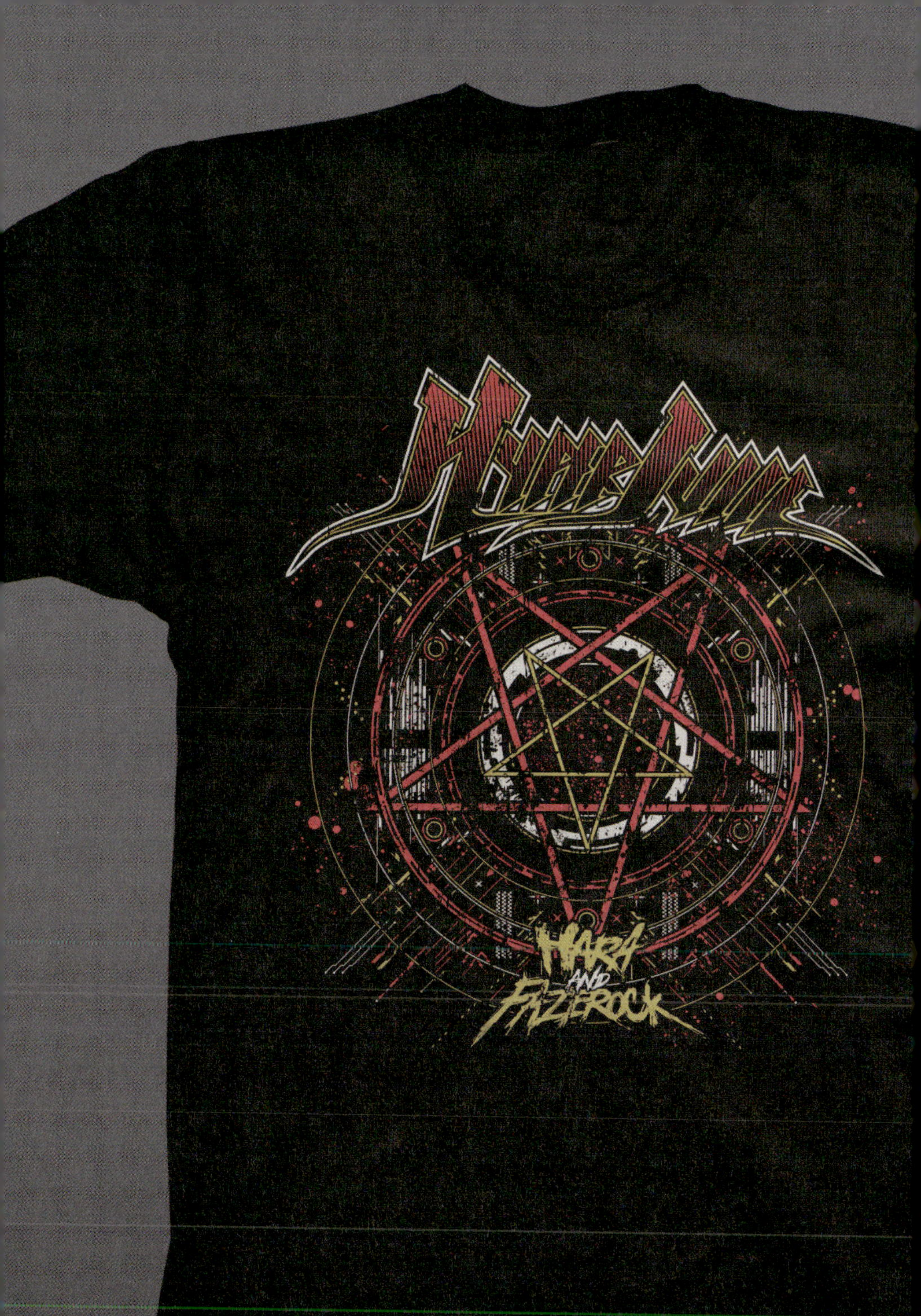

HyperJuice
Tシャツ | 2015

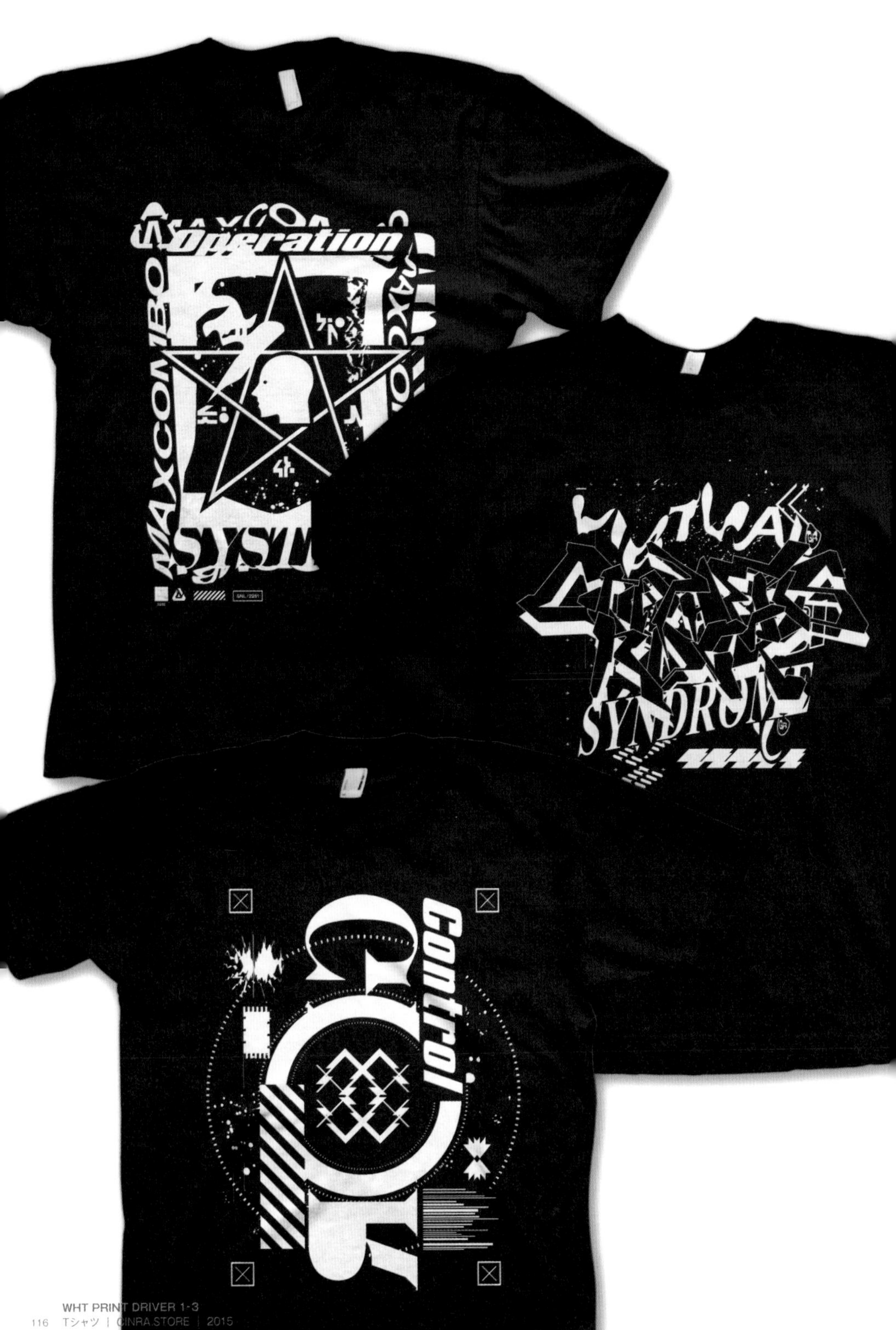

WHT PRINT DRIVER 1-3
Tシャツ | CINRA.STORE | 2015

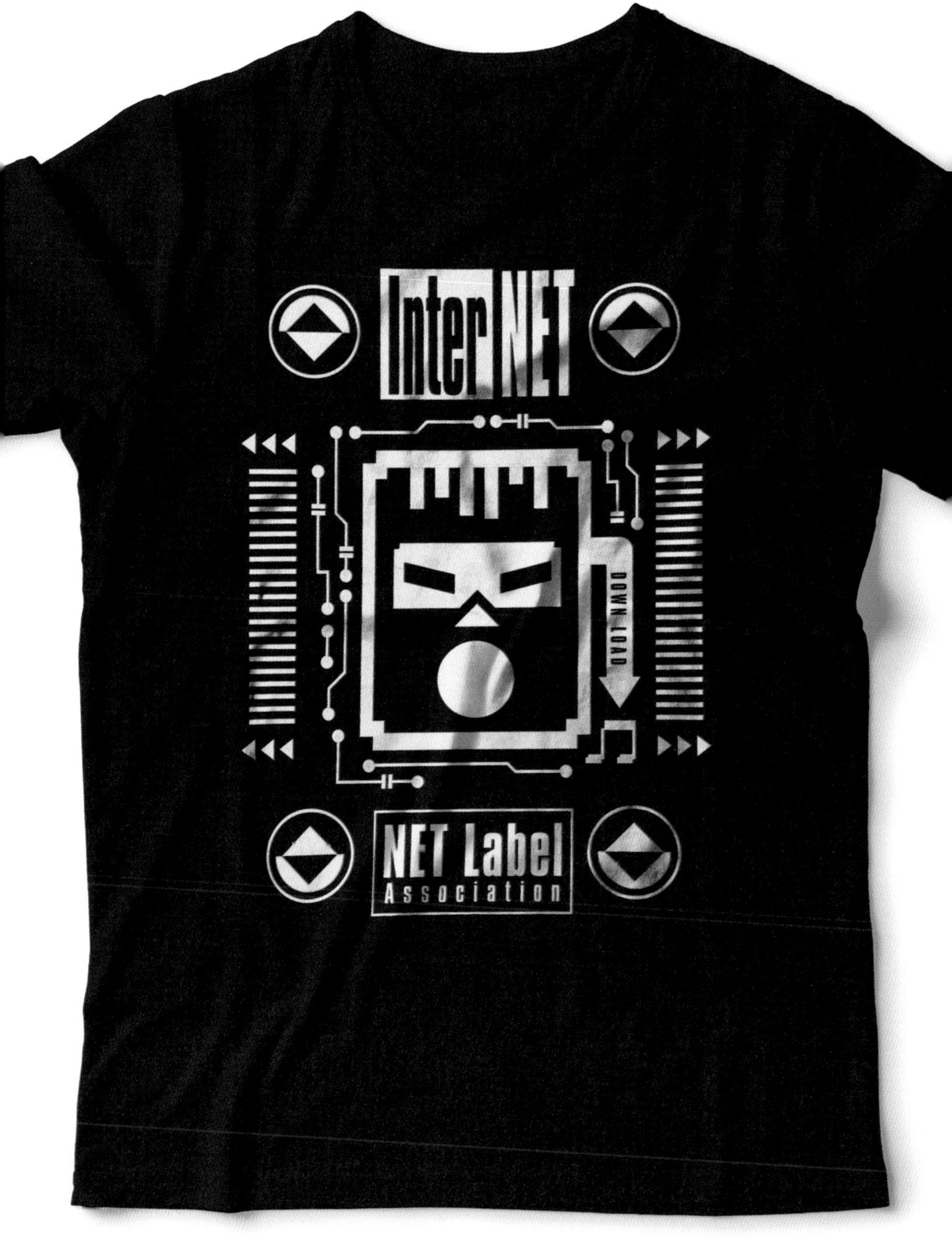

大ネットレーベル祭
Tシャツ ｜ 2013

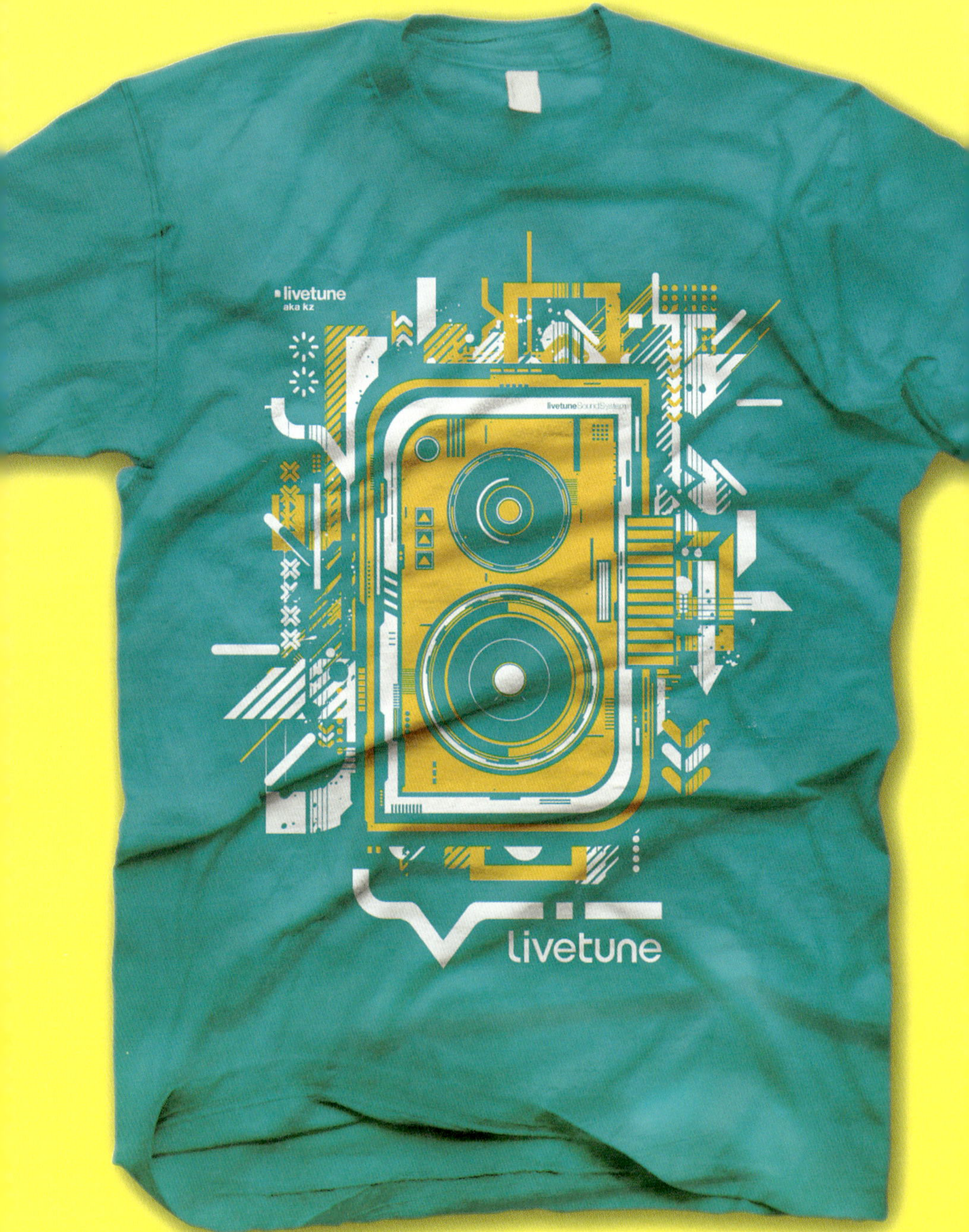

livetune
Tシャツ | インクストゥーエンター | 2010

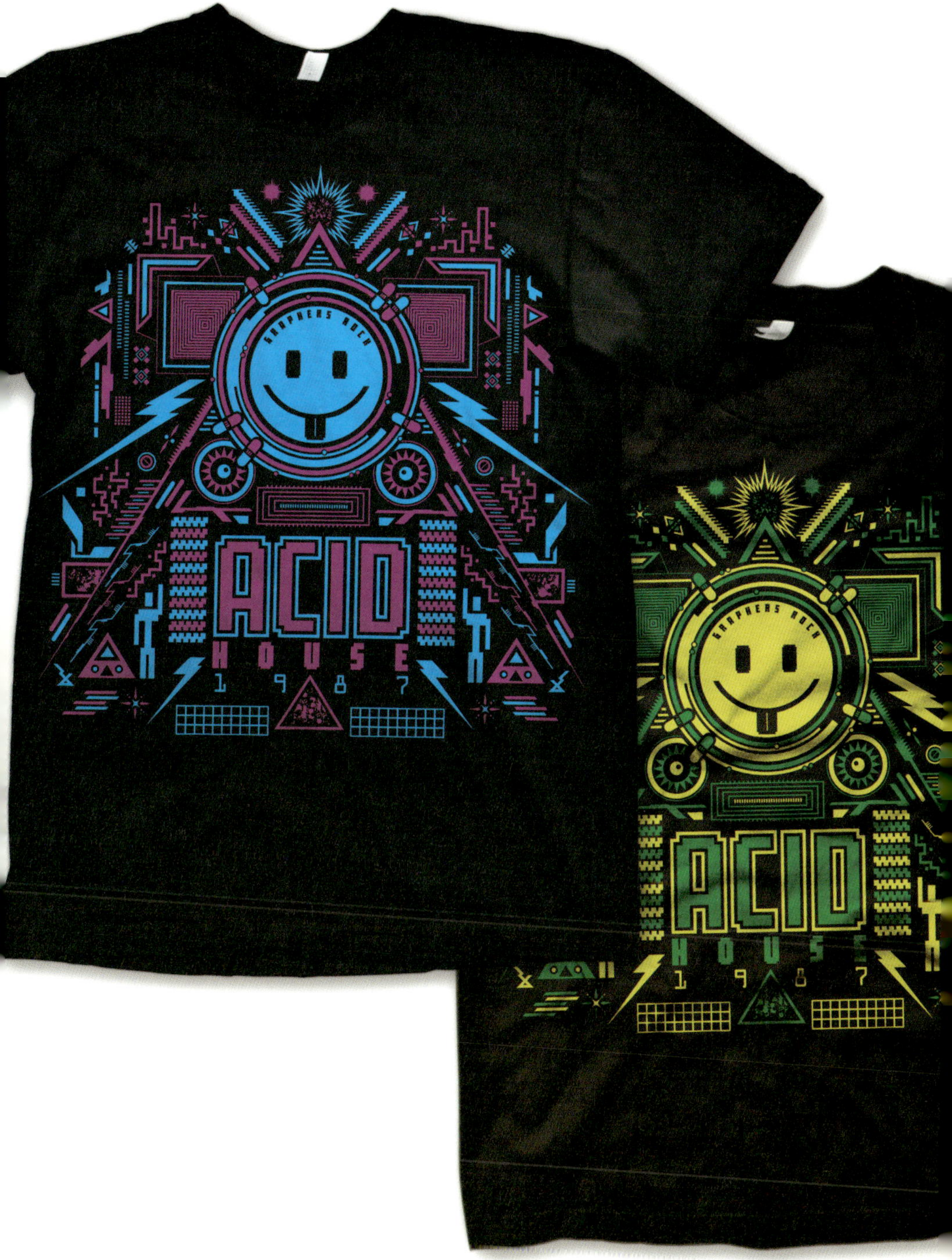

ACID HOUSE
Tシャツ | GraphersRock | 2011

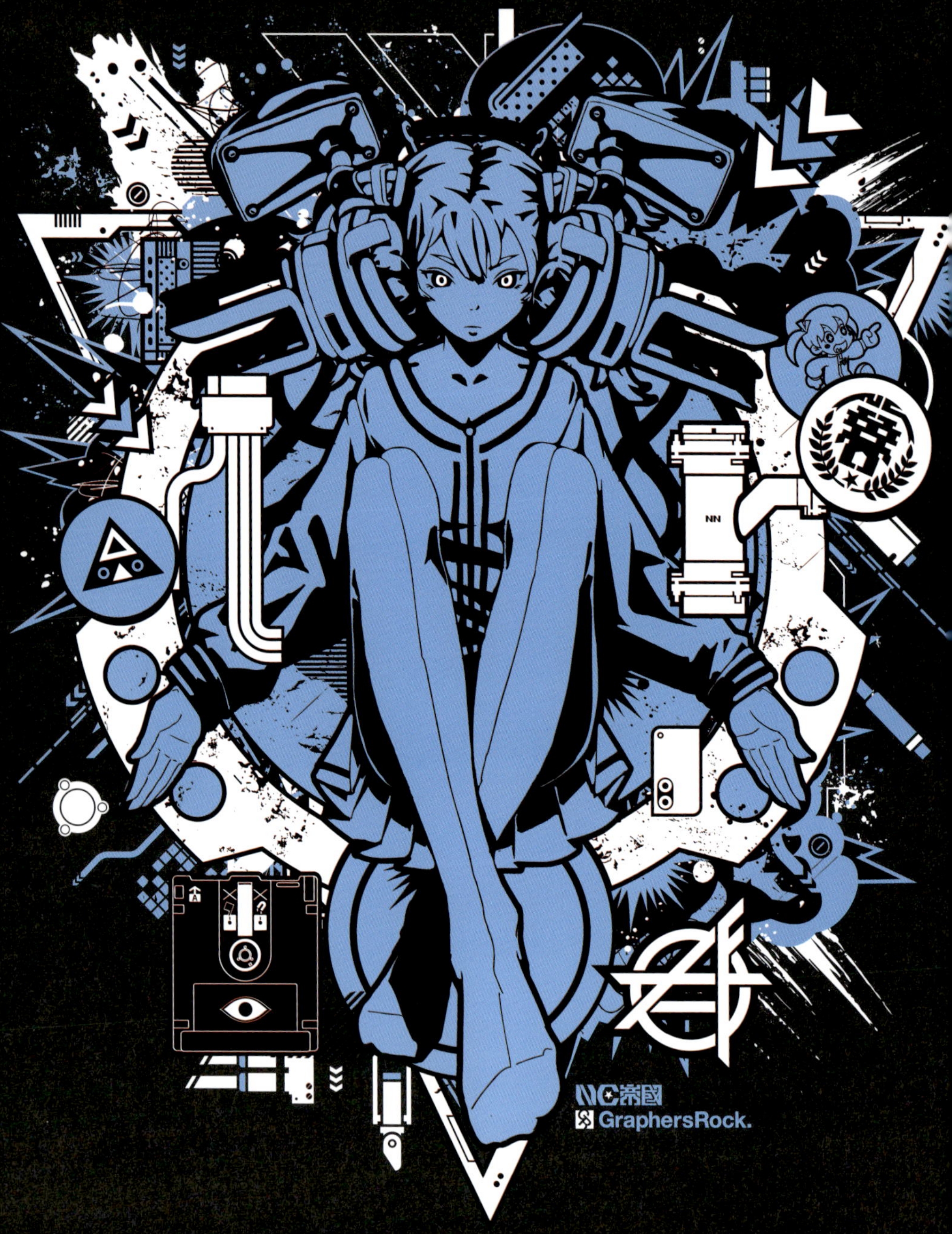

GraphersRock x NC帝國

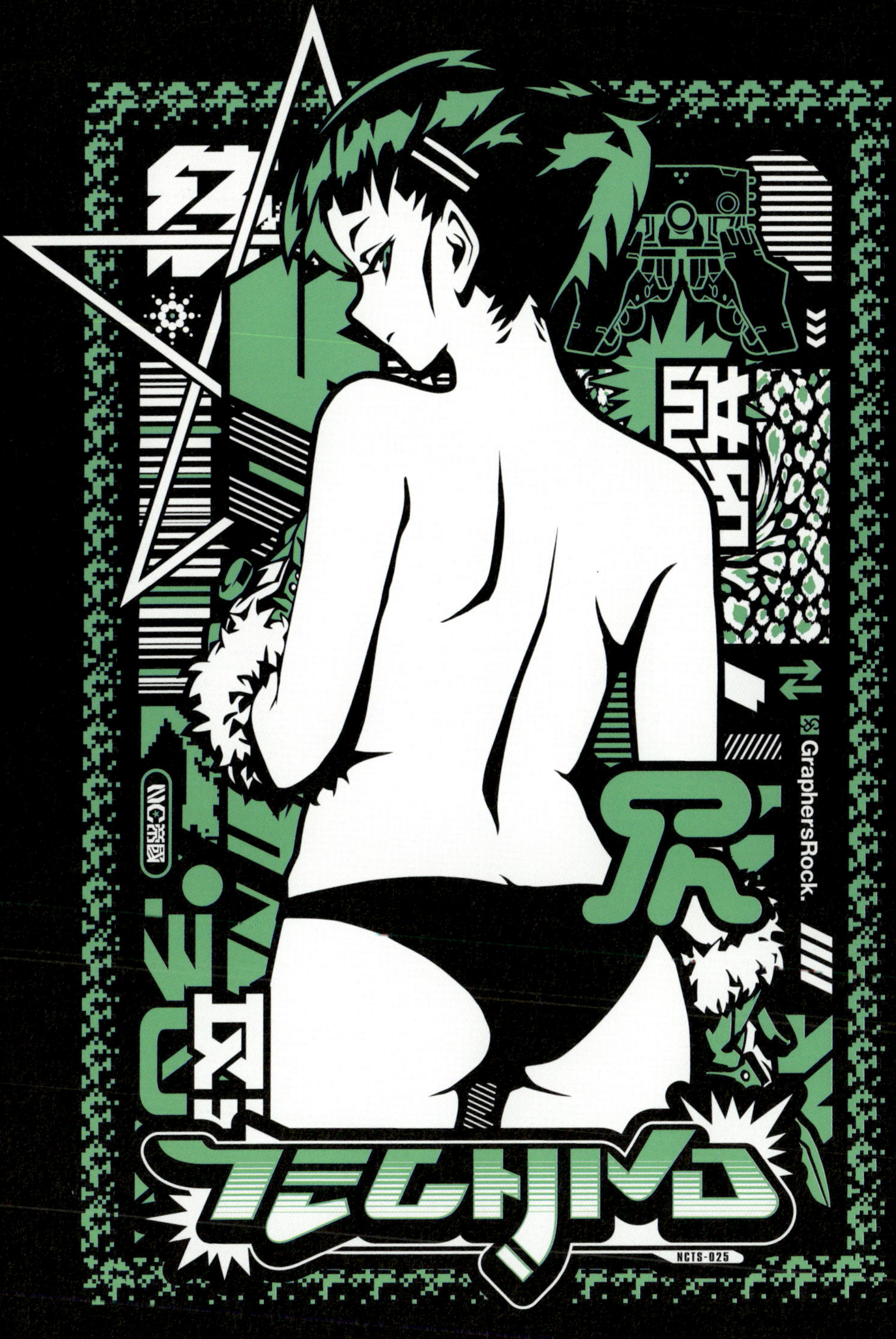
GraphersRock.
NC帝國
NCTS-025

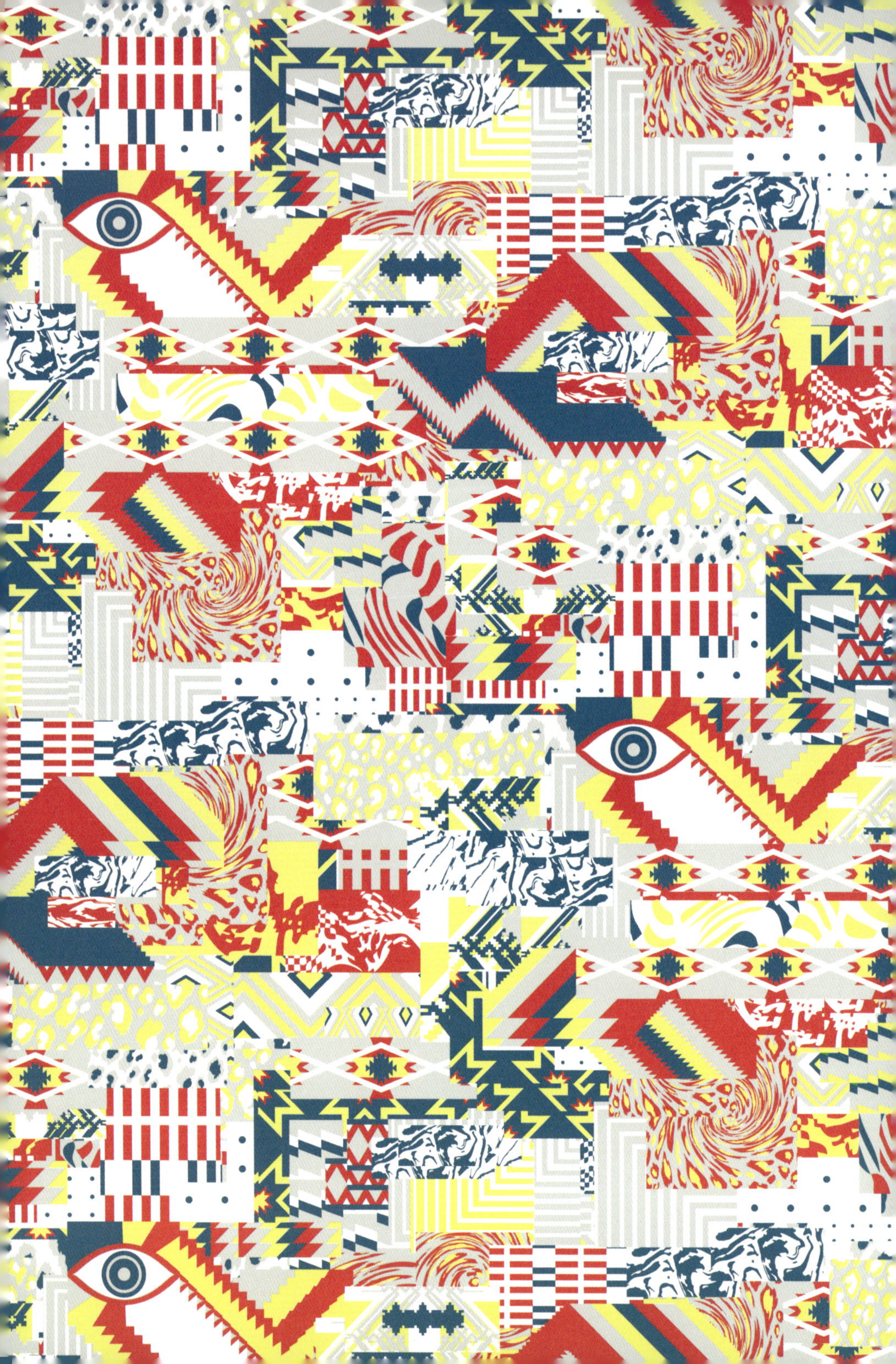

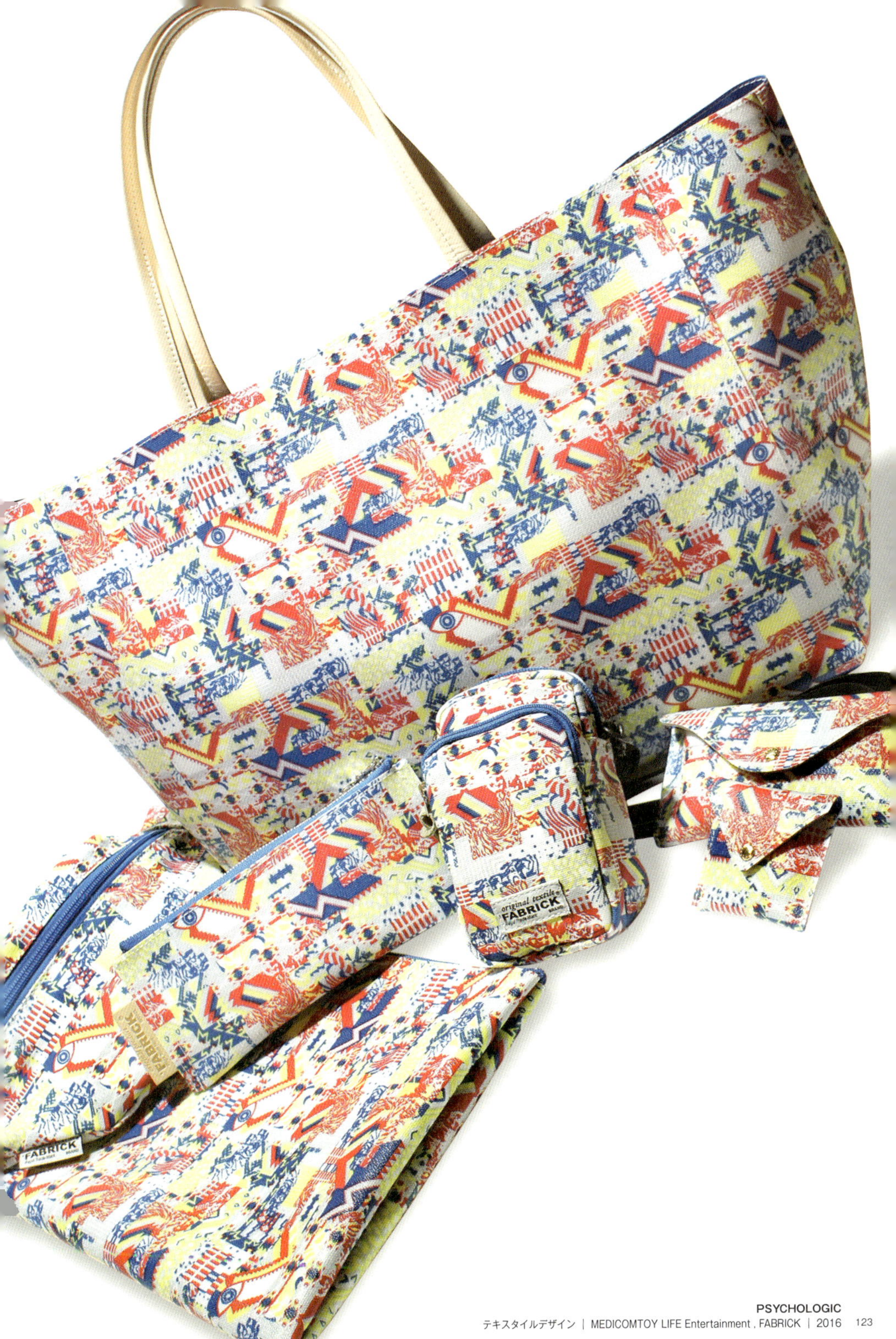
original textile
FABRICK
FABRICK
FABRICK

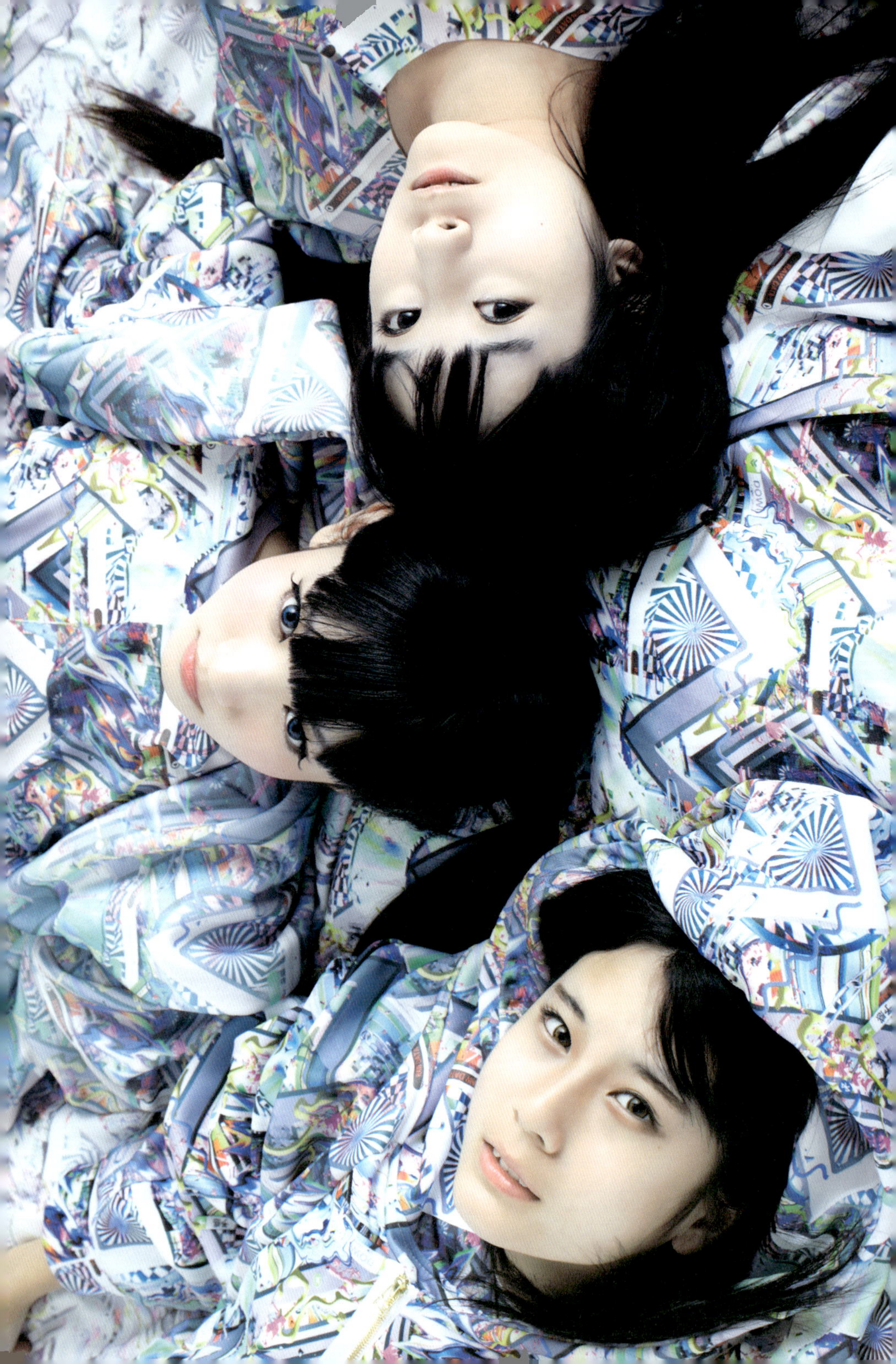

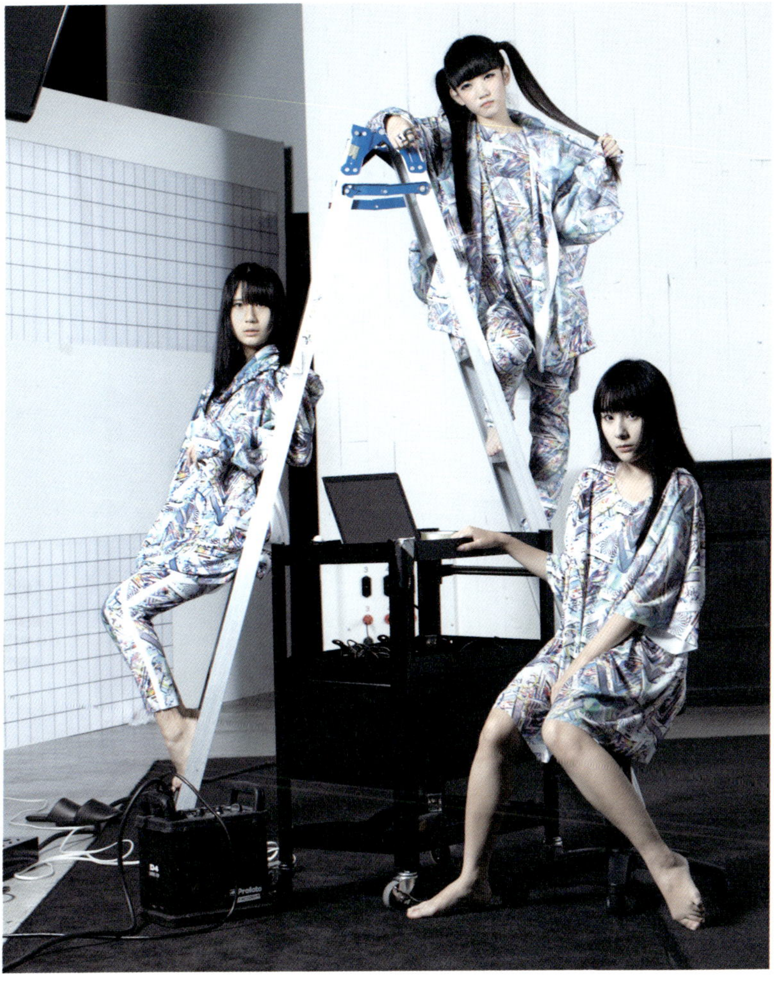

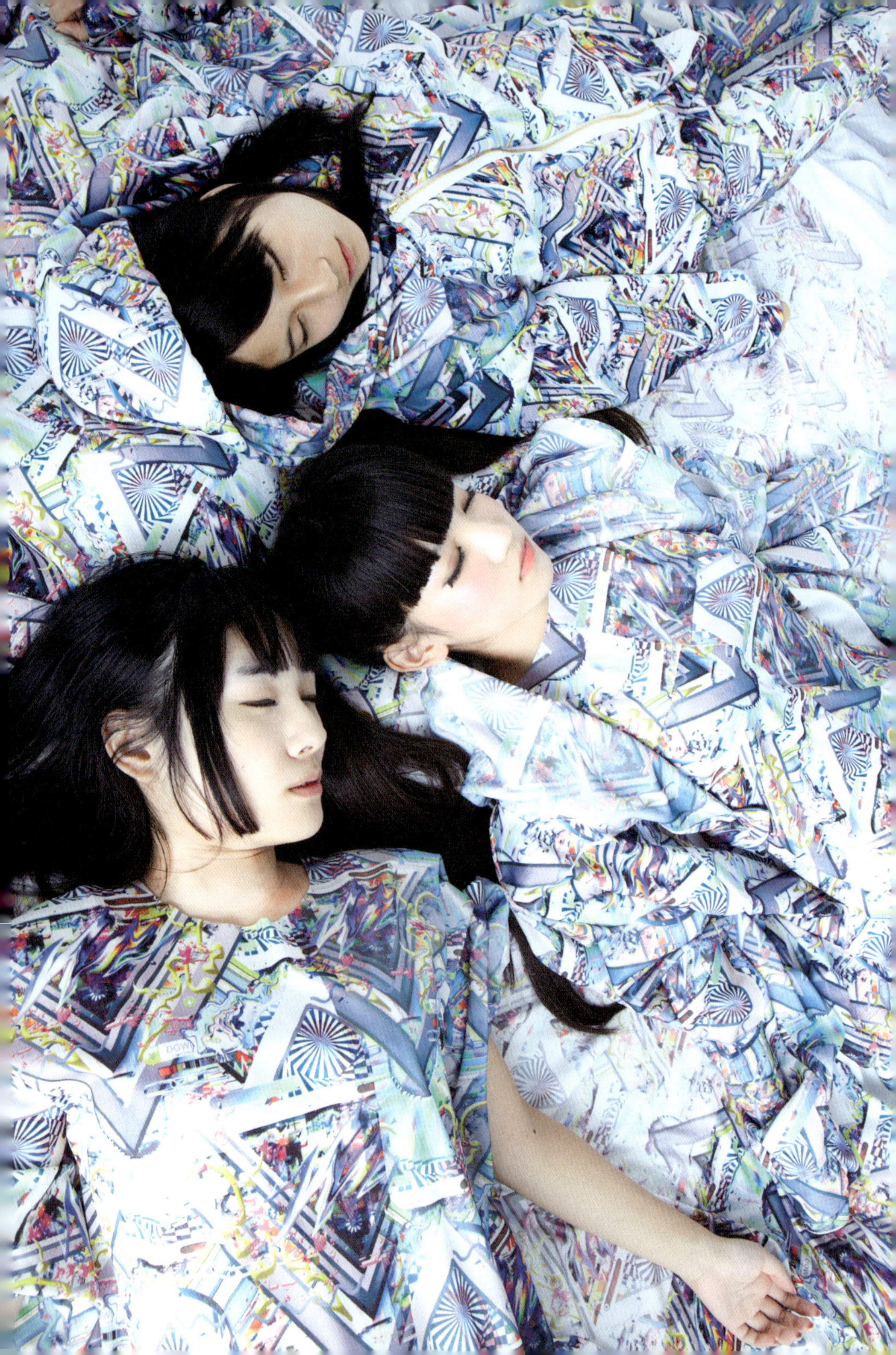

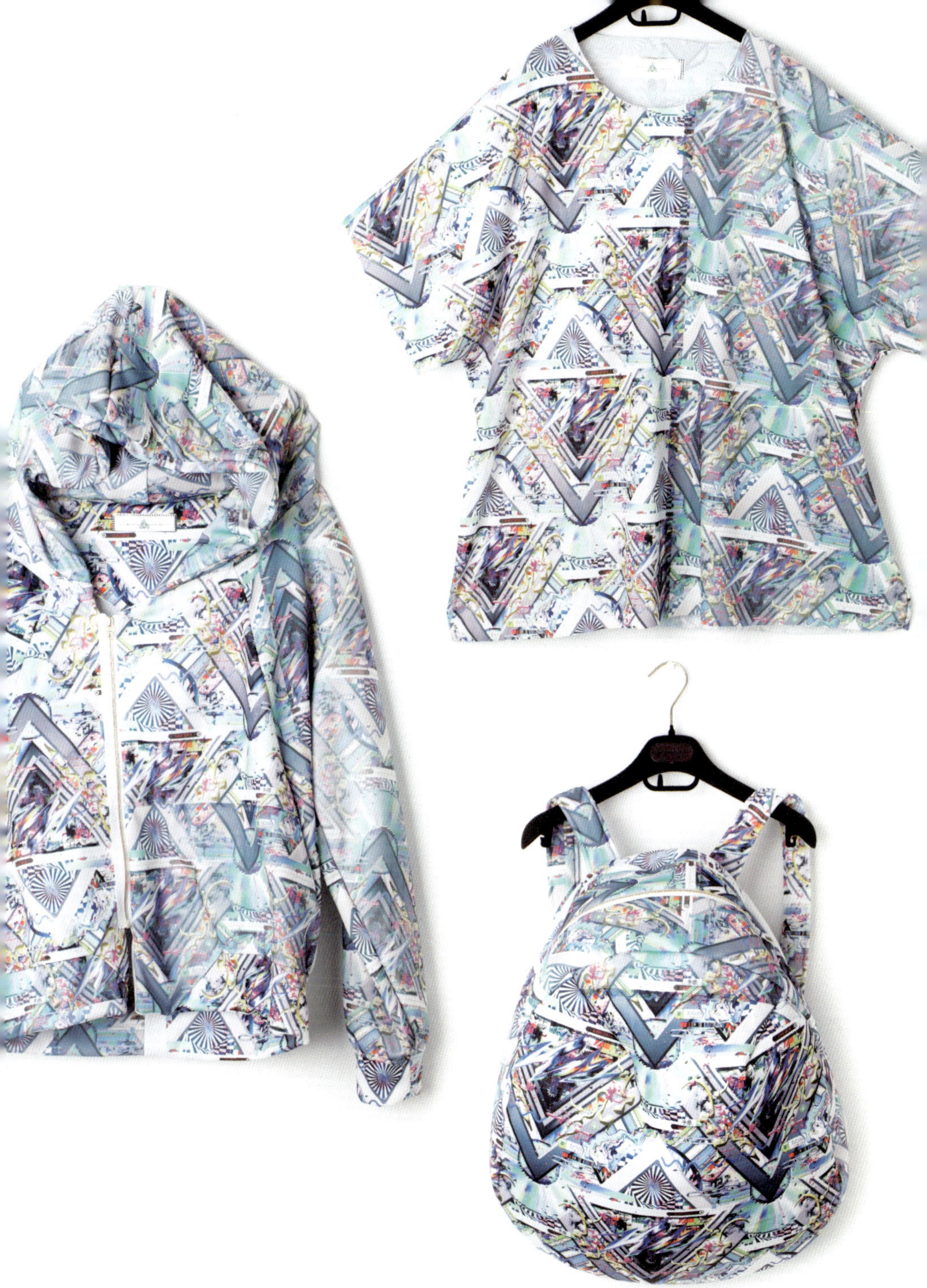

BALMUNG x GraphersRock x Zigg
テキスタイルデザイン | Zigg | 2013

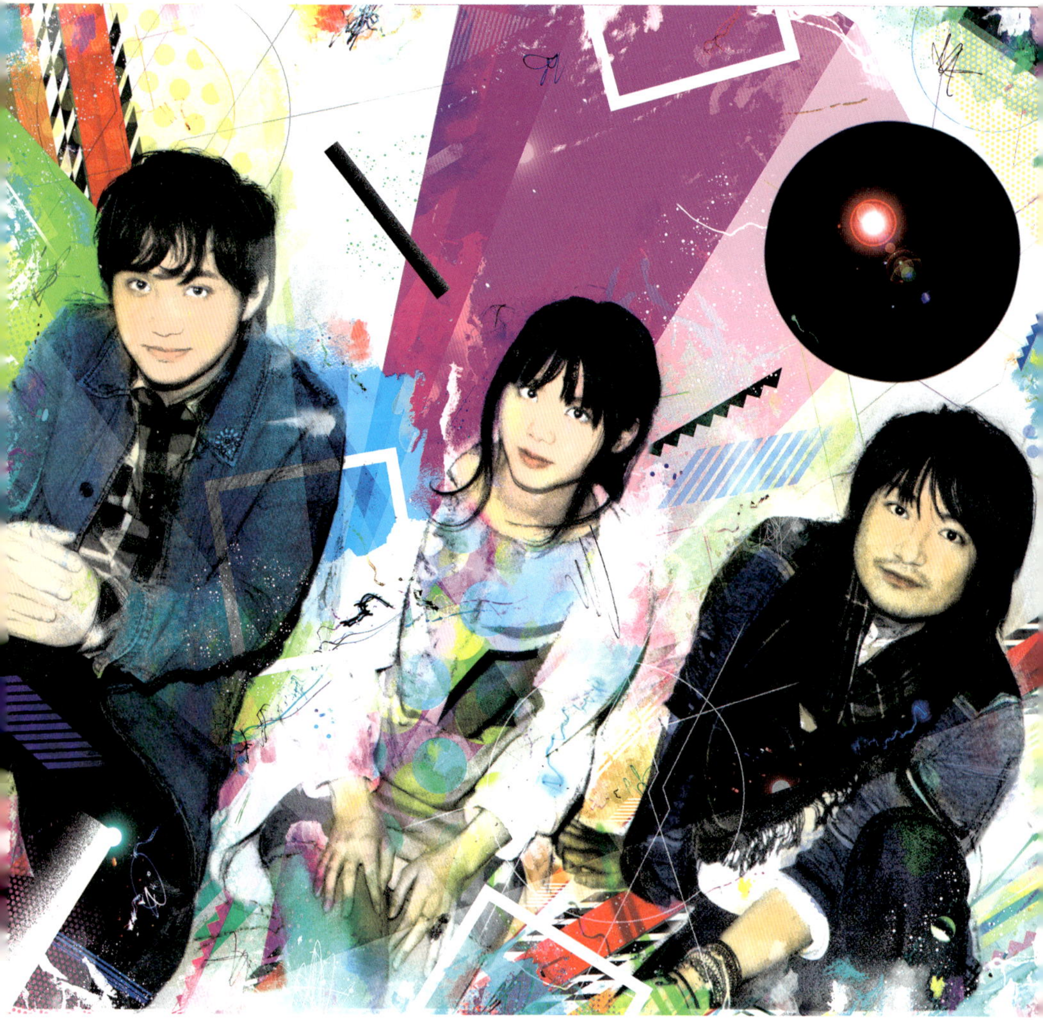

いきものがかり 5th アルバム「NEWTRAL」
初回生産限定盤特典ポストカード用グラフィック
エピックレコードジャパン ｜ 2012
©2012 Epic Records Japan

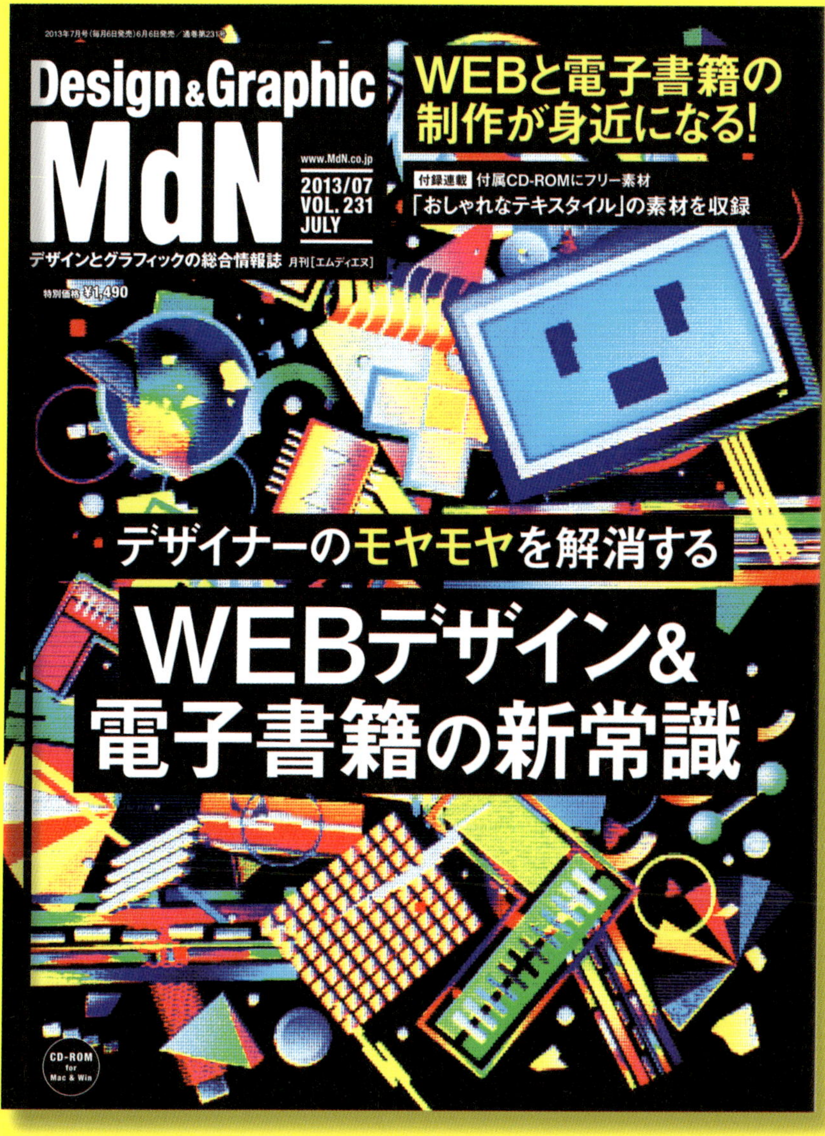

月刊MdN 2013年7月号

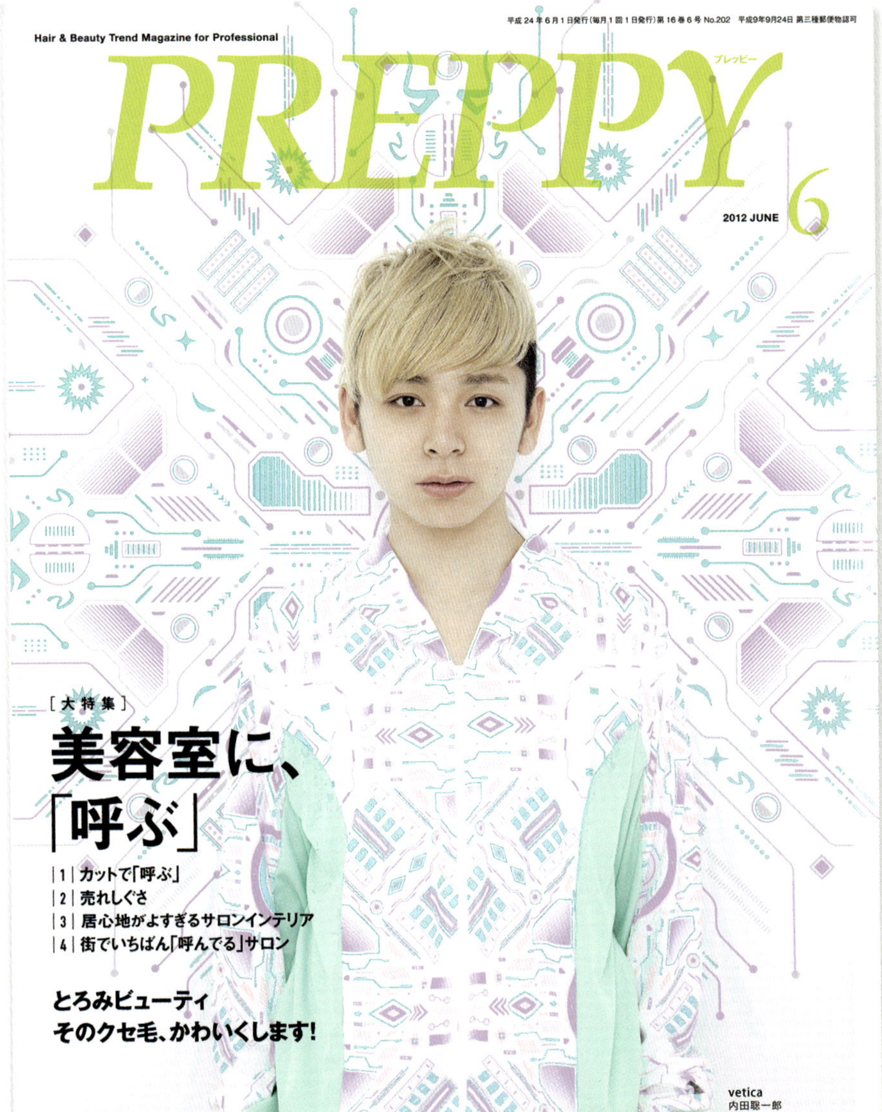
平成24年6月1日発行（毎月1回1日発行）第16巻6号 No.202 平成9年9月24日 第三種郵便物認可

Hair & Beauty Trend Magazine for Professional

PREPPY プレッピー

2012 JUNE 6

［大特集］

美容室に、「呼ぶ」

|1| カットで「呼ぶ」
|2| 売れしぐさ
|3| 居心地がよすぎるサロンインテリア
|4| 街でいちばん「呼んでる」サロン

とろみビューティ
そのクセ毛、かわいくします！

vetica
内田聡一郎

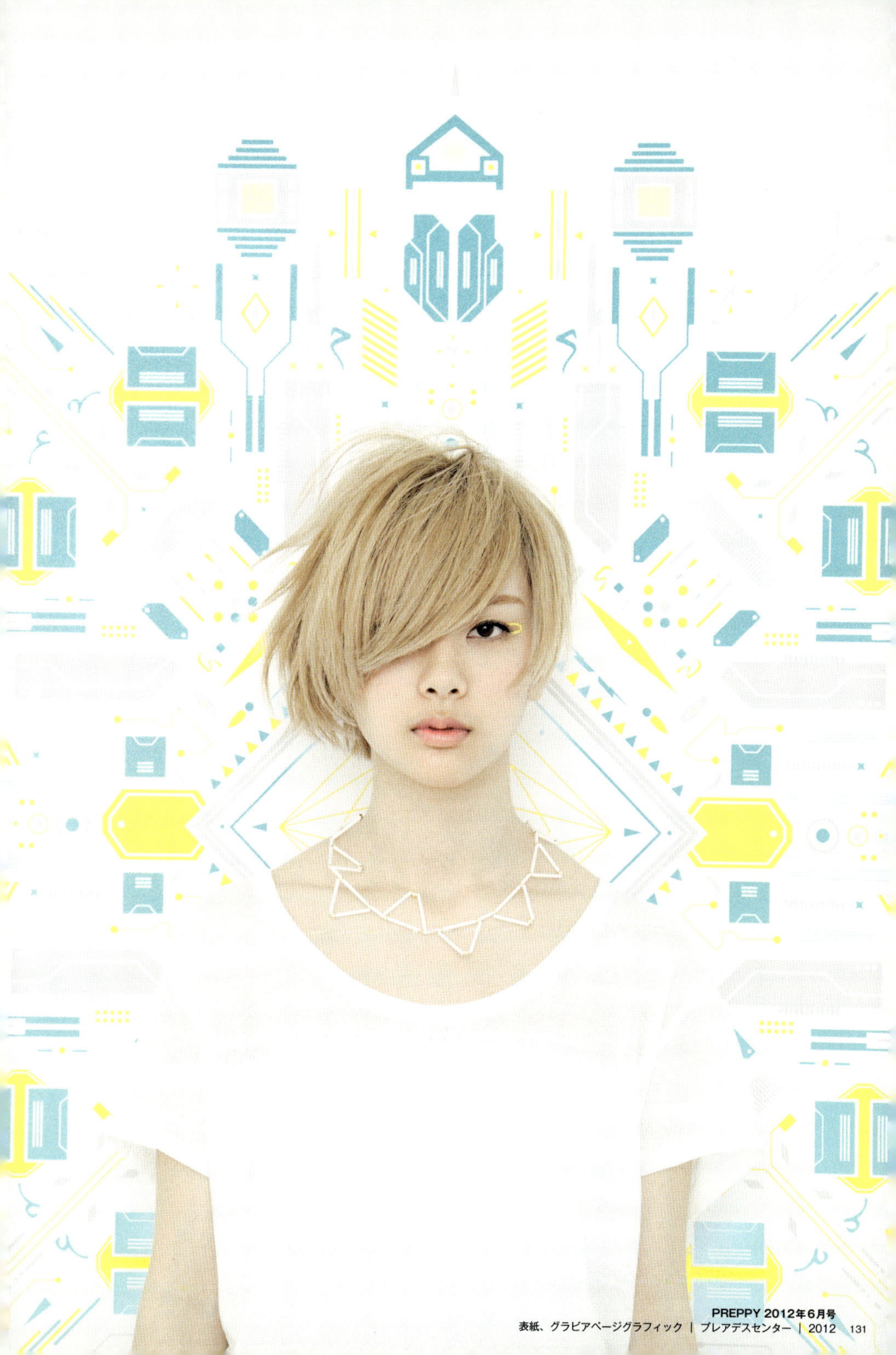

PREPPY 2012年6月号
表紙、グラビアページグラフィック | プレアデスセンター | 2012

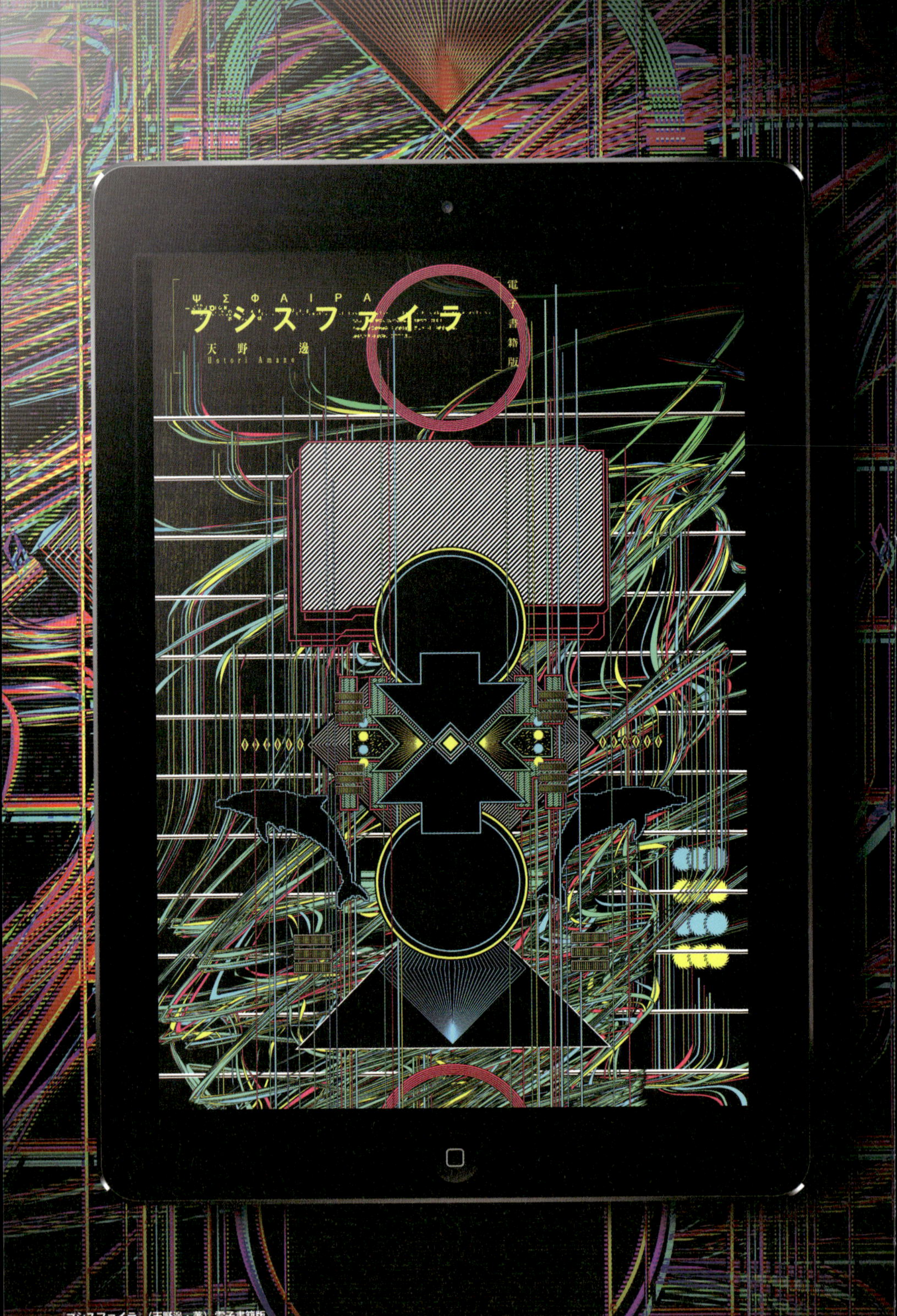

「プシスファイラ」（天野邊・著）電子書籍版

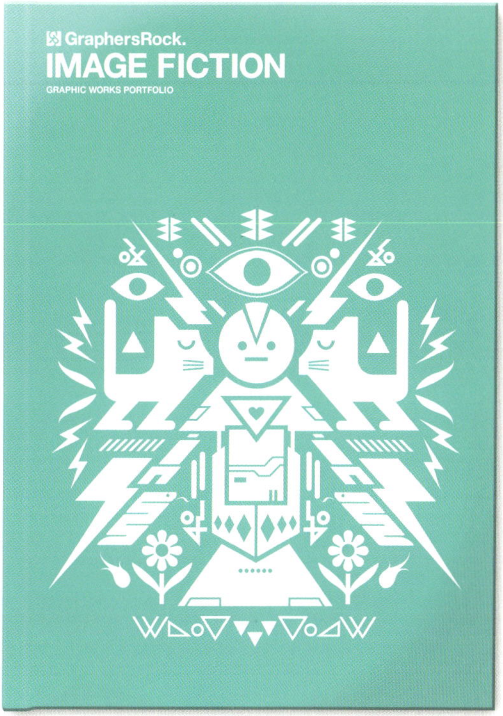

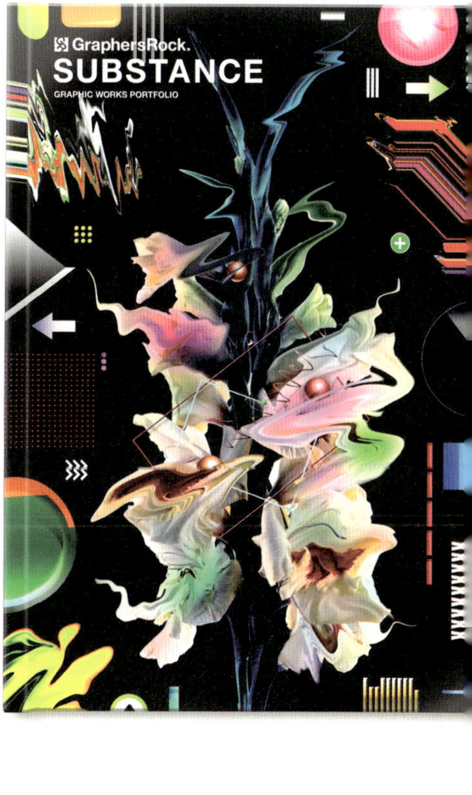

IMAGE FICTION
作品集 | GraphersRock | 2011

SUBSTANCE
作品集 | GraphersRock | 2014

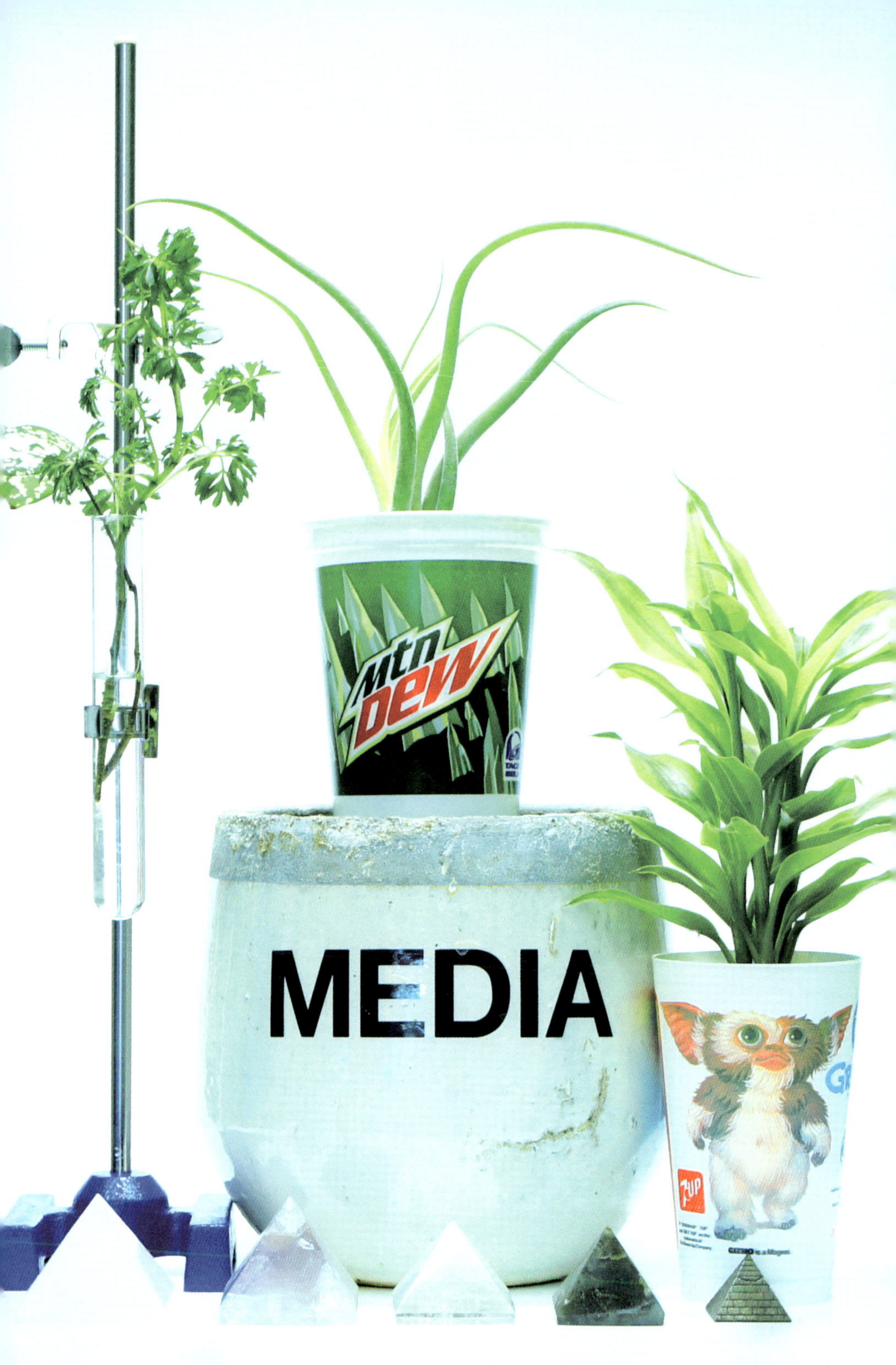
MEDIA
Mtn Dew
7UP

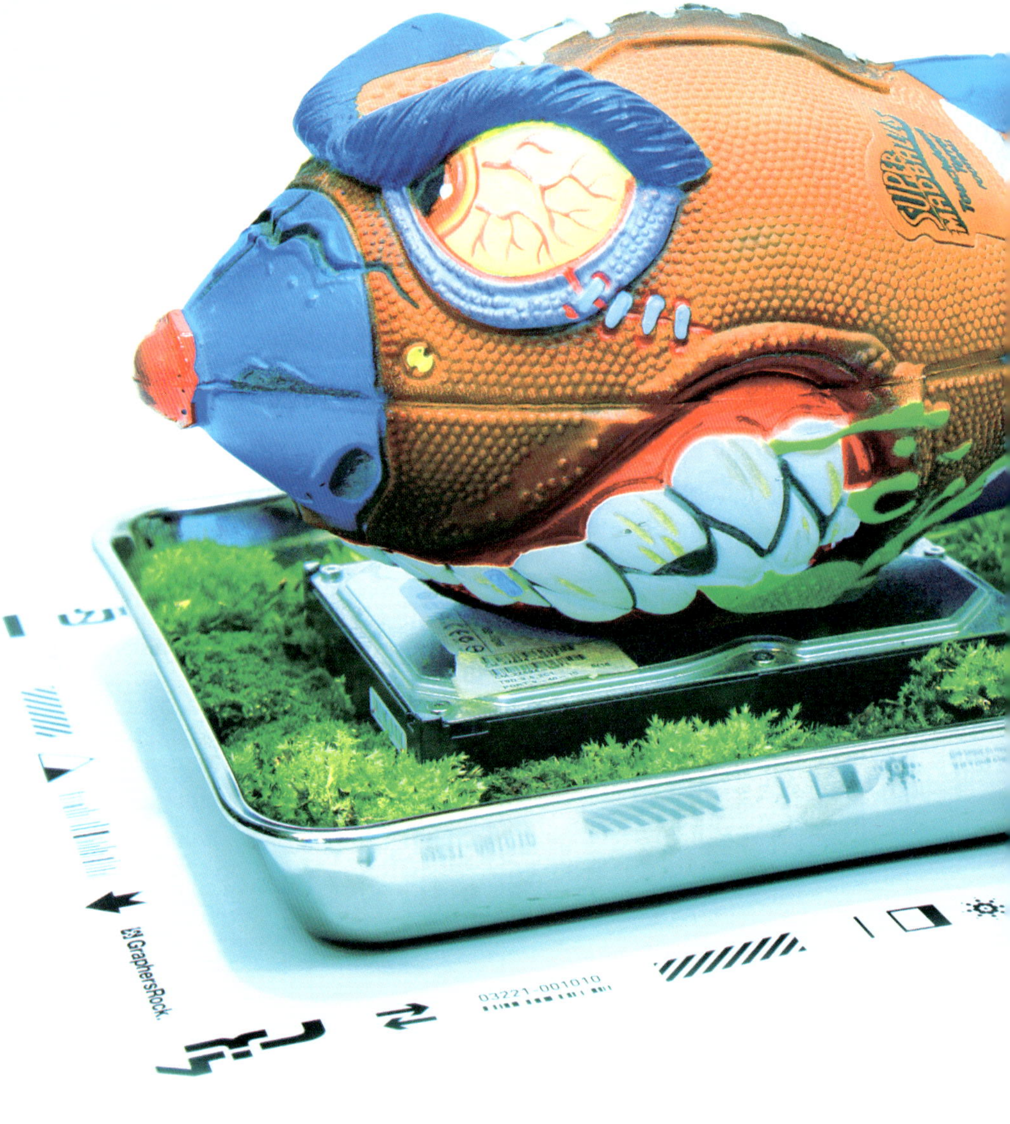
GraphersRock.
03221-001010

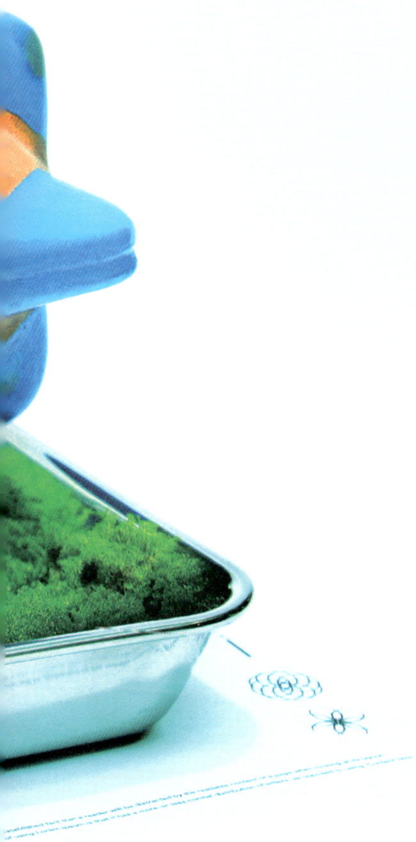

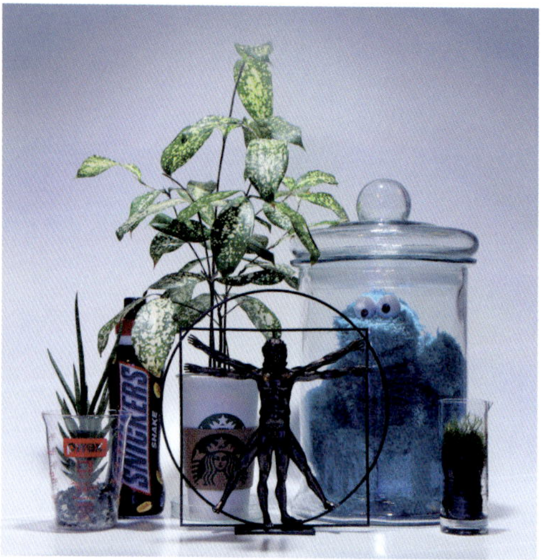
SNICKERS
SHAKE

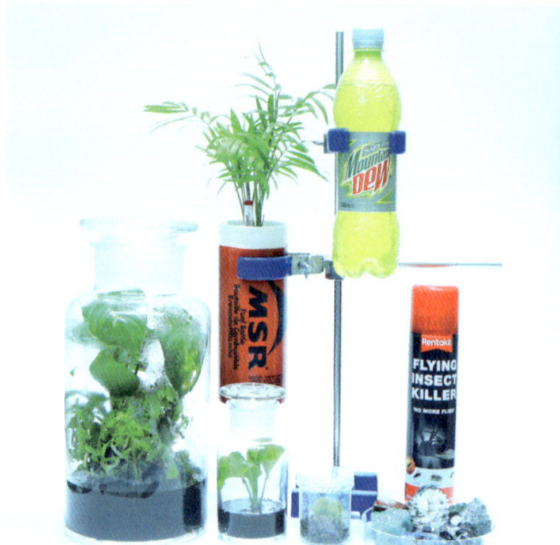
MSR
Rentokil
FLYING
INSECT
KILLER
NO MORE FLIES

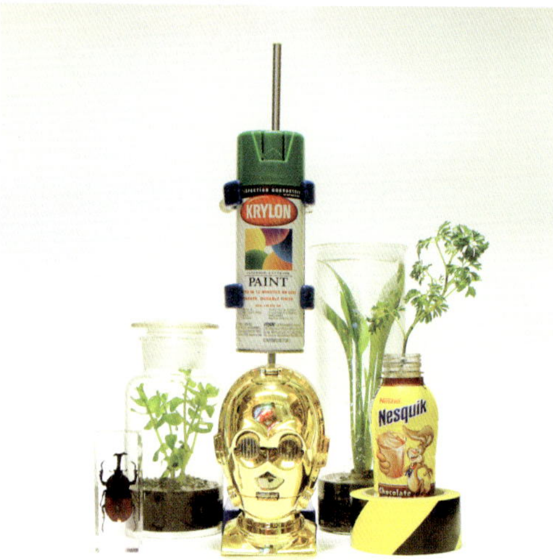
KRYLON
PAINT
Nesquik
Chocolate

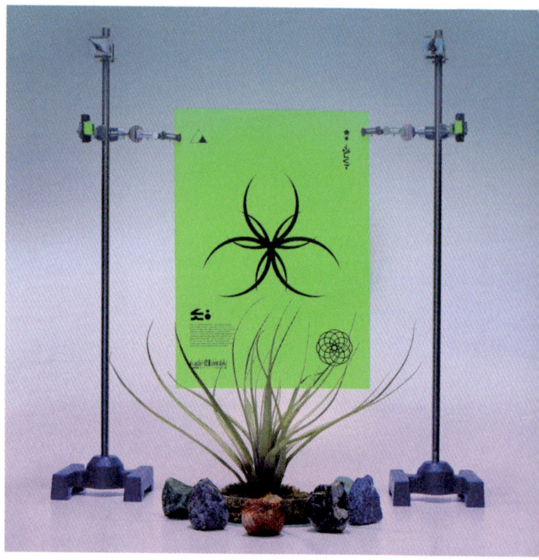

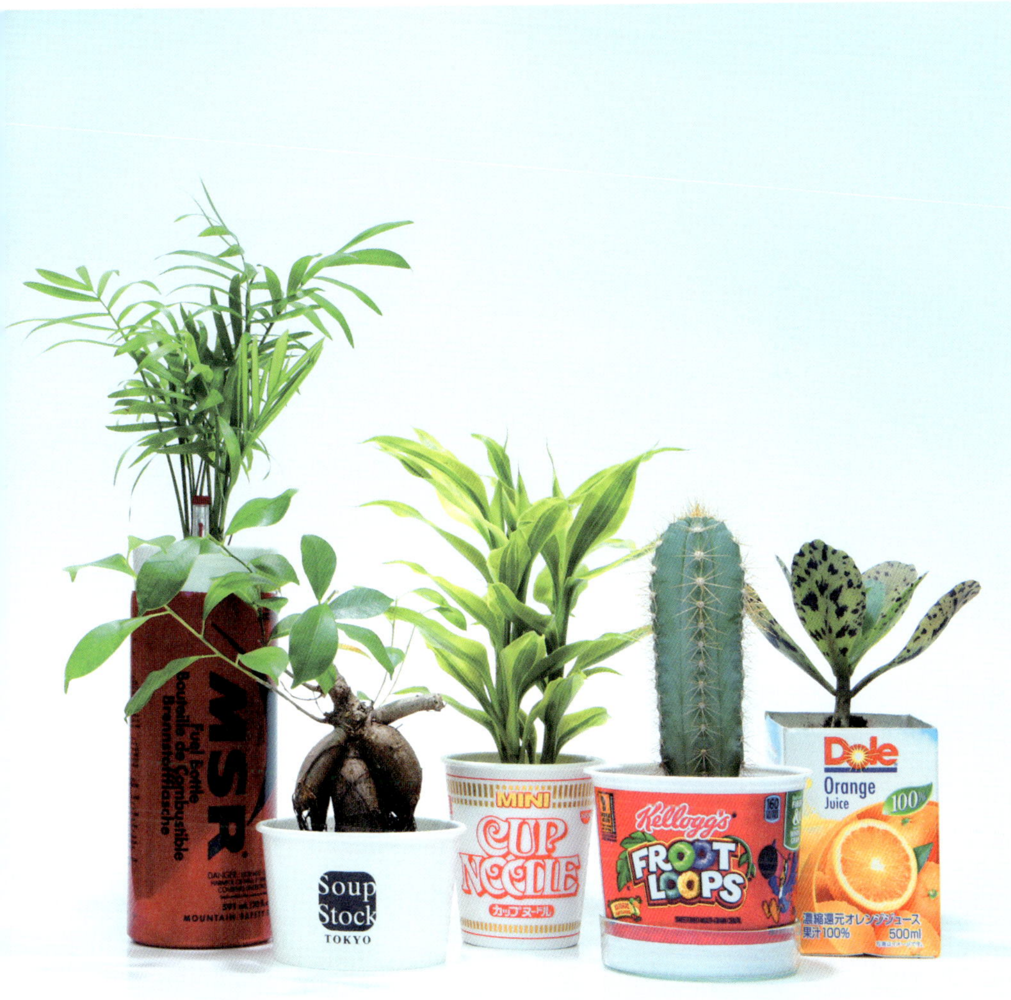

Group Shot 1-5

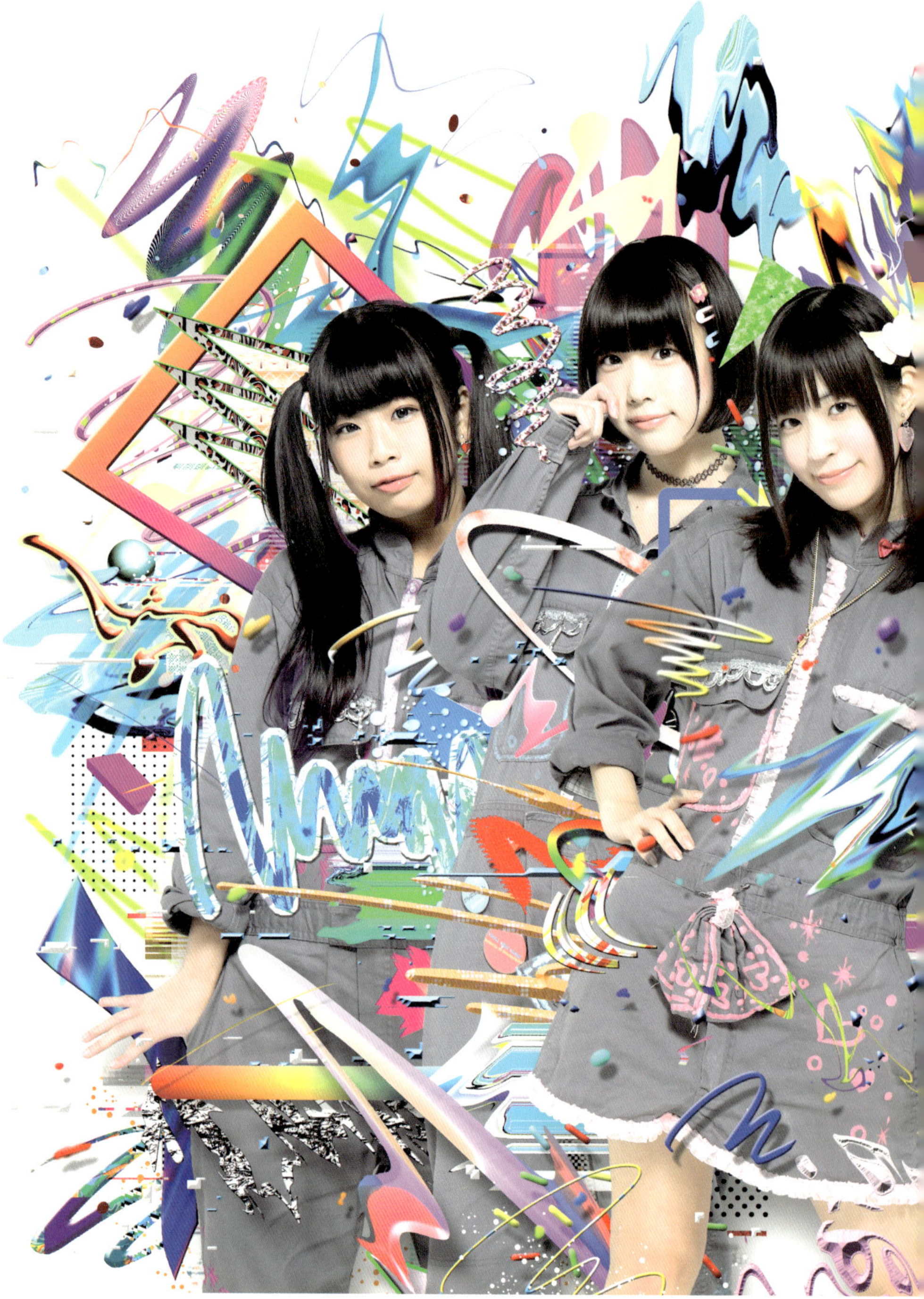

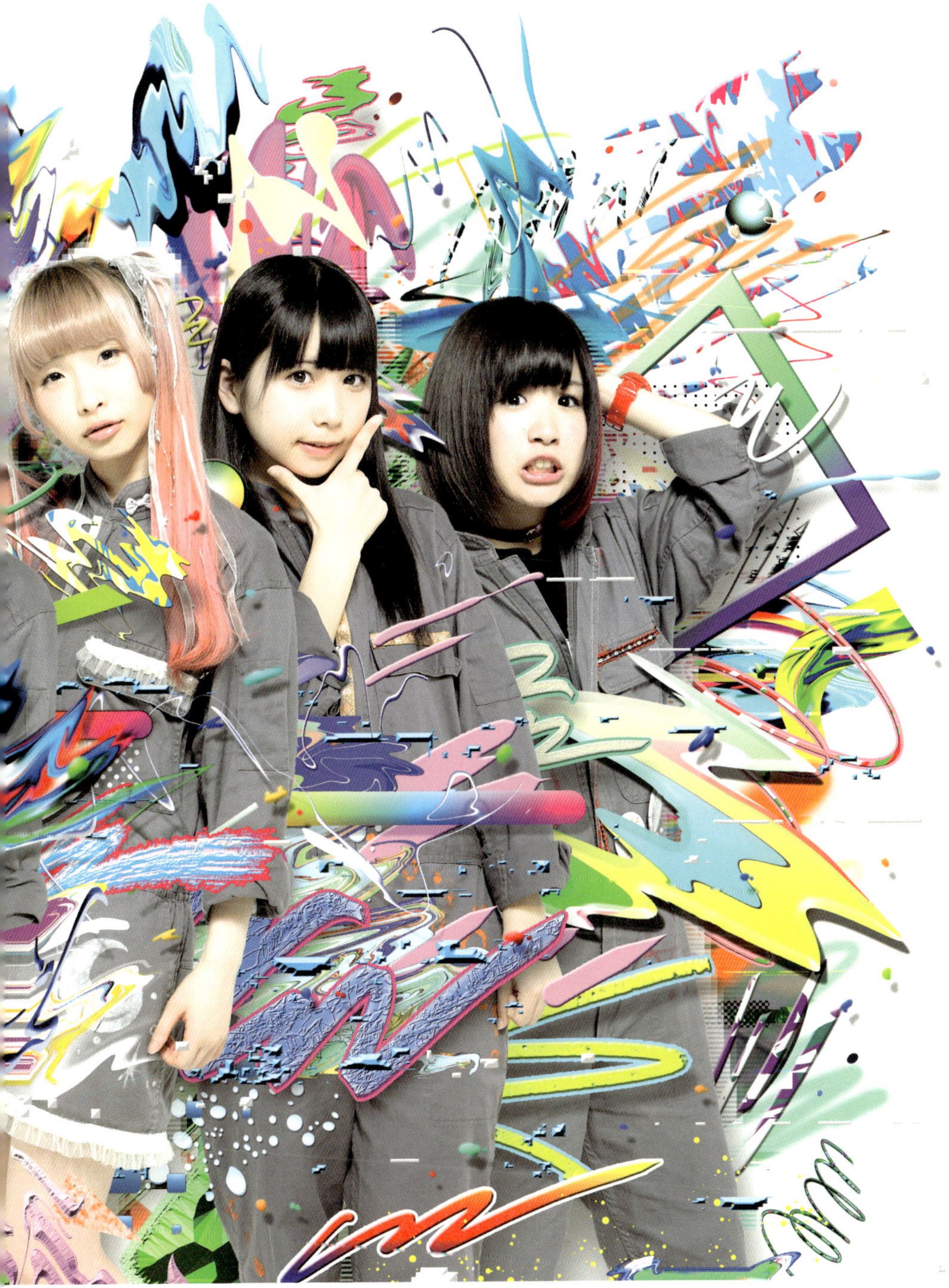

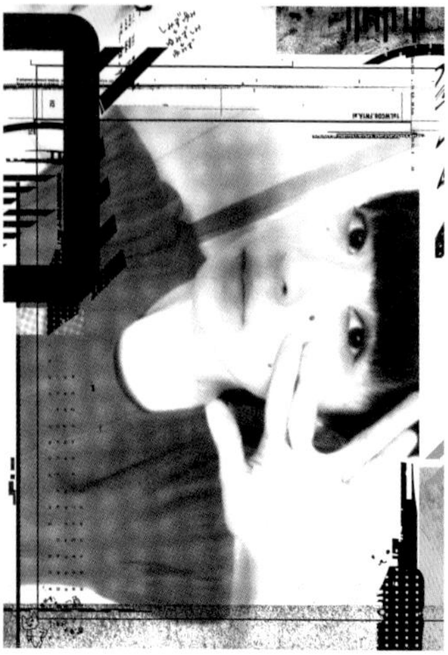
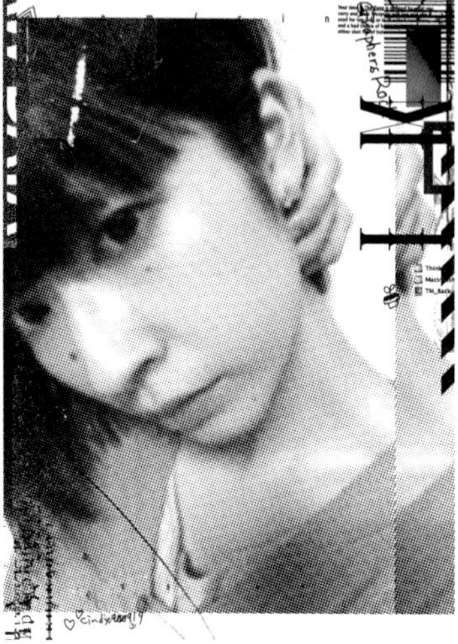
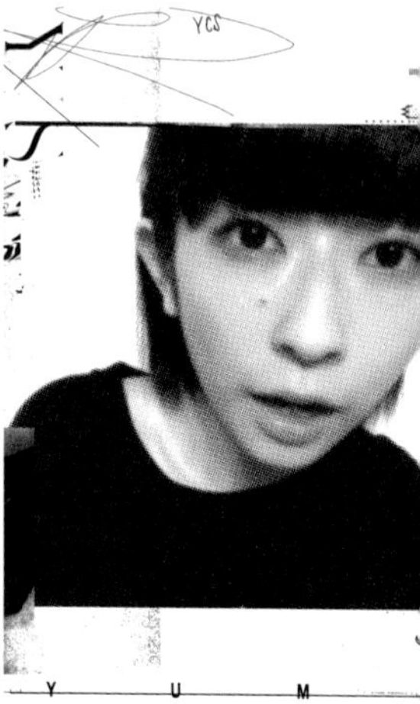
YCS
Y U M
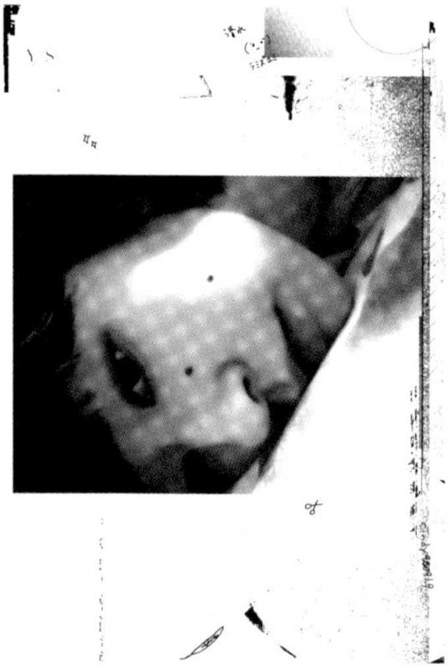
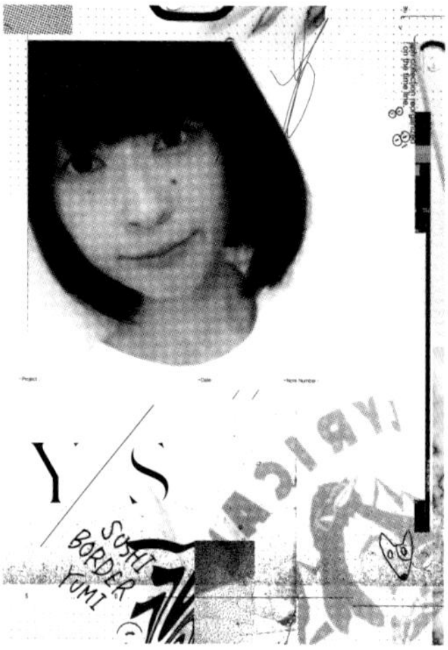
Y/S
SUSHI
BORDER
YUMI
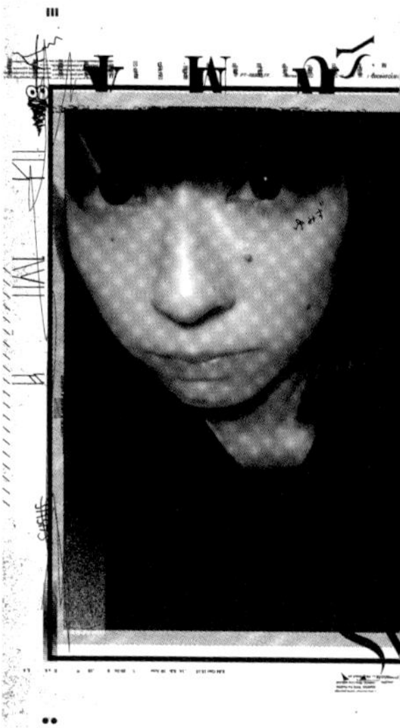
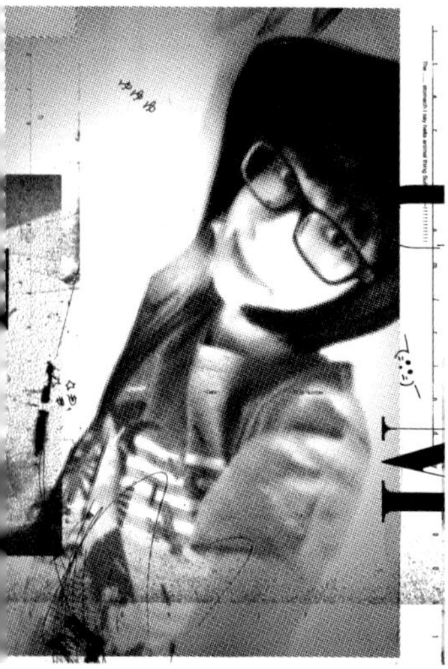
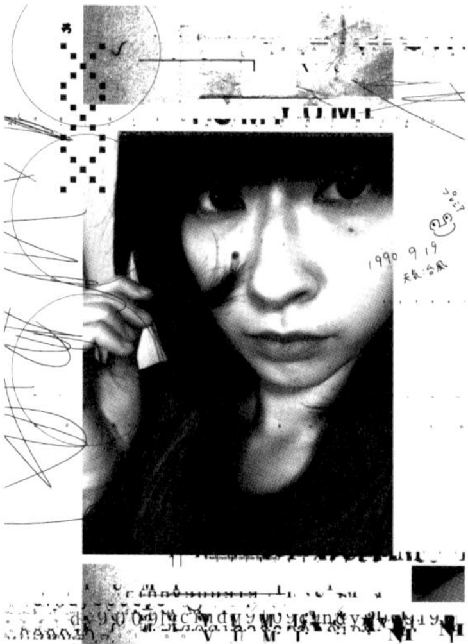
1990 9 19
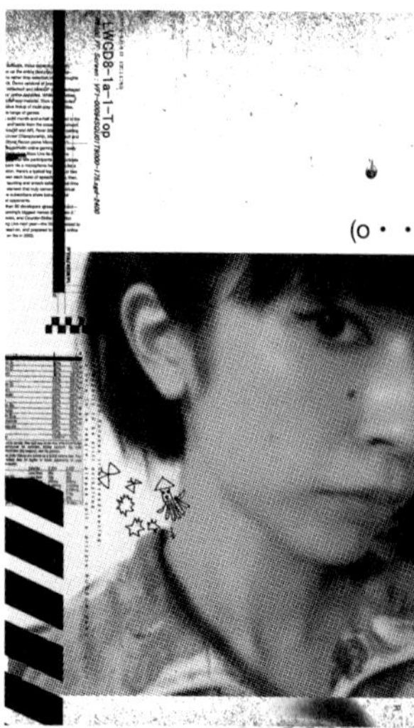
(o・・

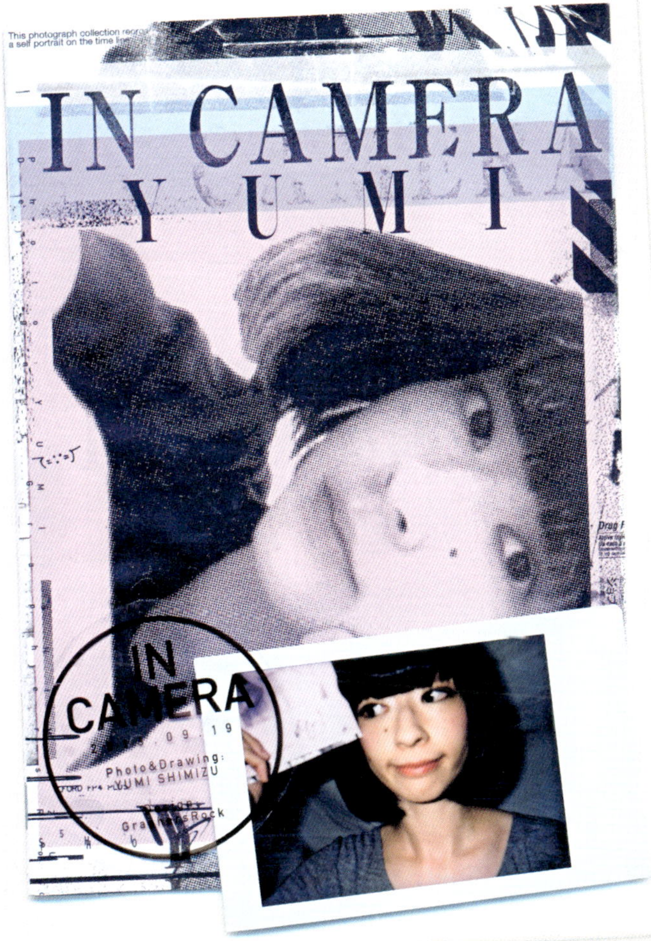
This photograph collection reorg
a self portrait on the time lin
IN CAMERA
YUMI
IN
CAMERA
Photo&Drawing:
YUMI SHIMIZU

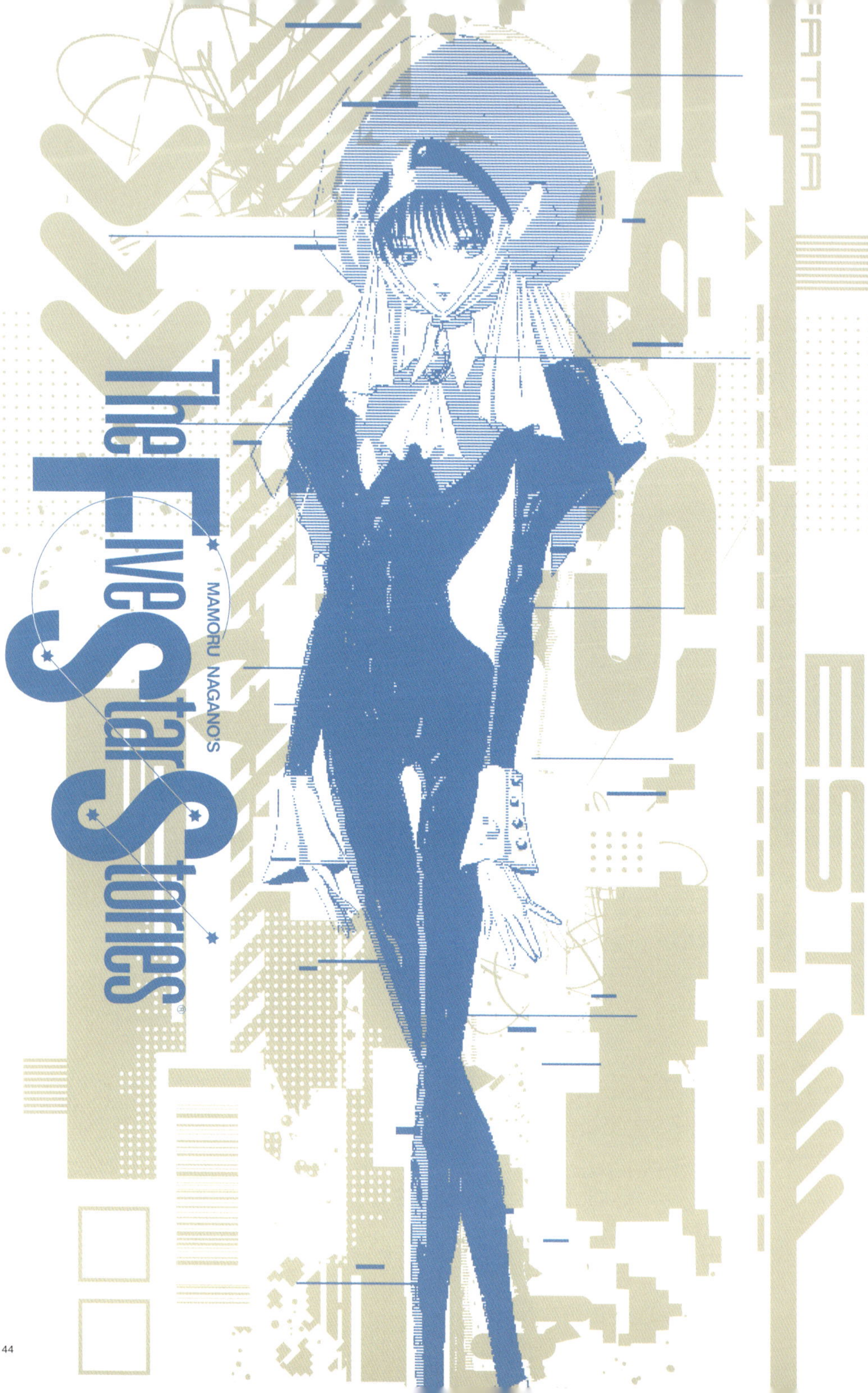
MAMORU NAGANO'S
The Five Star Stories®
FATIMA
EST

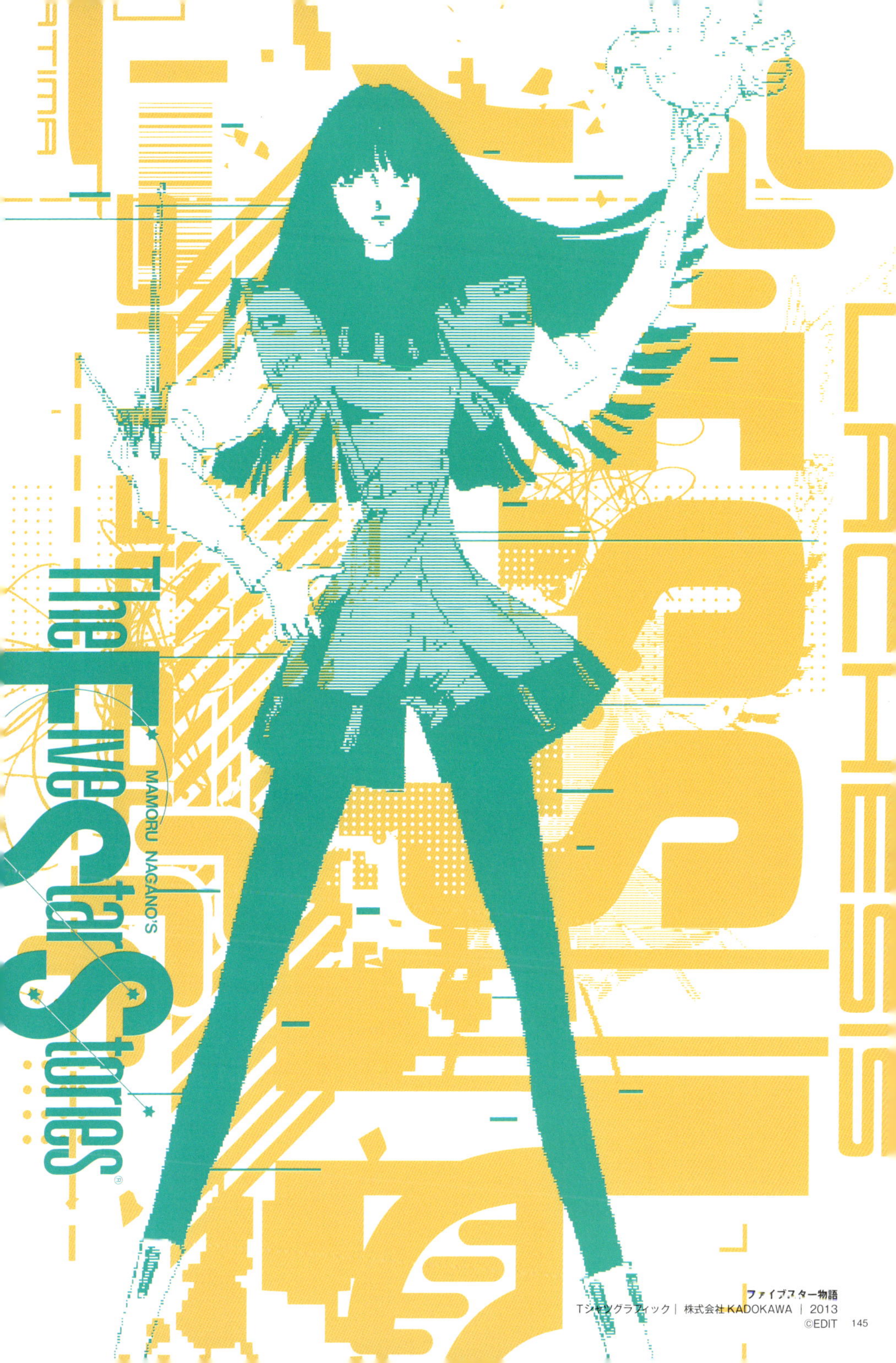

ファイブスター物語
Tシャツグラフィック｜株式会社KADOKAWA｜2013
©EDIT

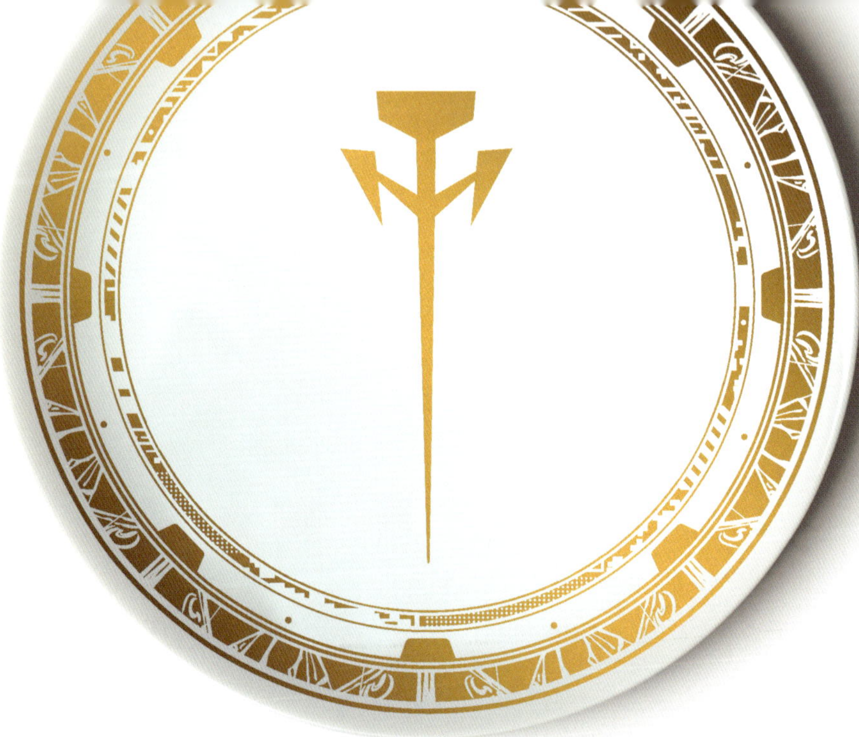

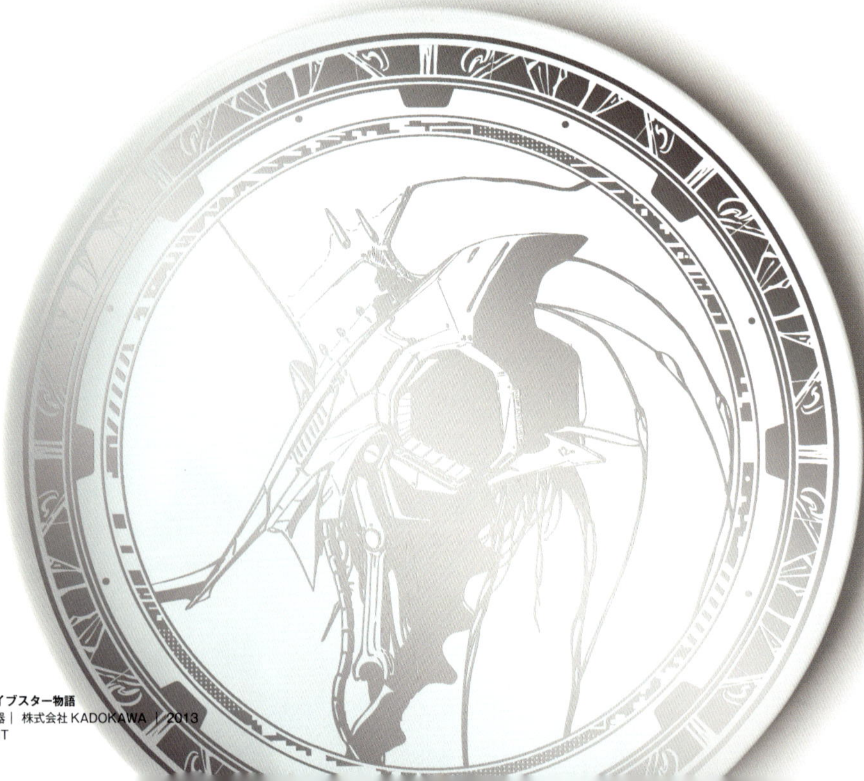

ファイブスター物語
陶磁器｜ 株式会社 KADOKAWA ｜2013
©EDIT

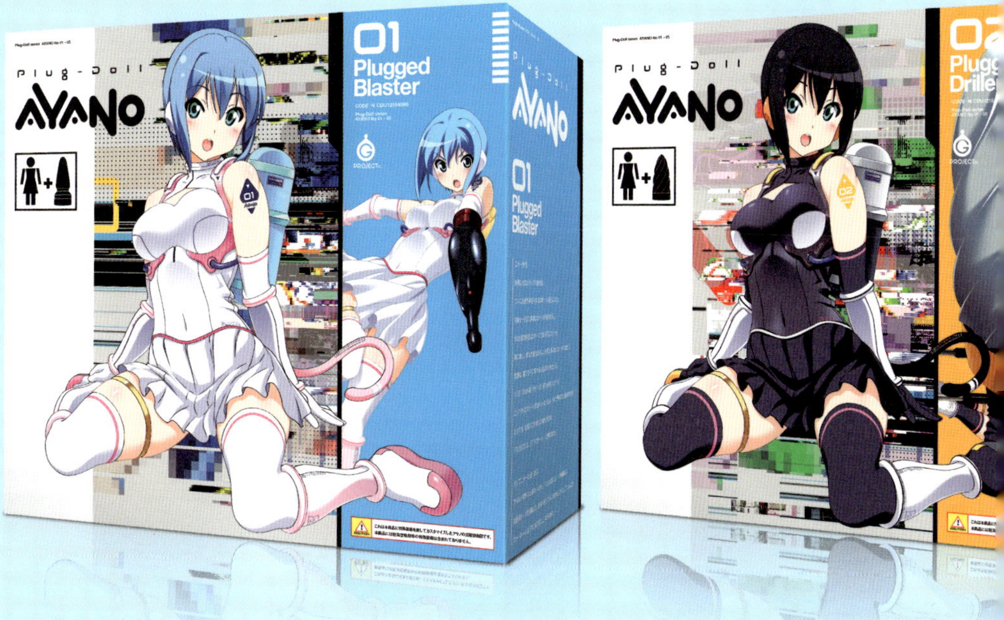
Plug-Doll
AYANO
01
Plugged
Blaster
Plug-Doll
AYANO
01
Plugged
Blaster
Plug-Doll
AYANO

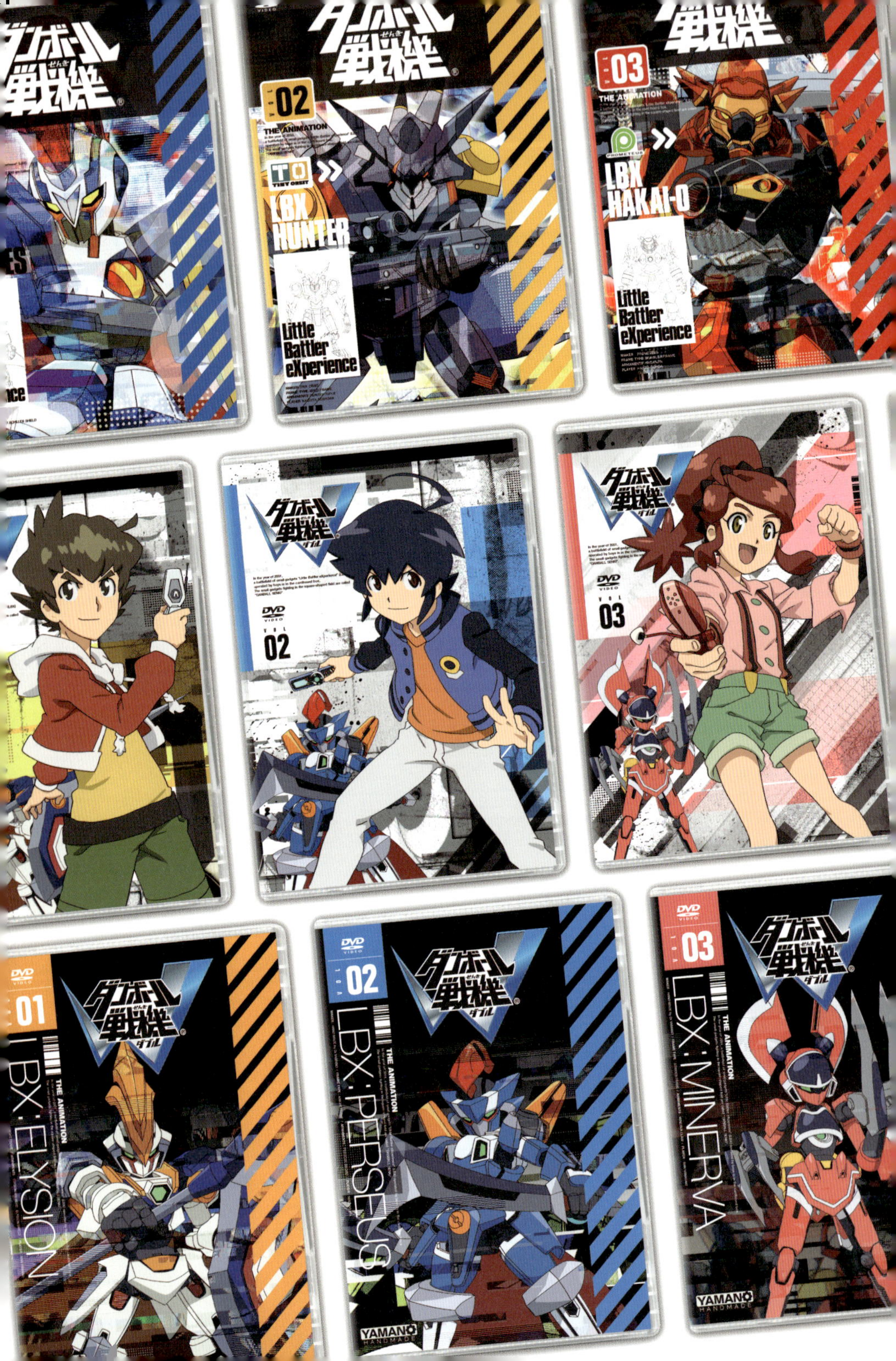

ダンボール戦機
02
THE ANIMATION
LBX HUNTER
Little Battler eXperience
03
THE ANIMATION
LBX HAKAI-O
Little Battler eXperience
ダンボール戦機W
DVD VIDEO 02
ダンボール戦機W
DVD VIDEO 03
DVD VIDEO 01
ダンボール戦機W
THE ANIMATION
LBX:ELYSION
DVD VIDEO 02
ダンボール戦機W
THE ANIMATION
LBX:PERSEUS
YAMANO HANDMADE
DVD VIDEO 03
ダンボール戦機W
THE ANIMATION
LBX:MINERVA
YAMANO HANDMADE

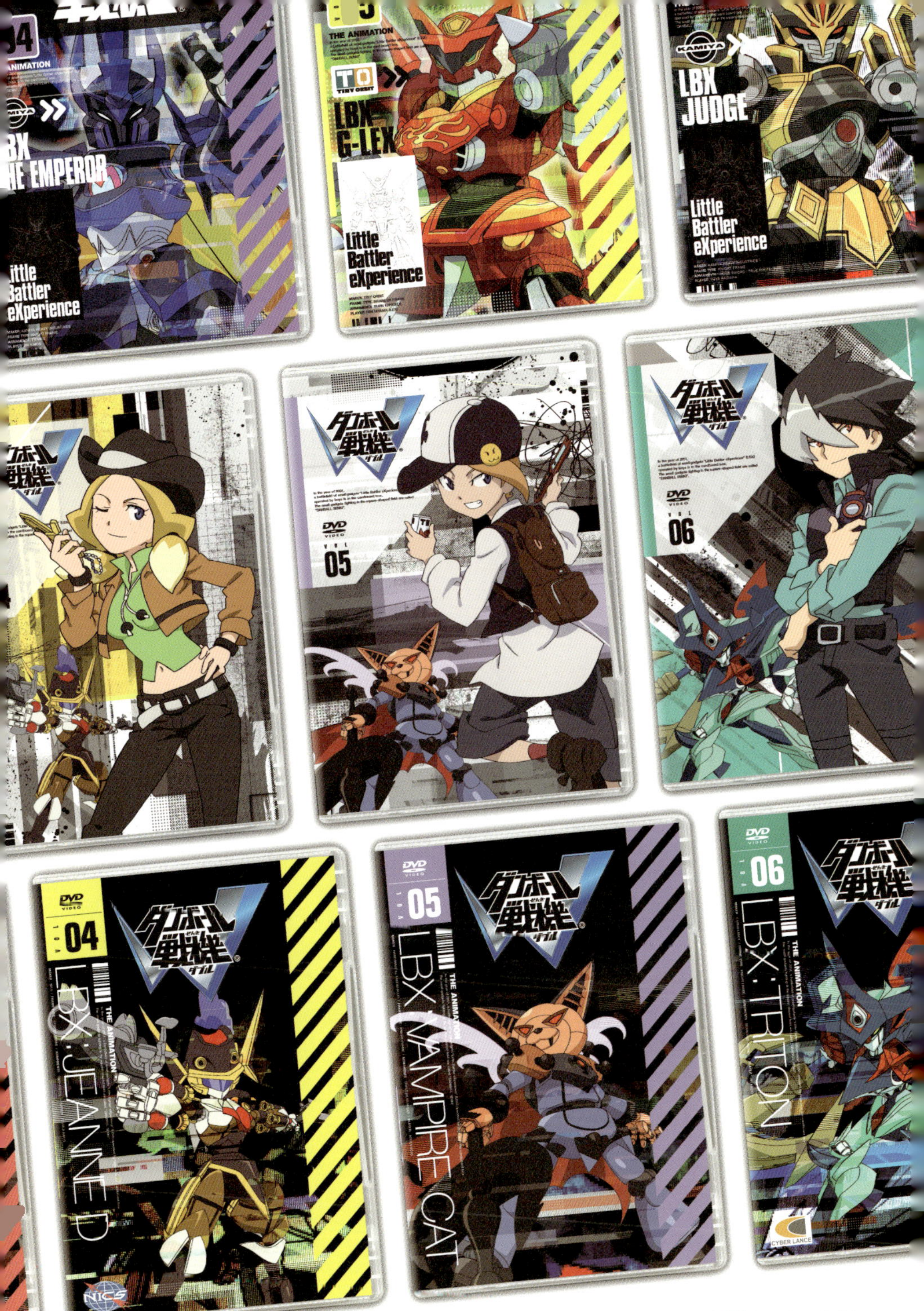

ダンボール戦機、ダンボール戦機ダブル
DVDジャケット ｜ 株式会社KADOKAWA メディアファクトリー ｜ 2011-2013
©L5/PDS·TX

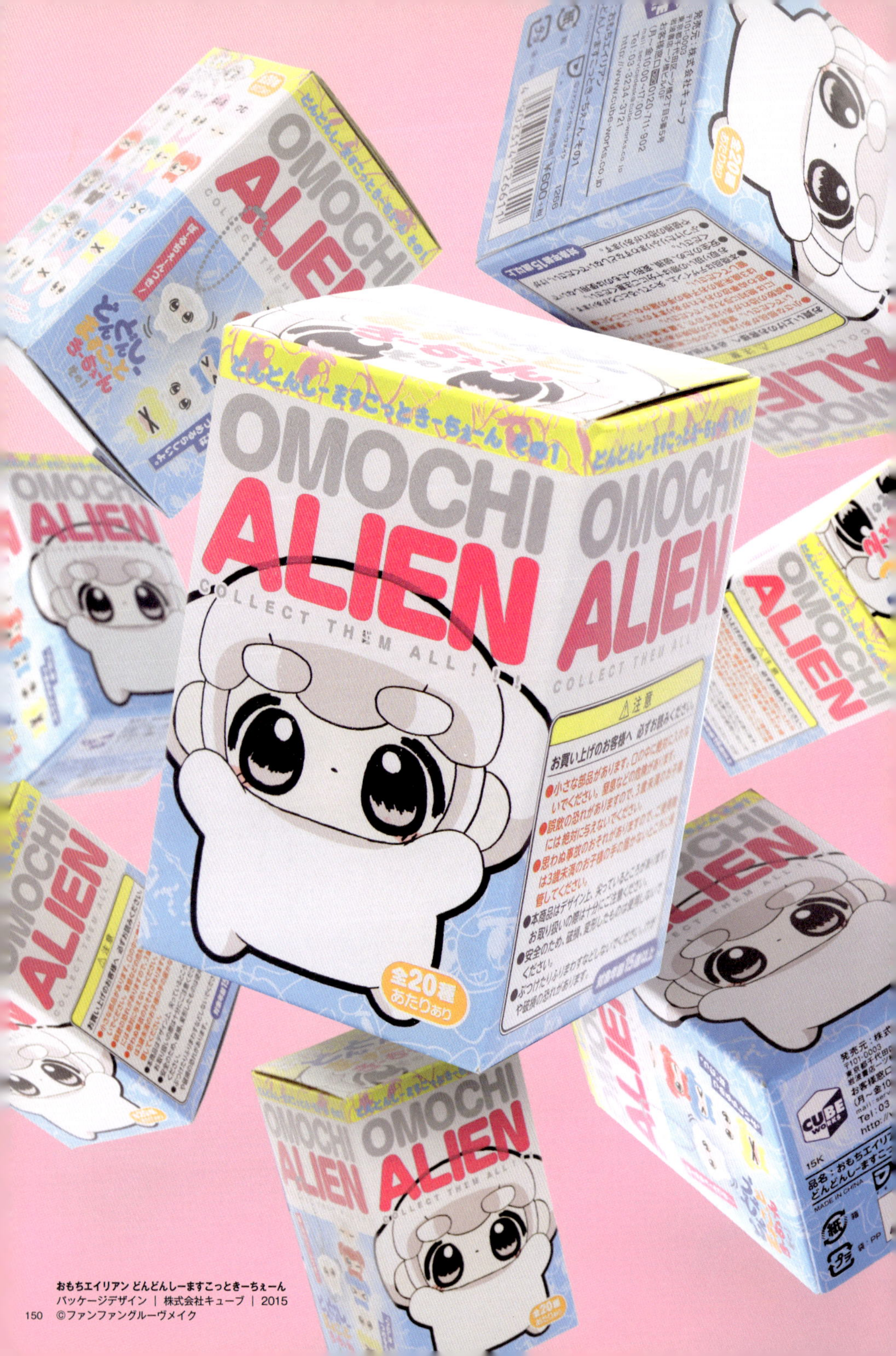

おもちエイリアン どんどんしーますこっときーちぇーん
パッケージデザイン | 株式会社キューブ | 2015
©ファンファングルーヴメイク

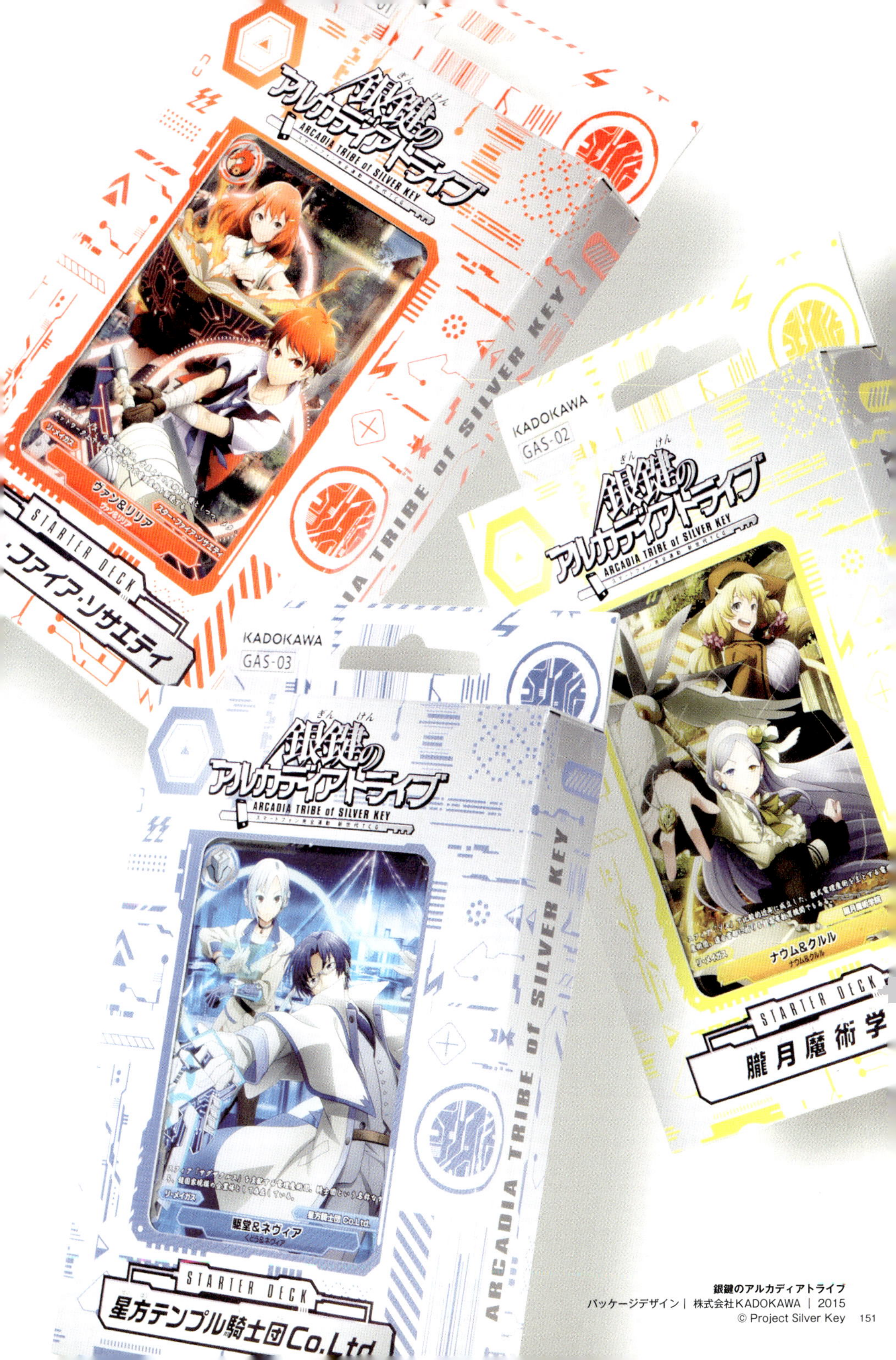

銀鍵のアルカディアトライブ
パッケージデザイン｜ 株式会社KADOKAWA ｜ 2015
© Project Silver Key

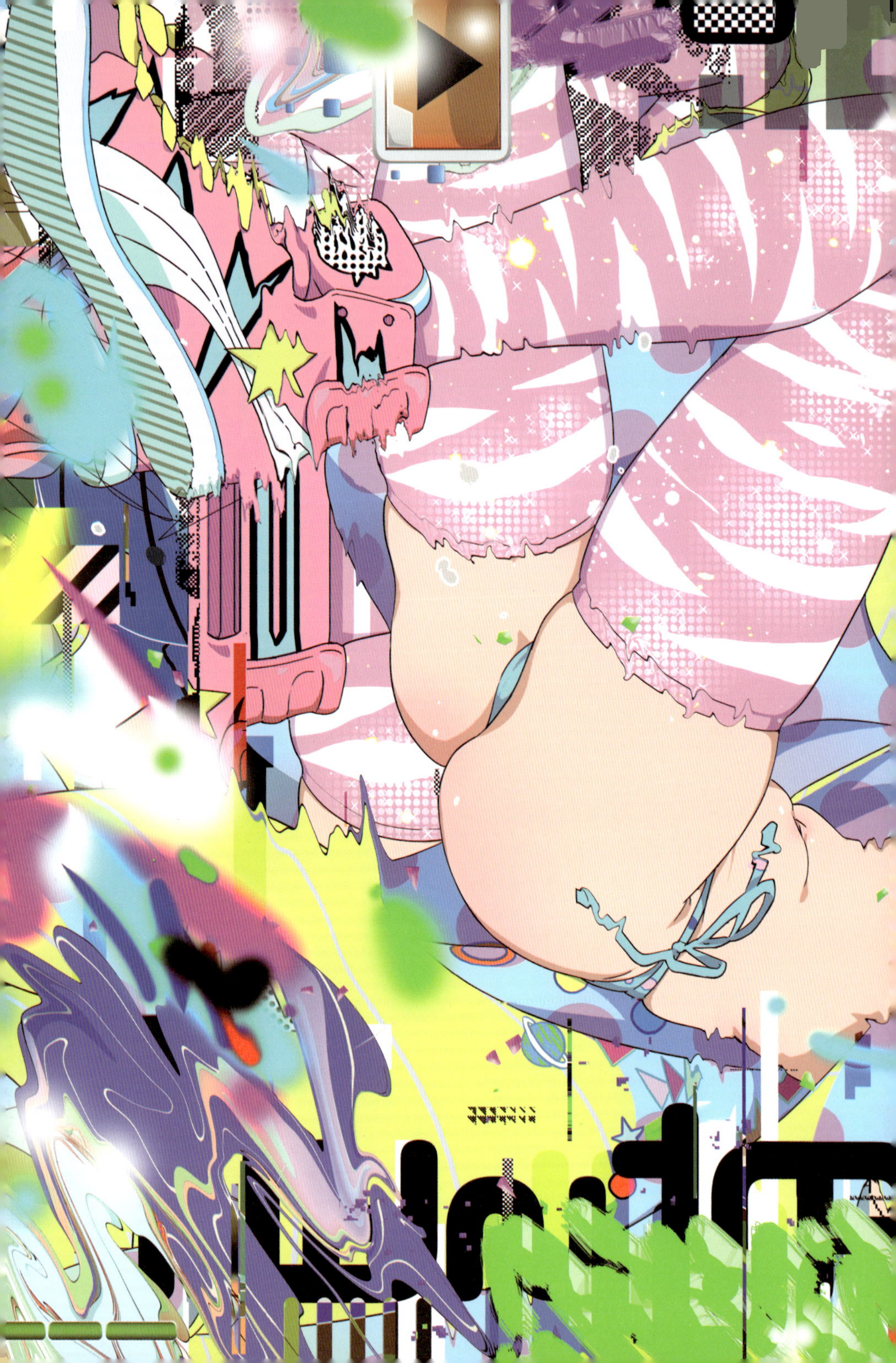

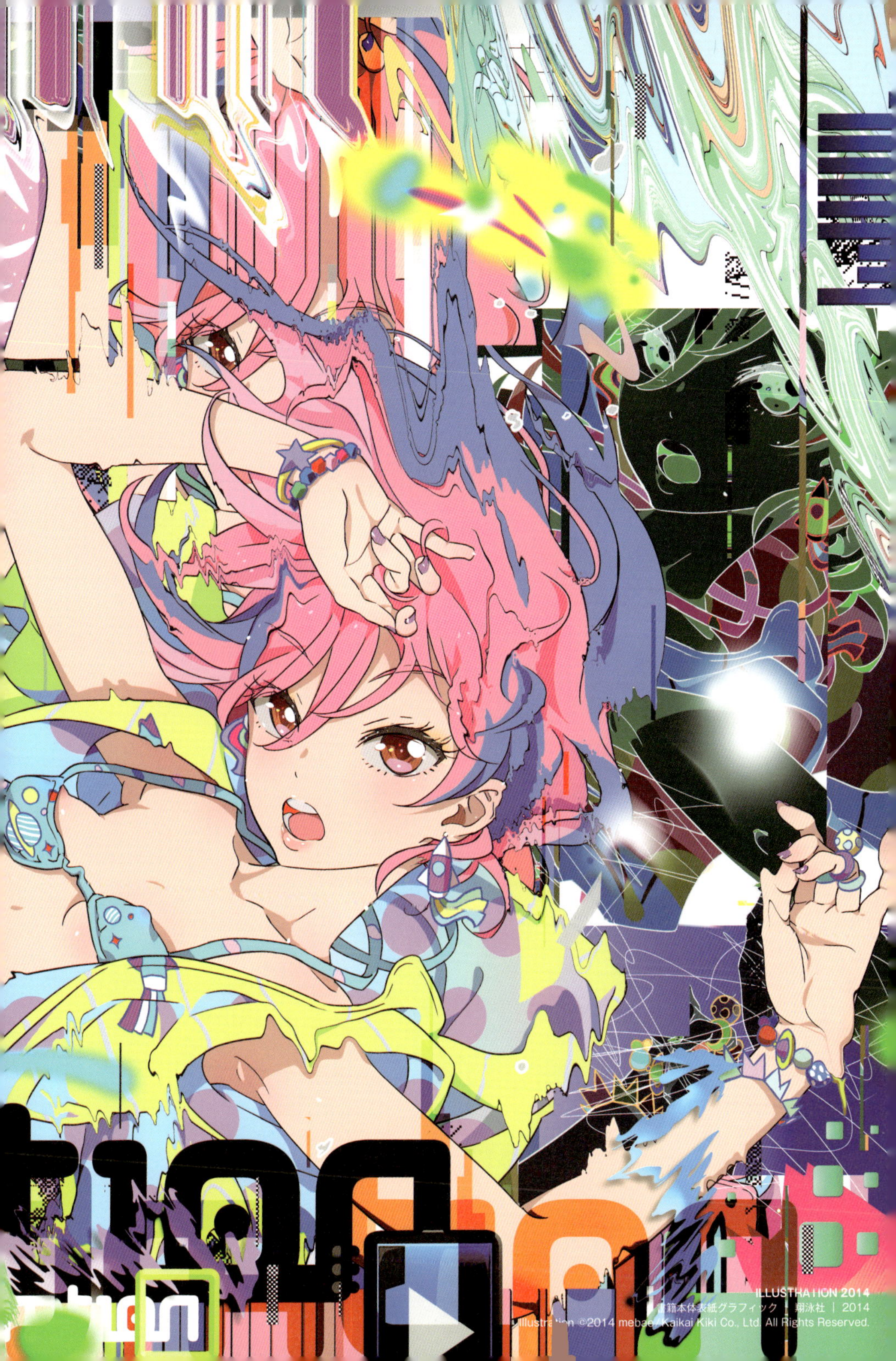

ILLUSTRATION 2014
書籍本体表紙グラフィック | 翔泳社 | 2014
Illustration ©2014 mebae / Kaikai Kiki Co., Ltd. All Rights Reserved.

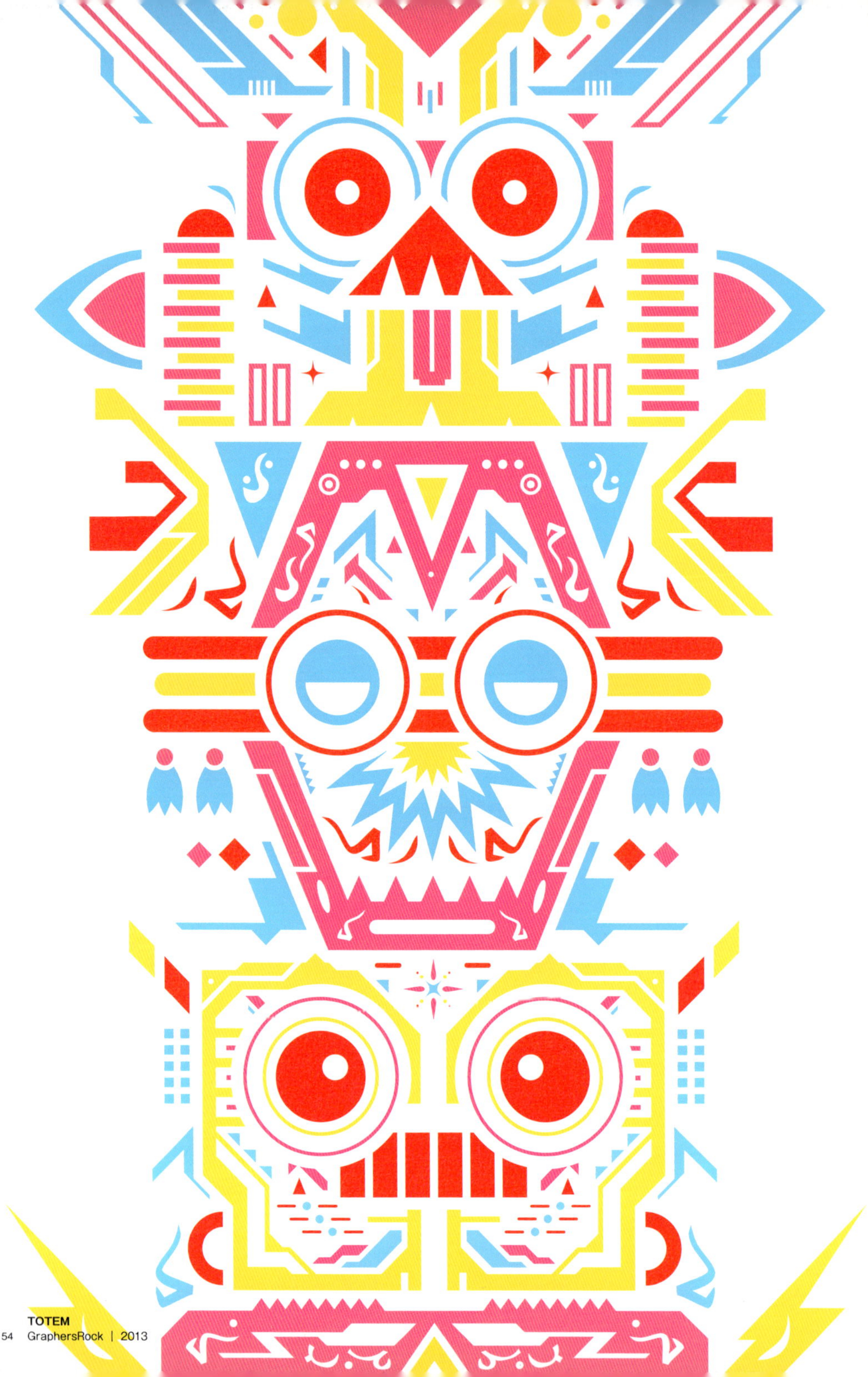

TOTEM

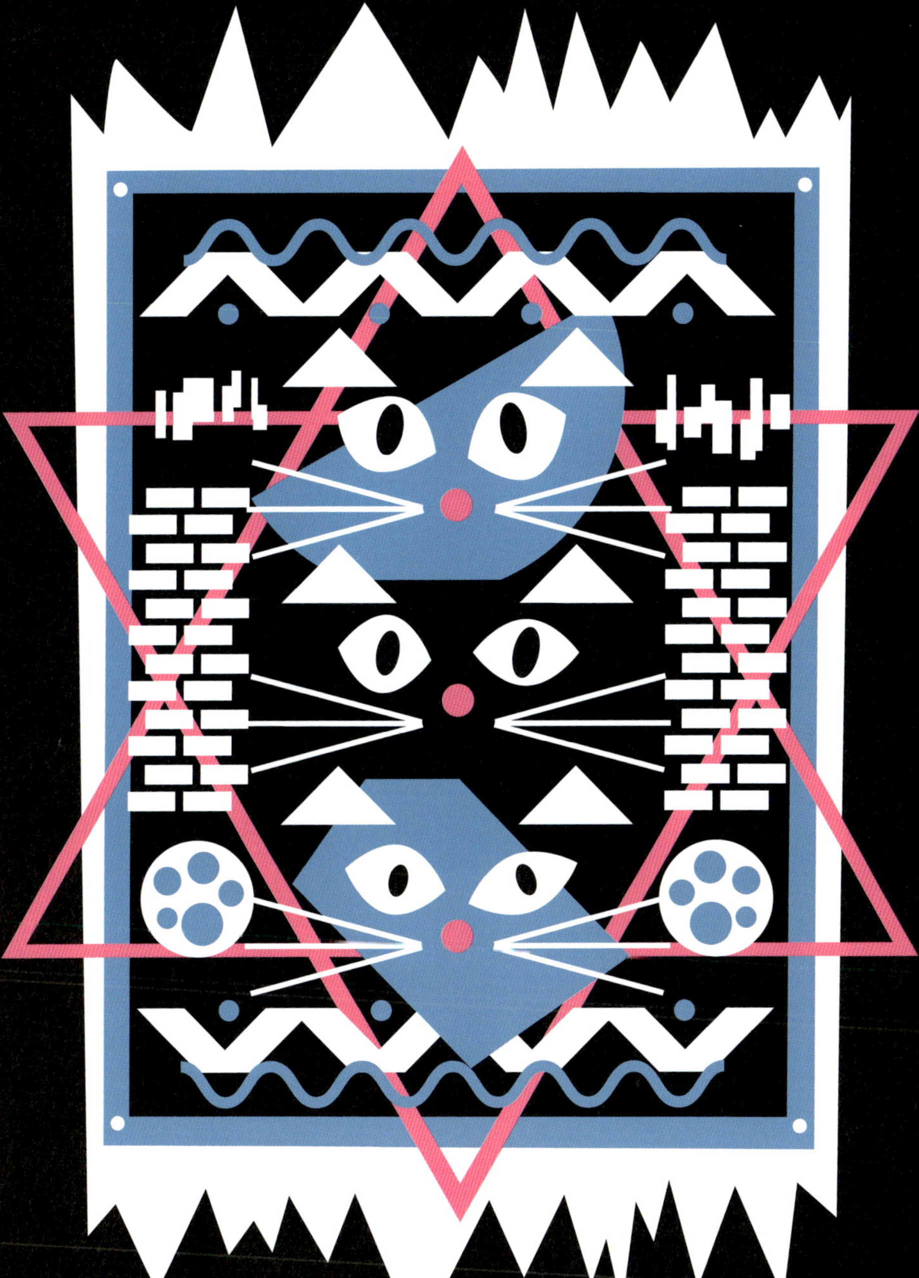

Catty Magic
GraphersRock | 2014

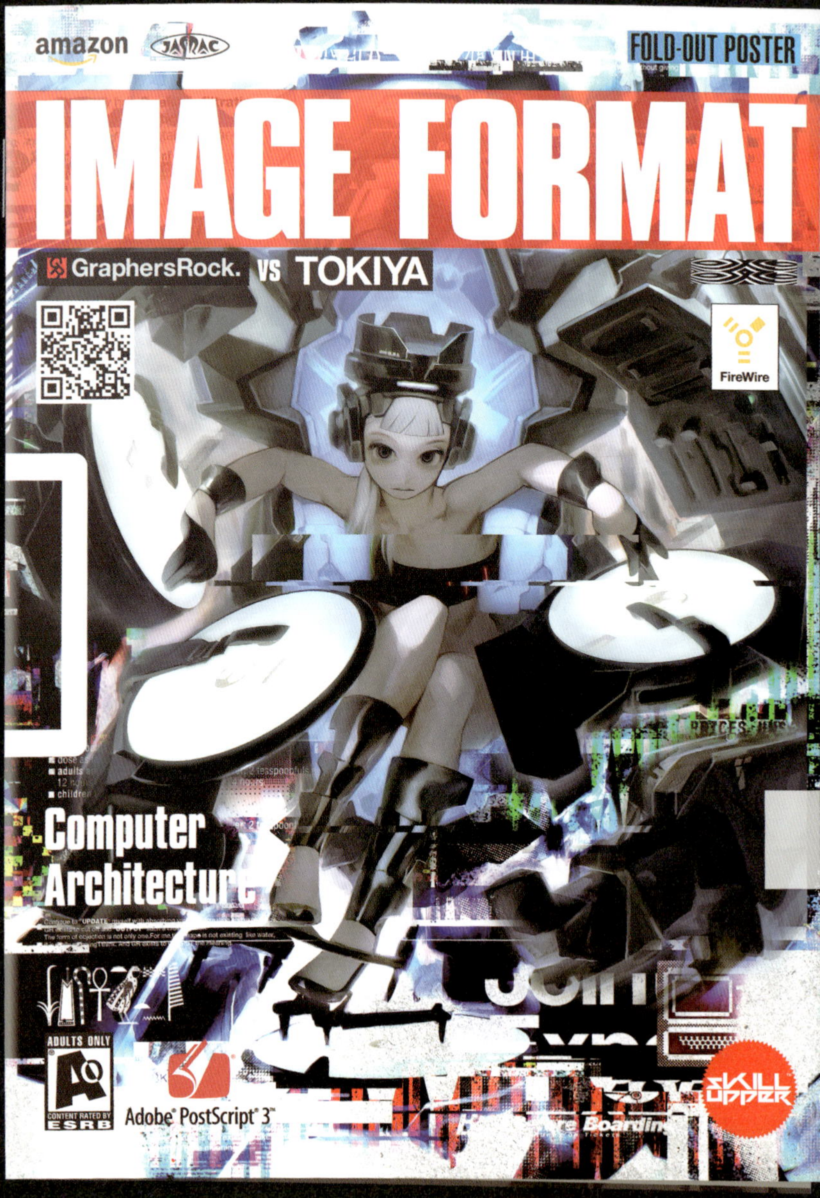

GraphersRock x TOKIYA / IMAGE FORMAT
Zine | GraphersRock | 2012

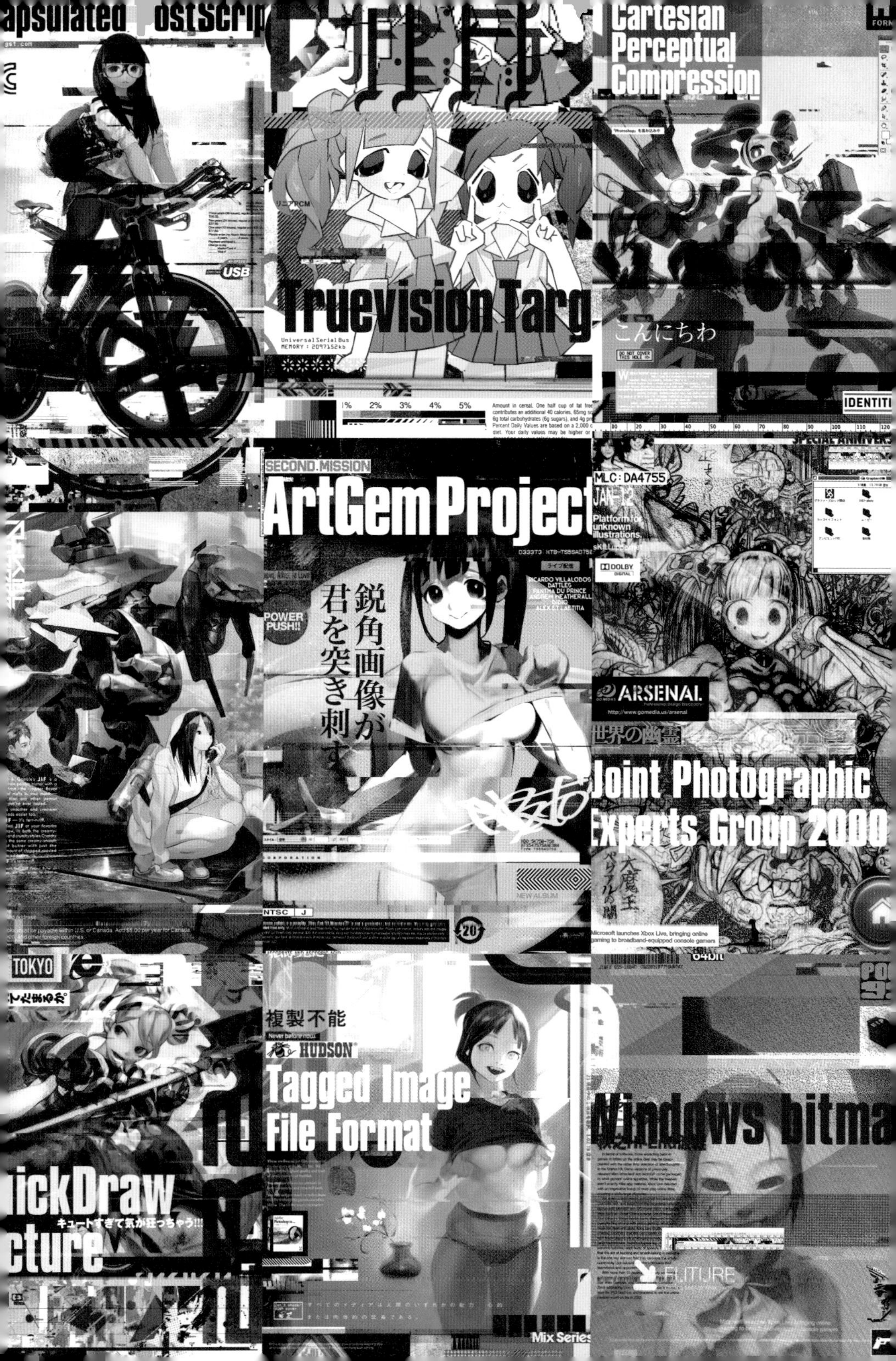

apsulated PostScrip
Truevision Targ
Universal Serial Bus
MEMORY : 2097152kb
USB
リニアPCM
Cartesian
Perceptual
Compression
こんにちわ
DO NOT COVER THIS HOLE
IDENTITI
1% 2% 3% 4% 5%
Amount in cersal. One half cup of fat free contributes an additional 40 calories, 65mg so 6g total carbohydrates (6g sugars), and 4g pr Percent Daily Values are based on a 2,000 c diet. Your daily values may be higher or
SECOND.MISSION
ArtGem Project
POWER PUSH!!
鋭角画像が
君を突き刺す
RICARDO VILLALOBOS
DATTLES
PANTHA DU PRINCE
ANDREW WEATHERALL
BIDIO
ALEX ET LAETITIA
ライブ配信
NEW ALBUM
NTSC J
MLC : DA4755
JAN-12
Platform for unknown illustrations.
DOLBY DIGITAL
ARSENAL
http://www.gomedia.us/arsenal
世界の幽霊
Joint Photographic
Experts Group 2000
大魔王
Microsoft launches Xbox Live, bringing online gaming to broadband-equipped console gamers
TOKYO
複製不能
Never before now.
HUDSON
Tagged Image
File Format
ickDraw
キュートすぎて気が狂っちゃう!!!
cture
Windows bitma
FUTURE
Mix Series

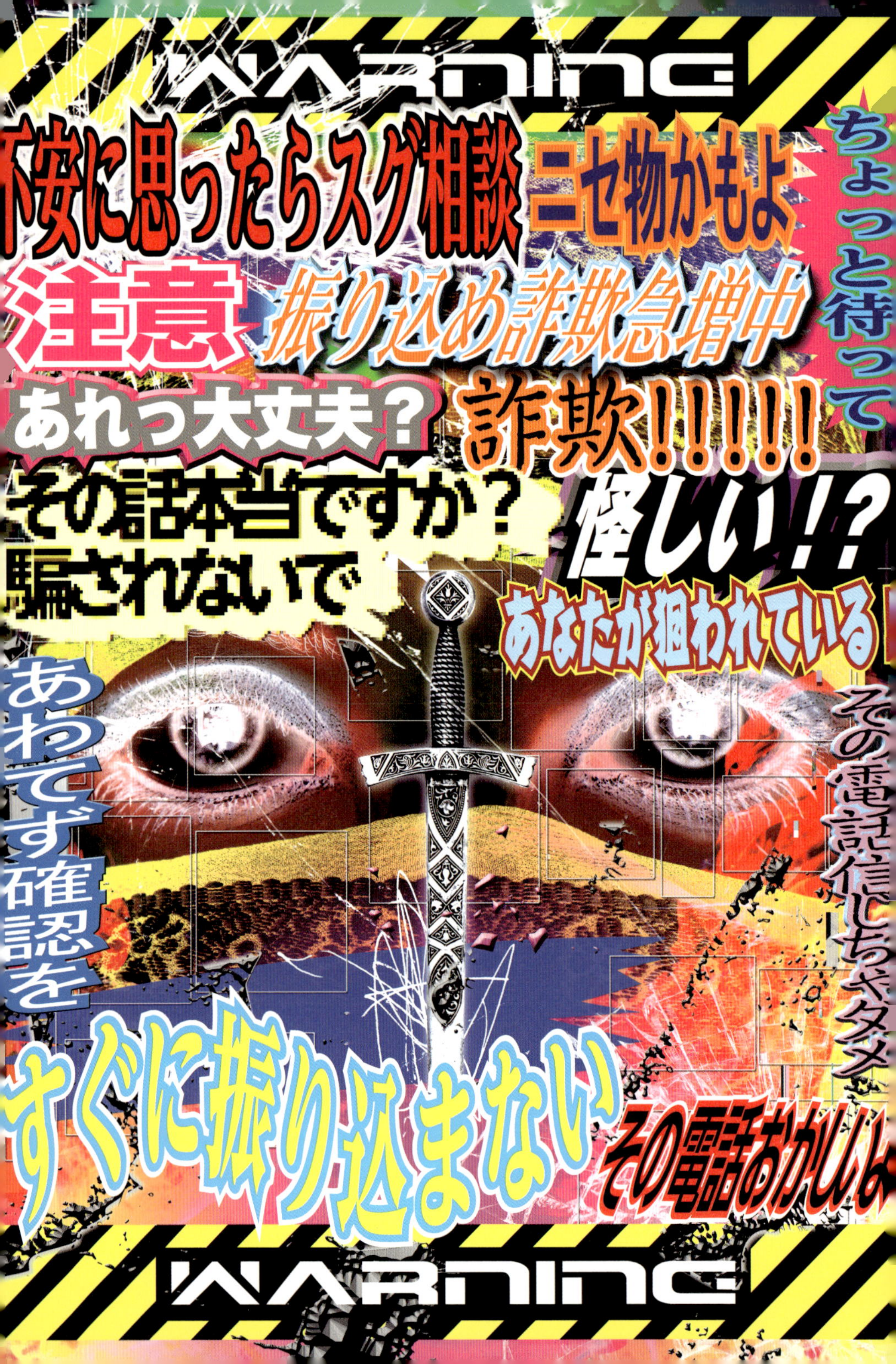
WARNING
不安に思ったらスグ相談
ニセ物かもよ
ちょっと待って
注意
振り込め詐欺急増中
あれっ大丈夫？
詐欺！！！！！
その話本当ですか？
怪しい！？
騙されないで
あなたが狙われている！
あわてず確認を
その電話信じちゃダメ
すぐに振り込まない
その電話おかしいよ
WARNING

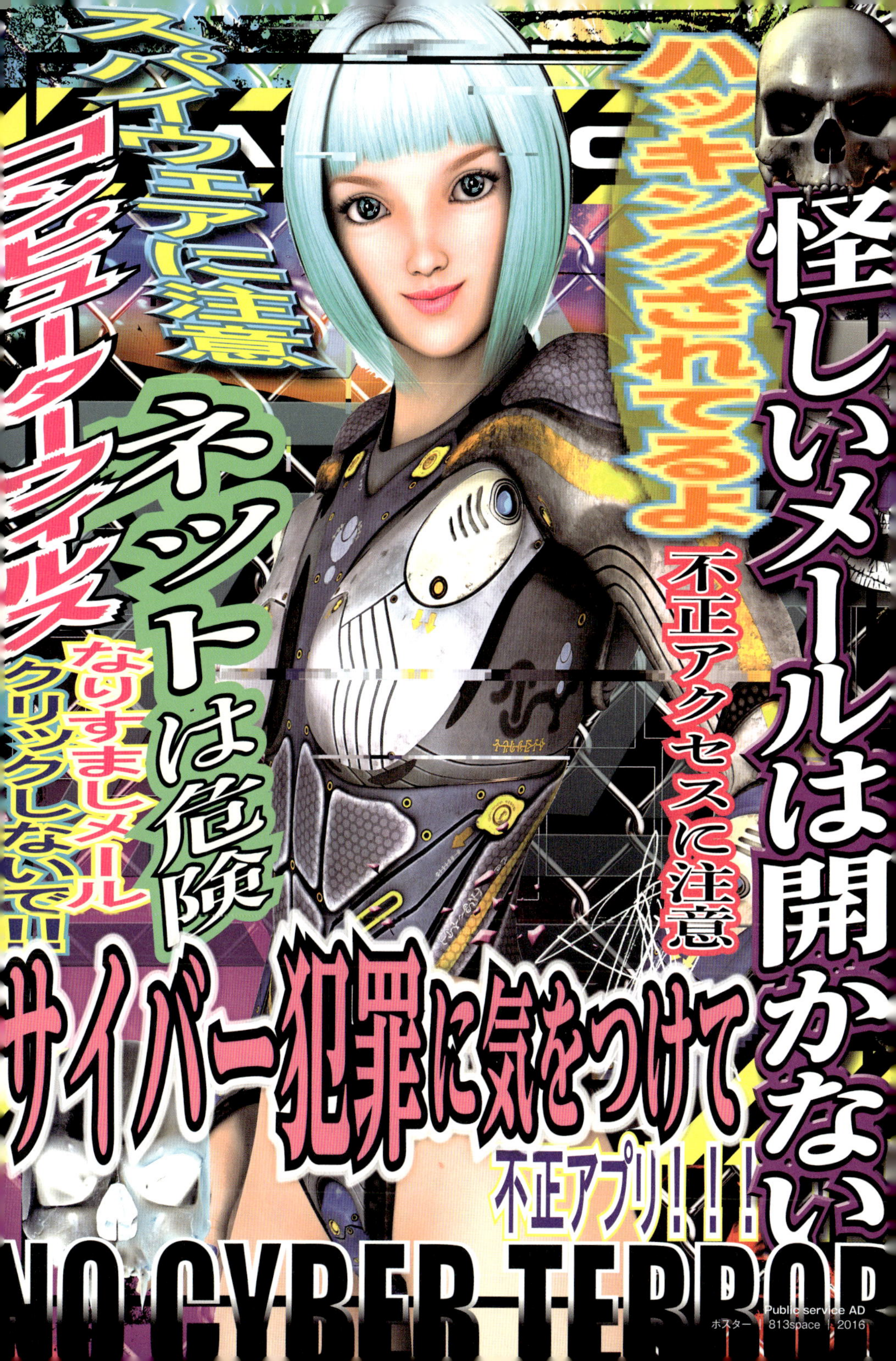

Public service AD
ポスター | 813space | 2016

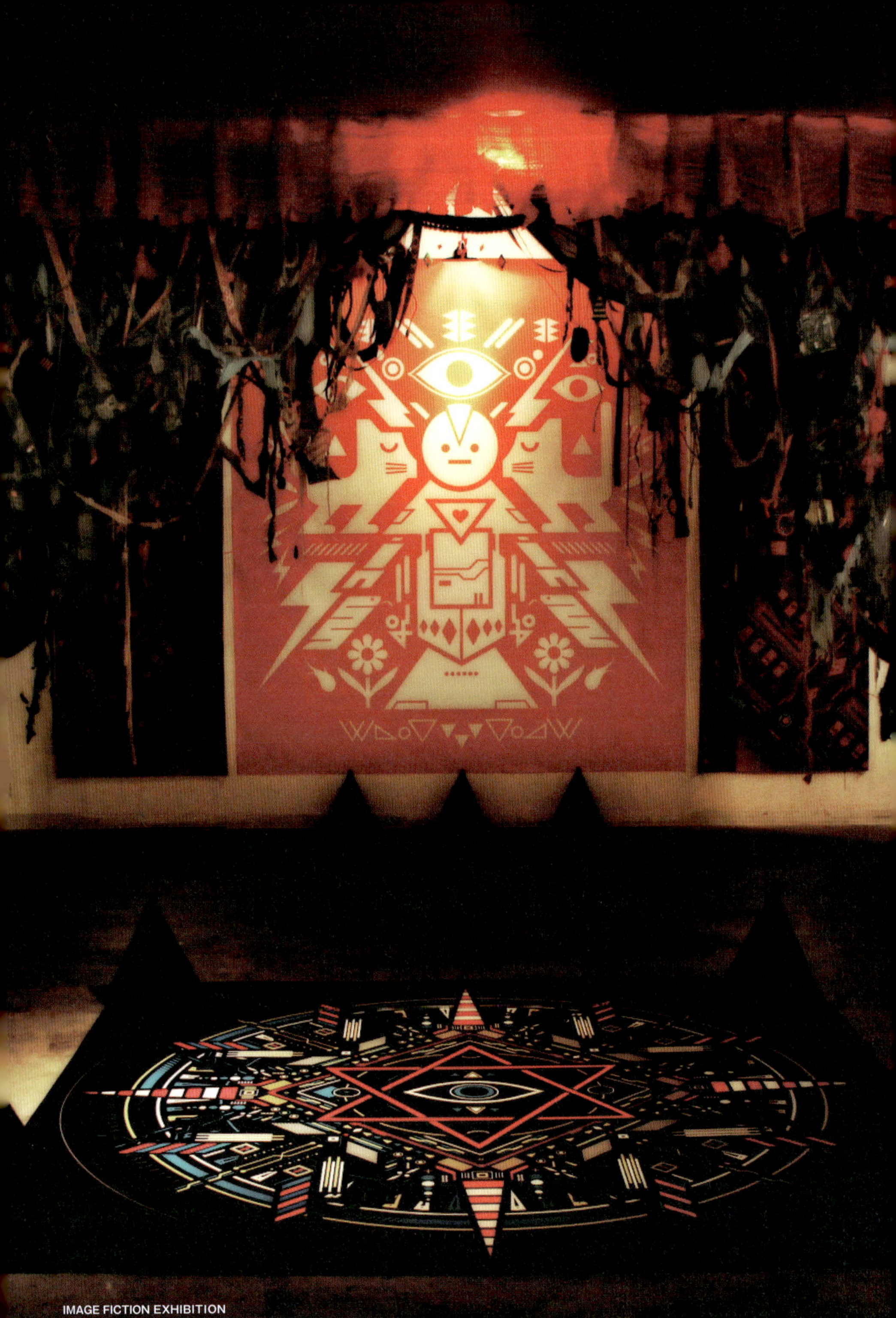

IMAGE FICTION EXHIBITION
展示、インスタレーション | GraphersRock | 2011

GraphersRock

RASTERIZE

Desktop SESSION

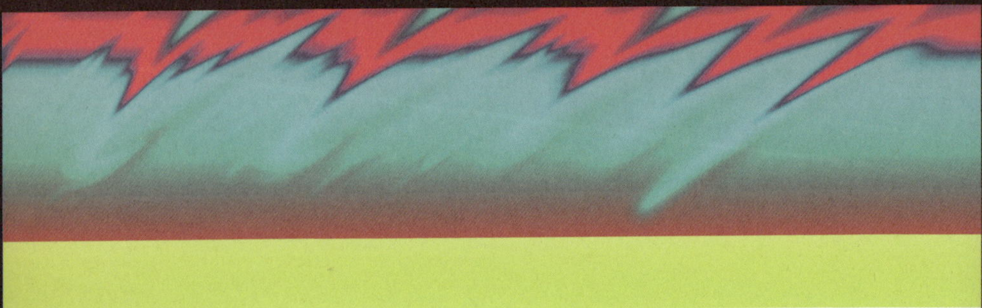

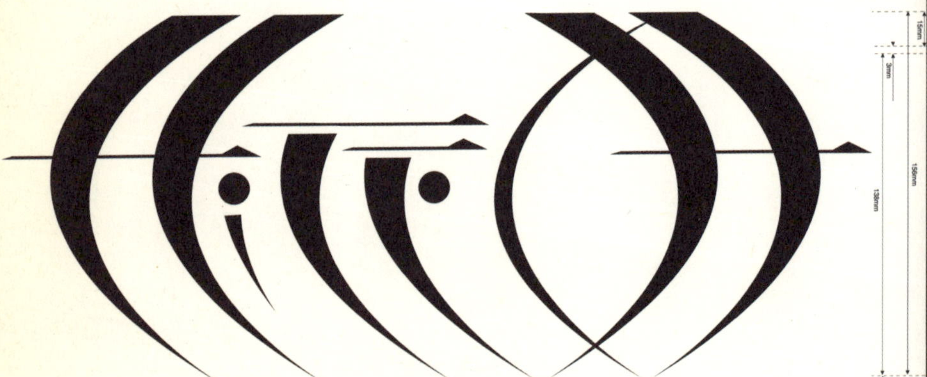

Your time in The Zone is defined by what you carry and wear. Weapons will jam mid-clip if used for too long or in ill-suited conditions, and a bad choice of hazard suit will see you either shot full of holes or microwaved

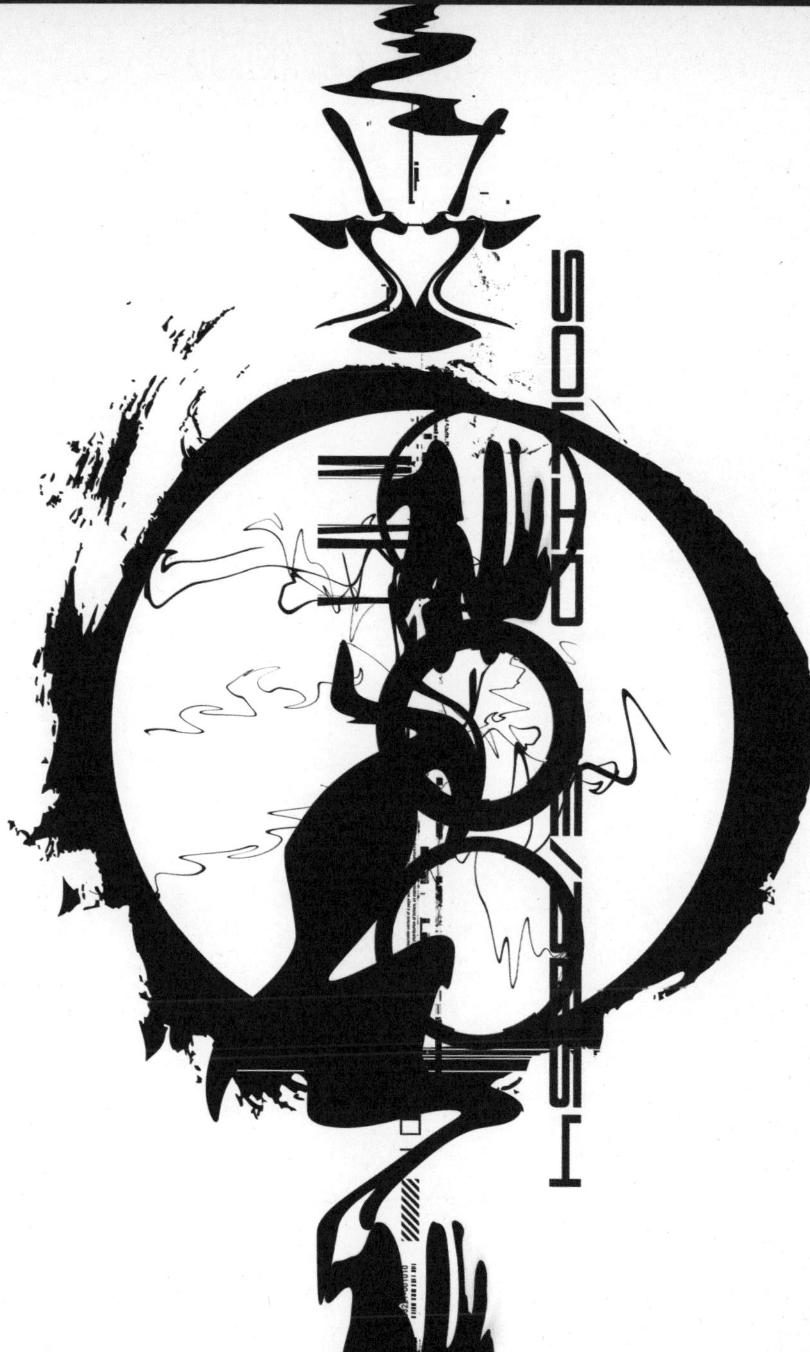

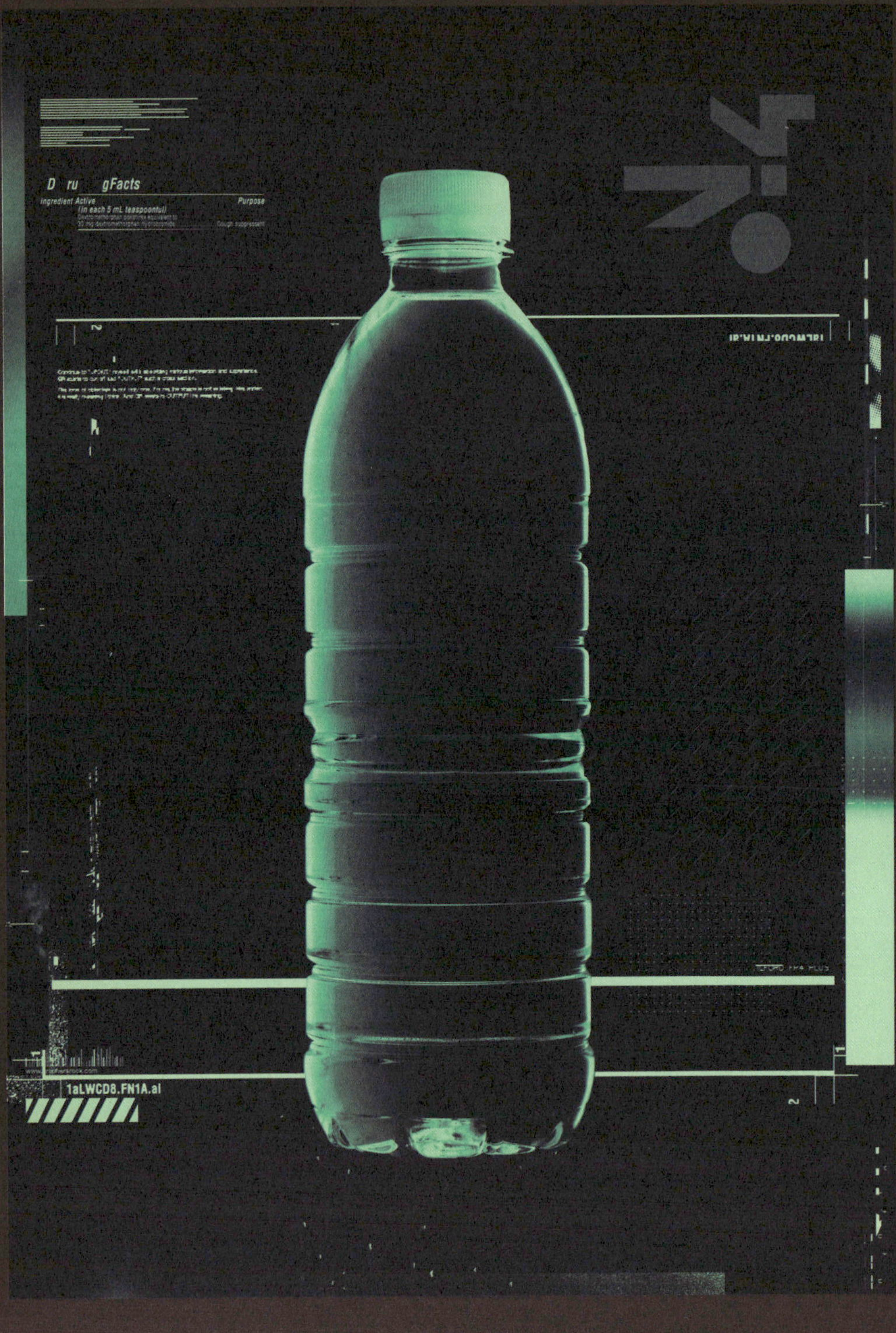
D ru gFacts
Ingredient Active
(in each 5 mL teaspoonful)
Purpose
1aLWCD8.FN1A.al

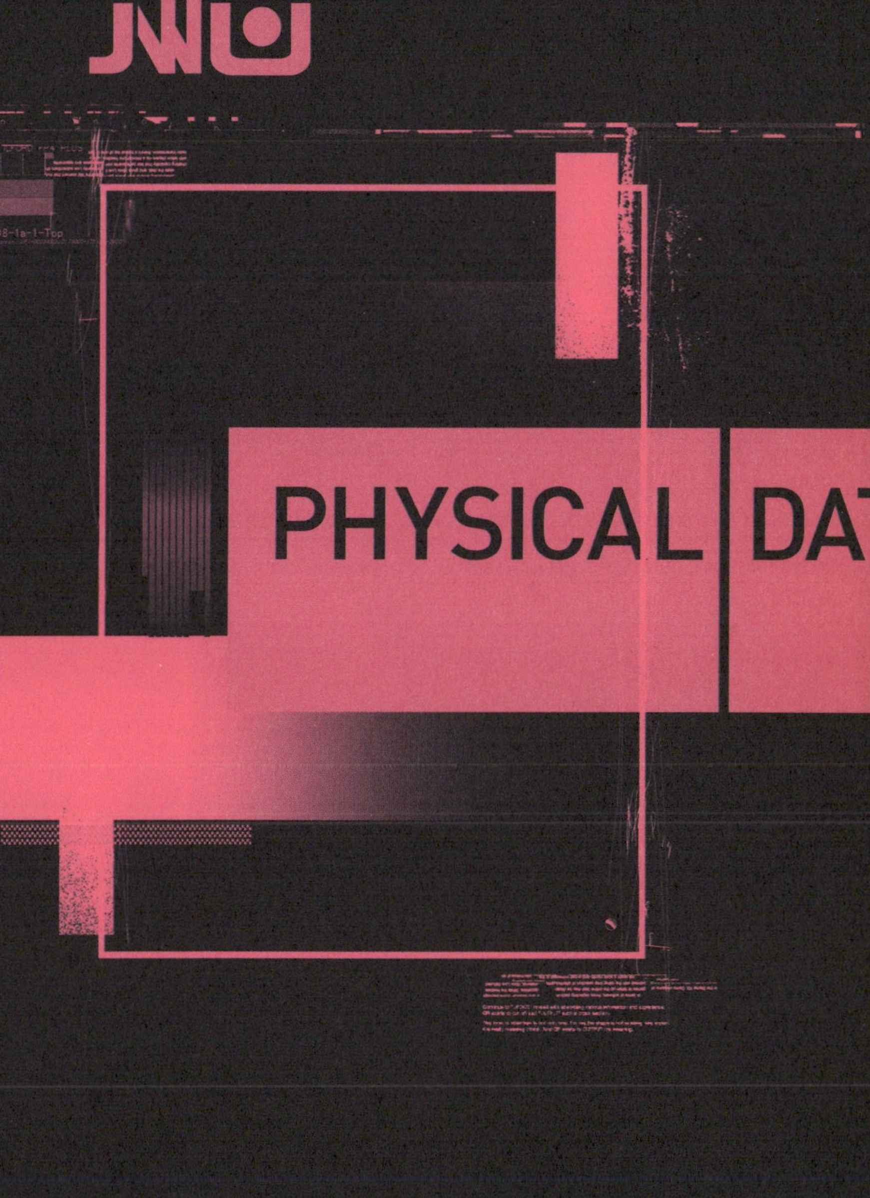
PHYSICAL DAT

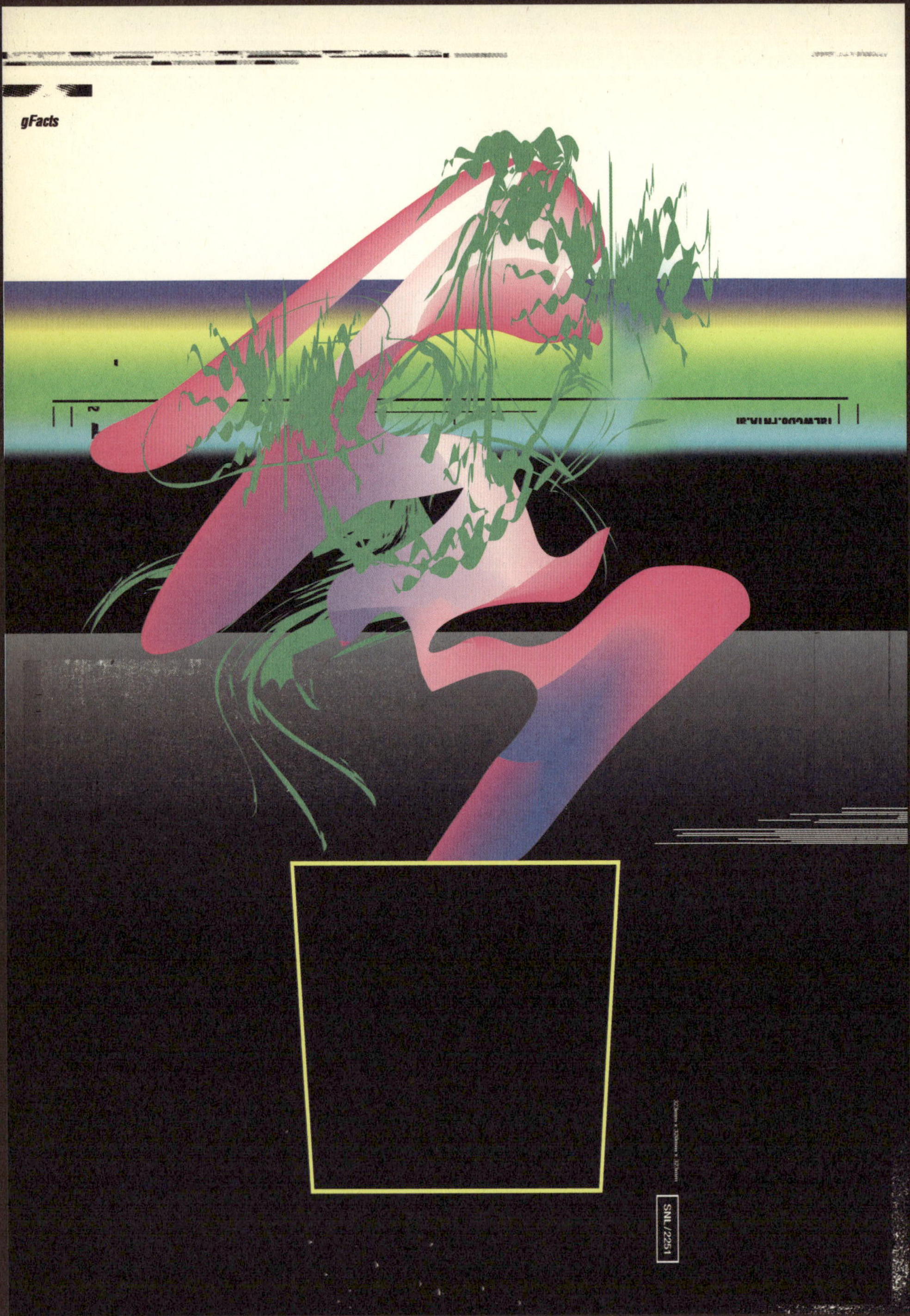
gFacts
SNL/2251

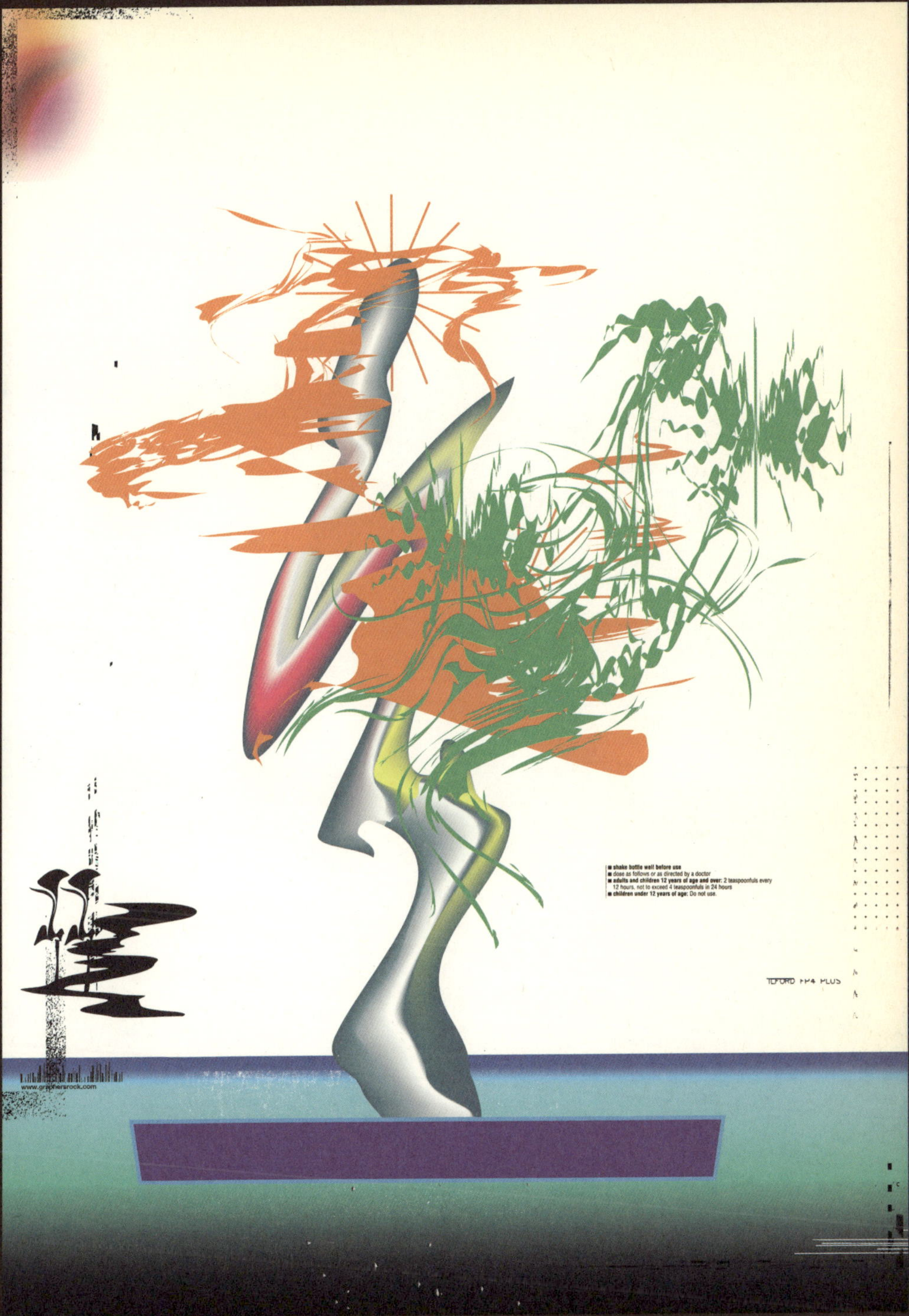
shake bottle well before use
dose as follows or as directed by a doctor
adults and children 12 years of age and over: 2 teaspoonfuls every 12 hours, not to exceed 4 teaspoonfuls in 24 hours
children under 12 years of age: Do not use.
www.graphersrock.com

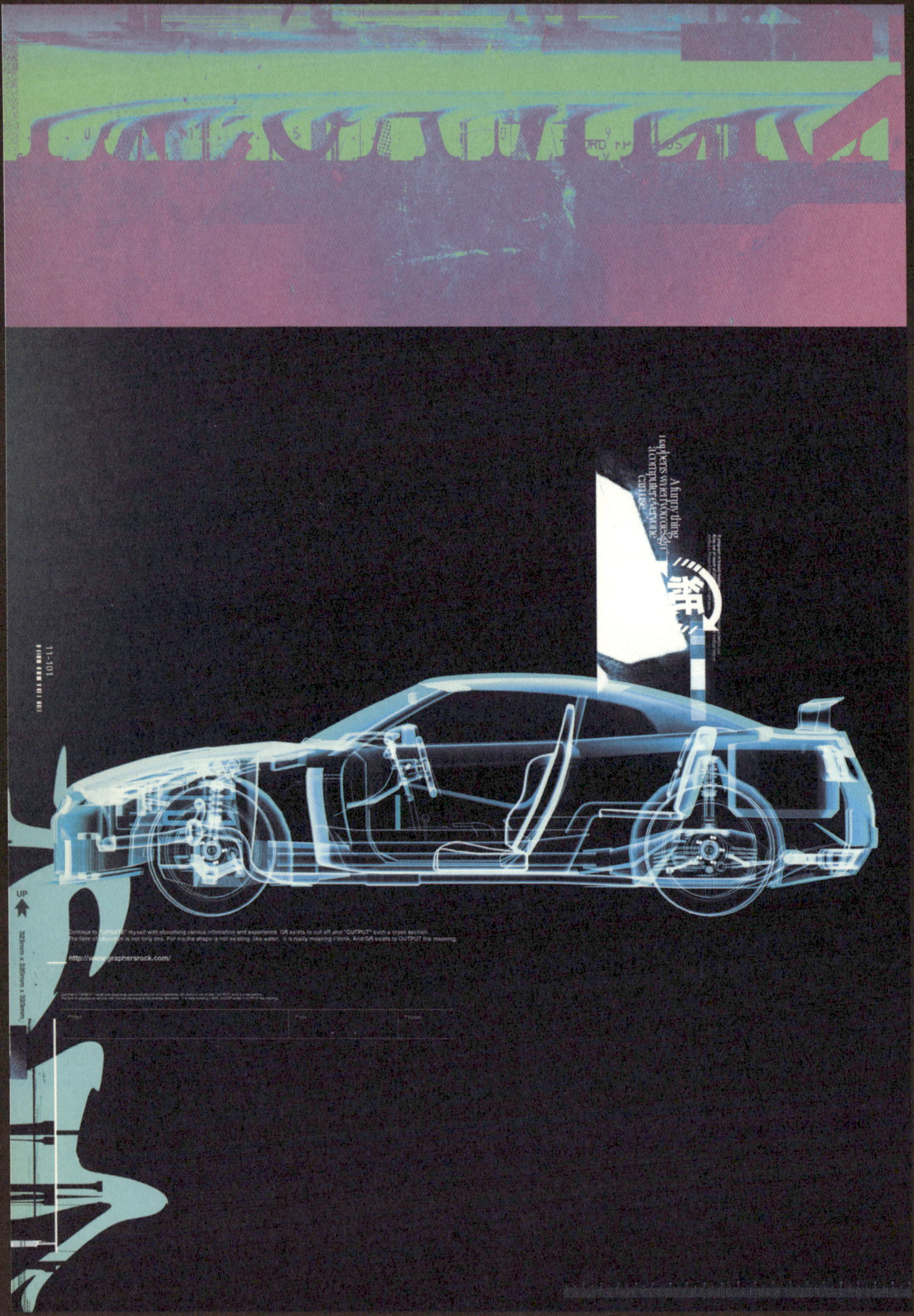
UP
http://www.graphersrock.com/
11-101

情報機器

System

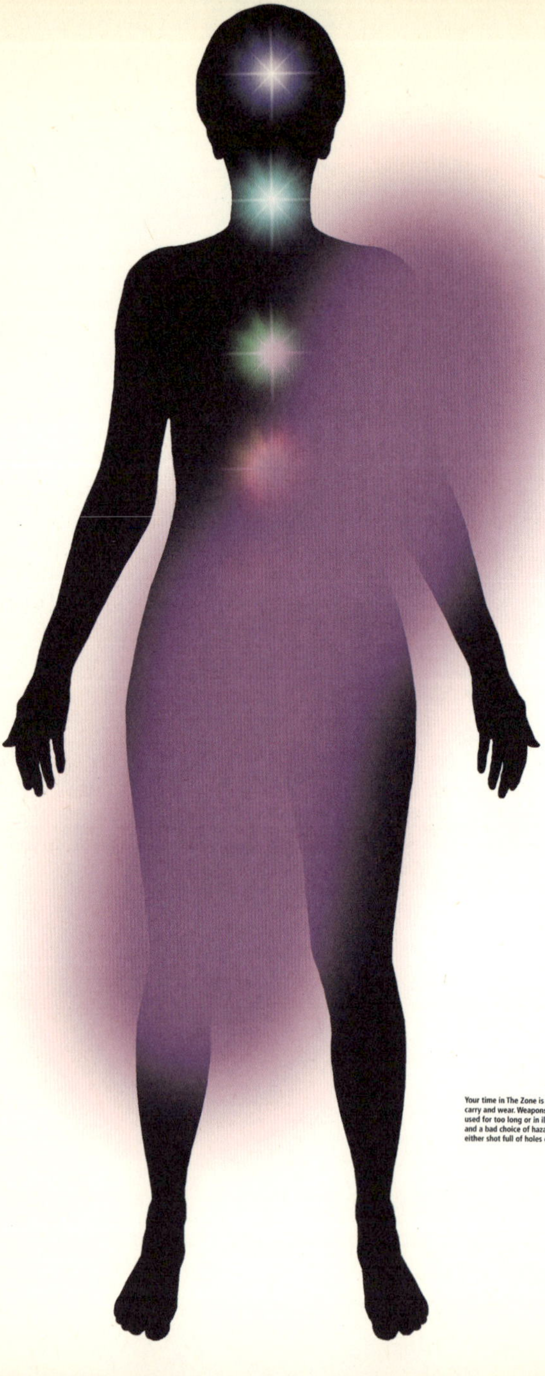

Your time in The Zone is defined by what you carry and wear. Weapons will jam mid-clip if used for too long or in ill-suited conditions, and a bad choice of hazard suit will see you either shot full of holes or microwaved

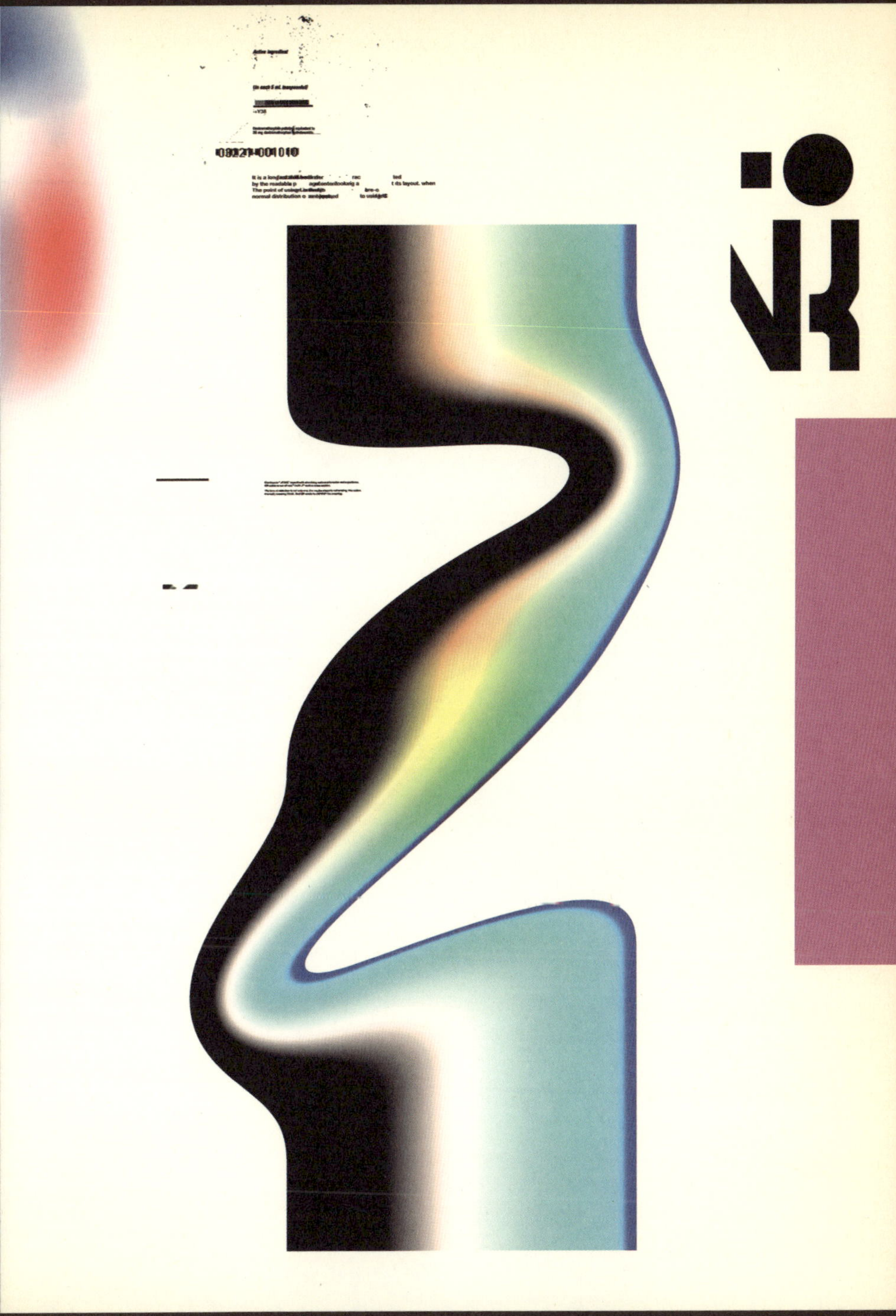

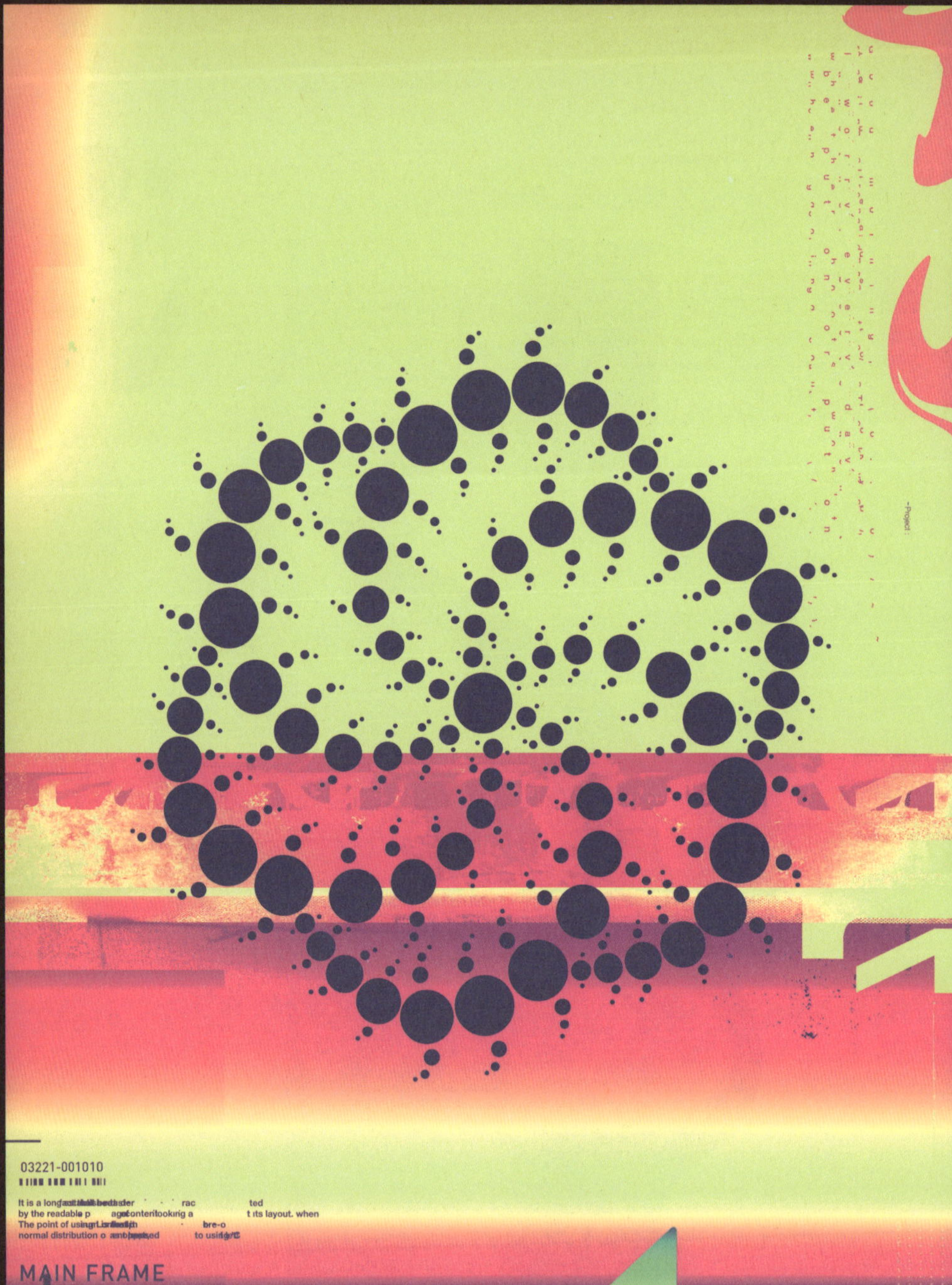
-Project:
03221-001010
MAIN FRAME

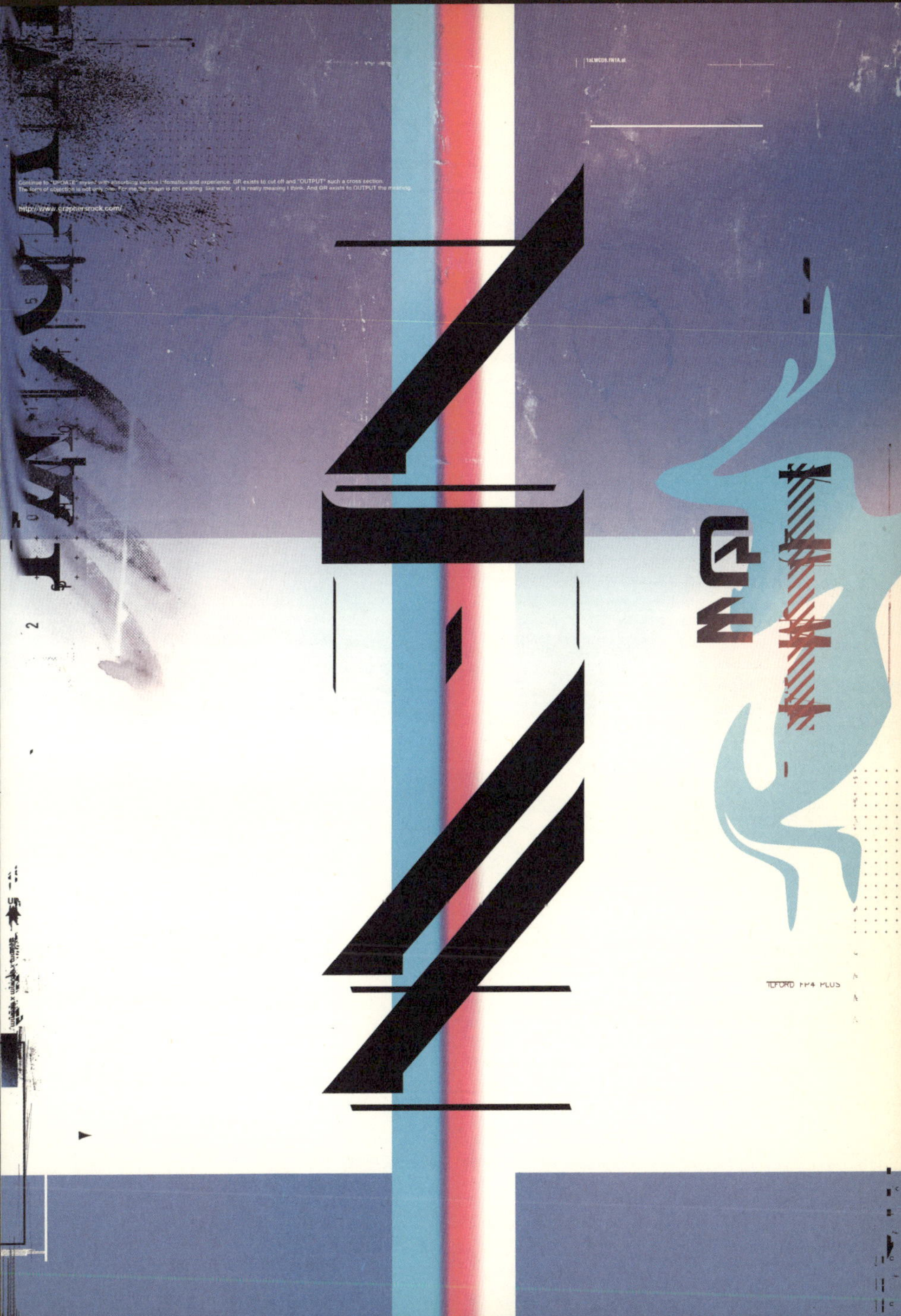
Continue to "UPDATE" myself with absorbing various information and experience. GR exists to cut off and "OUTPUT" such a cross section.
The form of objection is not only one. For me, the shape is not existing like water, it is really meaning I think. And GR exists to OUTPUT the meaning.
http://www.graphersrock.com/
ILFORD FP4 PLUS

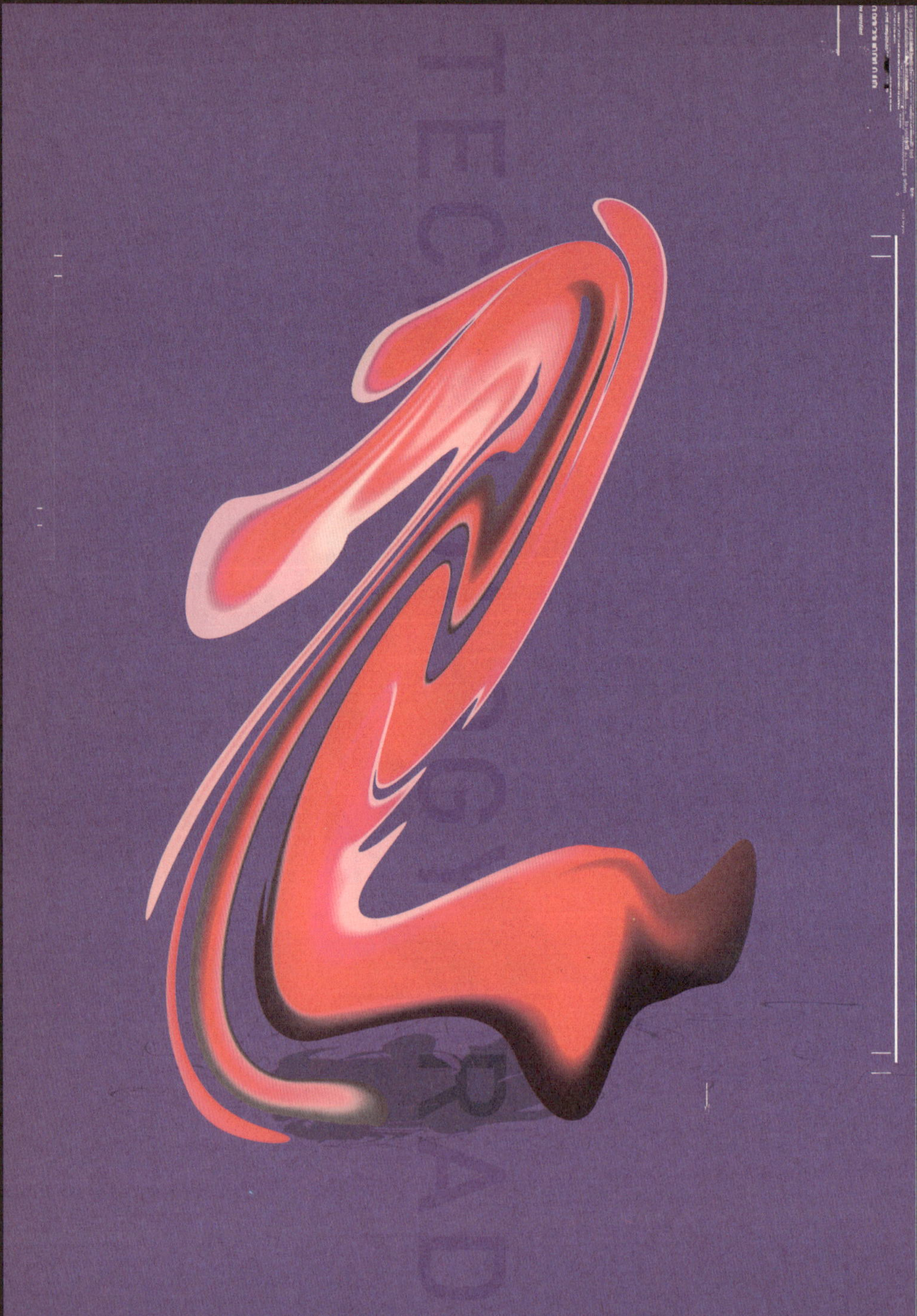

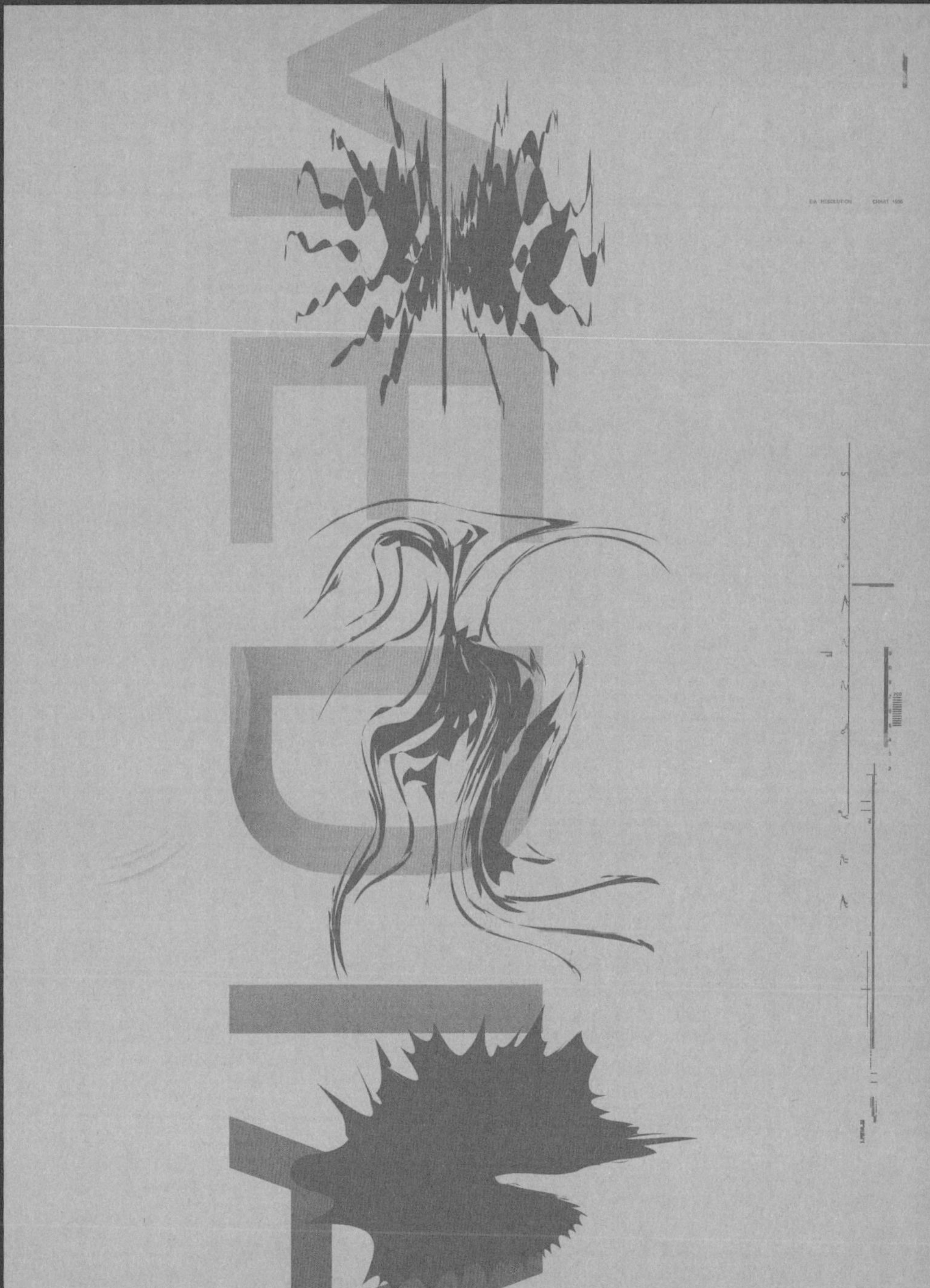
EIA RESOLUTION CHART 1956

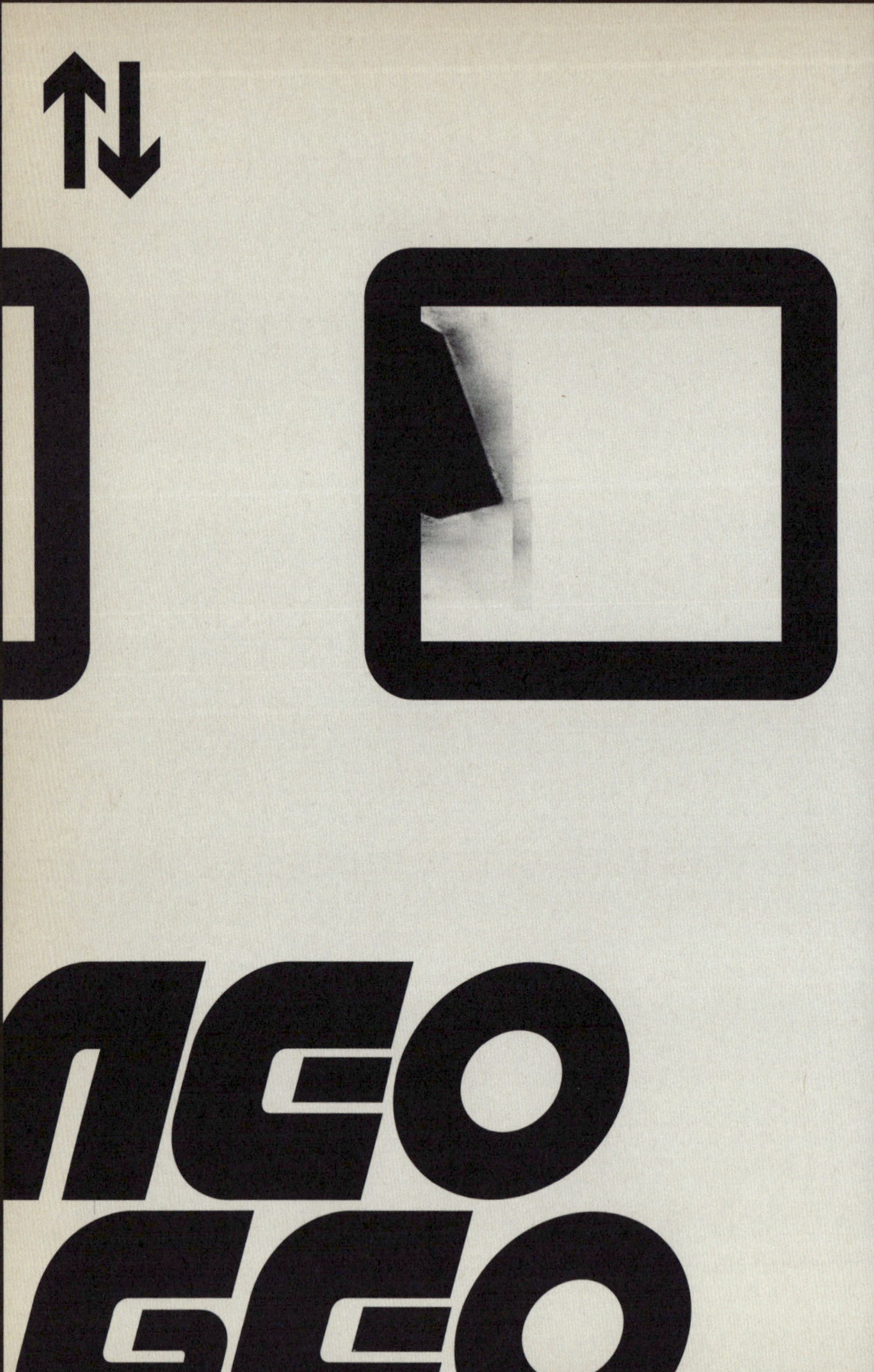

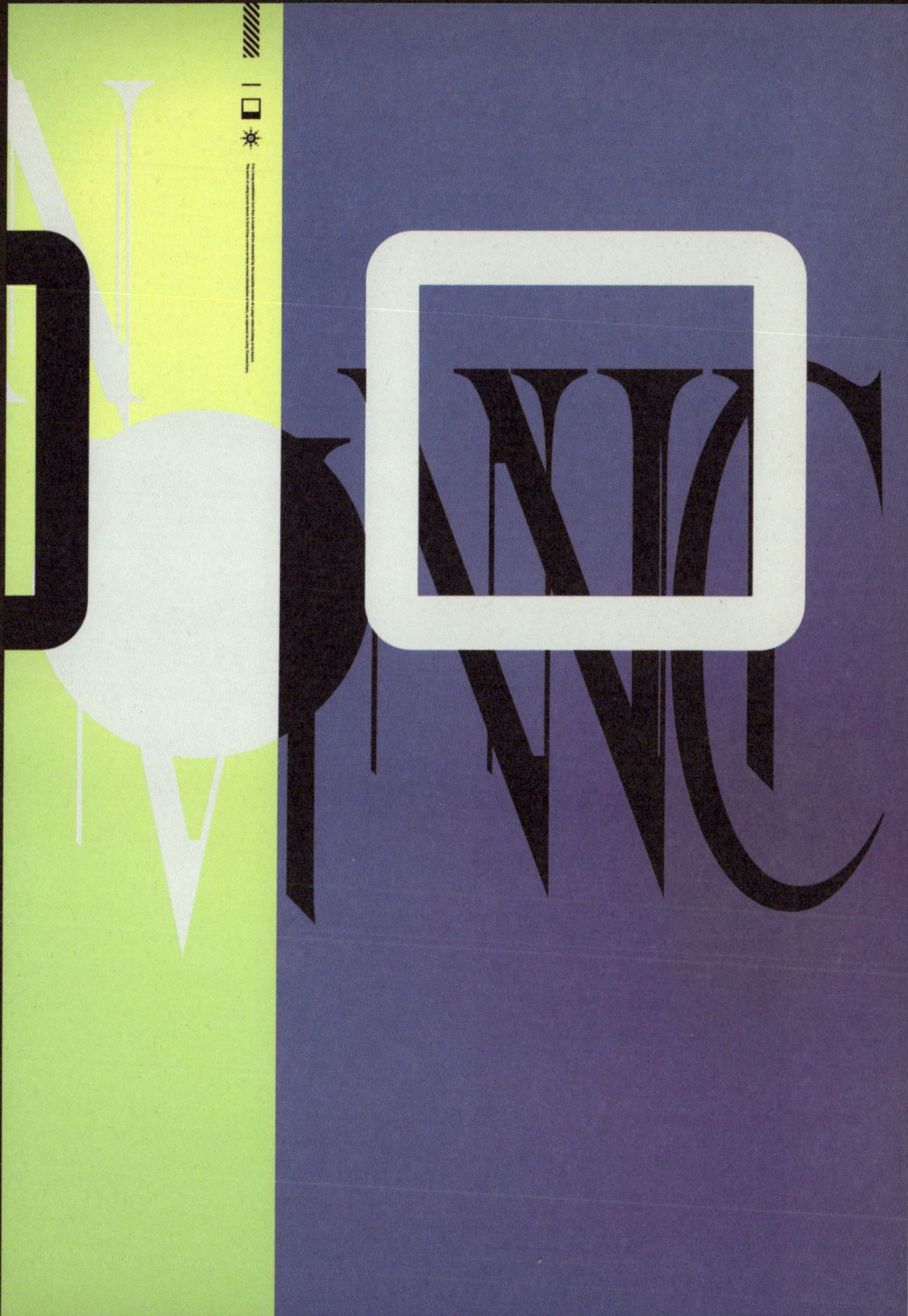

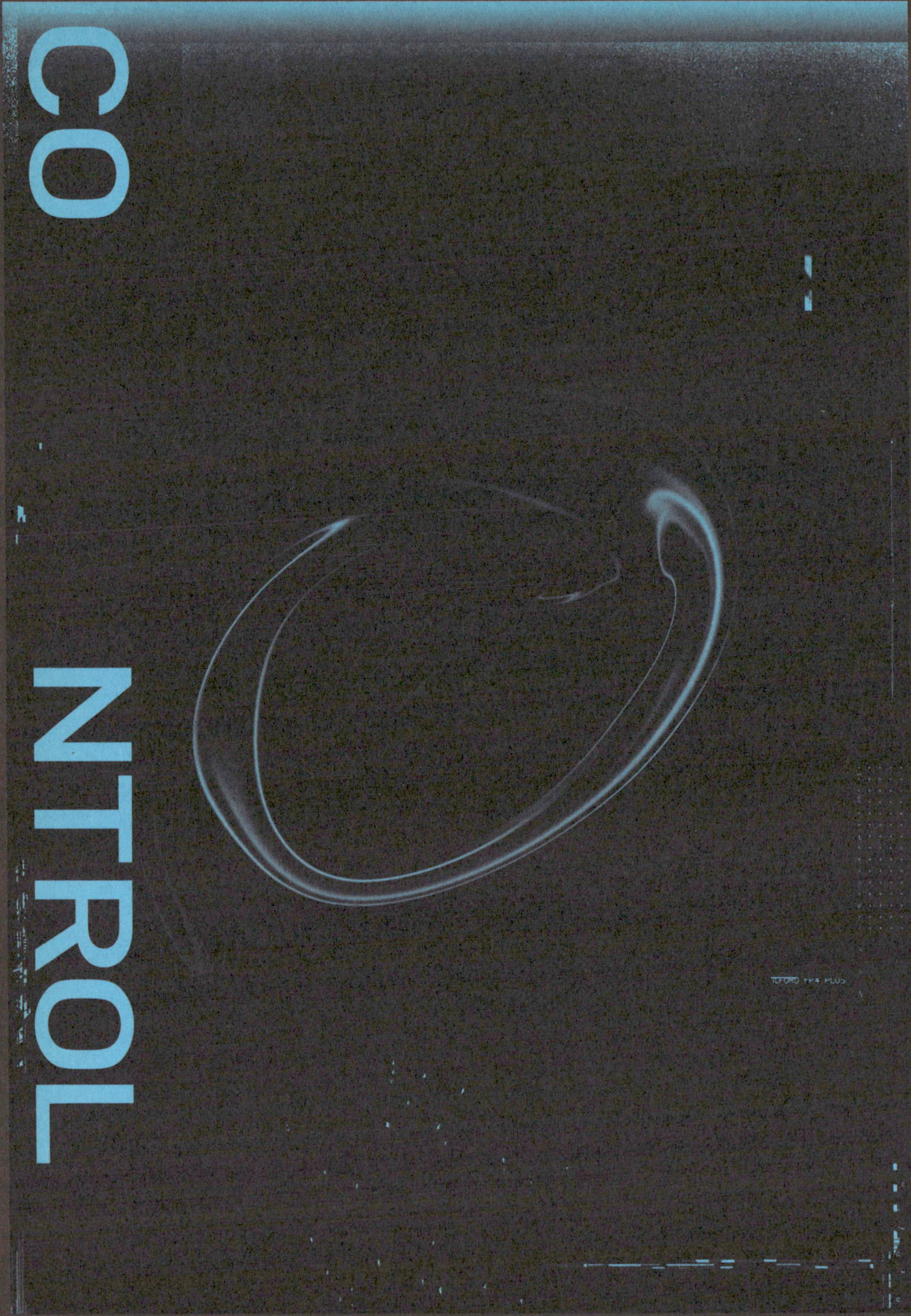
CONTROL

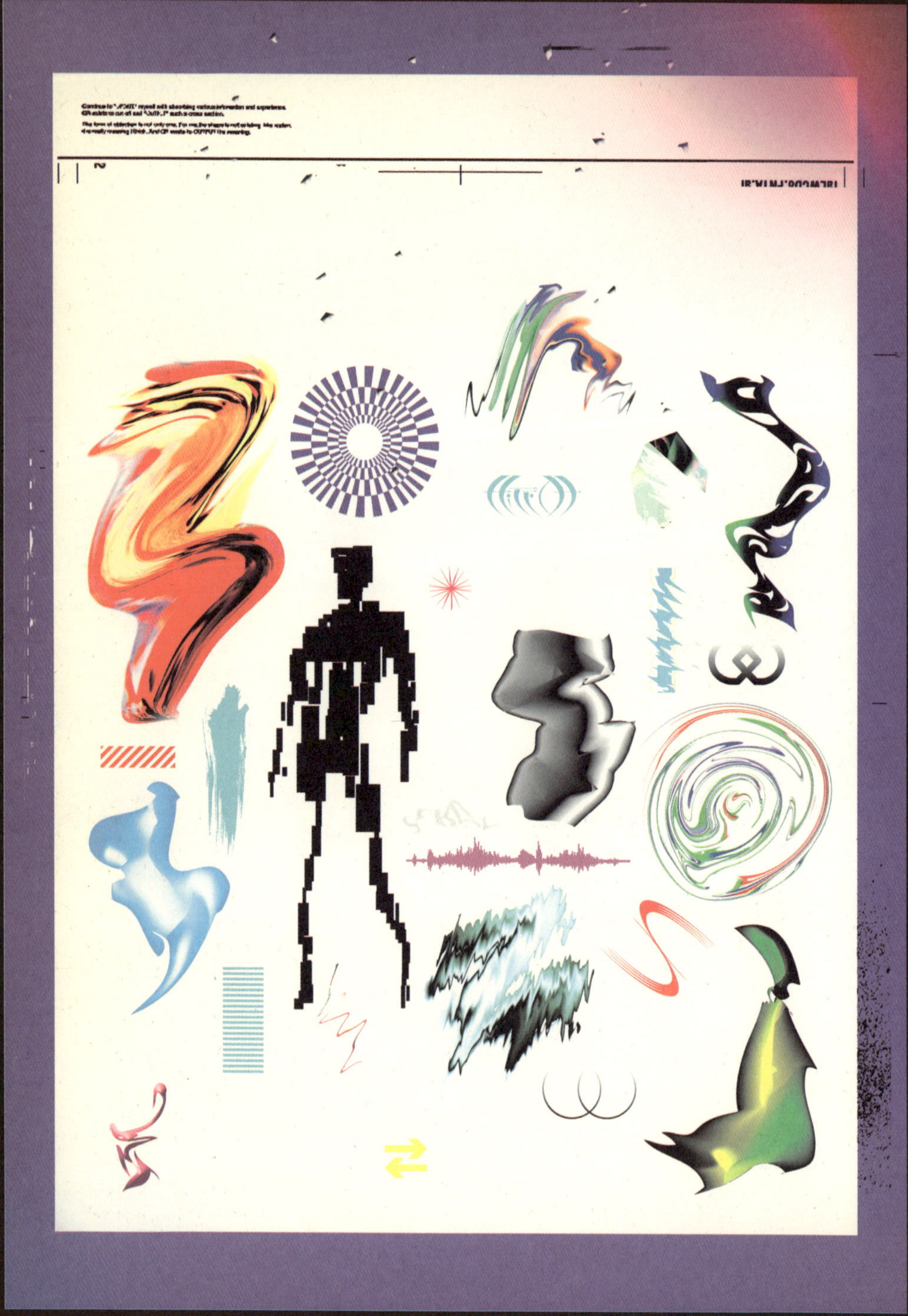

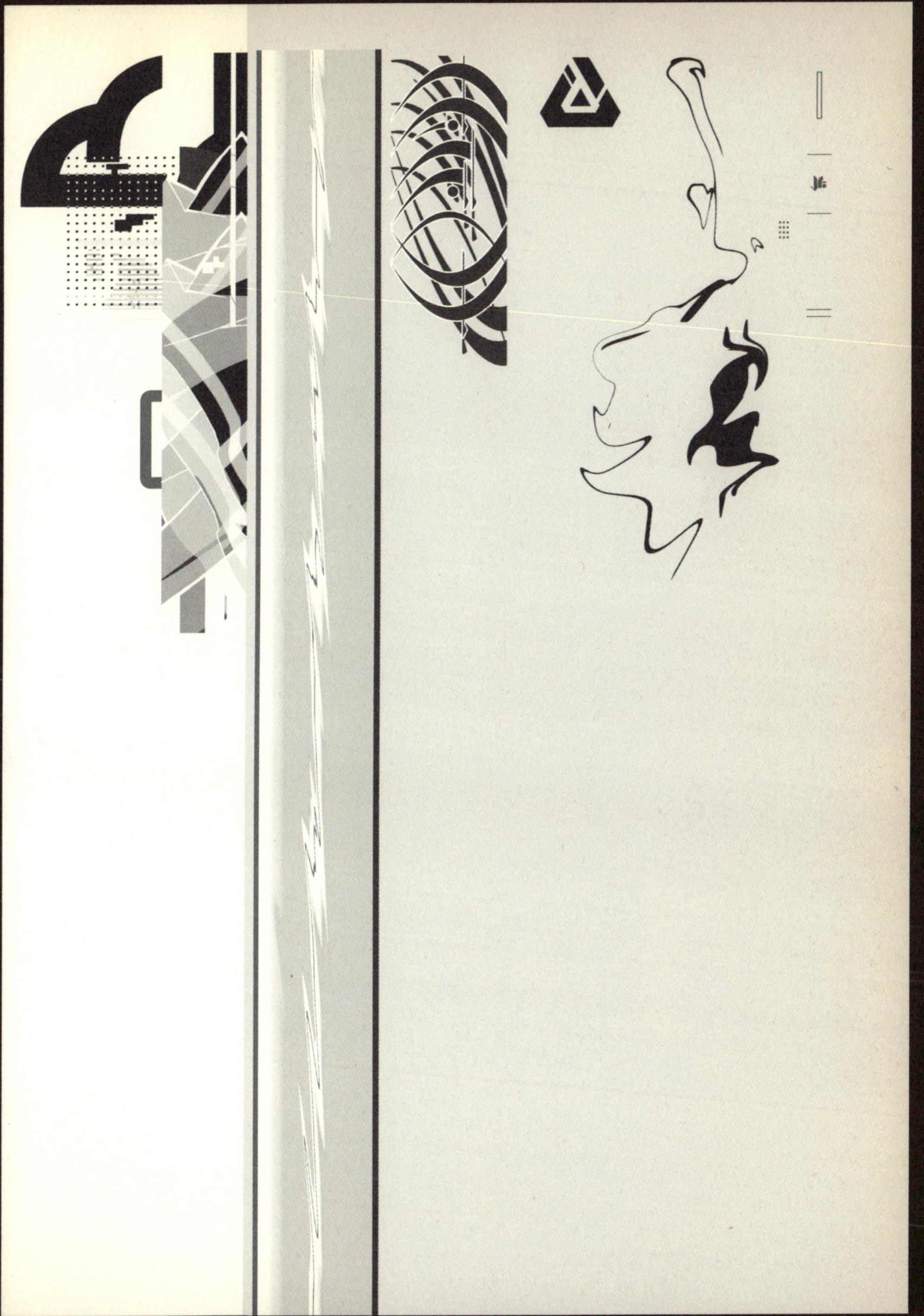

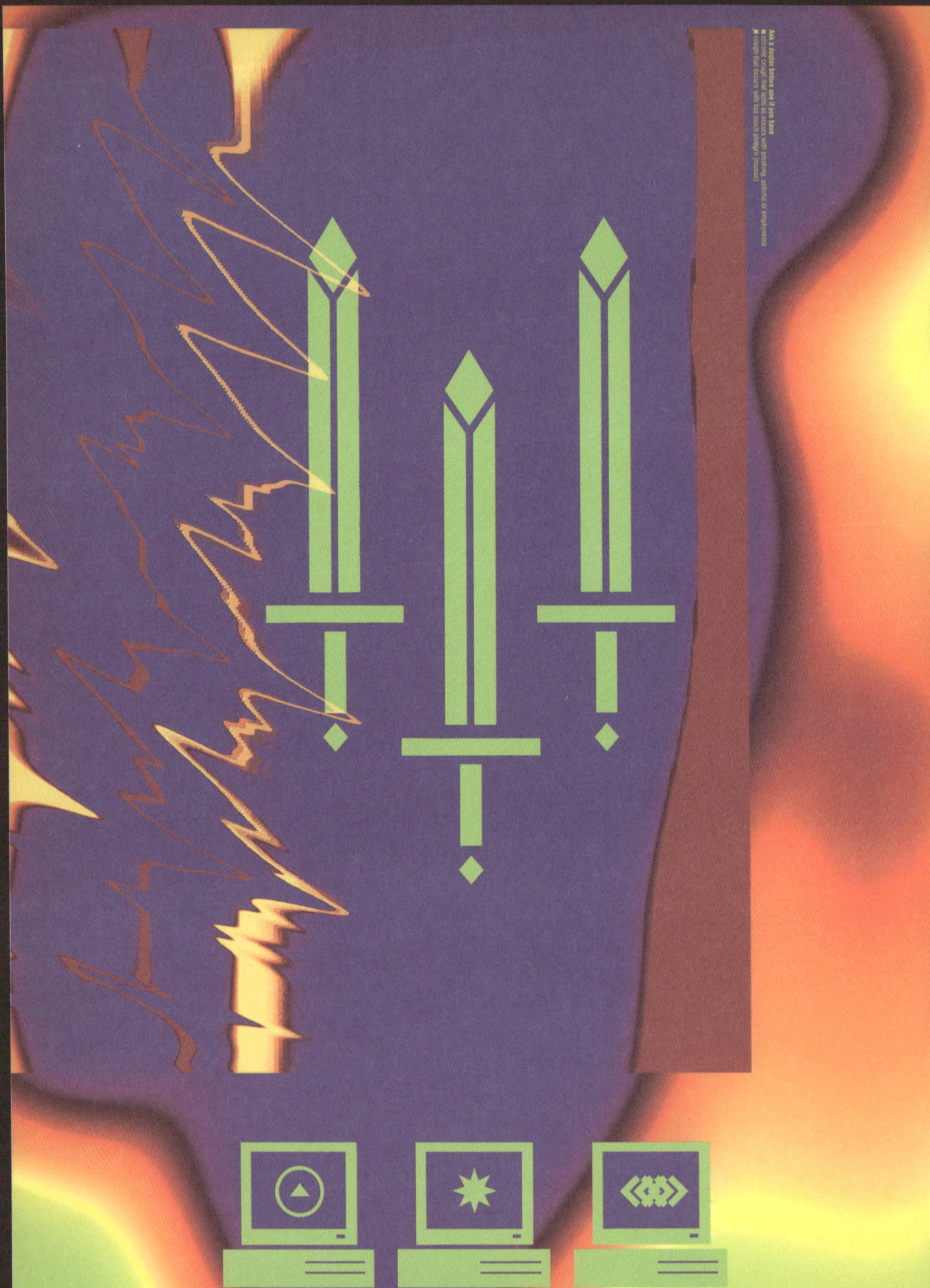
Ask a doctor before use if you have
■ chronic cough that lasts as occurs with smoking, asthma or emphysema
■ cough that occurs with too much phlegm (mucus)

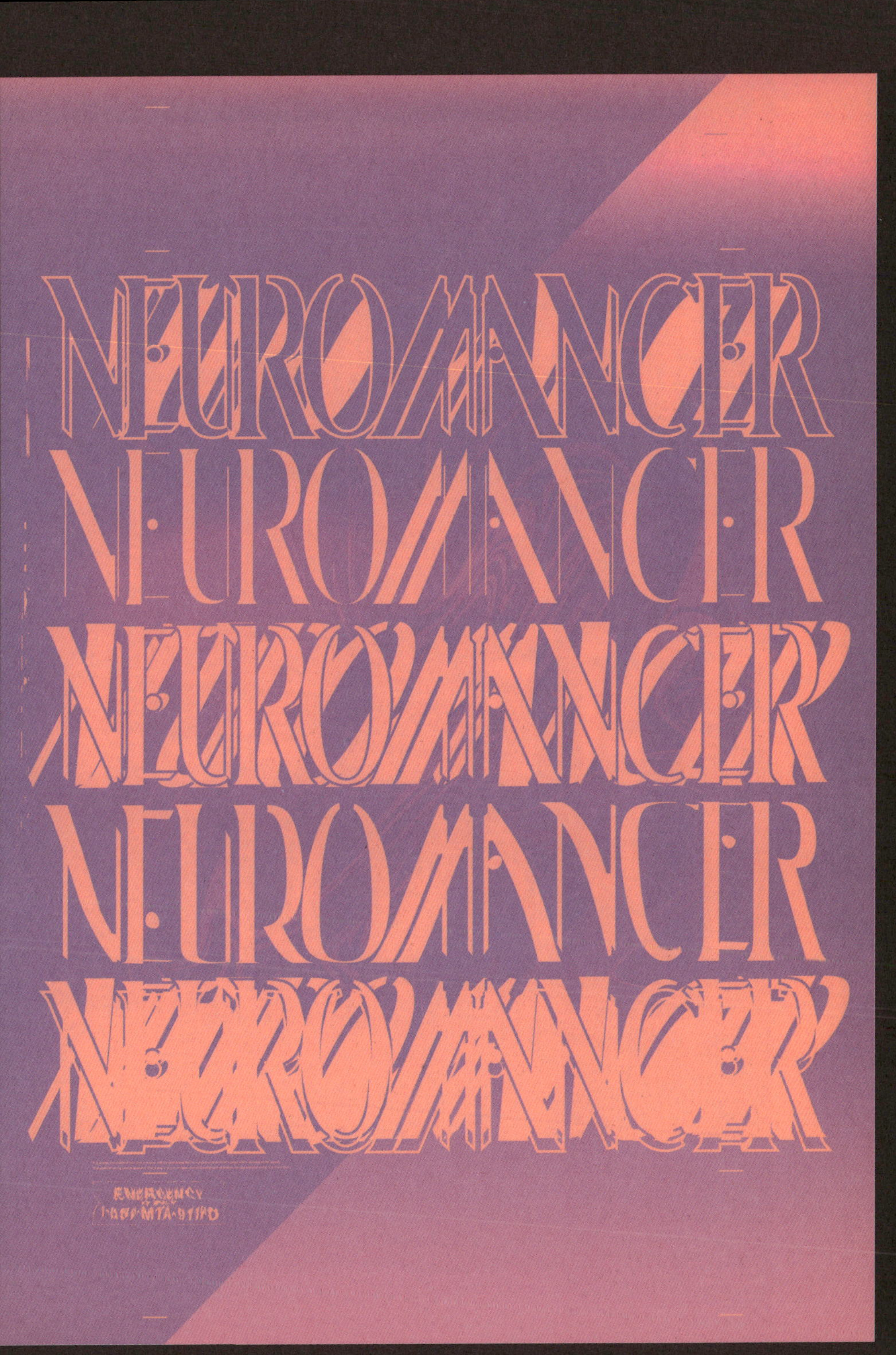
NEUROMANCER
NEUROMANCER
NEUROMANCER
NEUROMANCER
NEUROMANCER

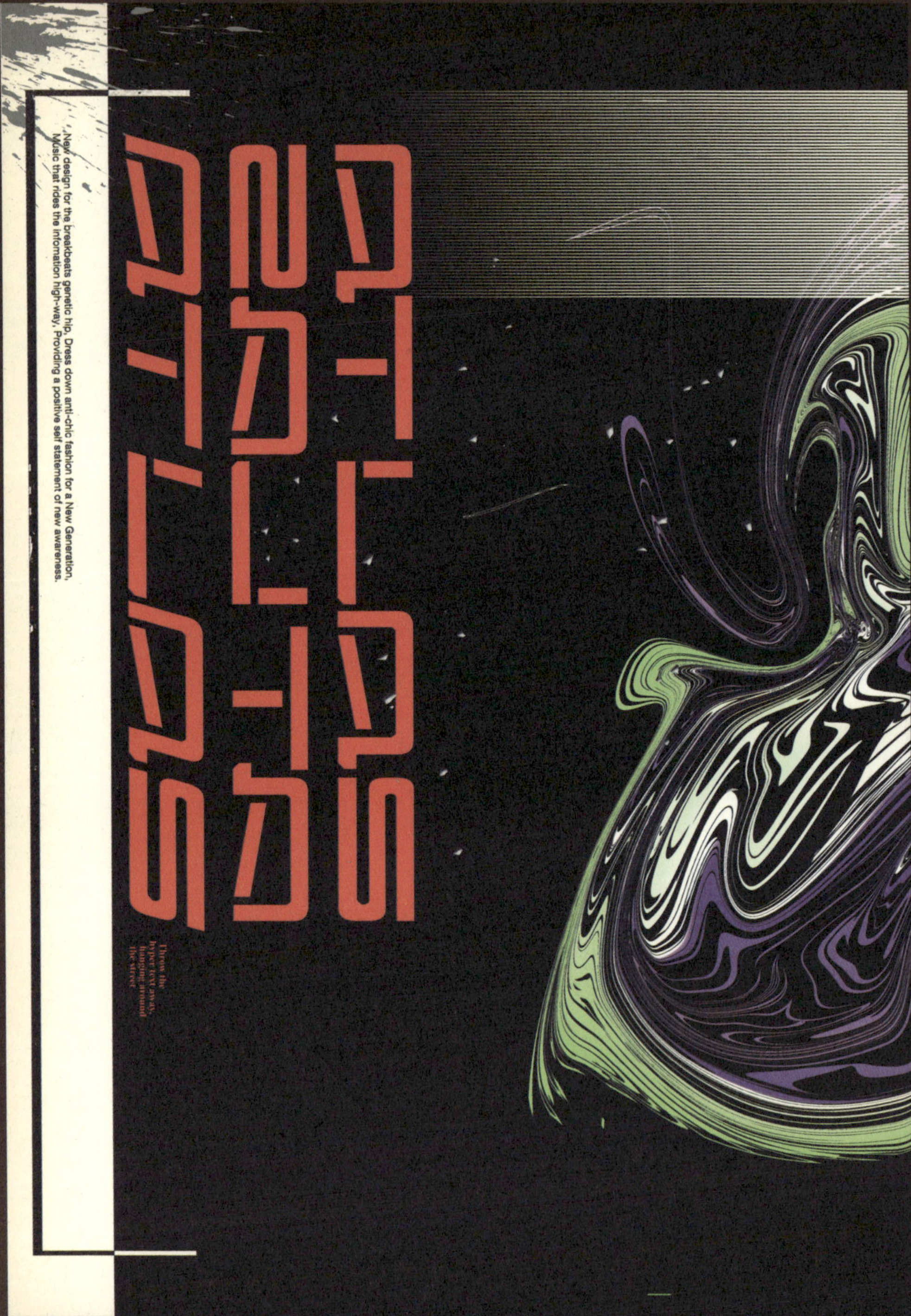
ATLAS
ATLAS
Throw the hyper text away, hanging around the street
New design for the breakbeats genetic hip, Dress down anti-chic fashion for a New Generation,
Music that rides the infomation high-way, Providing a positive self statement of new awareness.

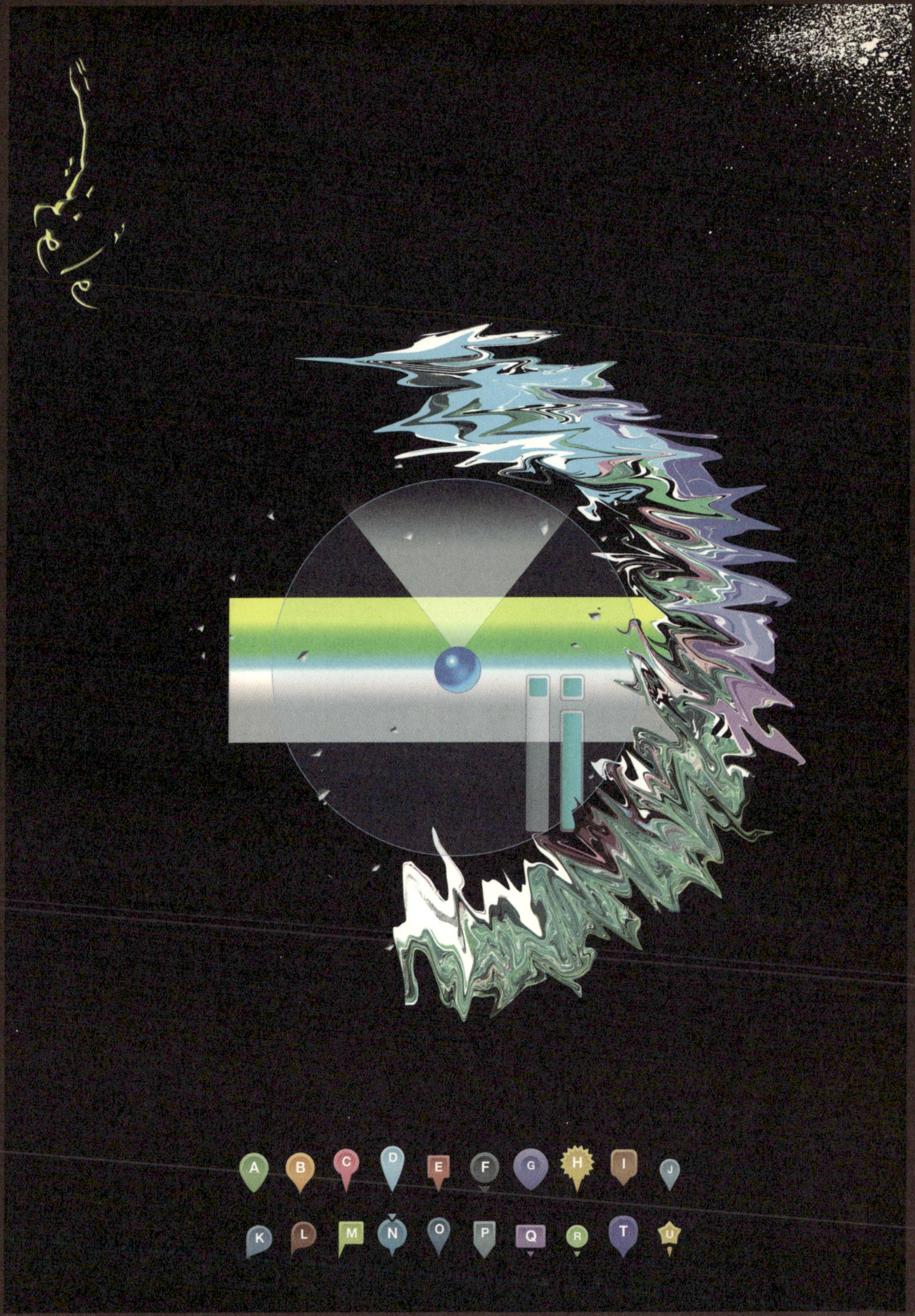
A B C D E F G H I J
K L M N O P Q R T U

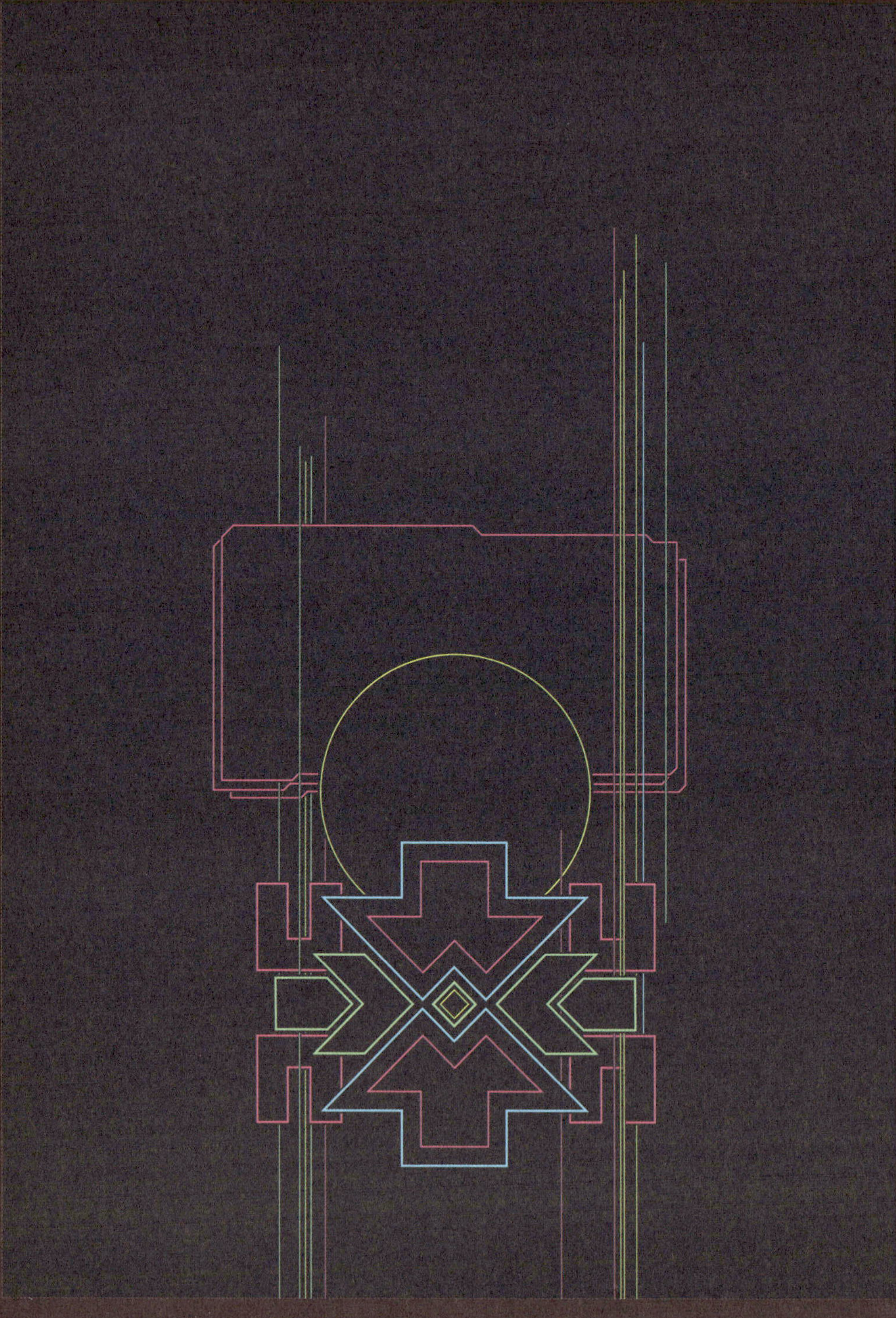

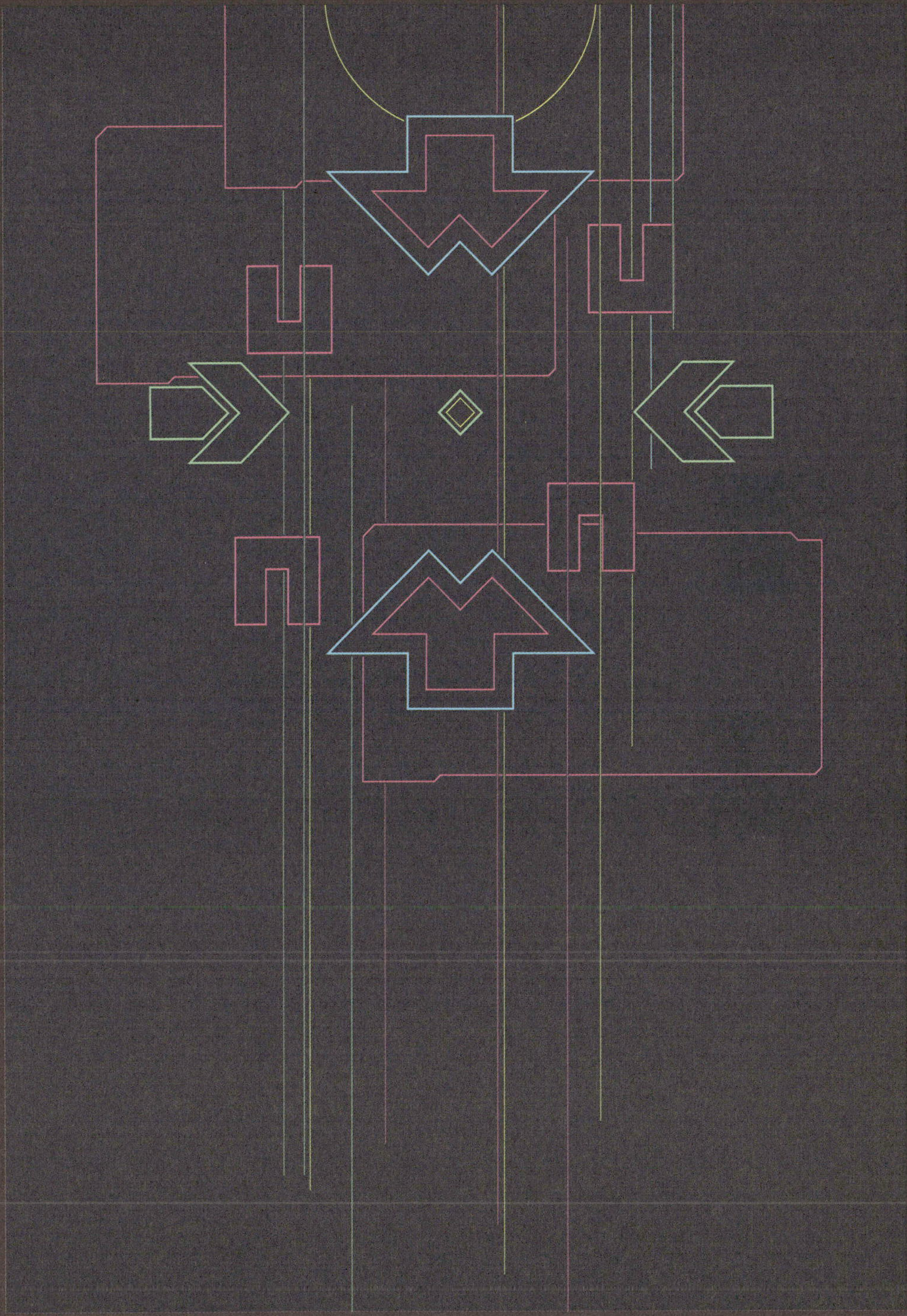

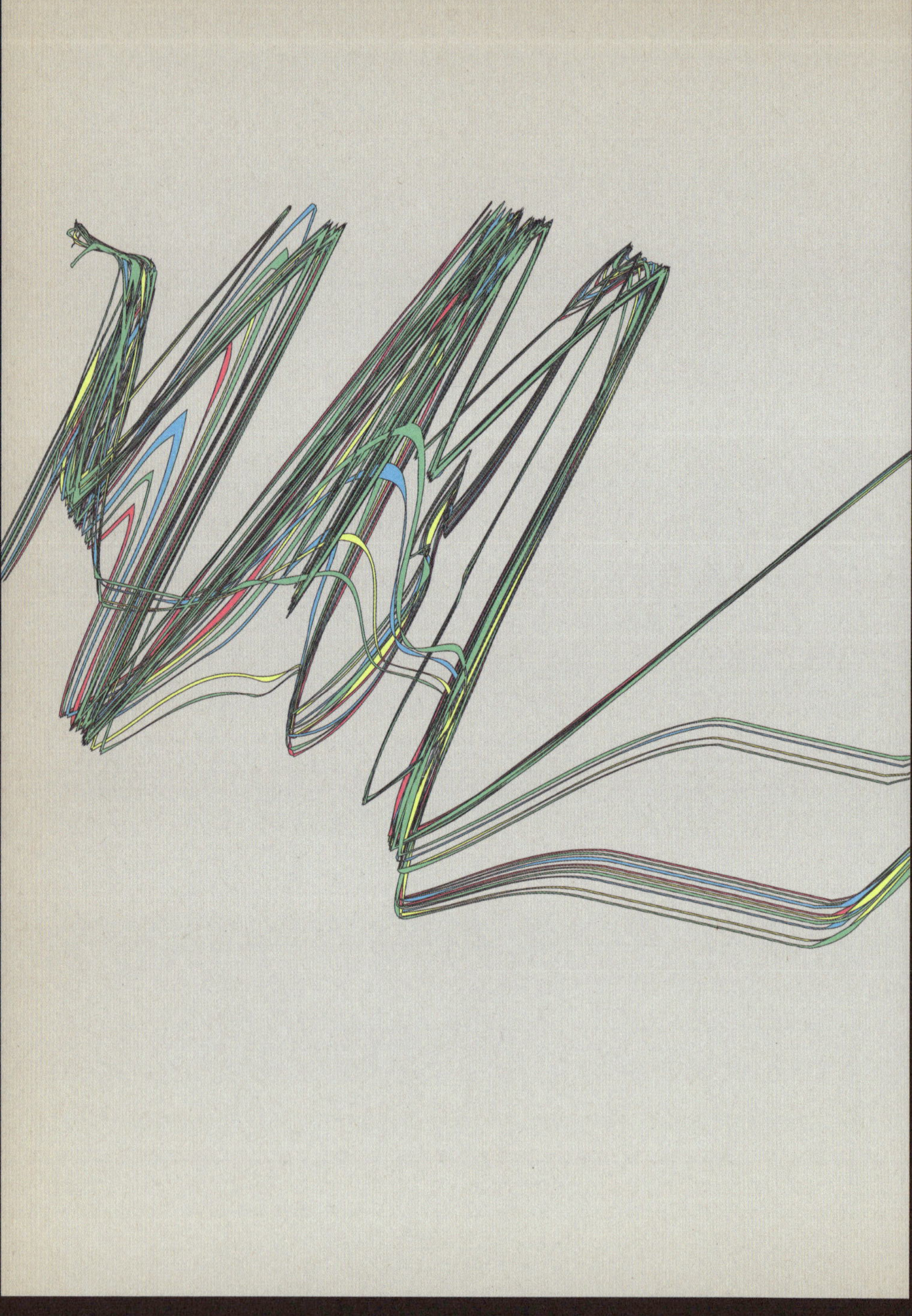

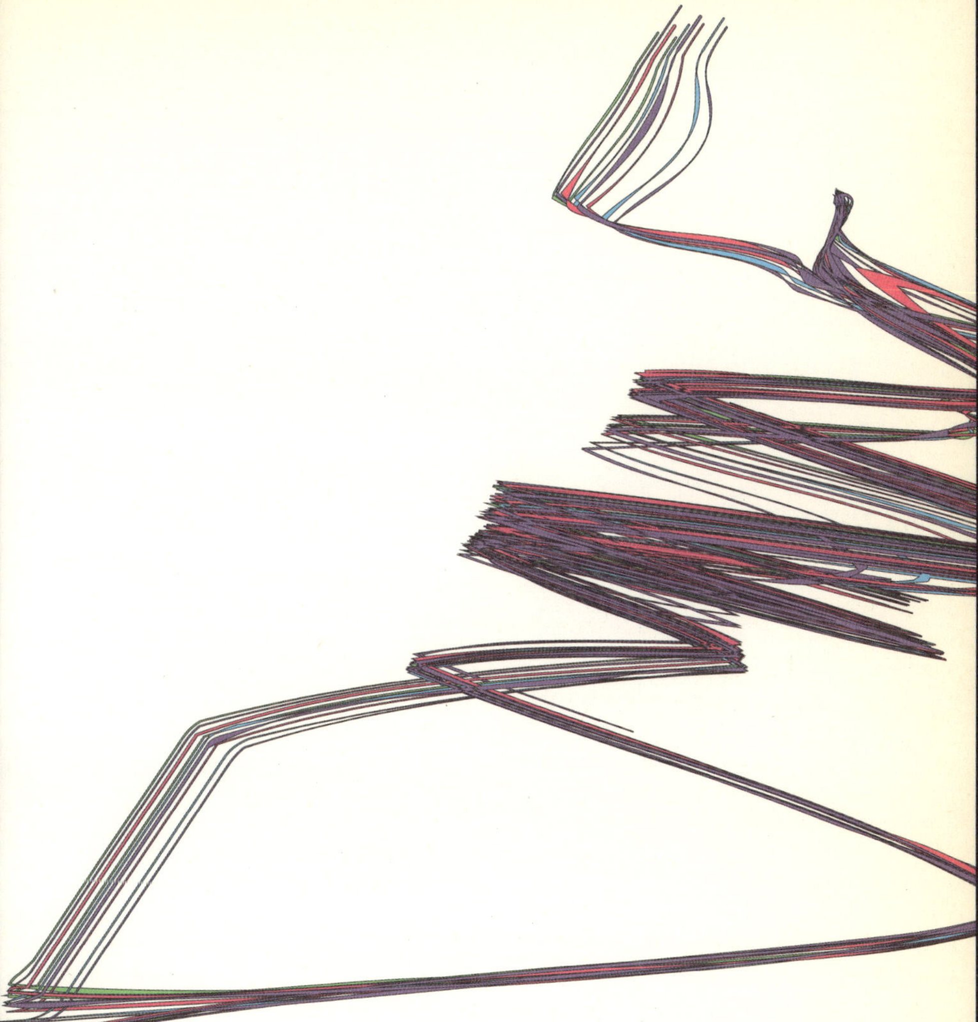

GraphersRock Interview

質問制作 / tomad (Maltine Records)

1. 何がきっかけでグラフィックデザイナーを志しましたか？

幼少から、絵を描いたり工作をしたり、何か作る遊びを繰り返してきて漠然と「モノづくり」に携わる仕事に就こうと思っていました。7歳の時に、つくば万博に連れていってもらったことがきっかけで、科学力の絶対感、コンピューターの全能感を強烈に植え付けられ、何かコンピューターを使った仕事をしたいと思うようになり90年末期のDTPブームを経てグラフィックデザイナーを志しました。

常々デザインという作業においてコンピューターは単なる道具であり手段にすぎないと思っていますが、四六時中、Macと戯れていられる仕事をして、コンピューターを操った結果をグラフィックデザインという形でアウトプットしているという意識が強いです。そこが他のデザイナーとは根本的に違う部分かもしれません。

2. どのような時に制作のインスピレーションが湧きますか？

・寝起きでボケーっとシャワーを浴びているとき。
・集めているお菓子のパッケージをファイリングしているとき。
・クラブで何も考えず音楽を楽しんでいる時。
・過去のラフや制作データを見直している時。

といくつか書きましたが、なんとなく湧いたインスピレーションをうまくデザインに収められることは稀で、実際は紙とペンを手にしながら云々と捻り出していることが多いです。

3. グラフィックを制作する中で一番大切にしていることはなんですか？

グラフィックとして描かれているものが、描かれていないものを想起させることが出来るかどうか。制作されたグラフィックはあくまでそのトリガーに過ぎず、媒体に合わせてトリミングされたグラフィックの外の風景やストーリーを、受け手側にイメージしてもらう体験こそをデザインしたいと考えています。

4. 憧れているもしくは影響を受けたグラフィックデザイナーはいますか？

デザイナーズ・リパブリック、tomato、ピーター・サヴィル、粟津 潔、GROOVISIONS、STEREOTYPE PRODUKTS、SKATE THING、宇川直宏、イルドーザー、針谷建二郎

思いつくグラフィックデザイナーを挙げさせてもらいましたが、映画や映像、音楽、現代美術、ファッション、オモチャ、本、プロダクトデザイン、食品など、グラフィックデザインではないジャンルから影響を受けていることの方が多く、別の分野で得た発想をグラフィックに転用、リミックスできないかと常に意識しています。

5. 音楽関連のアートワークを多く手掛けていますが、音楽が制作に与える影響はありますか？

沢山ありますが、うまく言語化できませんでした。何か新しい制作がスタートする際にはまずプロジェクトのイメージに合ったBGMを選曲します。

6.TwitterやFacebook、TumblrといったSNSによって自身の制作に変化はありましたか？

出来上がったものを自分やユーザーがSNSに投稿したくなるかどうか？という判断基準ができました。音楽ジャケット等は、スマートフォンの画面サイズやSNSのタイムラインに表示され

た場合にどう映るのか、というのも重要になっています。Instagram や Tumblr は反応がダイレクトに返ってくるのでフィードバックを獲やすいのですが、その反面、良くも悪くも SNS のスピード感で消費されるサイクルが早くなってしまっていることに恐怖を感じています。

7. 難しい質問かもしれませんが、今までの作品の中で一番自分のやりたいことができたものはどれですか？

制作の中で設定している着地点は様々なので一概にこれが一番だと言い切ることはできないのですが、「プロジェクトを通してまったく新しい経験を積むことができた」という点を一番やりたいことと設定し、印象に残ったプロジェクトを３つ挙げておきます。

・JR 大久保駅 壁画プロジェクト
大久保駅高架の約 80m に渡る巨大な壁にグラフィックを施しました。特定のターゲットではなく、駅周辺地域を利用する不特定多数に向けての公共物というレギュレーションに乗っ取った制作は普段の「見てもらう」ことを意識したデザインではなく「見えてしまう」というまったく真逆の思考からのスタートでだったこと、また地域をデザインするという意識など、とても貴重な経験をすることができました。またデスクトップの狭い画面の中でデザインしたものが実世界の 80 m の壁に展開されていく様は非常に快感でした。

・PUMA x GraphersRock
世界規模のクライアントと世界展開する商品を作ることの楽しさと難しさを経験させてもらいました。それまでのスニーカーカルチャーには無かったガジェット感やオタク感などをモチーフに両社のコラボレーションでなければ絶対に生まれなかったものを制作することができたと思っています。また単に商品をデザインして終わりではく、どう PR し販売していくのか、マーケティング的な部分や店舗での什器制作など、２～３年がかりのプロジェクト全体を通して関わらせてもらい、様々な刺激を得ることができました。

・ダンボール戦機シリーズ
レベルファイブ制作の男児向けアニメ DVD のパッケージデザイン。毎月コンスタントに１巻ずつ発売され、３シリーズ約４年間にわたりデザインをさせてもらいました。同じフォーマット内で巻数を積み重ねていくデザインの難しさや、フォーマット制作の重要さ、また子供という、なじみのないターゲットへ向けてデザインできたことも新しい経験でした。

8. 近年、今までの方向性からは意外な植物などの有機的なモチーフを使うことがありますがどういう意図がありますか？

ステレオタイプなテクノ感＝無機的というところから少し離れて、有機的なモノが入り込むことによって、無機的なモノが引き立つような、スイカに塩をふりかけるような感覚だったり、電子的なものとは違う、バイオテクノロジーのイメージに新たなテクノ感を見出している部分もあります。また父の趣味が園芸で、植物に囲まれて育った記憶が、今になって大きく影響を及ぼしてきました。

9. 世間の流行りと自分の制作との距離感についてどう考えていますか？

自分の根本は商業デザイナーだと思っているので、世間の流行にある程度乗っかることが重要だと思っています。今の流行を切り取って可視化することもデザインの役割であると思うと同時に次の流行を作るのもデザインの役割だと思っているので、うまくバランスのとれた歩調で、かつそこに GraphersRock の視点を注入していきたいです。

10. 今後、どのような活動をしていきたいですか？　目標や夢などあれば教えて下さい。

保ち続けることの難しさを考えるようになりました。ペースを崩さず、しかし変化に対応しながら、多様なクライアントと共謀し続けたいです。

Credit

4 **tofubeats / Don't Stop The Music**
Illustration : 山根慶丈

6 **tofubeats / ディスコの神様**
Illustration : 山根慶丈

7 **tofubeats / TOWER RECORDS POWER PUSH**
Photo : オノツトム
Styling : 高杉賢太郎 (CONDE NAST JAPAN)
Hair & make up : 内田聡一郎 (vetica)

8 **tofubeats / First Album**
Illustration : 山根慶丈

10 **tofubeats / POSITIVE**
Illustration : 山根慶丈

13 **tofubeats / POSITIVE feat. Dream Ami**
Illustration : 山根慶丈

14 **tofubeats / POSITIVE Remixes**
Illustration : 山根慶丈

17 **tofubeats / University of Remix**
Model : 松本ゆい
Photo : オノツトム

17 **tofubeats / College of Remix**
Illustration : 白根ゆたんぽ

28 **Maltine Records Photo Session "VERSION"**
Model : 玉城ティナ
Photo : 神藤剛
Costume : HATRA
Styling : 山口壮太
Hair & make up : 信沢Hitoshi

52 **でんぱ組.inc / サクラあっぱれーしょん**
Photo : 太田好治

58 **PUMA x GraphersRock**
Model : 守谷周人 , 小谷実由
Photo : オノツトム
Styling : 高橋エイジ
Hair & make up : 内田聡一郎 (vetica)

74 **GIRLS LAB X 2.5D**
Model : 松井玲奈
Photo : オノツトム
Styling : セイショーコ
Hair & make up : コバヤシジュンコ

78 **MONALISA OVERDRIVE**
Model : 夢眠ねむ
Photo : オノツトム
Hair & make up : 内田聡一郎 (vetica)

94 **HARDCORE SYNDROME シリーズ**
Illustration : KEI

98 **DJ TECHNORCH / STRAIGHT**
Illustration : TOKIYA

98 **DJ TECHNORCH / RUNNING COST**
Illustration : TOKIYA

126 **BALMUNG x GraphersRock x Zigg**
Model : 天川宇宙 , 緑川百々子 , りにょ
Photo : 深谷 亘

152 **ILLUSTRATION 2014**
Illustration : mebae

156 **GraphersRock x TOKIYA / IMAGE FORMAT**
Illustration : TOKIYA

RASTERIZE
GraphersRock 作品集

2016年6月1日 初版発行
著者 GraphersRock

デザイン GraphersRock
編集 筒井奈々(DU BOOKS)

発行者 広畑雅彦
発行元 DU BOOKS
発売元 株式会社ディスクユニオン
東京都千代田区九段南 3-9-14
編集 tel 03-3511-9970 / fax 03-3511-9938
営業 tel 03-3511-2722 / fax 03-3511-9941
http://diskunion.net/dubooks/

印刷・製本 シナノ印刷

ISBN978-4-907583-86-6
Printed in Japan

©2016 GraphersRock / disk union

万一、乱丁落丁の場合はお取り替えいたします。
定価はカバーに記してあります。
禁無断転載